CASE CLOSED

VOLUME 17

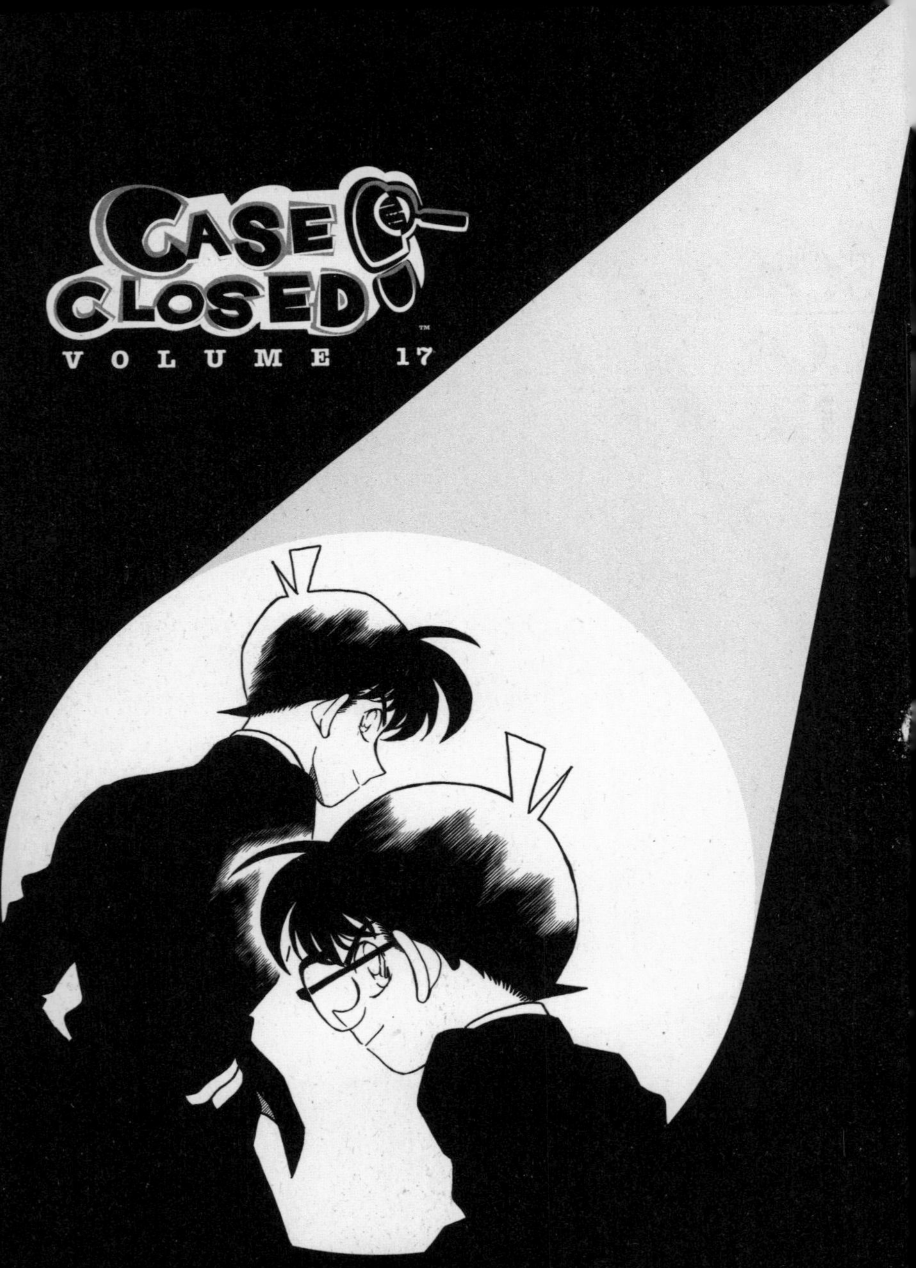

Gosho Aoyama

Case Briefing:

Subject:
Occupation:
Special Skills:
Equipment:

Jimmy Kudo, a.k.a. Conan Edogawa
High School Student/Detective
Analytical thinking and deductive reasoning, Soccer
Bow Tie Voice Transmitter, Super Sneakers,
Homing Glasses, Stretchy Suspenders

The subject is hot on the trail of a pair of suspicious men in black when he is attacked from behind and administered a strange substance which physically transforms him into a first grader. When the subject confides in the eccentric inventor Dr. Agasa, they decide to keep the subject's true identity a secret for the safety of everyone around him. Assuming the new identity of first-grader Conan Edogawa, the subject continues to assist the police force on their most baffling cases. The only problem is that most crime-solving professionals won't take a little kid's advice!

Table of Contents

CONFIDEN

CASE CLOSED

Volume 17 • VIZ Media Edition

GOSHO AOYAMA

Translation
Naoko Amemiya

Touch-up & Lettering
Walden Wong

Cover & Graphics Design
Andrea Rice

Editors
Joel Enos & Shaenon K. Garrity

Editor in Chief, Books **Alvin Lu**
Editor in Chief, Magazines **Marc Weidenbaum**
VP of Publishing Licensing **Rika Inouye**
VP of Sales **Gonzalo Ferreyra**
Sr. VP of Marketing **Liza Coppola**
Publisher **Hyoe Narita**

store.viz.com

VIZ
MEDIA

www.viz.com

Printed in the U.S.A.
Published by VIZ Media, LLC
P.O. Box 77010
San Francisco, CA 94107

10 9 8 7 6 5 4 3 2
First printing, May 2007
Second printing, February 2008

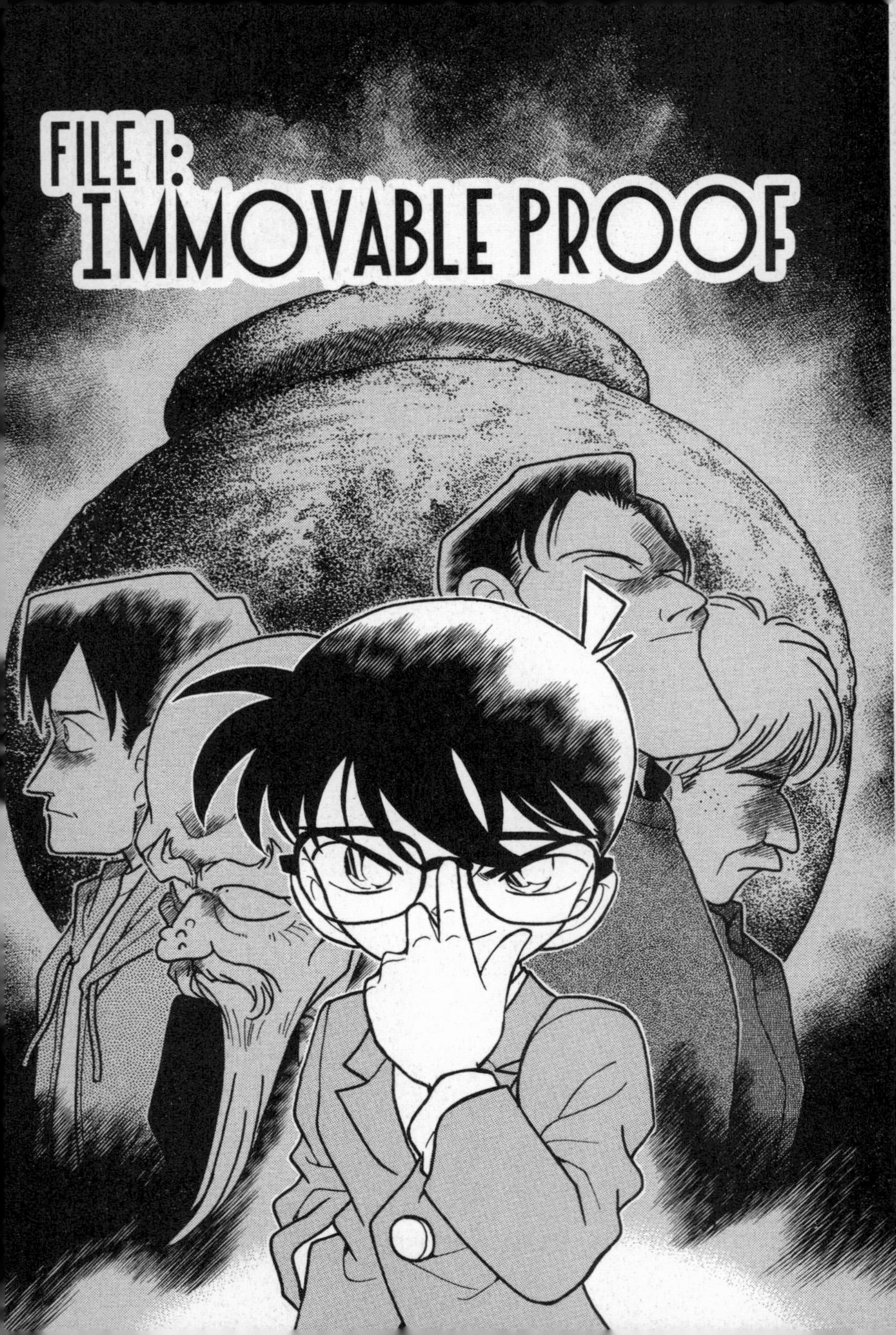
FILE 1:
IMMOVABLE PROOF

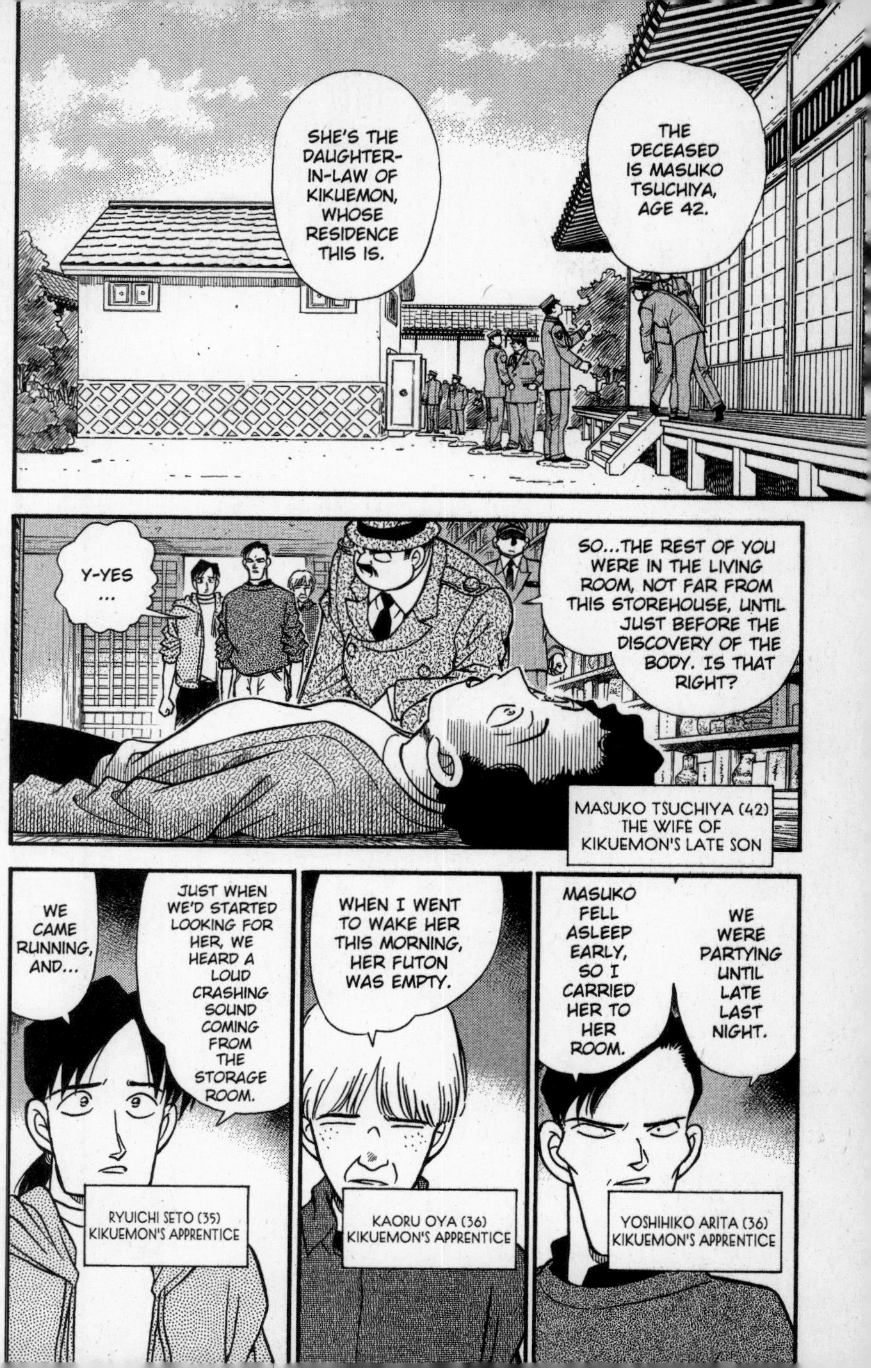
THE DECEASED IS MASUKO TSUCHIYA, AGE 42.
SHE'S THE DAUGHTER-IN-LAW OF KIKUEMON, WHOSE RESIDENCE THIS IS.
SO...THE REST OF YOU WERE IN THE LIVING ROOM, NOT FAR FROM THIS STOREHOUSE, UNTIL JUST BEFORE THE DISCOVERY OF THE BODY. IS THAT RIGHT?
Y-YES ...
MASUKO TSUCHIYA (42) THE WIFE OF KIKUEMON'S LATE SON
WE WERE PARTYING UNTIL LATE LAST NIGHT.
MASUKO FELL ASLEEP EARLY, SO I CARRIED HER TO HER ROOM.
YOSHIHIKO ARITA (36) KIKUEMON'S APPRENTICE
WHEN I WENT TO WAKE HER THIS MORNING, HER FUTON WAS EMPTY.
KAORU OYA (36) KIKUEMON'S APPRENTICE
JUST WHEN WE'D STARTED LOOKING FOR HER, WE HEARD A LOUD CRASHING SOUND COMING FROM THE STORAGE ROOM.
WE CAME RUNNING, AND...
RYUICHI SETO (35) KIKUEMON'S APPRENTICE

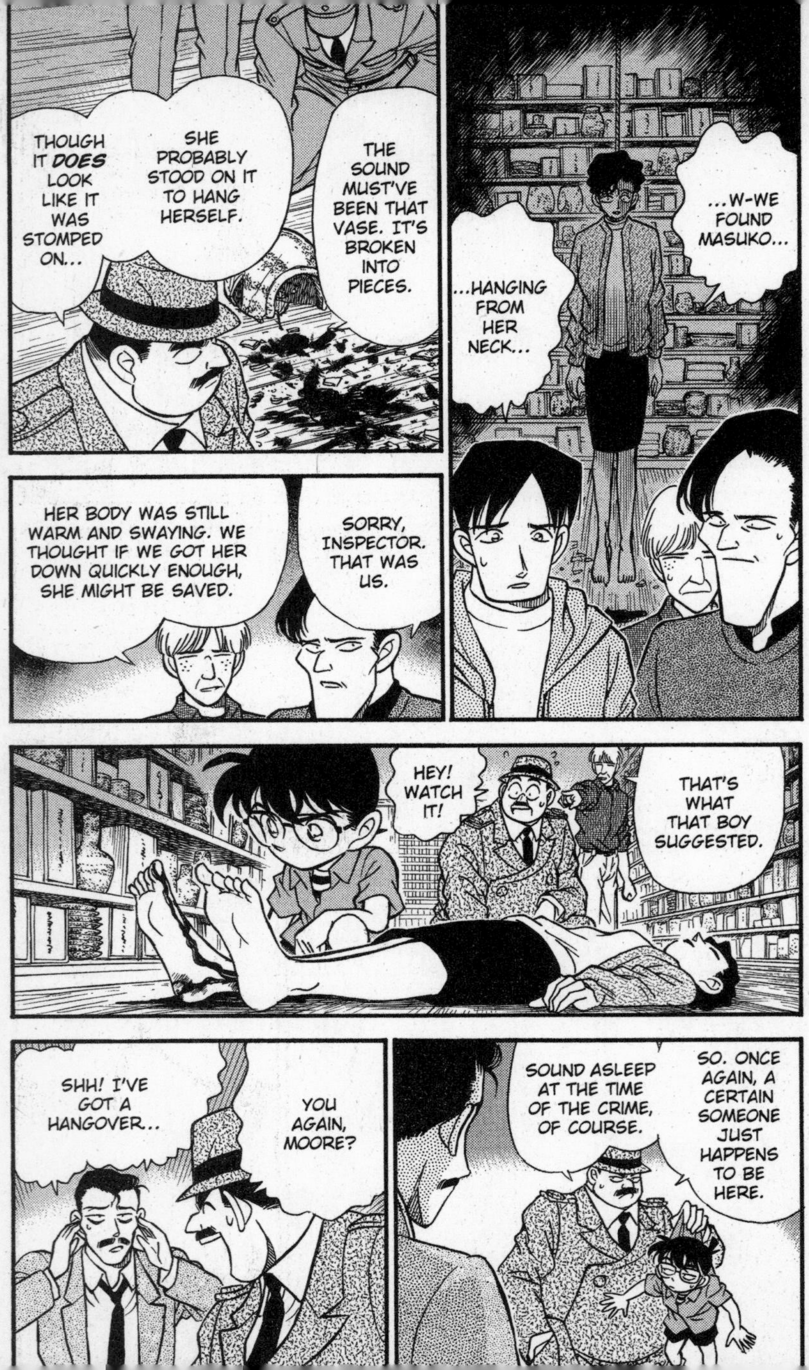
...W-WE FOUND MASUKO...
...HANGING FROM HER NECK...
THE SOUND MUST'VE BEEN THAT VASE. IT'S BROKEN INTO PIECES.
SHE PROBABLY STOOD ON IT TO HANG HERSELF.
THOUGH IT *DOES* LOOK LIKE IT WAS STOMPED ON...
SORRY, INSPECTOR. THAT WAS US.
HER BODY WAS STILL WARM AND SWAYING. WE THOUGHT IF WE GOT HER DOWN QUICKLY ENOUGH, SHE MIGHT BE SAVED.
THAT'S WHAT THAT BOY SUGGESTED.
HEY! WATCH IT!
SO. ONCE AGAIN, A CERTAIN SOMEONE JUST HAPPENS TO BE HERE.
SOUND ASLEEP AT THE TIME OF THE CRIME, OF COURSE.
YOU AGAIN, MOORE?
SHH! I'VE GOT A HANGOVER...

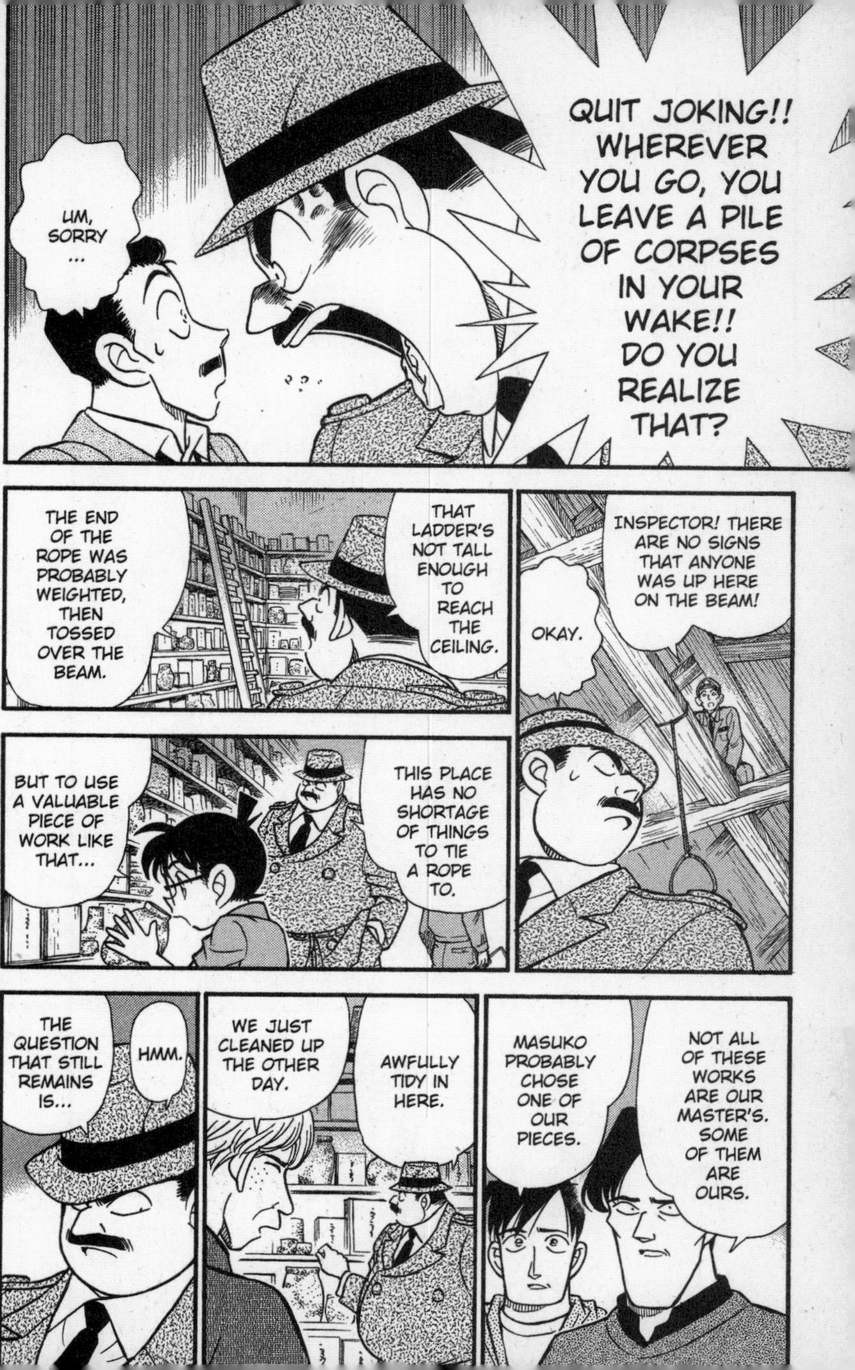
QUIT JOKING!! WHEREVER YOU GO, YOU LEAVE A PILE OF CORPSES IN YOUR WAKE!! DO YOU REALIZE THAT?
UM, SORRY ...
INSPECTOR! THERE ARE NO SIGNS THAT ANYONE WAS UP HERE ON THE BEAM!
OKAY.
THAT LADDER'S NOT TALL ENOUGH TO REACH THE CEILING.
THE END OF THE ROPE WAS PROBABLY WEIGHTED, THEN TOSSED OVER THE BEAM.
THIS PLACE HAS NO SHORTAGE OF THINGS TO TIE A ROPE TO.
BUT TO USE A VALUABLE PIECE OF WORK LIKE THAT...
NOT ALL OF THESE WORKS ARE OUR MASTER'S. SOME OF THEM ARE OURS.
MASUKO PROBABLY CHOSE ONE OF OUR PIECES.
AWFULLY TIDY IN HERE.
WE JUST CLEANED UP THE OTHER DAY.
HMM.
THE QUESTION THAT STILL REMAINS IS...

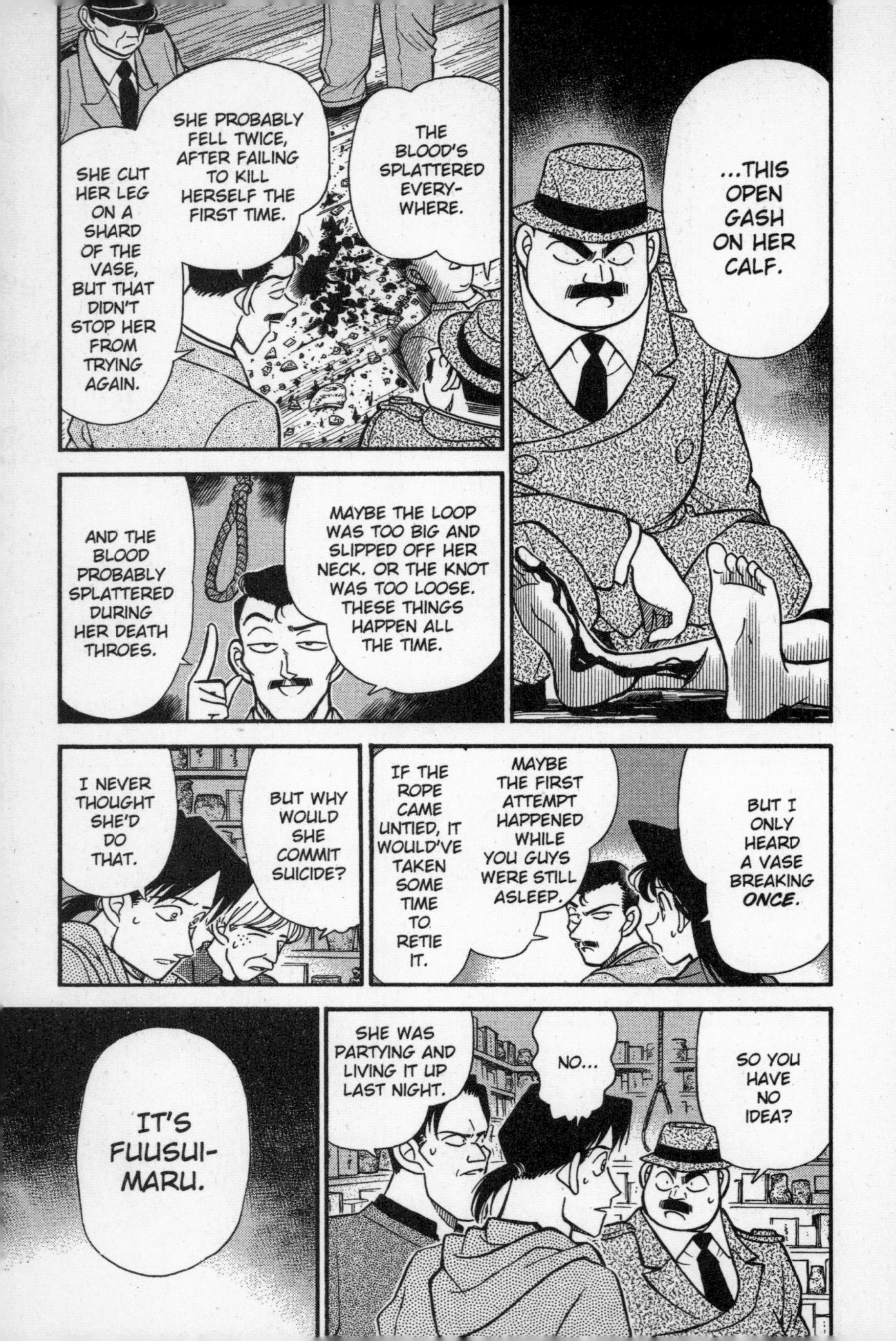
...THIS OPEN GASH ON HER CALF.
THE BLOOD'S SPLATTERED EVERYWHERE.
SHE PROBABLY FELL TWICE, AFTER FAILING TO KILL HERSELF THE FIRST TIME.
SHE CUT HER LEG ON A SHARD OF THE VASE, BUT THAT DIDN'T STOP HER FROM TRYING AGAIN.
MAYBE THE LOOP WAS TOO BIG AND SLIPPED OFF HER NECK. OR THE KNOT WAS TOO LOOSE. THESE THINGS HAPPEN ALL THE TIME.
AND THE BLOOD PROBABLY SPLATTERED DURING HER DEATH THROES.
BUT I ONLY HEARD A VASE BREAKING *ONCE*.
MAYBE THE FIRST ATTEMPT HAPPENED WHILE YOU GUYS WERE STILL ASLEEP.
IF THE ROPE CAME UNTIED, IT WOULD'VE TAKEN SOME TIME TO RETIE IT.
BUT WHY WOULD SHE COMMIT SUICIDE?
I NEVER THOUGHT SHE'D DO THAT.
SO YOU HAVE NO IDEA?
NO...
SHE WAS PARTYING AND LIVING IT UP LAST NIGHT.
IT'S FUUSUI-MARU.

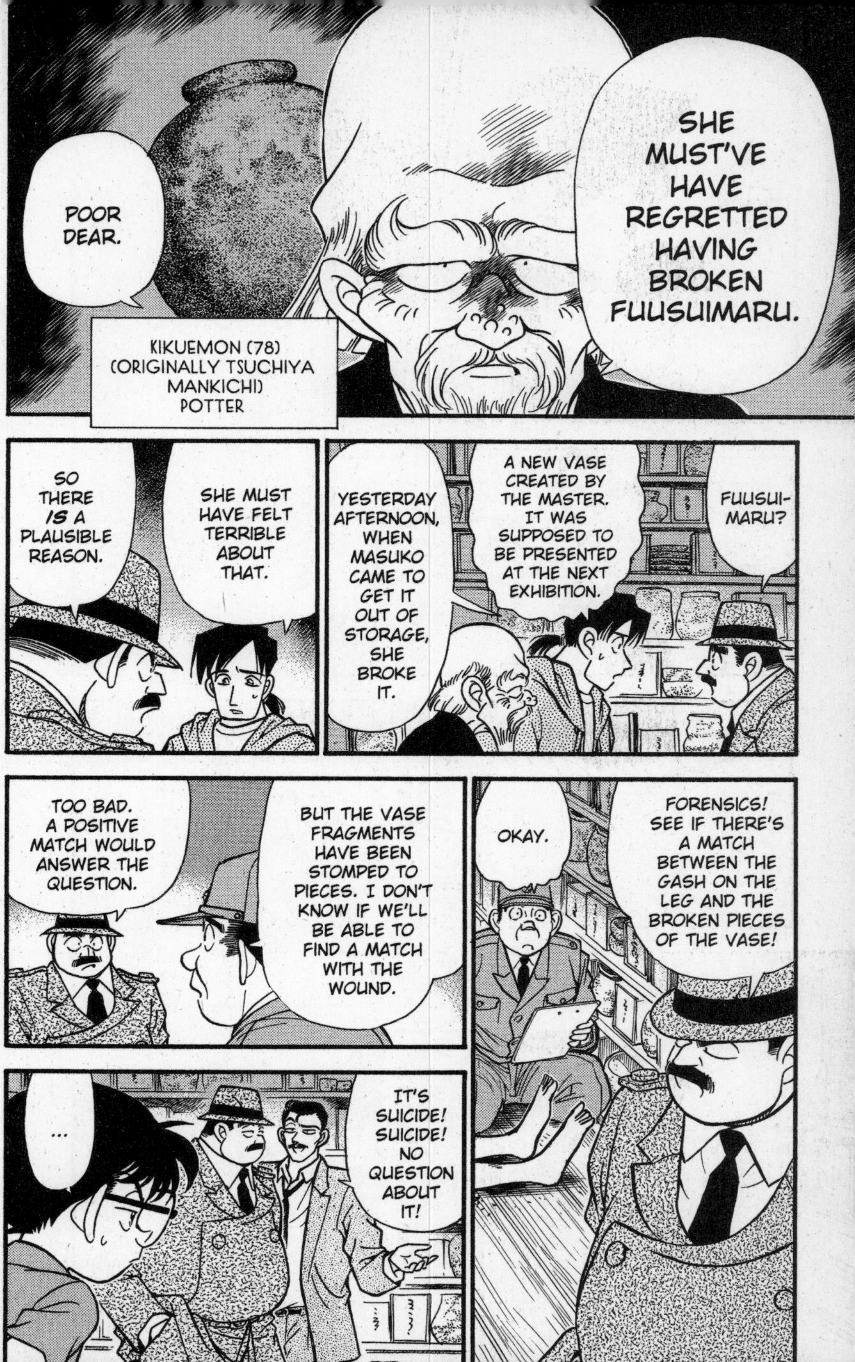
SHE MUST'VE HAVE REGRETTED HAVING BROKEN FUUSUIMARU.
POOR DEAR.
KIKUEMON (78) (ORIGINALLY TSUCHIYA MANKICHI) POTTER
FUUSUI-MARU?
A NEW VASE CREATED BY THE MASTER. IT WAS SUPPOSED TO BE PRESENTED AT THE NEXT EXHIBITION.
YESTERDAY AFTERNOON, WHEN MASUKO CAME TO GET IT OUT OF STORAGE, SHE BROKE IT.
SHE MUST HAVE FELT TERRIBLE ABOUT THAT.
SO THERE *IS* A PLAUSIBLE REASON.
FORENSICS! SEE IF THERE'S A MATCH BETWEEN THE GASH ON THE LEG AND THE BROKEN PIECES OF THE VASE!
OKAY.
BUT THE VASE FRAGMENTS HAVE BEEN STOMPED TO PIECES. I DON'T KNOW IF WE'LL BE ABLE TO FIND A MATCH WITH THE WOUND.
TOO BAD. A POSITIVE MATCH WOULD ANSWER THE QUESTION.
IT'S SUICIDE! SUICIDE! NO QUESTION ABOUT IT!
...

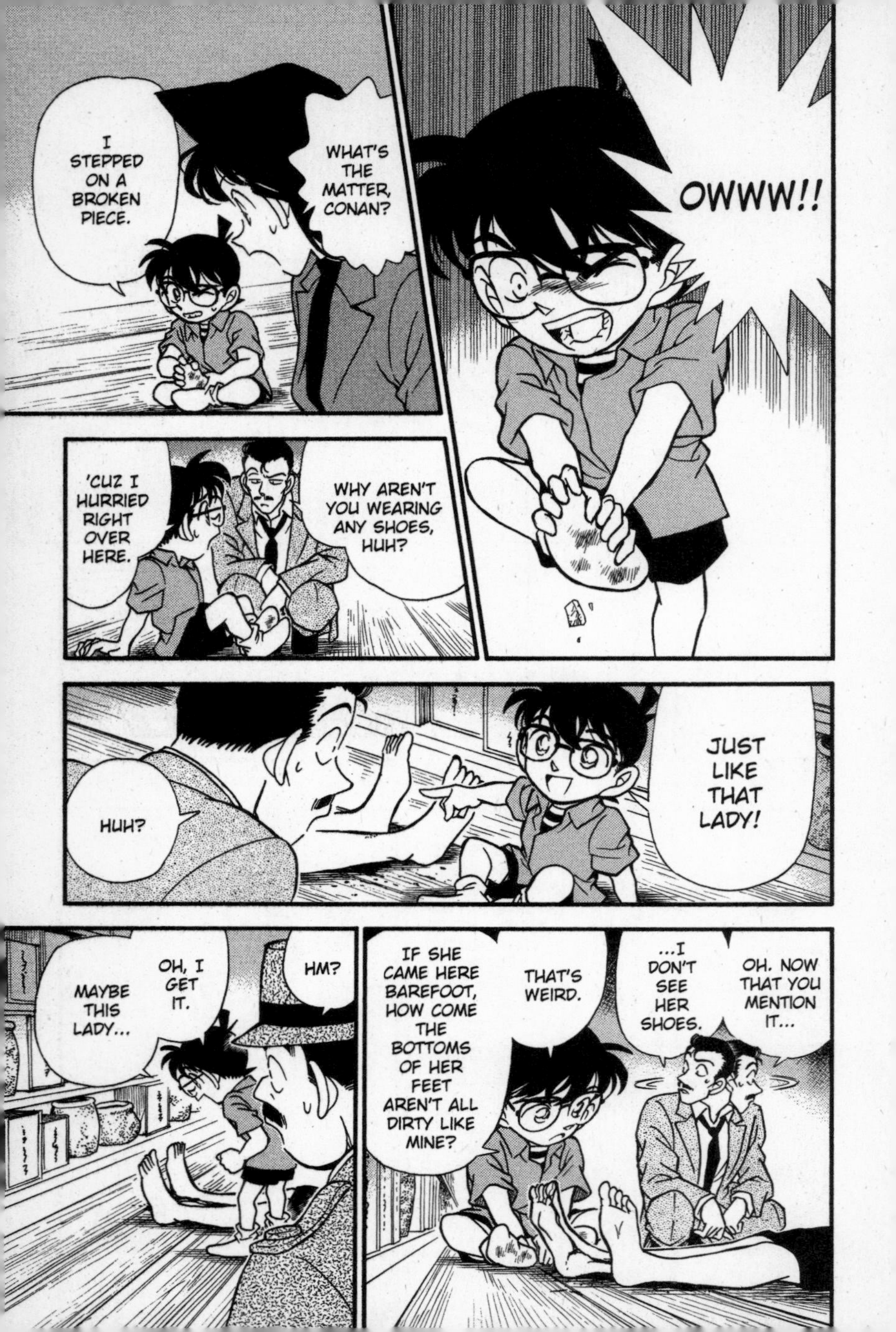
OWWW!!
WHAT'S THE MATTER, CONAN?
I STEPPED ON A BROKEN PIECE.
WHY AREN'T YOU WEARING ANY SHOES, HUH?
'CUZ I HURRIED RIGHT OVER HERE.
JUST LIKE THAT LADY!
HUH?
OH. NOW THAT YOU MENTION IT...
...I DON'T SEE HER SHOES.
THAT'S WEIRD.
IF SHE CAME HERE BAREFOOT, HOW COME THE BOTTOMS OF HER FEET AREN'T ALL DIRTY LIKE MINE?
HM?
OH, I GET IT.
MAYBE THIS LADY...

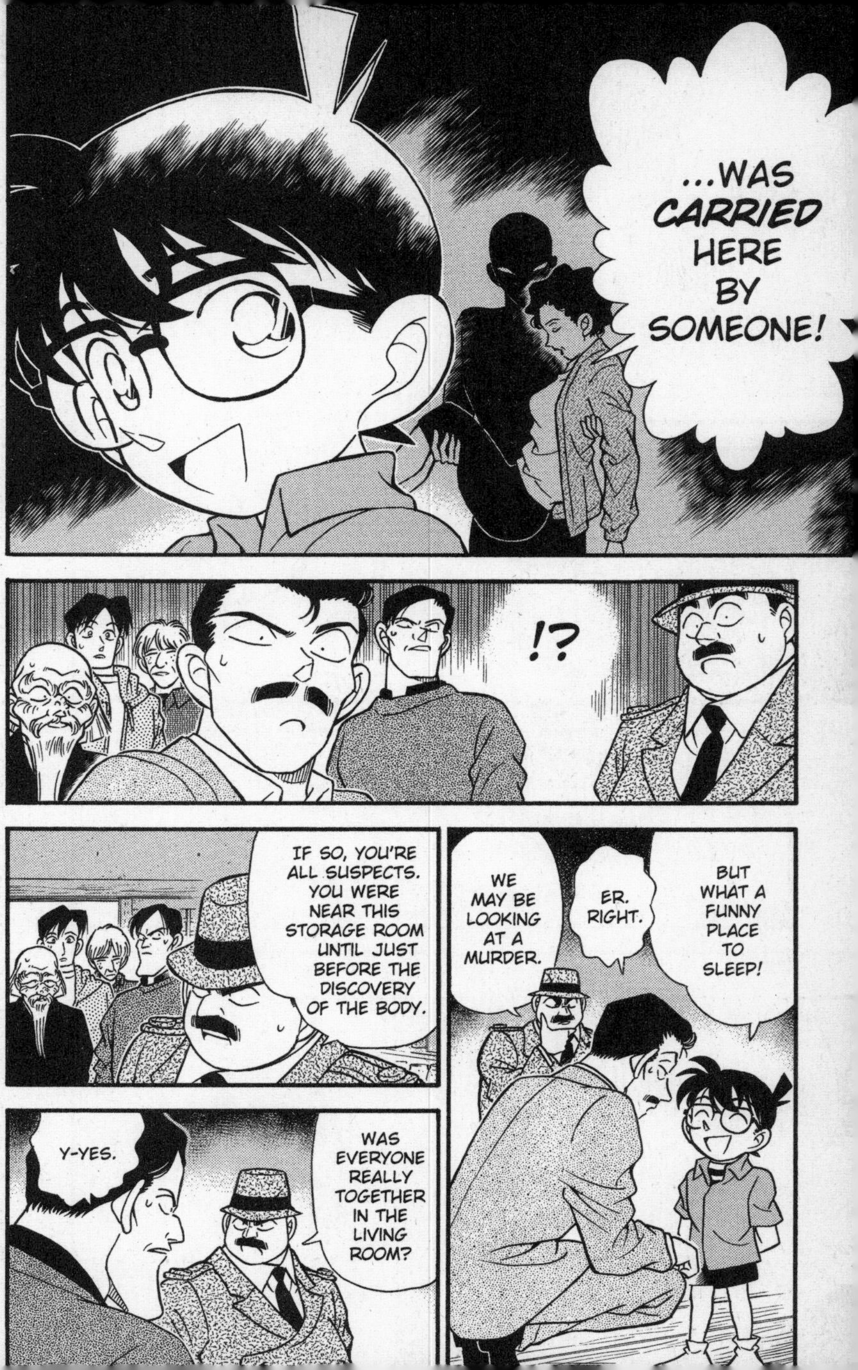
...WAS CARRIED HERE BY SOMEONE!
!?
BUT WHAT A FUNNY PLACE TO SLEEP!
ER. RIGHT.
WE MAY BE LOOKING AT A MURDER.
IF SO, YOU'RE ALL SUSPECTS. YOU WERE NEAR THIS STORAGE ROOM UNTIL JUST BEFORE THE DISCOVERY OF THE BODY.
WAS EVERYONE REALLY TOGETHER IN THE LIVING ROOM?
Y-YES.

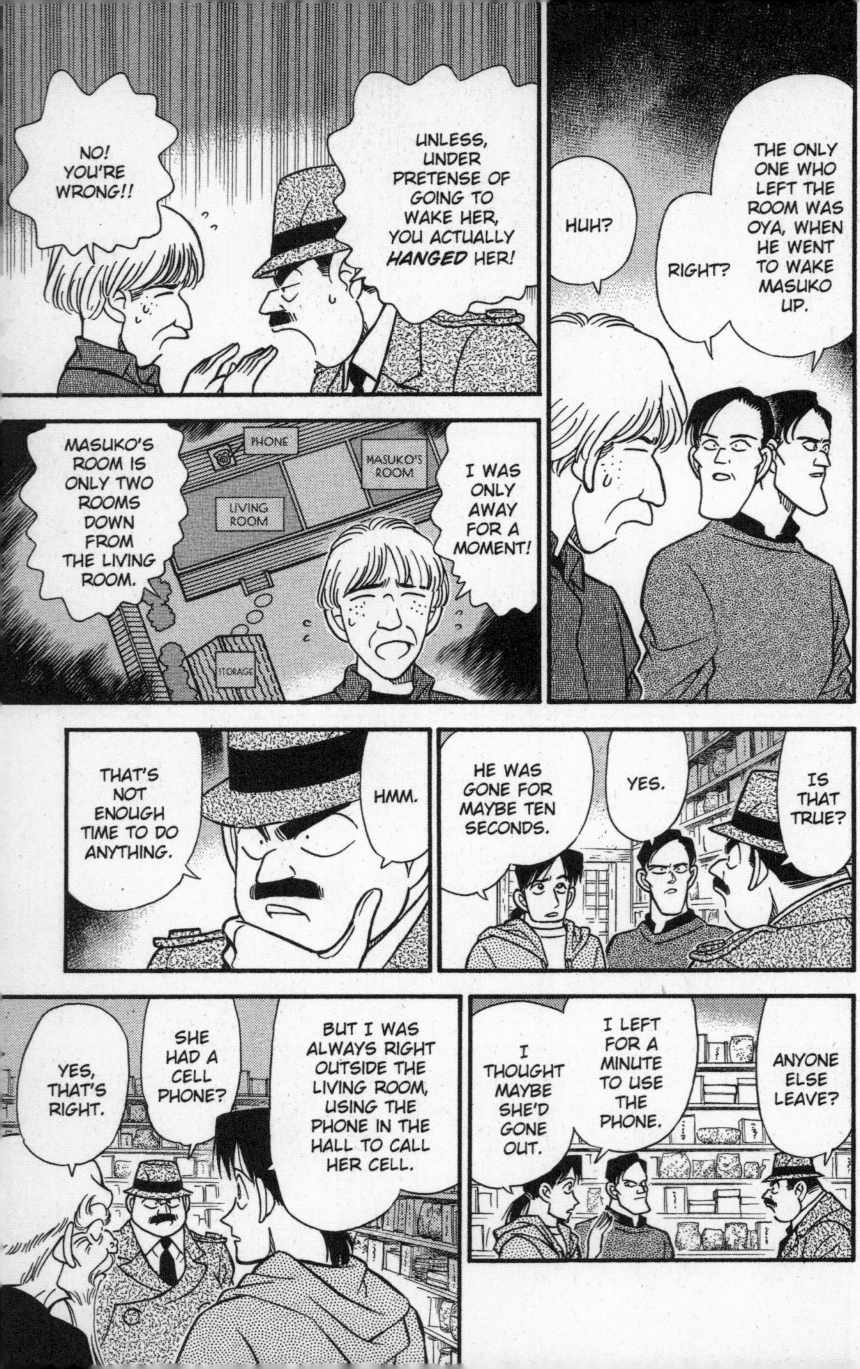
THE ONLY ONE WHO LEFT THE ROOM WAS OYA, WHEN HE WENT TO WAKE MASUKO UP.
RIGHT?
HUH?
UNLESS, UNDER PRETENSE OF GOING TO WAKE HER, YOU ACTUALLY **HANGED** HER!
NO! YOU'RE WRONG!!
I WAS ONLY AWAY FOR A MOMENT!
MASUKO'S ROOM IS ONLY TWO ROOMS DOWN FROM THE LIVING ROOM.
PHONE
MASUKO'S ROOM
LIVING ROOM
STORAGE
IS THAT TRUE?
YES.
HE WAS GONE FOR MAYBE TEN SECONDS.
HMM.
THAT'S NOT ENOUGH TIME TO DO ANYTHING.
ANYONE ELSE LEAVE?
I LEFT FOR A MINUTE TO USE THE PHONE.
I THOUGHT MAYBE SHE'D GONE OUT.
BUT I WAS ALWAYS RIGHT OUTSIDE THE LIVING ROOM, USING THE PHONE IN THE HALL TO CALL HER CELL.
SHE HAD A CELL PHONE?
YES, THAT'S RIGHT.

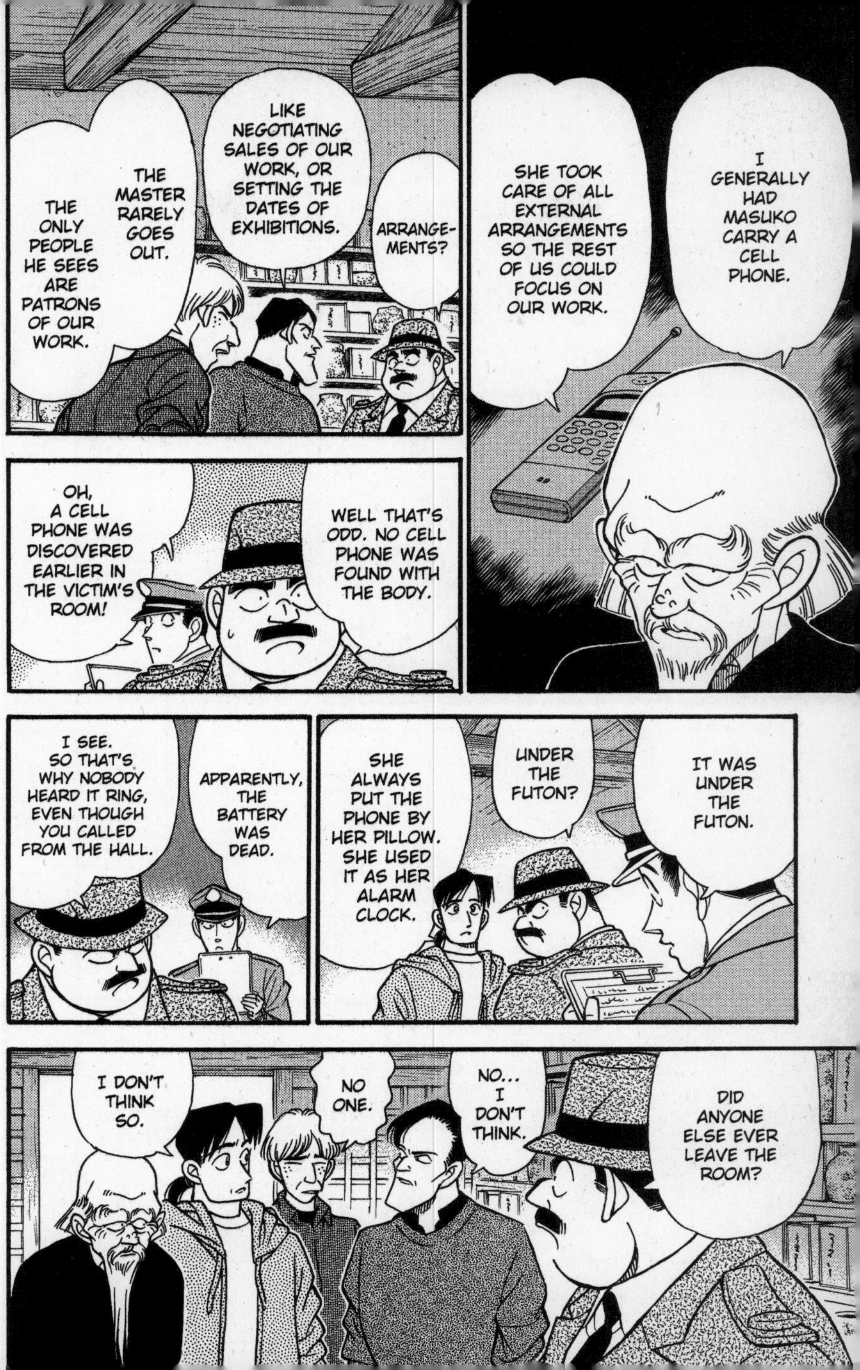
I GENERALLY HAD MASUKO CARRY A CELL PHONE.
SHE TOOK CARE OF ALL EXTERNAL ARRANGEMENTS SO THE REST OF US COULD FOCUS ON OUR WORK.
ARRANGE-MENTS?
LIKE NEGOTIATING SALES OF OUR WORK, OR SETTING THE DATES OF EXHIBITIONS.
THE MASTER RARELY GOES OUT.
THE ONLY PEOPLE HE SEES ARE PATRONS OF OUR WORK.
WELL THAT'S ODD. NO CELL PHONE WAS FOUND WITH THE BODY.
OH, A CELL PHONE WAS DISCOVERED EARLIER IN THE VICTIM'S ROOM!
IT WAS UNDER THE FUTON.
UNDER THE FUTON?
SHE ALWAYS PUT THE PHONE BY HER PILLOW. SHE USED IT AS HER ALARM CLOCK.
APPARENTLY, THE BATTERY WAS DEAD.
I SEE. SO THAT'S WHY NOBODY HEARD IT RING, EVEN THOUGH YOU CALLED FROM THE HALL.
DID ANYONE ELSE EVER LEAVE THE ROOM?
NO... I DON'T THINK.
NO ONE.
I DON'T THINK SO.

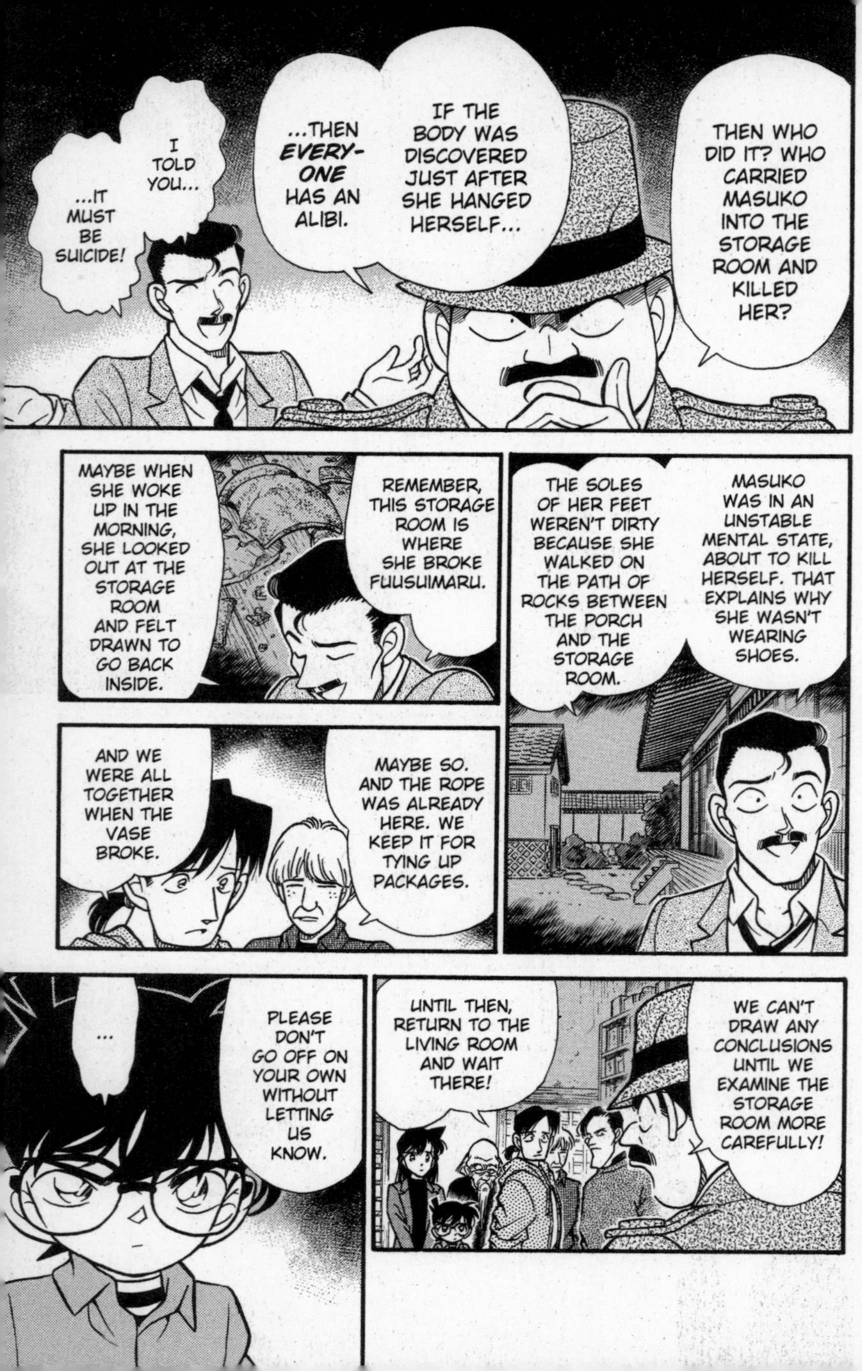
THEN WHO DID IT? WHO CARRIED MASUKO INTO THE STORAGE ROOM AND KILLED HER?
IF THE BODY WAS DISCOVERED JUST AFTER SHE HANGED HERSELF...
...THEN *EVERYONE* HAS AN ALIBI.
I TOLD YOU...
...IT MUST BE SUICIDE!
MASUKO WAS IN AN UNSTABLE MENTAL STATE, ABOUT TO KILL HERSELF. THAT EXPLAINS WHY SHE WASN'T WEARING SHOES.
THE SOLES OF HER FEET WEREN'T DIRTY BECAUSE SHE WALKED ON THE PATH OF ROCKS BETWEEN THE PORCH AND THE STORAGE ROOM.
REMEMBER, THIS STORAGE ROOM IS WHERE SHE BROKE FUUSUIMARU.
MAYBE WHEN SHE WOKE UP IN THE MORNING, SHE LOOKED OUT AT THE STORAGE ROOM AND FELT DRAWN TO GO BACK INSIDE.
MAYBE SO. AND THE ROPE WAS ALREADY HERE. WE KEEP IT FOR TYING UP PACKAGES.
AND WE WERE ALL TOGETHER WHEN THE VASE BROKE.
WE CAN'T DRAW ANY CONCLUSIONS UNTIL WE EXAMINE THE STORAGE ROOM MORE CAREFULLY!
UNTIL THEN, RETURN TO THE LIVING ROOM AND WAIT THERE!
PLEASE DON'T GO OFF ON YOUR OWN WITHOUT LETTING US KNOW.
...

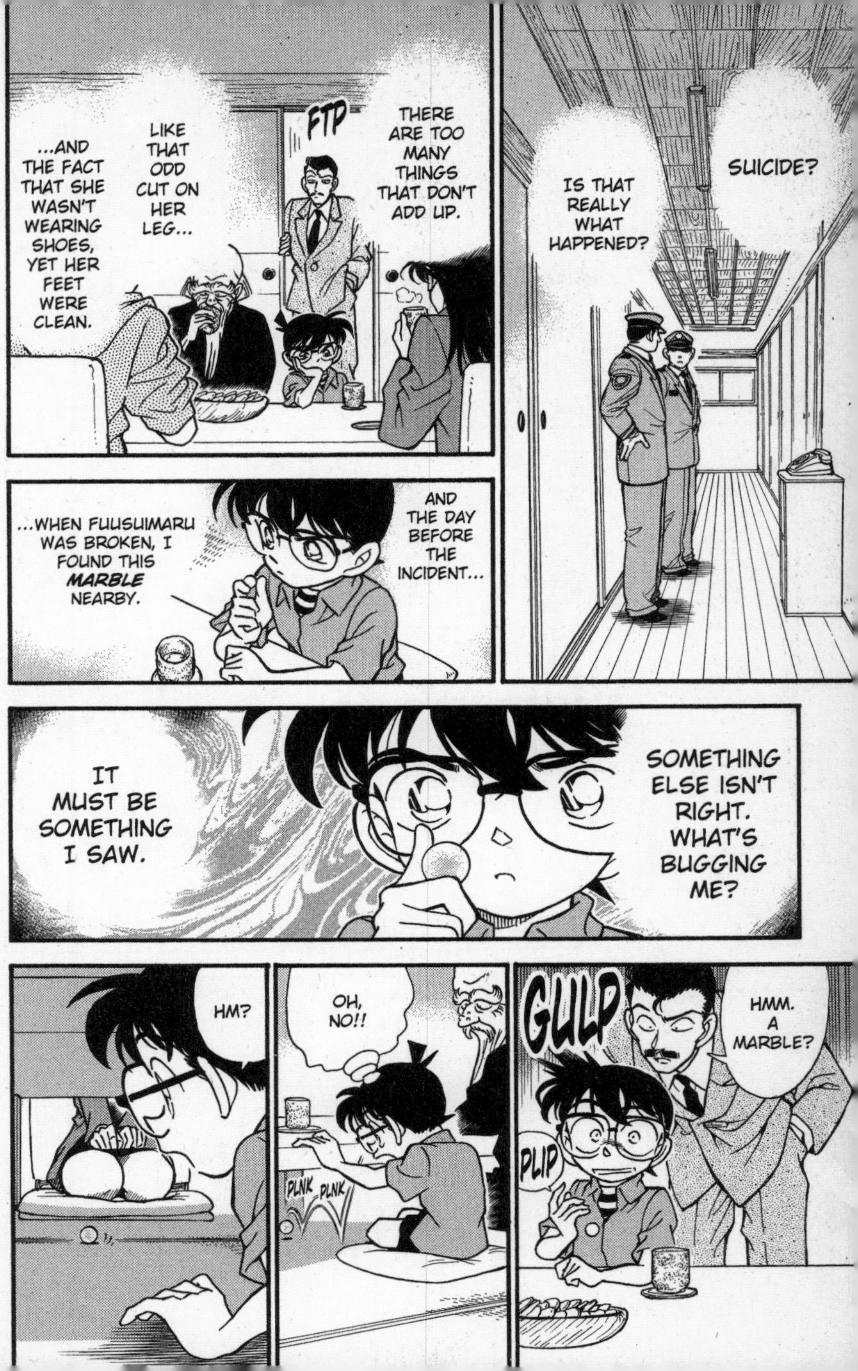
SUICIDE?
IS THAT REALLY WHAT HAPPENED?
THERE ARE TOO MANY THINGS THAT DON'T ADD UP.
FTP
LIKE THAT ODD CUT ON HER LEG...
...AND THE FACT THAT SHE WASN'T WEARING SHOES, YET HER FEET WERE CLEAN.
AND THE DAY BEFORE THE INCIDENT...
...WHEN FUUSUIMARU WAS BROKEN, I FOUND THIS MARBLE NEARBY.
SOMETHING ELSE ISN'T RIGHT. WHAT'S BUGGING ME?
IT MUST BE SOMETHING I SAW.
HMM. A MARBLE?
GULP
PLIP
OH, NO!!
PLNK PLNK
HM?

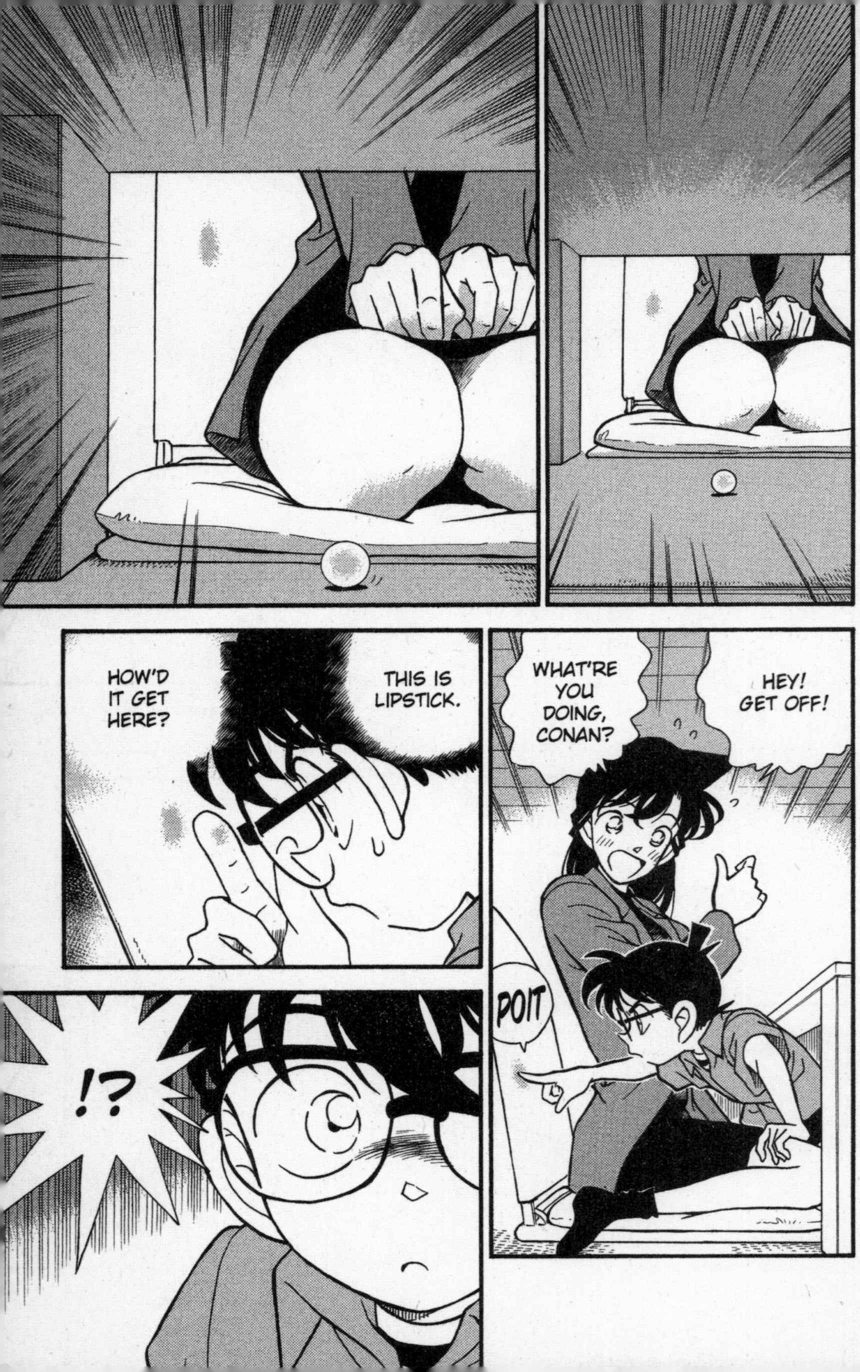
HEY! GET OFF!
WHAT'RE YOU DOING, CONAN?
POIT
THIS IS LIPSTICK.
HOW'D IT GET HERE?
!?

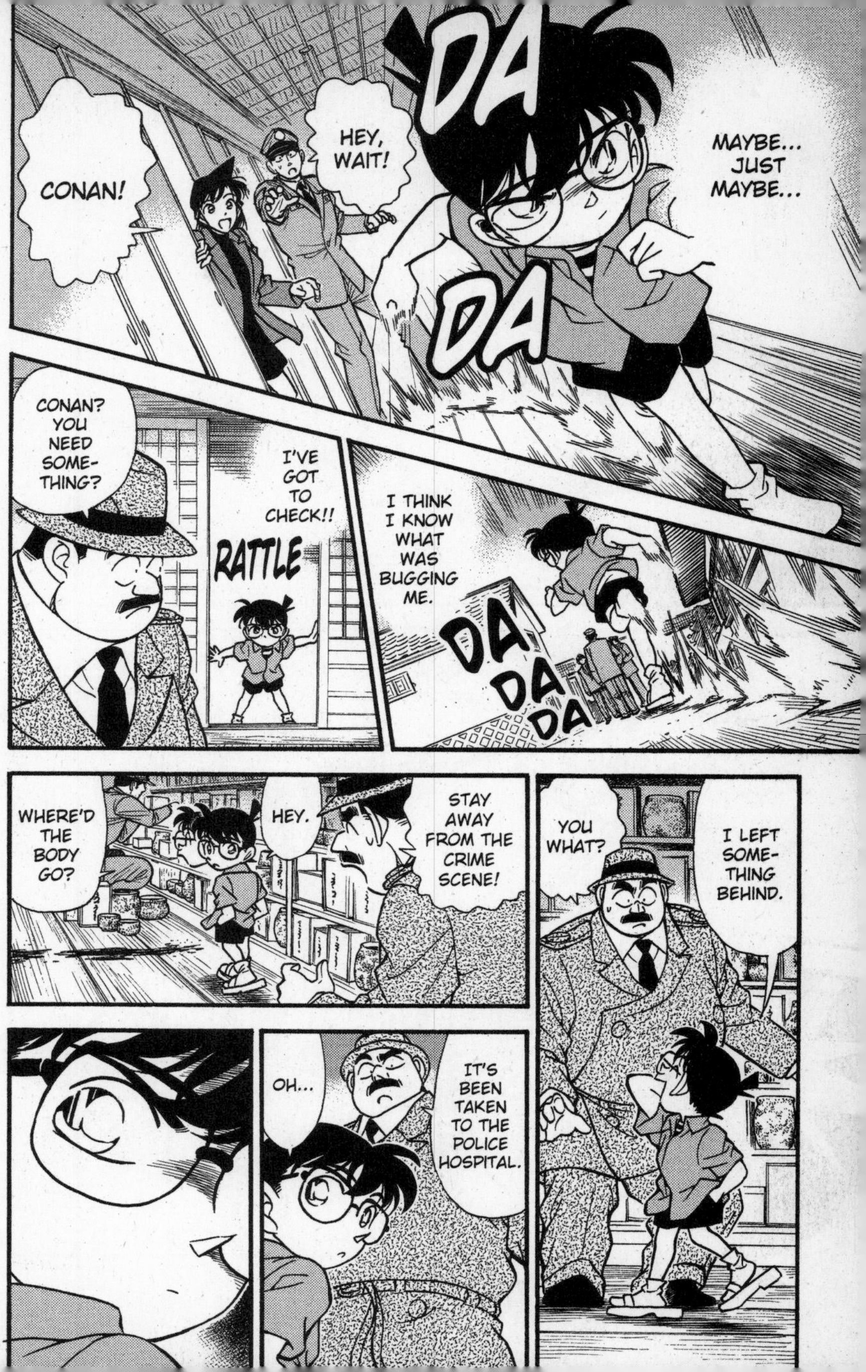
MAYBE... JUST MAYBE...
DA
DA
HEY, WAIT!
CONAN!
I THINK I KNOW WHAT WAS BUGGING ME.
DA DA DA
I'VE GOT TO CHECK!!
RATTLE
CONAN? YOU NEED SOME-THING?
I LEFT SOME-THING BEHIND.
YOU WHAT?
STAY AWAY FROM THE CRIME SCENE!
HEY.
WHERE'D THE BODY GO?
IT'S BEEN TAKEN TO THE POLICE HOSPITAL.
OH...

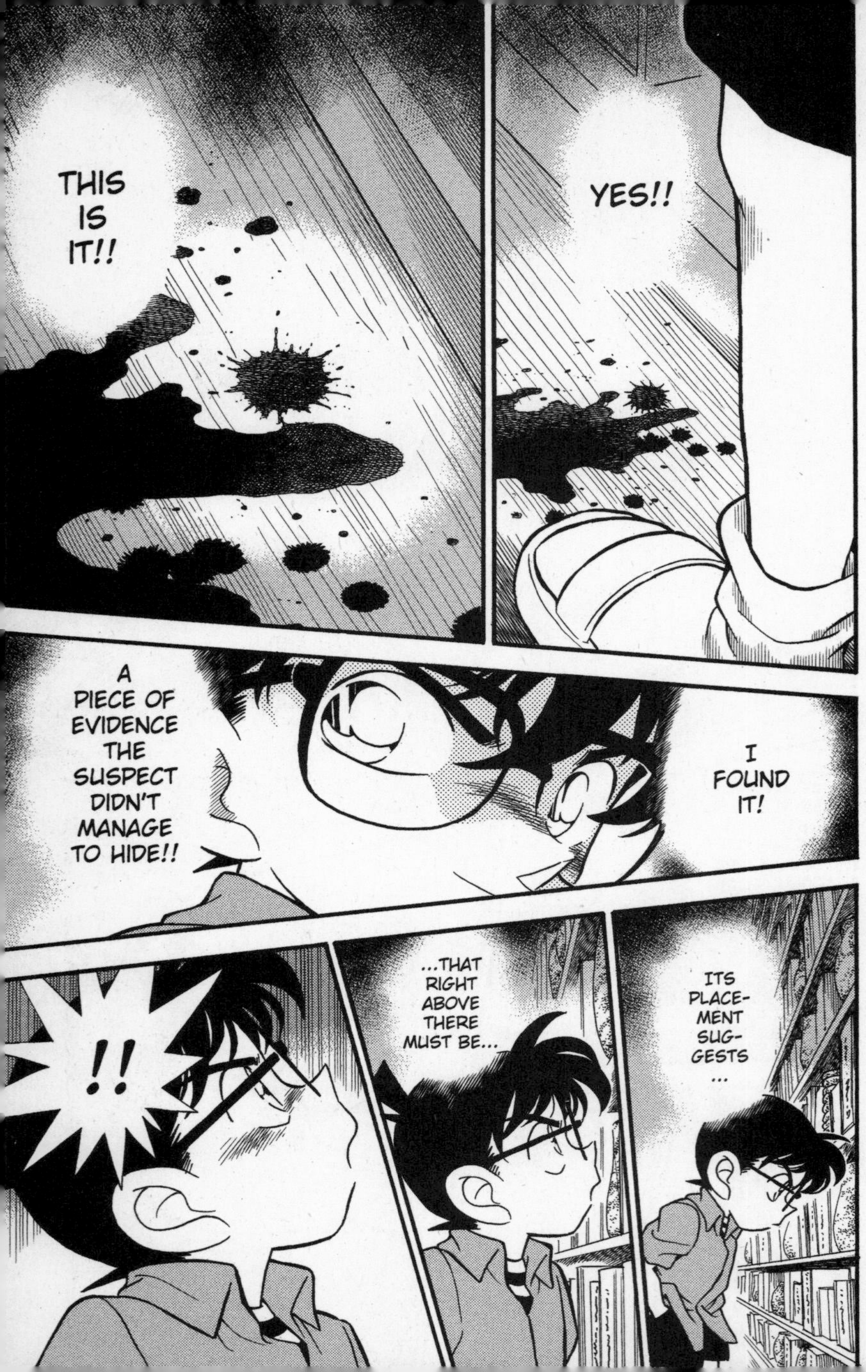
YES!!
THIS IS IT!!
I FOUND IT!
A PIECE OF EVIDENCE THE SUSPECT DIDN'T MANAGE TO HIDE!!
ITS PLACEMENT SUGGESTS...
...THAT RIGHT ABOVE THERE MUST BE...
!!

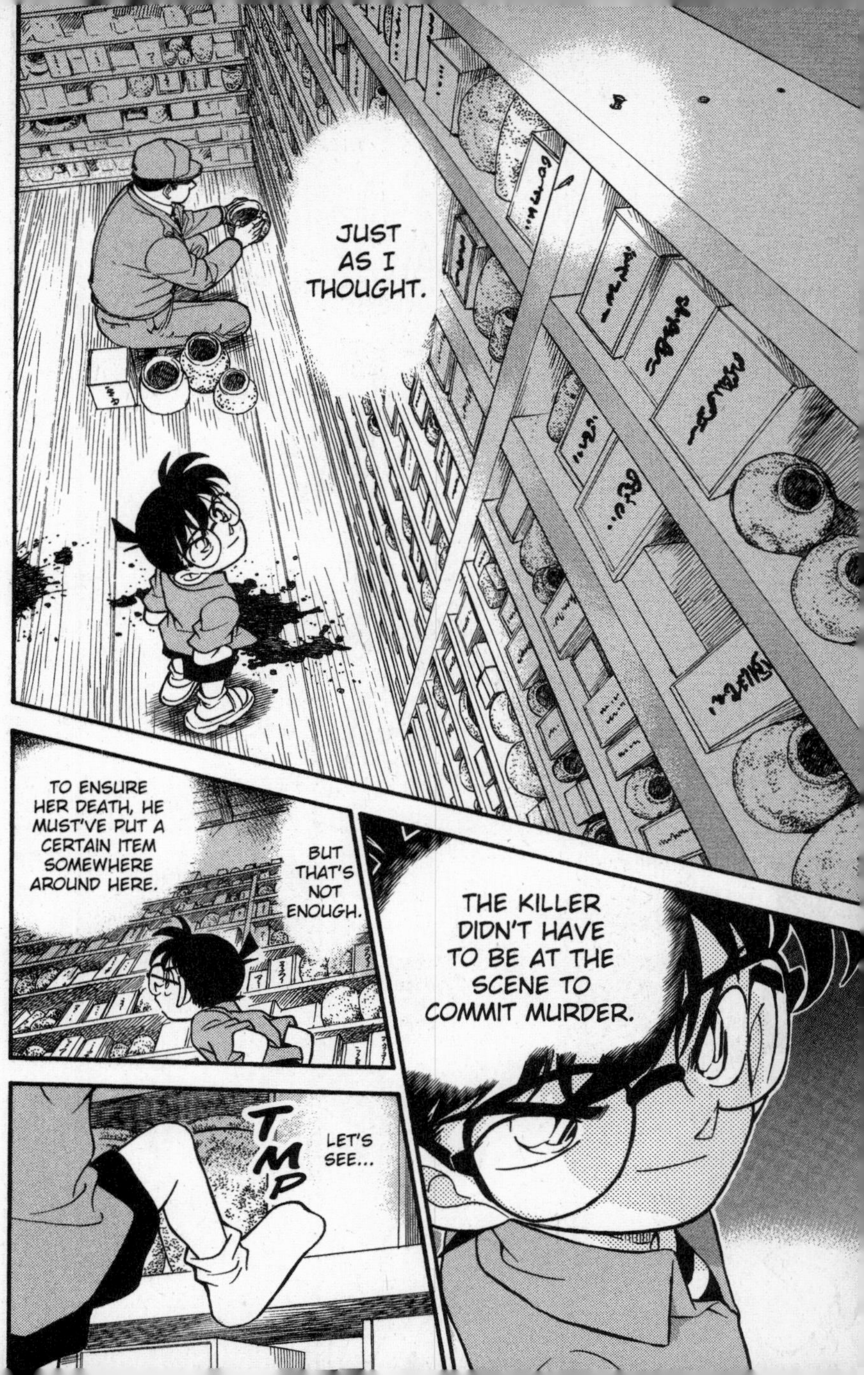
JUST AS I THOUGHT.
THE KILLER DIDN'T HAVE TO BE AT THE SCENE TO COMMIT MURDER.
TO ENSURE HER DEATH, HE MUST'VE PUT A CERTAIN ITEM SOMEWHERE AROUND HERE.
BUT THAT'S NOT ENOUGH.
LET'S SEE...
TMP

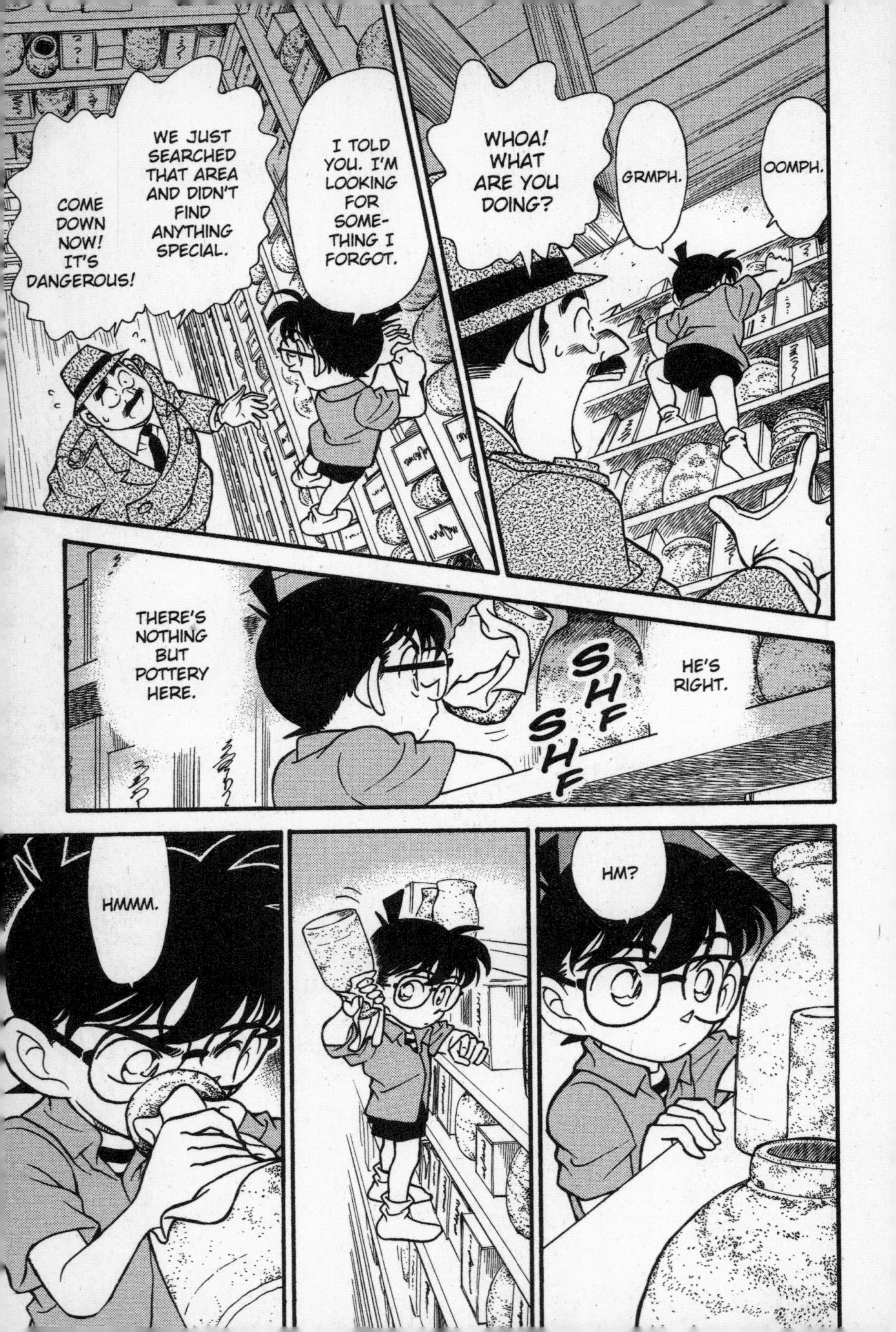
OOMPH.
GRMPH.
WHOA! WHAT ARE YOU DOING?
I TOLD YOU. I'M LOOKING FOR SOME-THING I FORGOT.
WE JUST SEARCHED THAT AREA AND DIDN'T FIND ANYTHING SPECIAL.
COME DOWN NOW! IT'S DANGEROUS!
HE'S RIGHT.
SHF SHF
THERE'S NOTHING BUT POTTERY HERE.
HM?
HMMM.

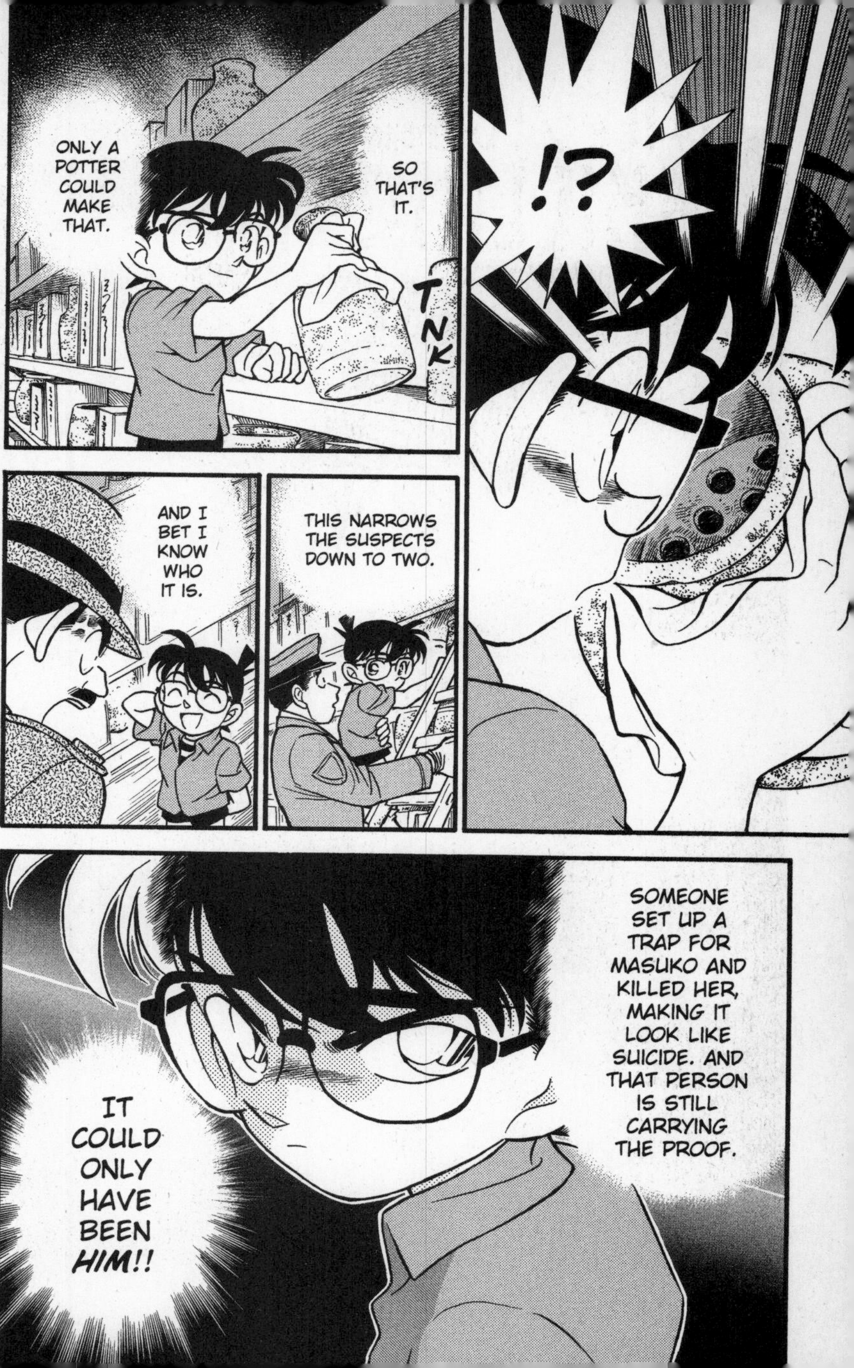
!?
SO THAT'S IT.
ONLY A POTTER COULD MAKE THAT.
TNK
THIS NARROWS THE SUSPECTS DOWN TO TWO.
AND I BET I KNOW WHO IT IS.
SOMEONE SET UP A TRAP FOR MASUKO AND KILLED HER, MAKING IT LOOK LIKE SUICIDE. AND THAT PERSON IS STILL CARRYING THE PROOF.
IT COULD ONLY HAVE BEEN *HIM*!!

FILE 2: KILLING WITH SOUND?

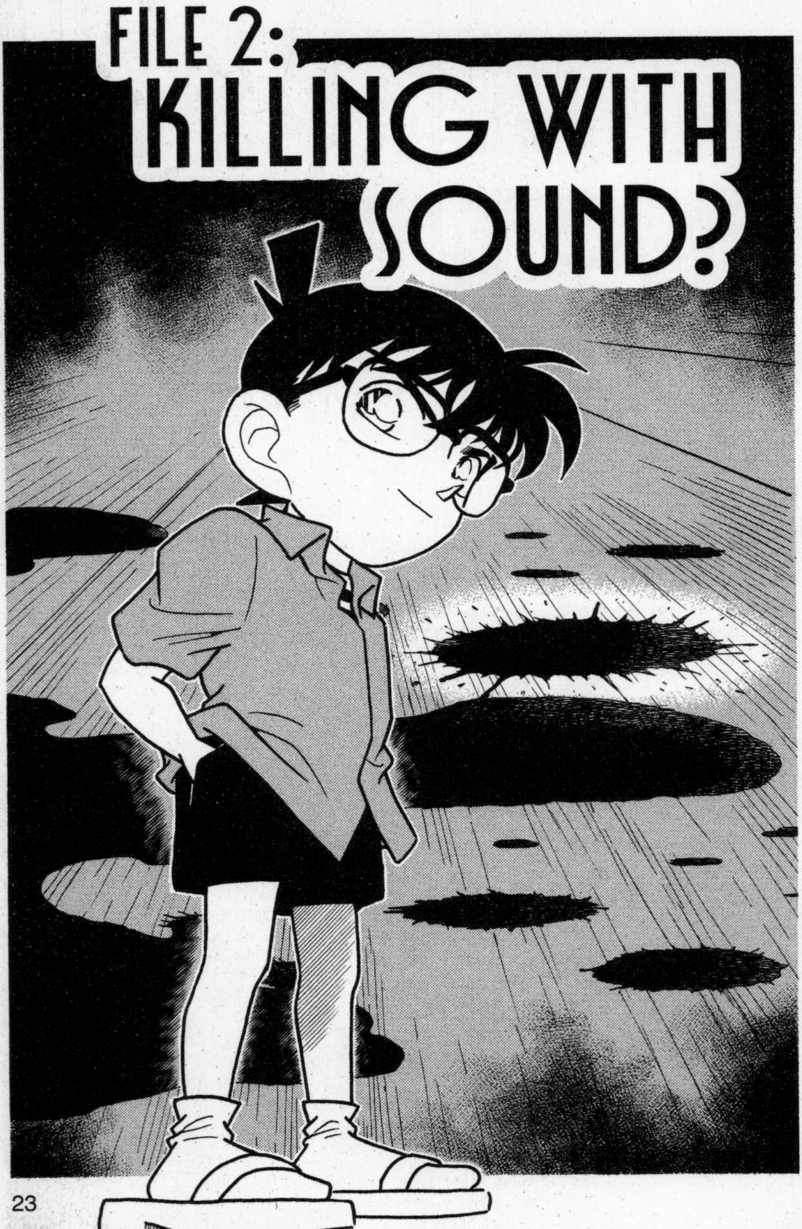

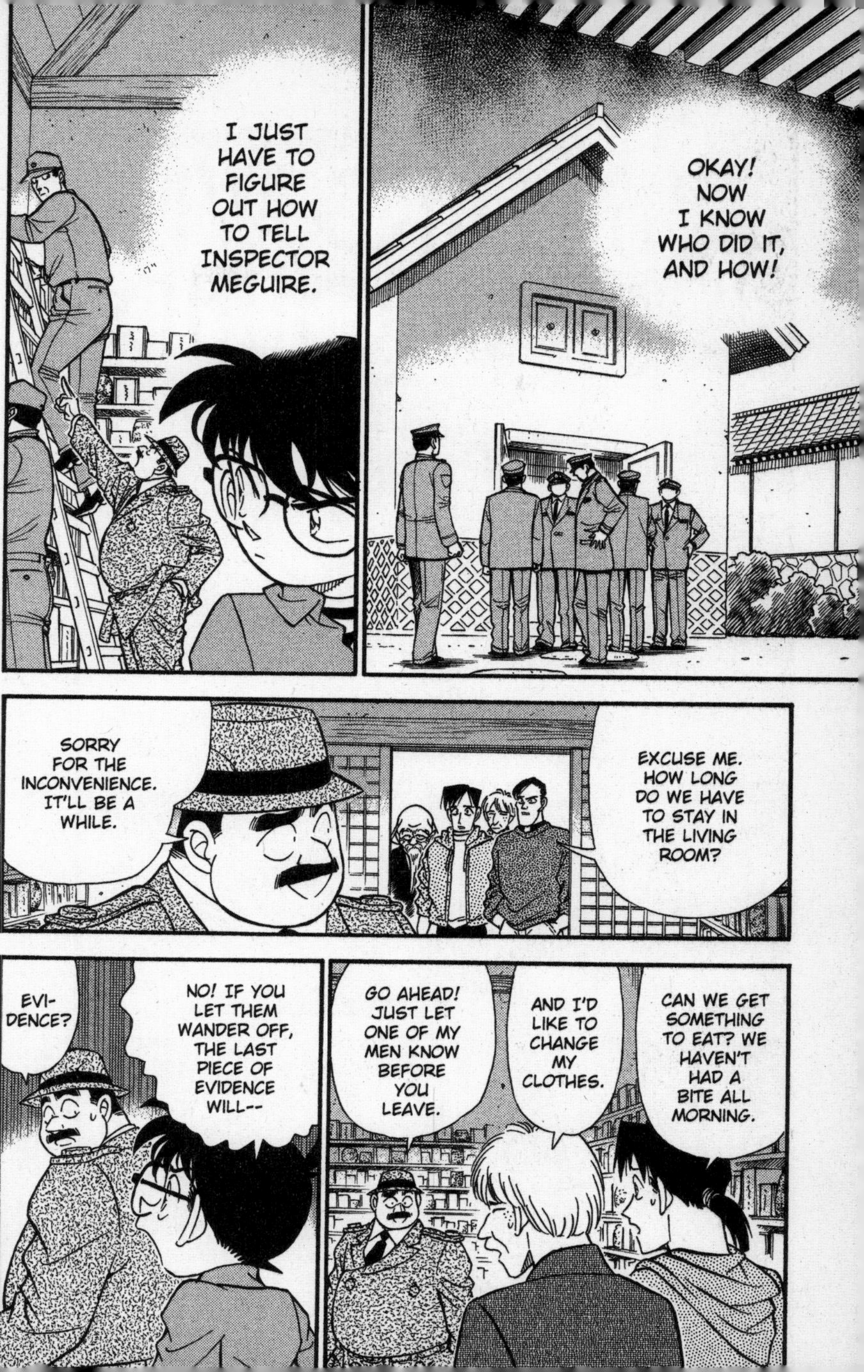
OKAY! NOW I KNOW WHO DID IT, AND HOW!
I JUST HAVE TO FIGURE OUT HOW TO TELL INSPECTOR MEGUIRE.
EXCUSE ME. HOW LONG DO WE HAVE TO STAY IN THE LIVING ROOM?
SORRY FOR THE INCONVENIENCE. IT'LL BE A WHILE.
CAN WE GET SOMETHING TO EAT? WE HAVEN'T HAD A BITE ALL MORNING.
AND I'D LIKE TO CHANGE MY CLOTHES.
GO AHEAD! JUST LET ONE OF MY MEN KNOW BEFORE YOU LEAVE.
NO! IF YOU LET THEM WANDER OFF, THE LAST PIECE OF EVIDENCE WILL--
EVI- DENCE?

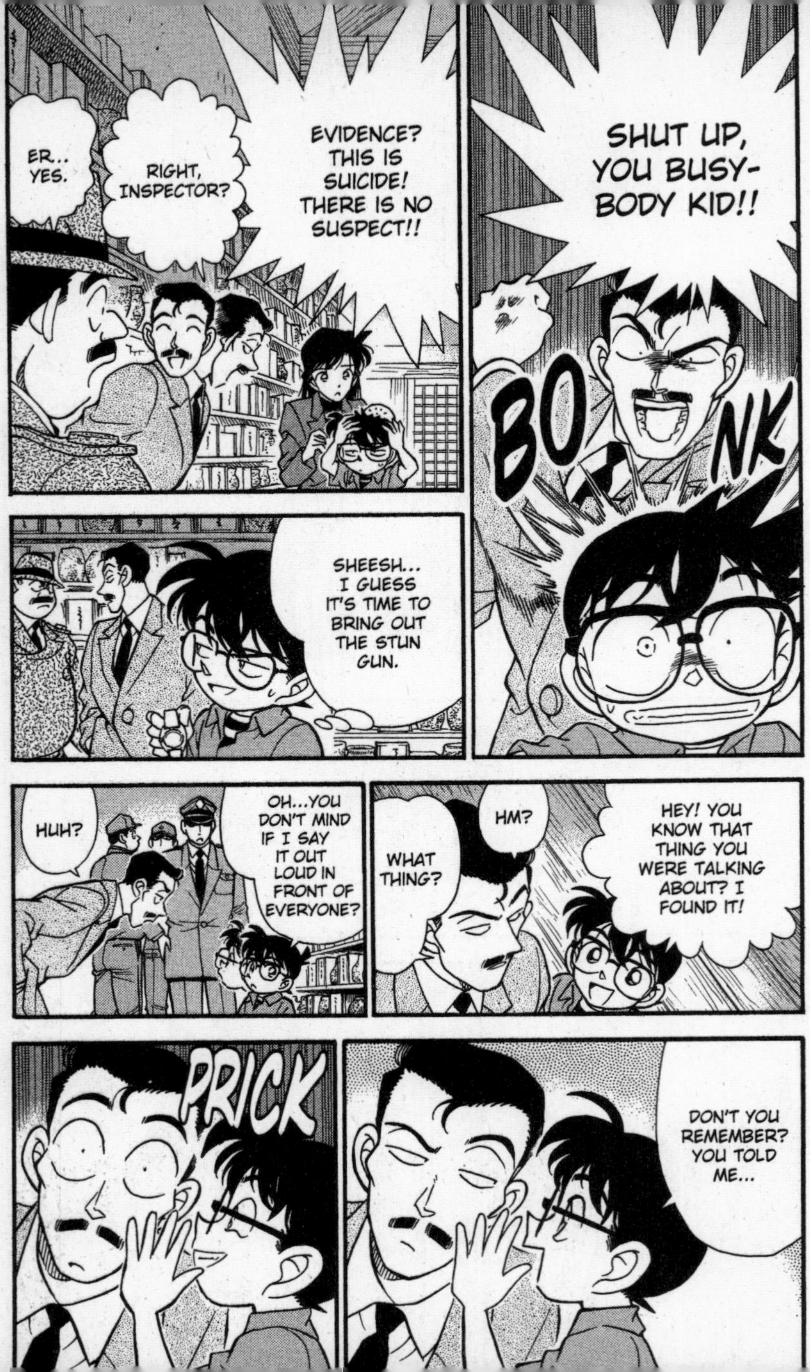
SHUT UP, YOU BUSY-BODY KID!!
BONK
EVIDENCE? THIS IS SUICIDE! THERE IS NO SUSPECT!!
RIGHT, INSPECTOR?
ER... YES.
SHEESH... I GUESS IT'S TIME TO BRING OUT THE STUN GUN.
HEY! YOU KNOW THAT THING YOU WERE TALKING ABOUT? I FOUND IT!
HM?
WHAT THING?
OH...YOU DON'T MIND IF I SAY IT OUT LOUD IN FRONT OF EVERYONE?
HUH?
DON'T YOU REMEMBER? YOU TOLD ME...
PRICK

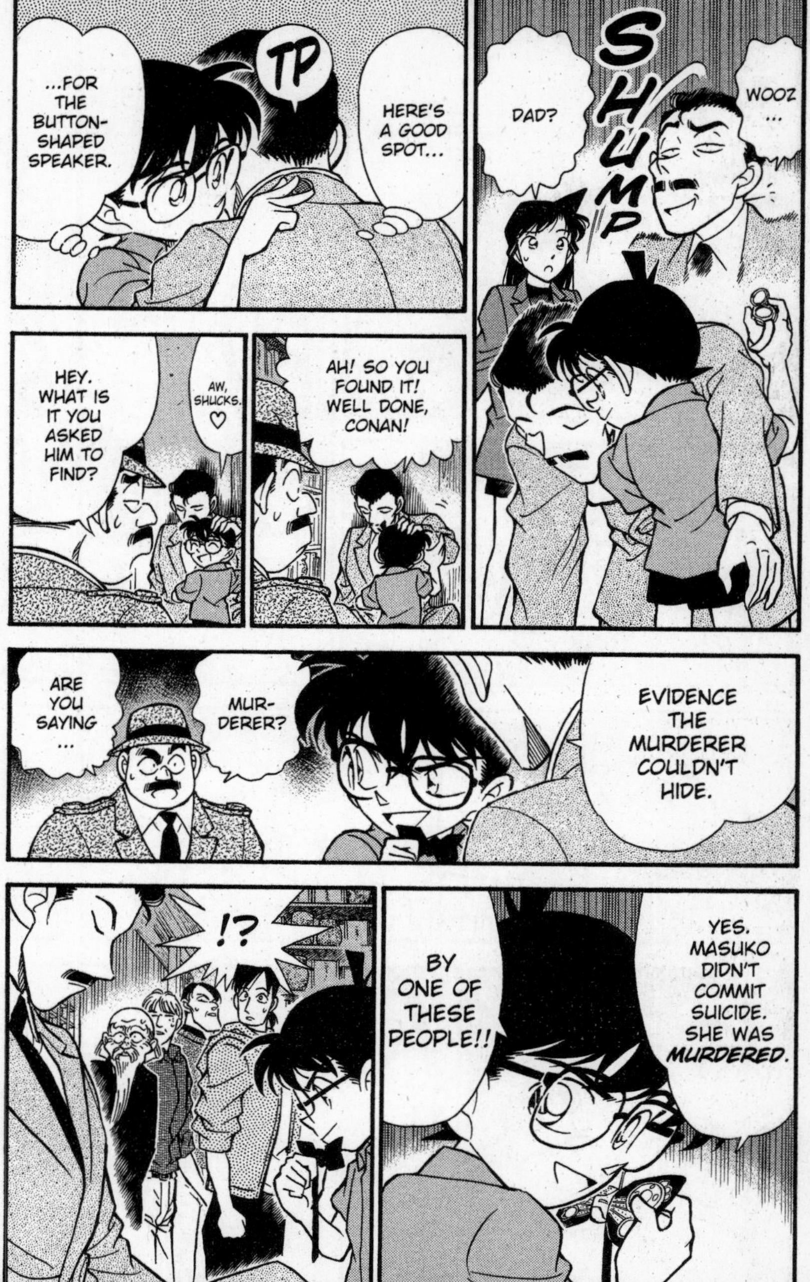
WOOZ ...
SHUMP
DAD?
HERE'S A GOOD SPOT...
TP
...FOR THE BUTTON-SHAPED SPEAKER.
AH! SO YOU FOUND IT! WELL DONE, CONAN!
AW, SHUCKS. ♡
HEY. WHAT IS IT YOU ASKED HIM TO FIND?
EVIDENCE THE MURDERER COULDN'T HIDE.
MUR-DERER?
ARE YOU SAYING ...
YES. MASUKO DIDN'T COMMIT SUICIDE. SHE WAS *MURDERED*.
BY ONE OF THESE PEOPLE!!
!?

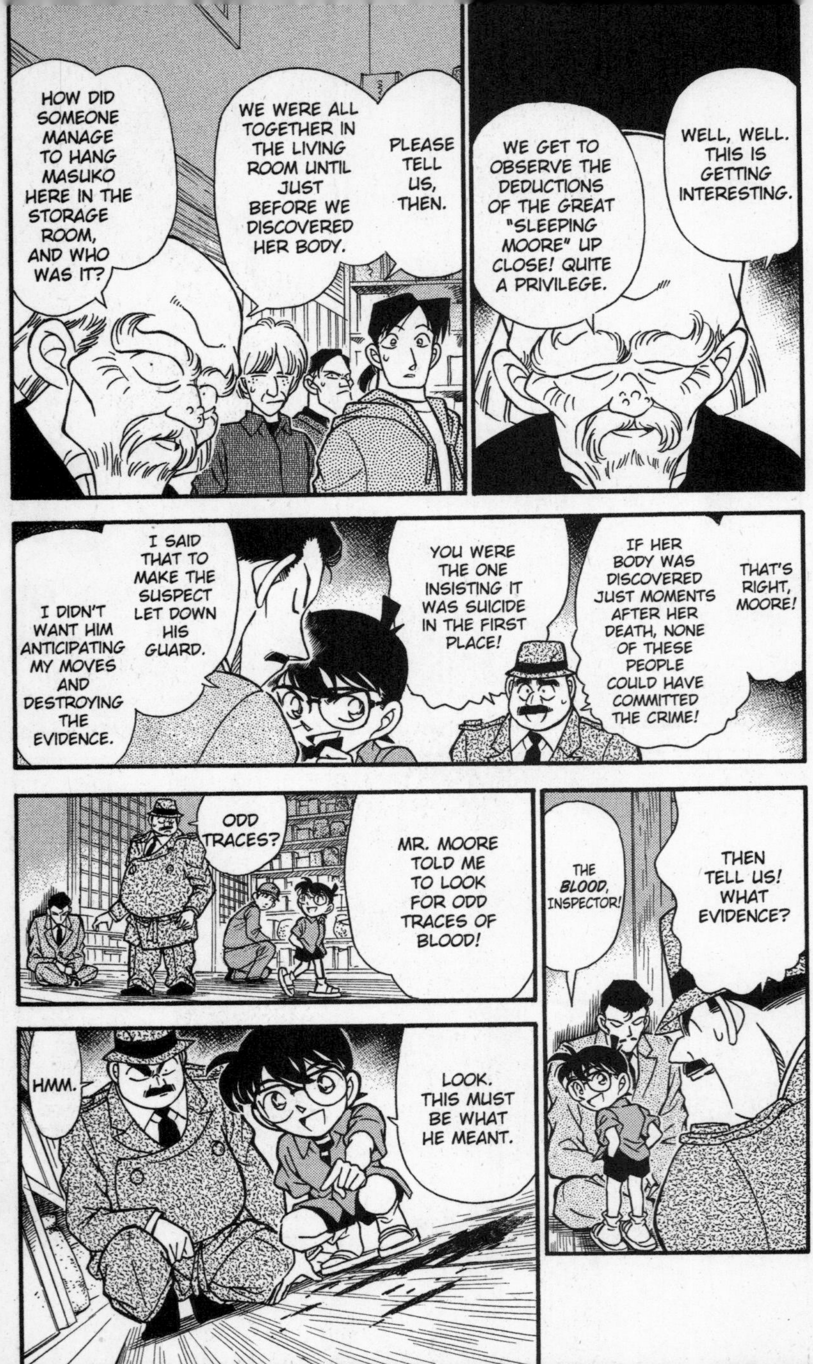
WELL, WELL. THIS IS GETTING INTERESTING.
WE GET TO OBSERVE THE DEDUCTIONS OF THE GREAT "SLEEPING MOORE" UP CLOSE! QUITE A PRIVILEGE.
PLEASE TELL US, THEN.
WE WERE ALL TOGETHER IN THE LIVING ROOM UNTIL JUST BEFORE WE DISCOVERED HER BODY.
HOW DID SOMEONE MANAGE TO HANG MASUKO HERE IN THE STORAGE ROOM, AND WHO WAS IT?
THAT'S RIGHT, MOORE!
IF HER BODY WAS DISCOVERED JUST MOMENTS AFTER HER DEATH, NONE OF THESE PEOPLE COULD HAVE COMMITTED THE CRIME!
YOU WERE THE ONE INSISTING IT WAS SUICIDE IN THE FIRST PLACE!
I SAID THAT TO MAKE THE SUSPECT LET DOWN HIS GUARD.
I DIDN'T WANT HIM ANTICIPATING MY MOVES AND DESTROYING THE EVIDENCE.
THEN TELL US! WHAT EVIDENCE?
THE *BLOOD*, INSPECTOR!
MR. MOORE TOLD ME TO LOOK FOR ODD TRACES OF BLOOD!
ODD TRACES?
LOOK. THIS MUST BE WHAT HE MEANT.
HMM.

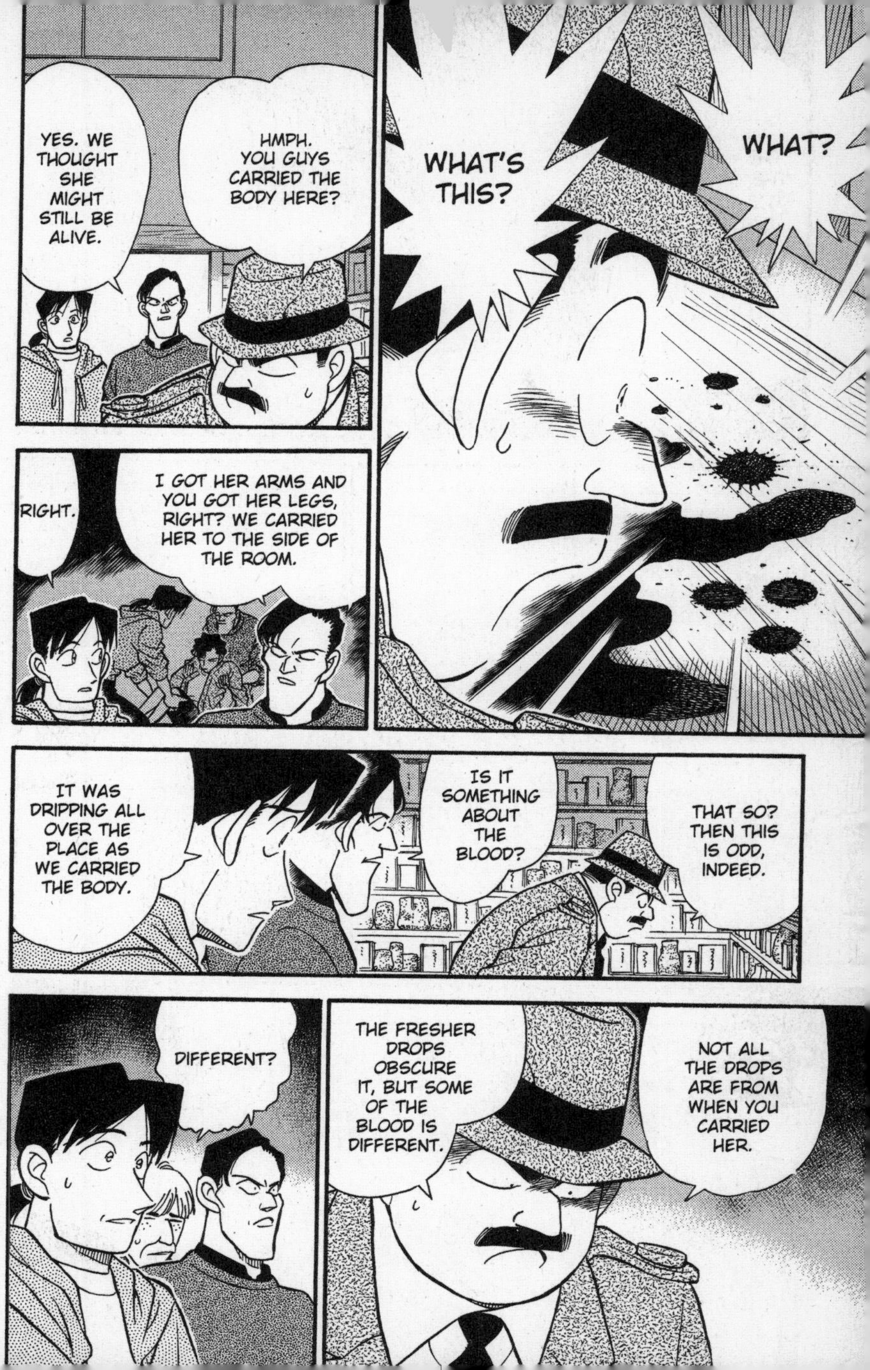
WHAT?
WHAT'S THIS?
HMPH. YOU GUYS CARRIED THE BODY HERE?
YES. WE THOUGHT SHE MIGHT STILL BE ALIVE.
I GOT HER ARMS AND YOU GOT HER LEGS, RIGHT? WE CARRIED HER TO THE SIDE OF THE ROOM.
RIGHT.
THAT SO? THEN THIS IS ODD, INDEED.
IS IT SOMETHING ABOUT THE BLOOD?
IT WAS DRIPPING ALL OVER THE PLACE AS WE CARRIED THE BODY.
NOT ALL THE DROPS ARE FROM WHEN YOU CARRIED HER.
THE FRESHER DROPS OBSCURE IT, BUT SOME OF THE BLOOD IS DIFFERENT.
DIFFERENT?

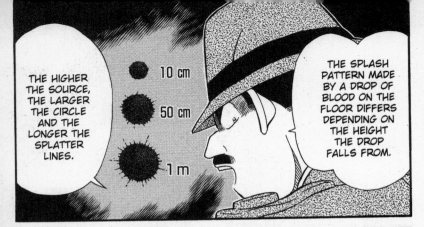

THE SPLASH PATTERN MADE BY A DROP OF BLOOD ON THE FLOOR DIFFERS DEPENDING ON THE HEIGHT THE DROP FALLS FROM.
10 cm
50 cm
1 m
THE HIGHER THE SOURCE, THE LARGER THE CIRCLE AND THE LONGER THE SPLATTER LINES.
IF YOU CARRIED HER BY THE ARMS AND LEGS, THE DISTANCE FROM HER TOES TO THE FLOOR WAS ABOUT 50 CENTI-METERS.
BUT THESE DROPS OBVIOUSLY FELL FROM A HEIGHT OF OVER ONE METER.
THAT'S CLEAR.
ARE YOU SAYING...
...SHE WAS ON TOP OF THESE SHELVES?
WHY WOULD SHE BE UP THERE?
!?
THAT'S RIGHT.

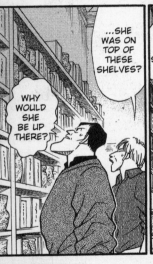

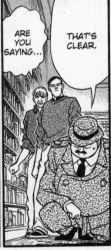

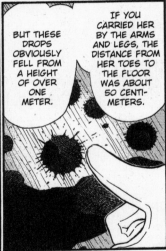

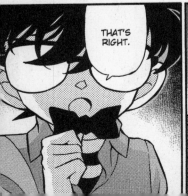

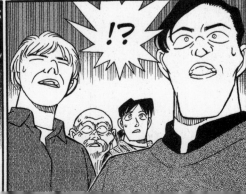

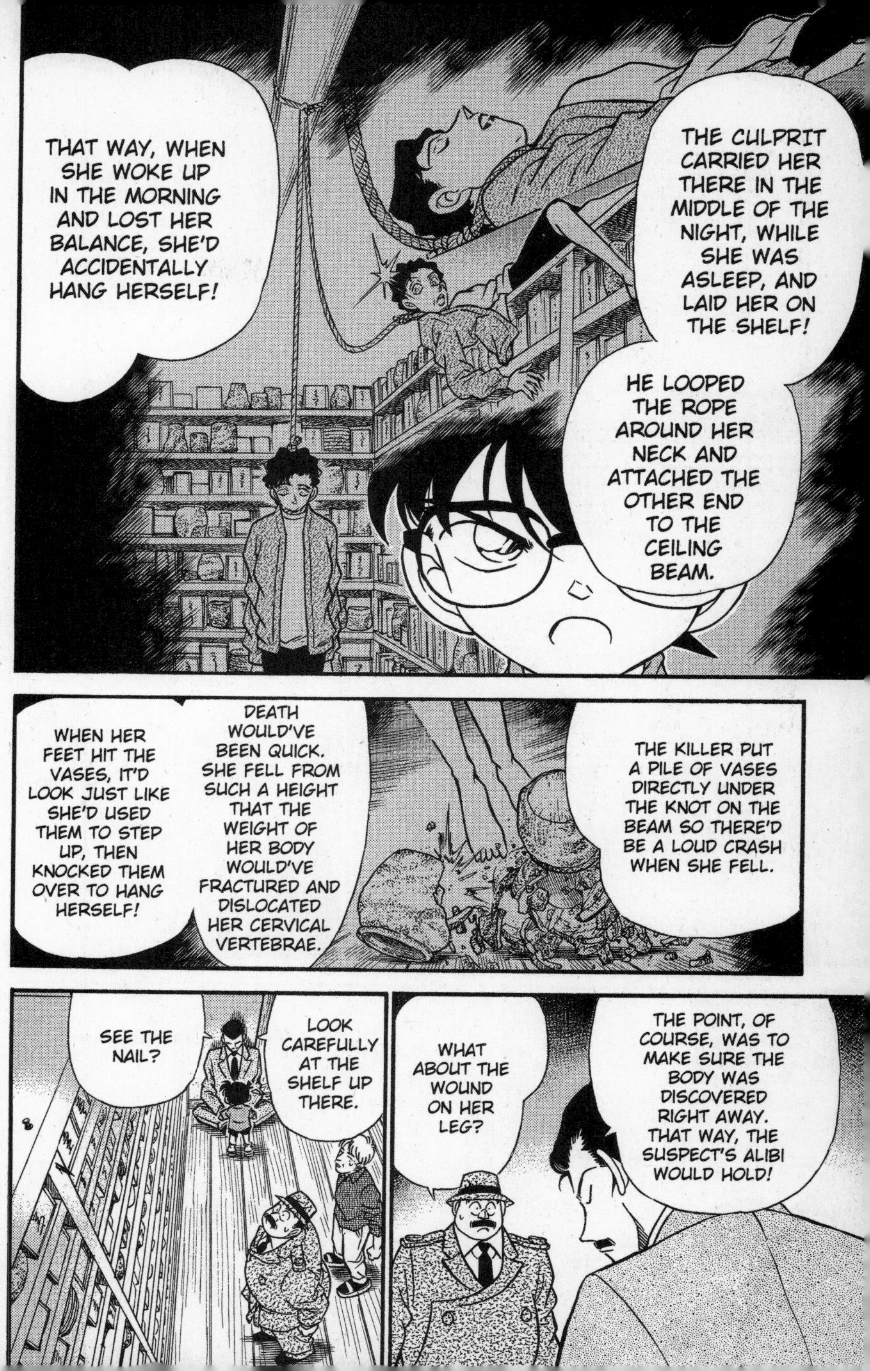
THE CULPRIT CARRIED HER THERE IN THE MIDDLE OF THE NIGHT, WHILE SHE WAS ASLEEP, AND LAID HER ON THE SHELF!
HE LOOPED THE ROPE AROUND HER NECK AND ATTACHED THE OTHER END TO THE CEILING BEAM.
THAT WAY, WHEN SHE WOKE UP IN THE MORNING AND LOST HER BALANCE, SHE'D ACCIDENTALLY HANG HERSELF!
THE KILLER PUT A PILE OF VASES DIRECTLY UNDER THE KNOT ON THE BEAM SO THERE'D BE A LOUD CRASH WHEN SHE FELL.
DEATH WOULD'VE BEEN QUICK. SHE FELL FROM SUCH A HEIGHT THAT THE WEIGHT OF HER BODY WOULD'VE FRACTURED AND DISLOCATED HER CERVICAL VERTEBRAE.
WHEN HER FEET HIT THE VASES, IT'D LOOK JUST LIKE SHE'D USED THEM TO STEP UP, THEN KNOCKED THEM OVER TO HANG HERSELF!
THE POINT, OF COURSE, WAS TO MAKE SURE THE BODY WAS DISCOVERED RIGHT AWAY. THAT WAY, THE SUSPECT'S ALIBI WOULD HOLD!
WHAT ABOUT THE WOUND ON HER LEG?
LOOK CAREFULLY AT THE SHELF UP THERE.
SEE THE NAIL?

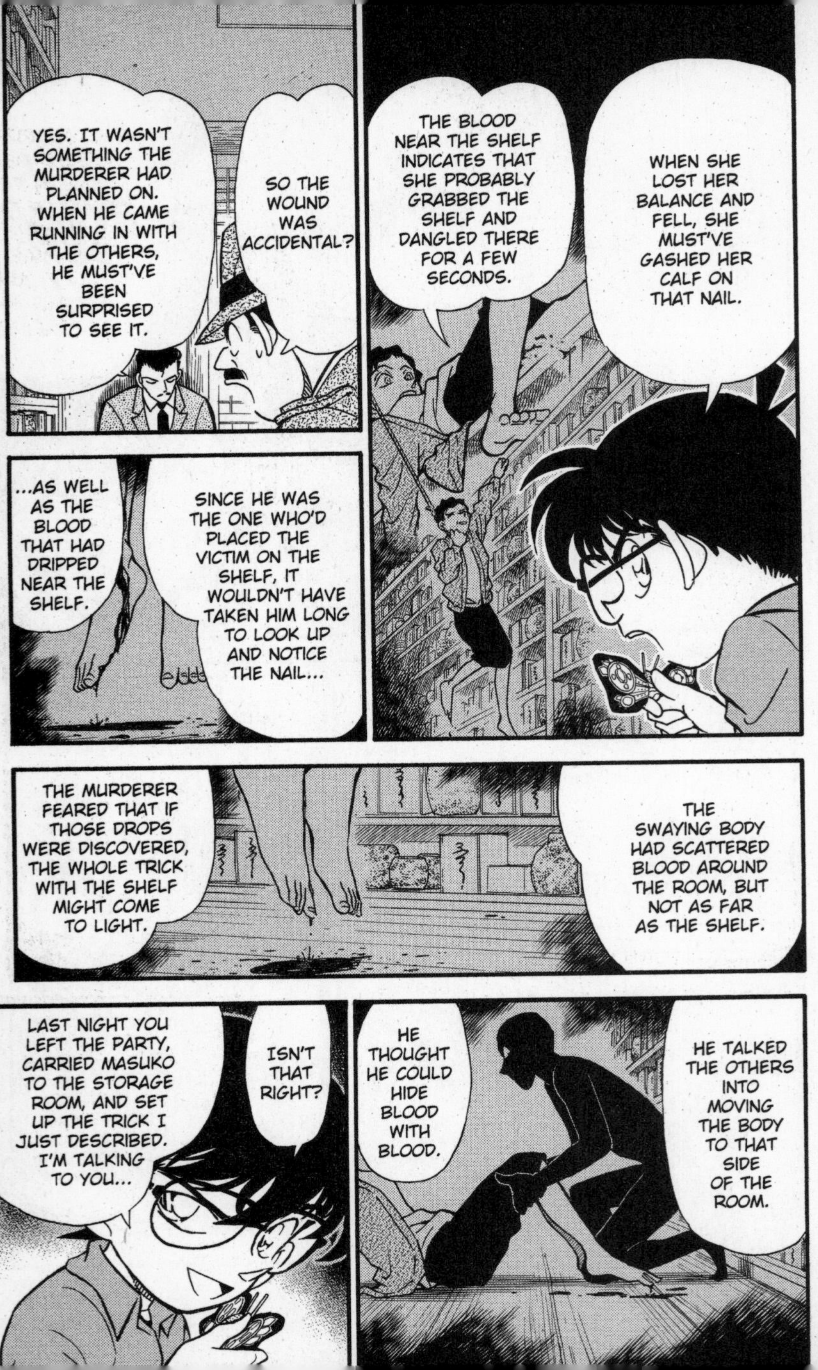
WHEN SHE LOST HER BALANCE AND FELL, SHE MUST'VE GASHED HER CALF ON THAT NAIL.
THE BLOOD NEAR THE SHELF INDICATES THAT SHE PROBABLY GRABBED THE SHELF AND DANGLED THERE FOR A FEW SECONDS.
SO THE WOUND WAS ACCIDENTAL?
YES. IT WASN'T SOMETHING THE MURDERER HAD PLANNED ON. WHEN HE CAME RUNNING IN WITH THE OTHERS, HE MUST'VE BEEN SURPRISED TO SEE IT.
SINCE HE WAS THE ONE WHO'D PLACED THE VICTIM ON THE SHELF, IT WOULDN'T HAVE TAKEN HIM LONG TO LOOK UP AND NOTICE THE NAIL...
...AS WELL AS THE BLOOD THAT HAD DRIPPED NEAR THE SHELF.
THE SWAYING BODY HAD SCATTERED BLOOD AROUND THE ROOM, BUT NOT AS FAR AS THE SHELF.
THE MURDERER FEARED THAT IF THOSE DROPS WERE DISCOVERED, THE WHOLE TRICK WITH THE SHELF MIGHT COME TO LIGHT.
HE TALKED THE OTHERS INTO MOVING THE BODY TO THAT SIDE OF THE ROOM.
HE THOUGHT HE COULD HIDE BLOOD WITH BLOOD.
LAST NIGHT YOU LEFT THE PARTY, CARRIED MASUKO TO THE STORAGE ROOM, AND SET UP THE TRICK I JUST DESCRIBED. I'M TALKING TO YOU...
ISN'T THAT RIGHT?

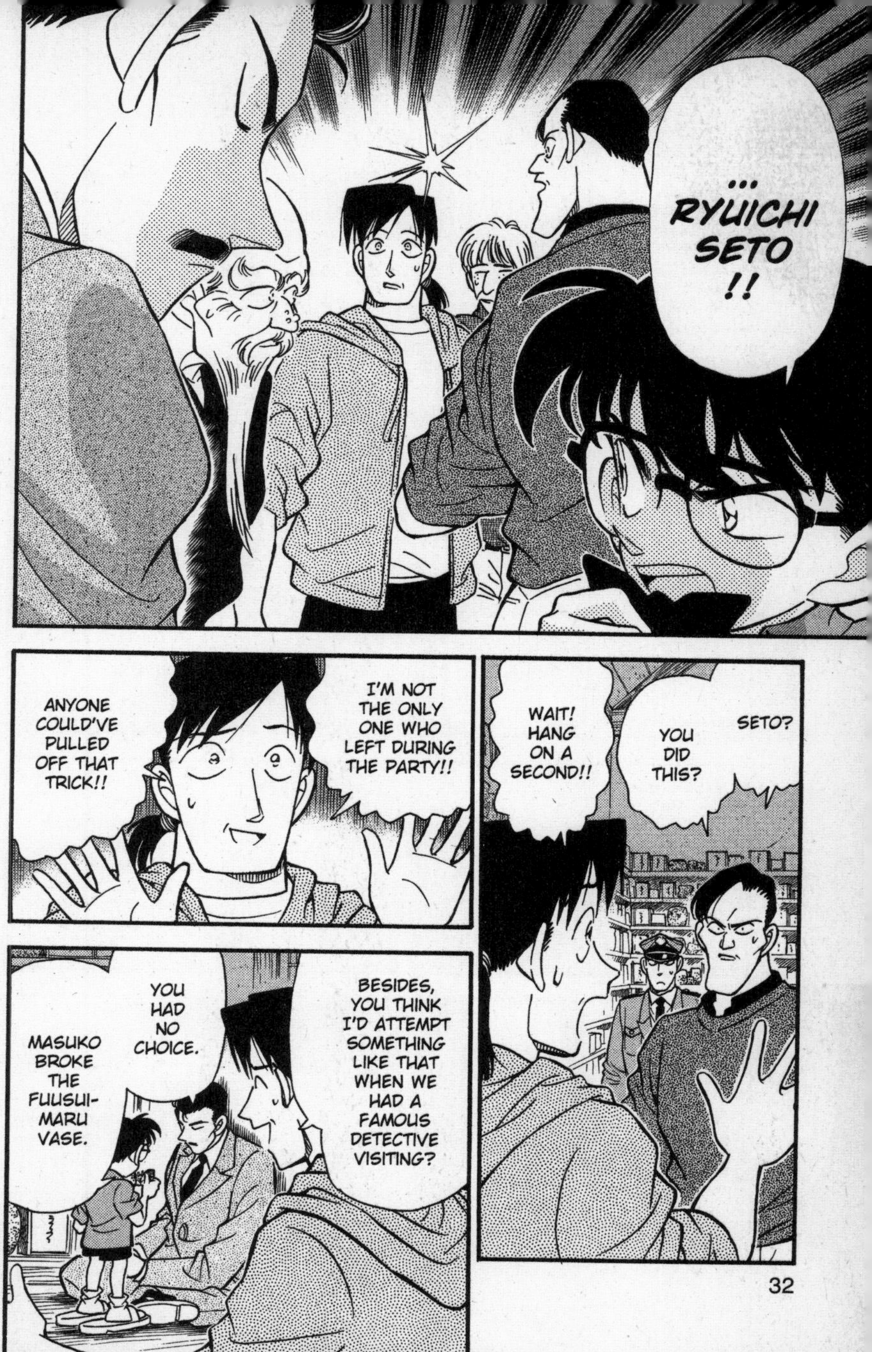
... RYUICHI SETO !!
SETO?
YOU DID THIS?
WAIT! HANG ON A SECOND!!
I'M NOT THE ONLY ONE WHO LEFT DURING THE PARTY!!
ANYONE COULD'VE PULLED OFF THAT TRICK!!
BESIDES, YOU THINK I'D ATTEMPT SOMETHING LIKE THAT WHEN WE HAD A FAMOUS DETECTIVE VISITING?
YOU HAD NO CHOICE.
MASUKO BROKE THE FUUSUI-MARU VASE.

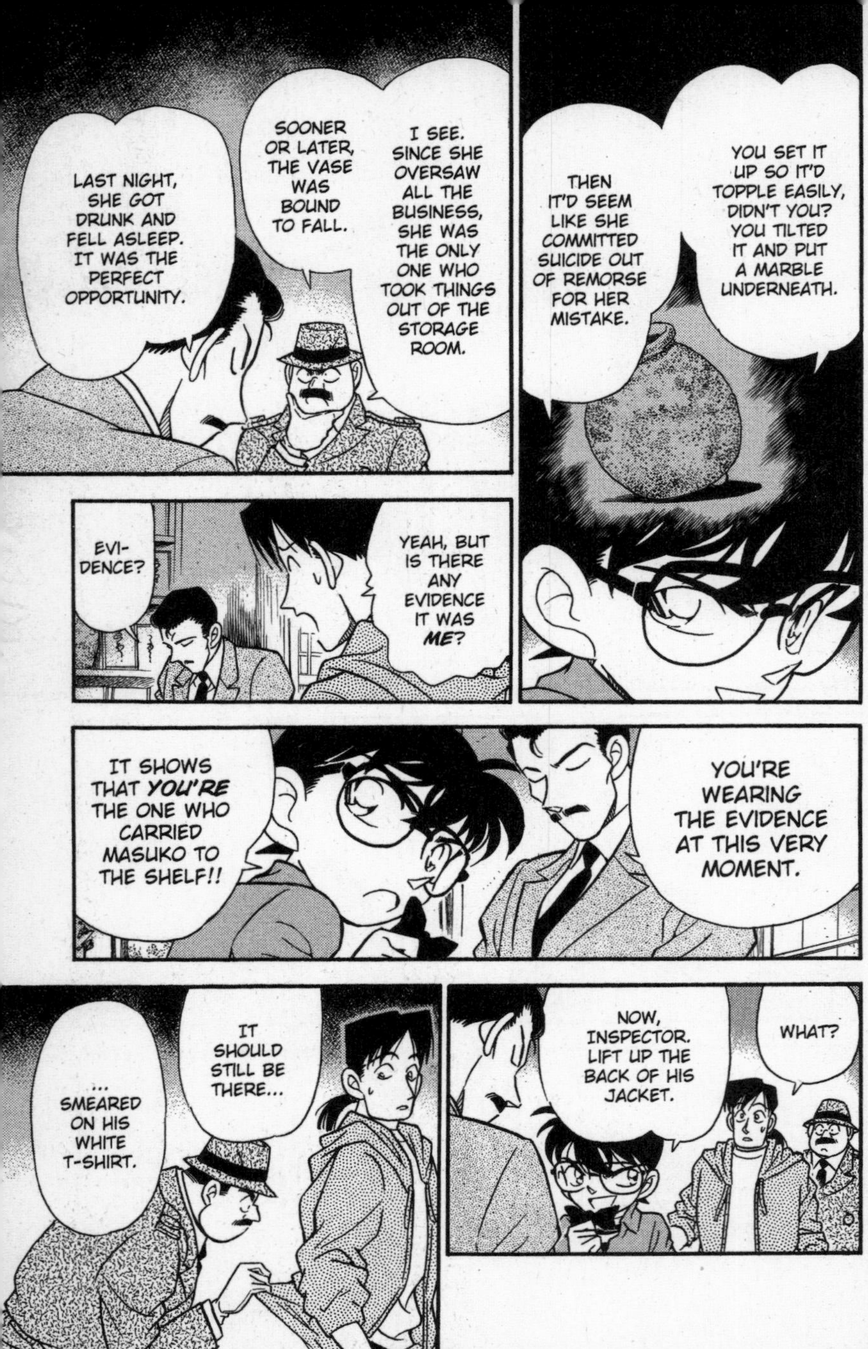
YOU SET IT UP SO IT'D TOPPLE EASILY, DIDN'T YOU? YOU TILTED IT AND PUT A MARBLE UNDERNEATH.
THEN IT'D SEEM LIKE SHE COMMITTED SUICIDE OUT OF REMORSE FOR HER MISTAKE.
I SEE. SINCE SHE OVERSAW ALL THE BUSINESS, SHE WAS THE ONLY ONE WHO TOOK THINGS OUT OF THE STORAGE ROOM.
SOONER OR LATER, THE VASE WAS BOUND TO FALL.
LAST NIGHT, SHE GOT DRUNK AND FELL ASLEEP. IT WAS THE PERFECT OPPORTUNITY.
YEAH, BUT IS THERE ANY EVIDENCE IT WAS *ME*?
EVI-DENCE?
YOU'RE WEARING THE EVIDENCE AT THIS VERY MOMENT.
IT SHOWS THAT *YOU'RE* THE ONE WHO CARRIED MASUKO TO THE SHELF!!
WHAT?
NOW, INSPECTOR. LIFT UP THE BACK OF HIS JACKET.
IT SHOULD STILL BE THERE...
... SMEARED ON HIS WHITE T-SHIRT.

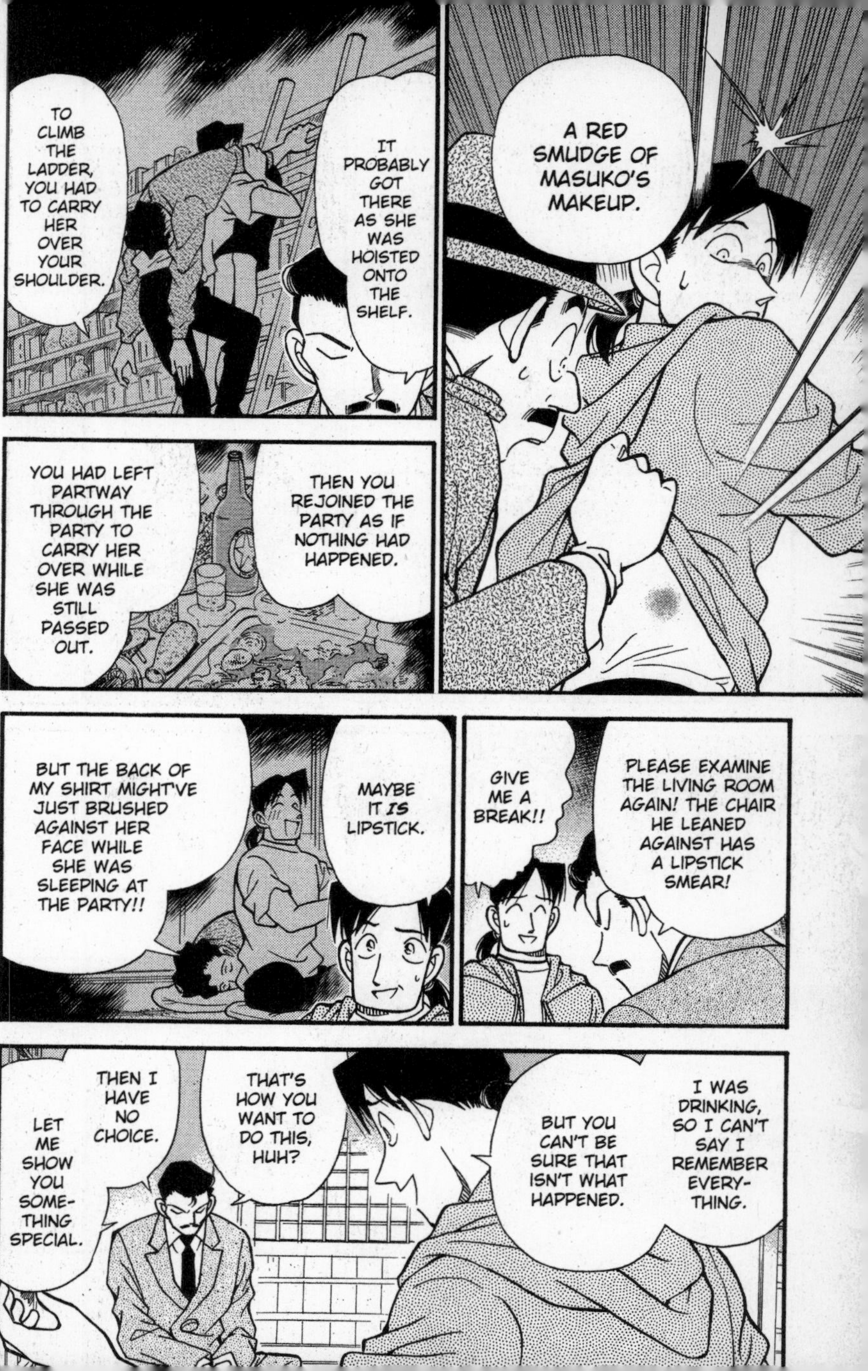
A RED SMUDGE OF MASUKO'S MAKEUP.
IT PROBABLY GOT THERE AS SHE WAS HOISTED ONTO THE SHELF.
TO CLIMB THE LADDER, YOU HAD TO CARRY HER OVER YOUR SHOULDER.
THEN YOU REJOINED THE PARTY AS IF NOTHING HAD HAPPENED.
YOU HAD LEFT PARTWAY THROUGH THE PARTY TO CARRY HER OVER WHILE SHE WAS STILL PASSED OUT.
PLEASE EXAMINE THE LIVING ROOM AGAIN! THE CHAIR HE LEANED AGAINST HAS A LIPSTICK SMEAR!
GIVE ME A BREAK!!
MAYBE IT *IS* LIPSTICK.
BUT THE BACK OF MY SHIRT MIGHT'VE JUST BRUSHED AGAINST HER FACE WHILE SHE WAS SLEEPING AT THE PARTY!!
I WAS DRINKING, SO I CAN'T SAY I REMEMBER EVERY-THING.
BUT YOU CAN'T BE SURE THAT ISN'T WHAT HAPPENED.
THAT'S HOW YOU WANT TO DO THIS, HUH?
THEN I HAVE NO CHOICE.
LET ME SHOW YOU SOME-THING SPECIAL.

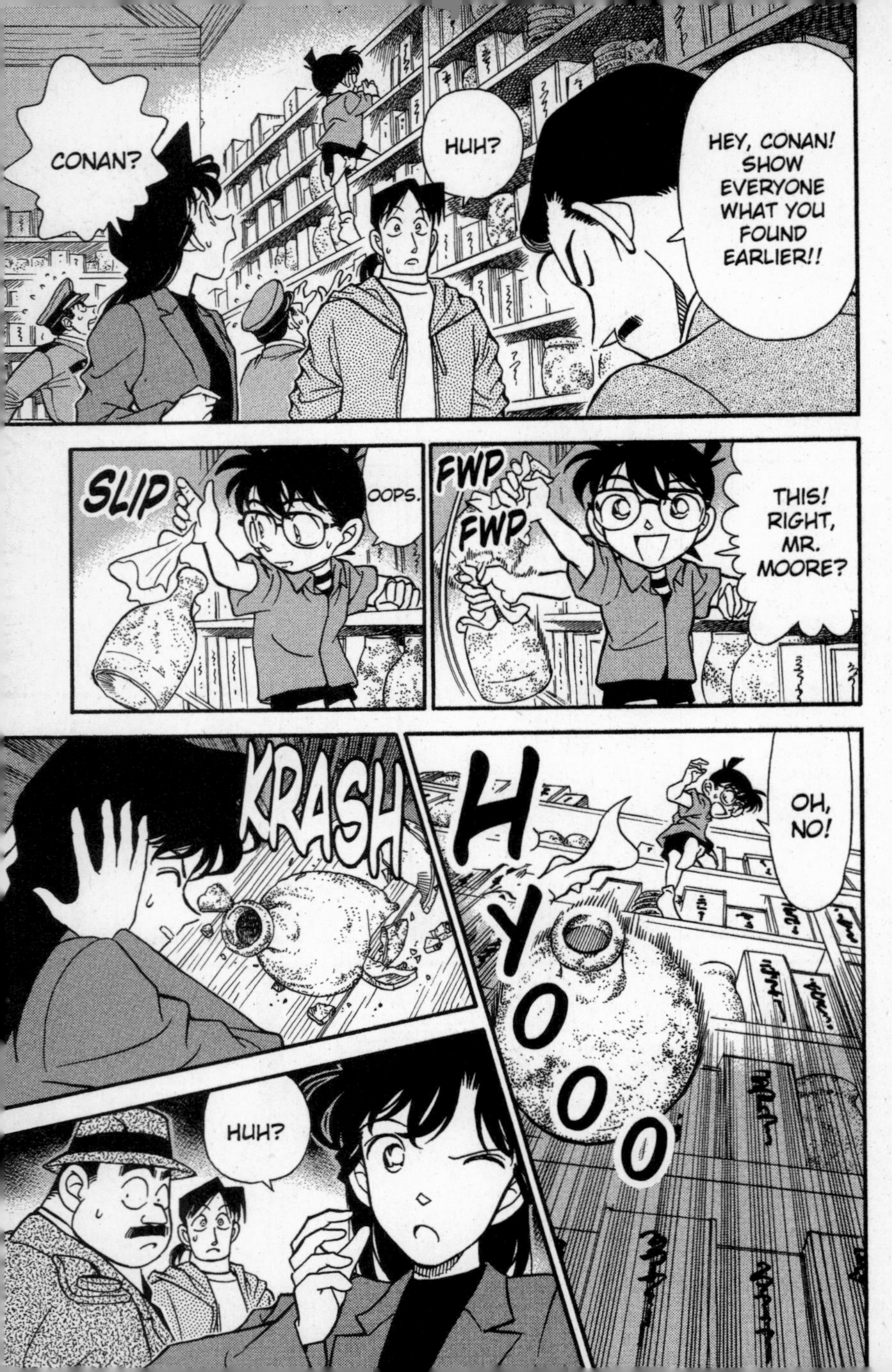
HEY, CONAN! SHOW EVERYONE WHAT YOU FOUND EARLIER!!
HUH?
CONAN?
THIS! RIGHT, MR. MOORE?
FWP
FWP
OOPS.
SLIP
OH, NO!
HYOOOO
KRASH
HUH?

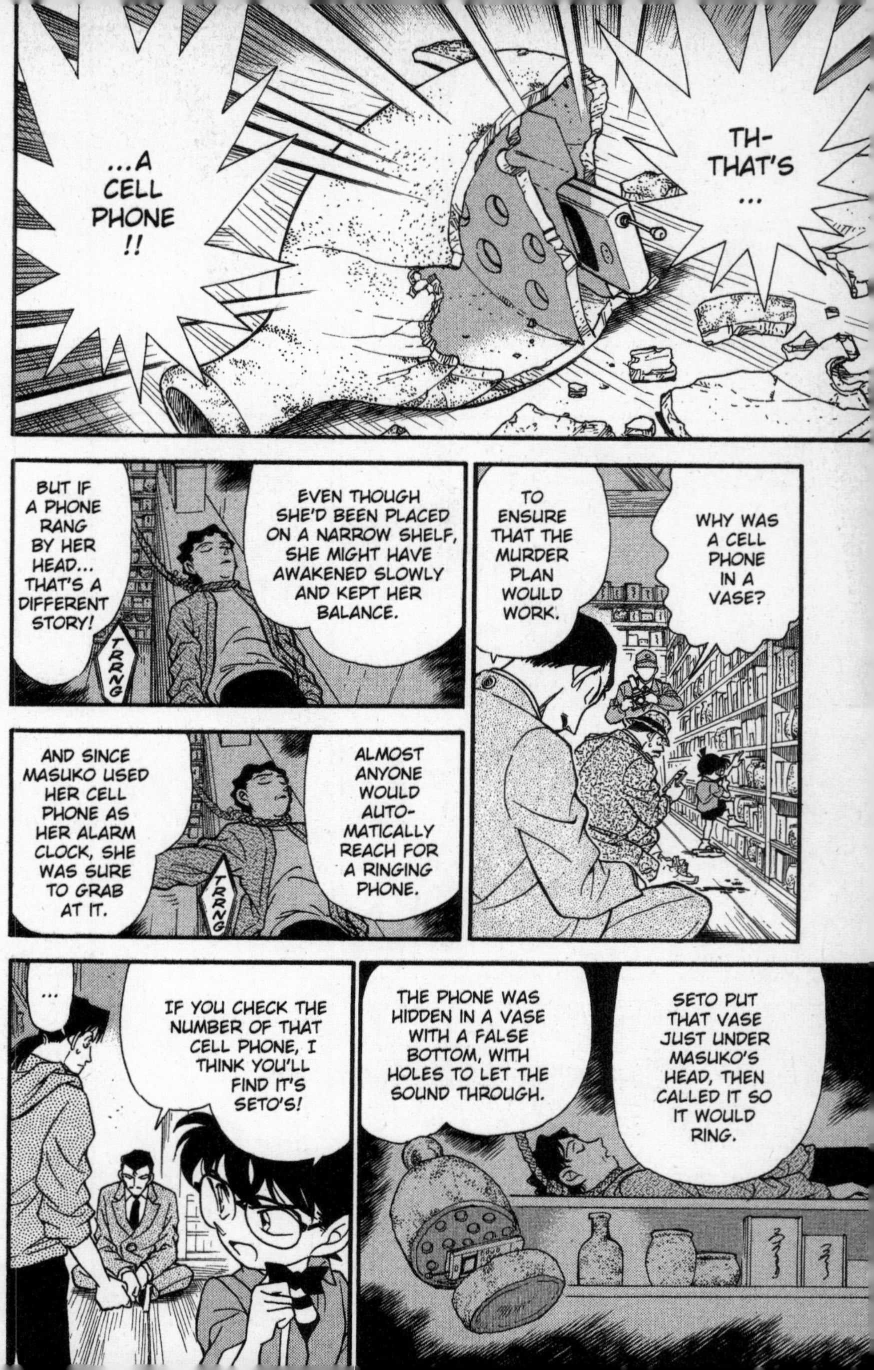
TH- THAT'S ...
...A CELL PHONE !!
WHY WAS A CELL PHONE IN A VASE?
TO ENSURE THAT THE MURDER PLAN WOULD WORK.
EVEN THOUGH SHE'D BEEN PLACED ON A NARROW SHELF, SHE MIGHT HAVE AWAKENED SLOWLY AND KEPT HER BALANCE.
BUT IF A PHONE RANG BY HER HEAD... THAT'S A DIFFERENT STORY!
TRRNG
ALMOST ANYONE WOULD AUTO-MATICALLY REACH FOR A RINGING PHONE.
AND SINCE MASUKO USED HER CELL PHONE AS HER ALARM CLOCK, SHE WAS SURE TO GRAB AT IT.
TRRNG
SETO PUT THAT VASE JUST UNDER MASUKO'S HEAD, THEN CALLED IT SO IT WOULD RING.
THE PHONE WAS HIDDEN IN A VASE WITH A FALSE BOTTOM, WITH HOLES TO LET THE SOUND THROUGH.
IF YOU CHECK THE NUMBER OF THAT CELL PHONE, I THINK YOU'LL FIND IT'S SETO'S!
...

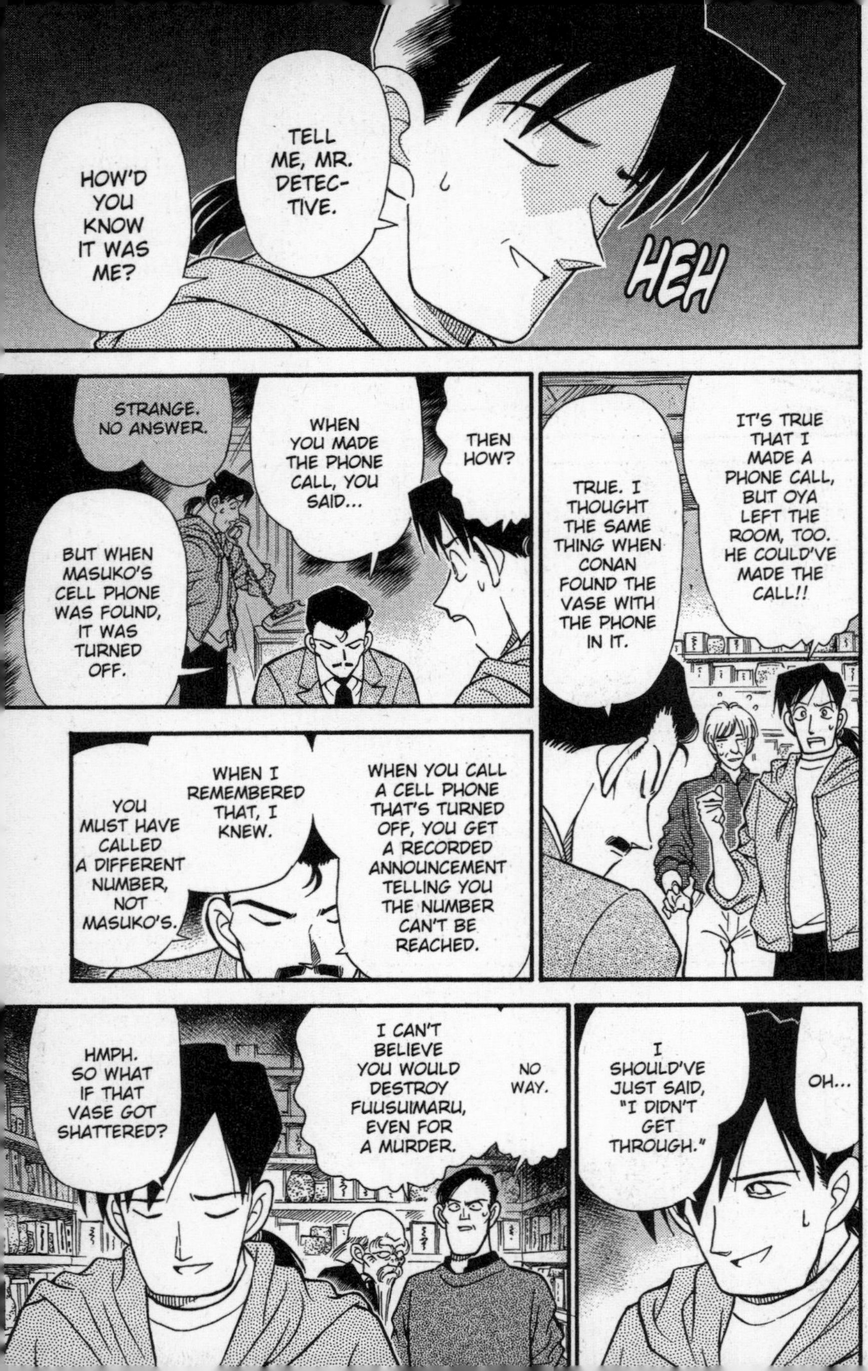
HEH
TELL ME, MR. DETECTIVE.
HOW'D YOU KNOW IT WAS ME?
IT'S TRUE THAT I MADE A PHONE CALL, BUT OYA LEFT THE ROOM, TOO. HE COULD'VE MADE THE CALL!!
TRUE. I THOUGHT THE SAME THING WHEN CONAN FOUND THE VASE WITH THE PHONE IN IT.
THEN HOW?
WHEN YOU MADE THE PHONE CALL, YOU SAID...
STRANGE. NO ANSWER.
BUT WHEN MASUKO'S CELL PHONE WAS FOUND, IT WAS TURNED OFF.
WHEN YOU CALL A CELL PHONE THAT'S TURNED OFF, YOU GET A RECORDED ANNOUNCEMENT TELLING YOU THE NUMBER CAN'T BE REACHED.
WHEN I REMEMBERED THAT, I KNEW.
YOU MUST HAVE CALLED A DIFFERENT NUMBER, NOT MASUKO'S.
OH...
I SHOULD'VE JUST SAID, "I DIDN'T GET THROUGH."
NO WAY.
I CAN'T BELIEVE YOU WOULD DESTROY FUUSUIMARU, EVEN FOR A MURDER.
HMPH. SO WHAT IF THAT VASE GOT SHATTERED?

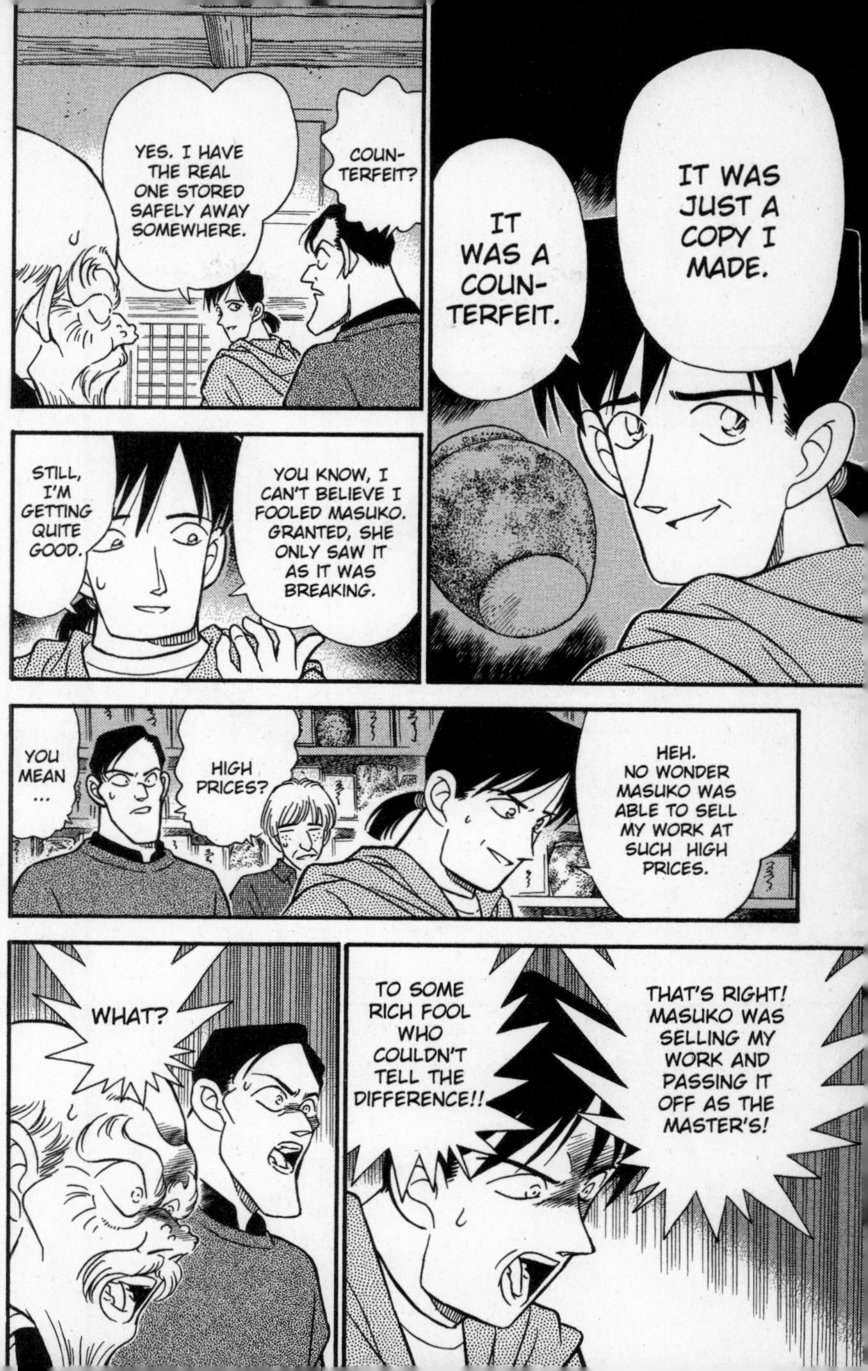
IT WAS JUST A COPY I MADE.
IT WAS A COUNTERFEIT.
COUNTERFEIT?
YES. I HAVE THE REAL ONE STORED SAFELY AWAY SOMEWHERE.
YOU KNOW, I CAN'T BELIEVE I FOOLED MASUKO. GRANTED, SHE ONLY SAW IT AS IT WAS BREAKING.
STILL, I'M GETTING QUITE GOOD.
HEH. NO WONDER MASUKO WAS ABLE TO SELL MY WORK AT SUCH HIGH PRICES.
HIGH PRICES?
YOU MEAN ...
THAT'S RIGHT! MASUKO WAS SELLING MY WORK AND PASSING IT OFF AS THE MASTER'S!
TO SOME RICH FOOL WHO COULDN'T TELL THE DIFFERENCE!!
WHAT?

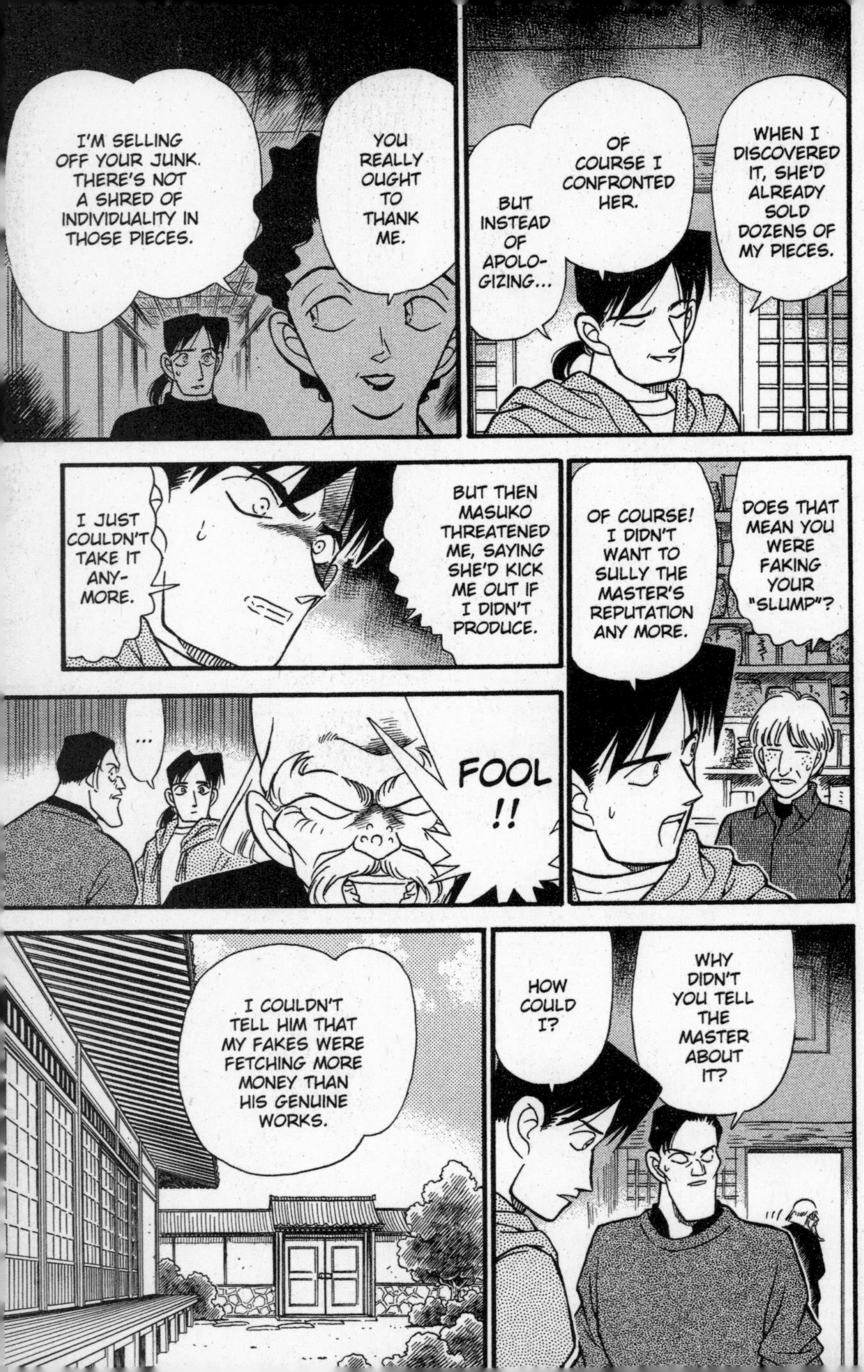
WHEN I DISCOVERED IT, SHE'D ALREADY SOLD DOZENS OF MY PIECES.
OF COURSE I CONFRONTED HER.
BUT INSTEAD OF APOLOGIZING...
YOU REALLY OUGHT TO THANK ME.
I'M SELLING OFF YOUR JUNK. THERE'S NOT A SHRED OF INDIVIDUALITY IN THOSE PIECES.
DOES THAT MEAN YOU WERE FAKING YOUR "SLUMP"?
OF COURSE! I DIDN'T WANT TO SULLY THE MASTER'S REPUTATION ANY MORE.
BUT THEN MASUKO THREATENED ME, SAYING SHE'D KICK ME OUT IF I DIDN'T PRODUCE.
I JUST COULDN'T TAKE IT ANY-MORE.
FOOL !!
...
WHY DIDN'T YOU TELL THE MASTER ABOUT IT?
HOW COULD I?
I COULDN'T TELL HIM THAT MY FAKES WERE FETCHING MORE MONEY THAN HIS GENUINE WORKS.

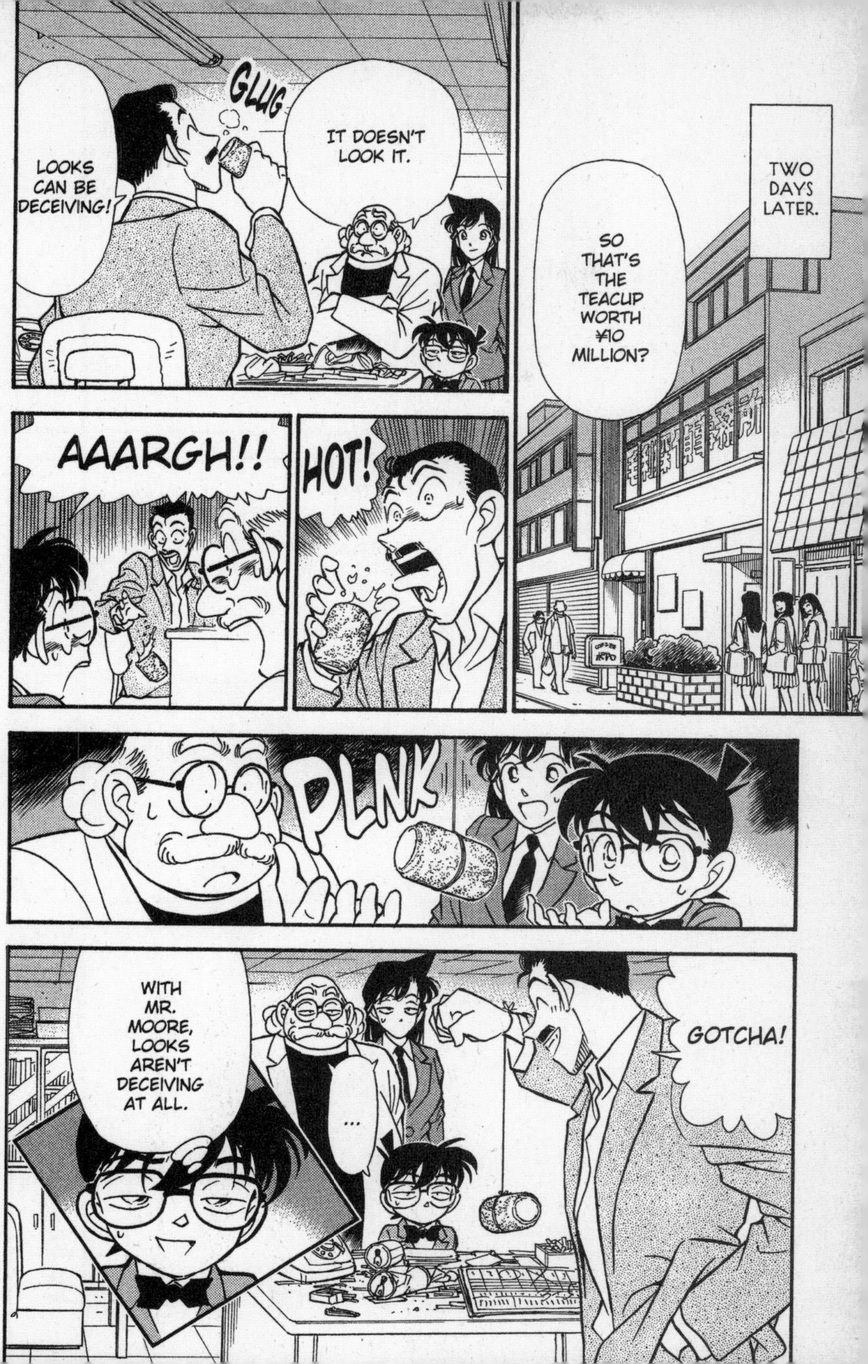
TWO DAYS LATER.
SO THAT'S THE TEACUP WORTH ¥10 MILLION?
IT DOESN'T LOOK IT.
GLUG
LOOKS CAN BE DECEIVING!
HOT!
AAARGH!!
PLNK
GOTCHA!
...
WITH MR. MOORE, LOOKS AREN'T DECEIVING AT ALL.

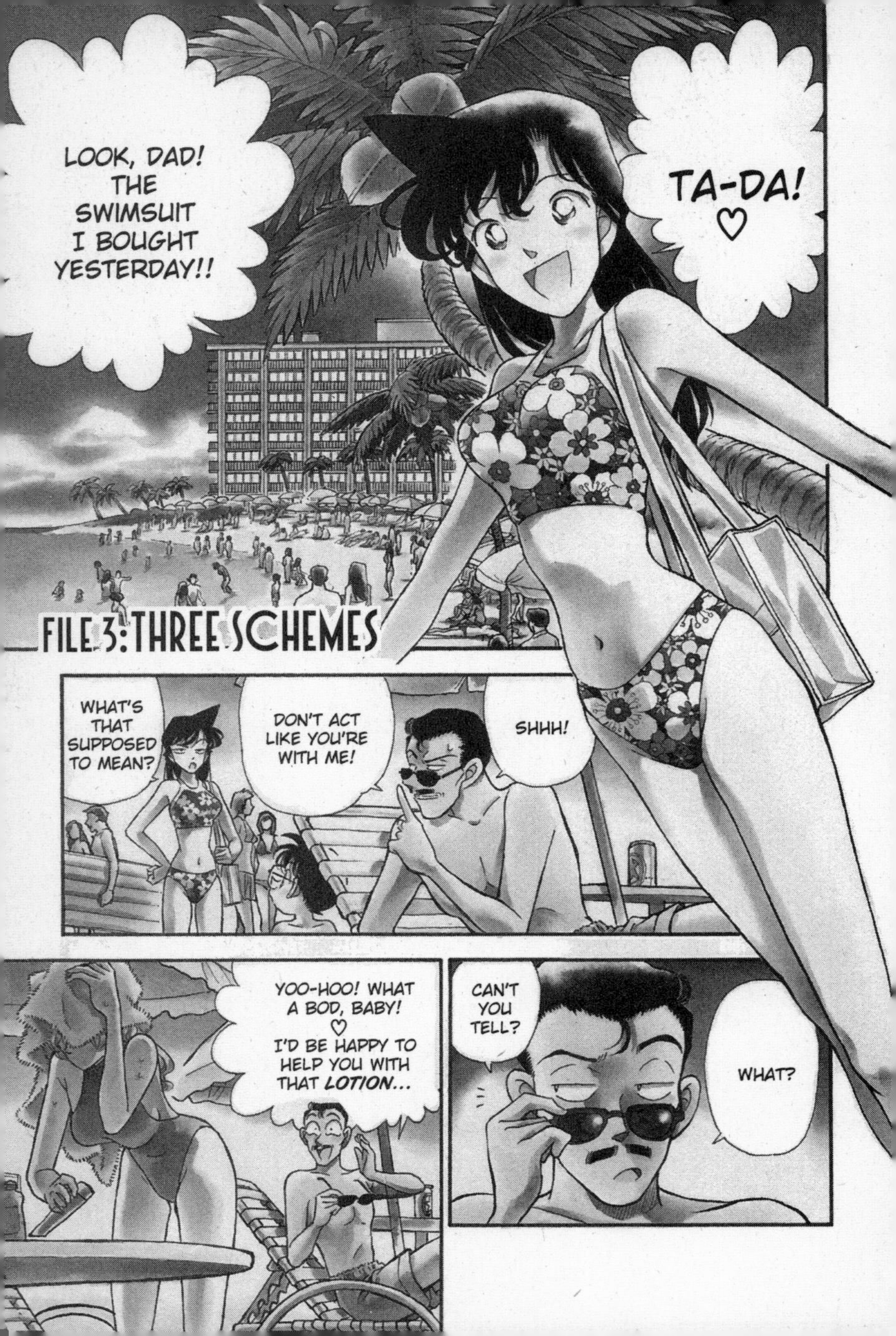
TA-DA! ♡
LOOK, DAD! THE SWIMSUIT I BOUGHT YESTERDAY!!
FILE 3: THREE SCHEMES
SHHH!
DON'T ACT LIKE YOU'RE WITH ME!
WHAT'S THAT SUPPOSED TO MEAN?
CAN'T YOU TELL?
WHAT?
YOO-HOO! WHAT A BOD, BABY! ♡ I'D BE HAPPY TO HELP YOU WITH THAT ***LOTION***...

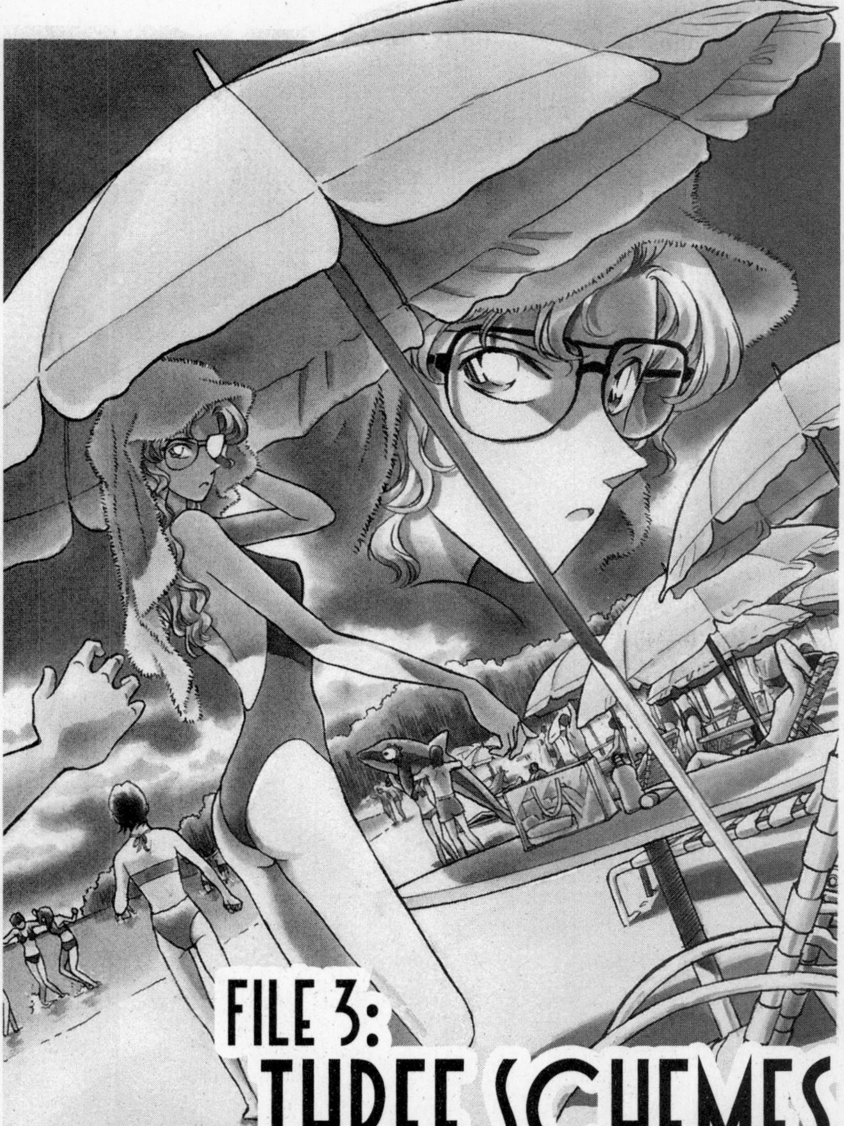
FILE 3:
THREE SCHEMES

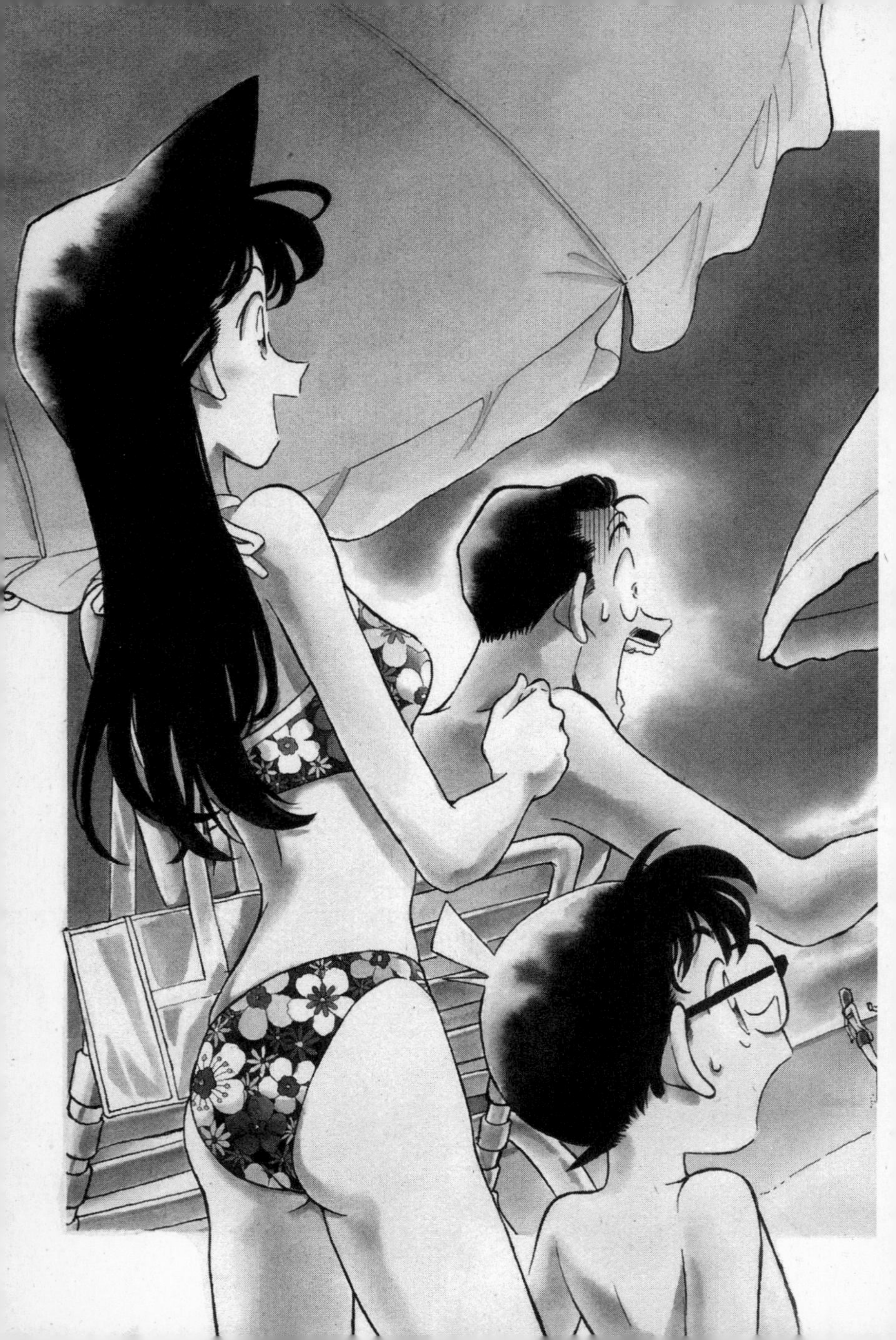

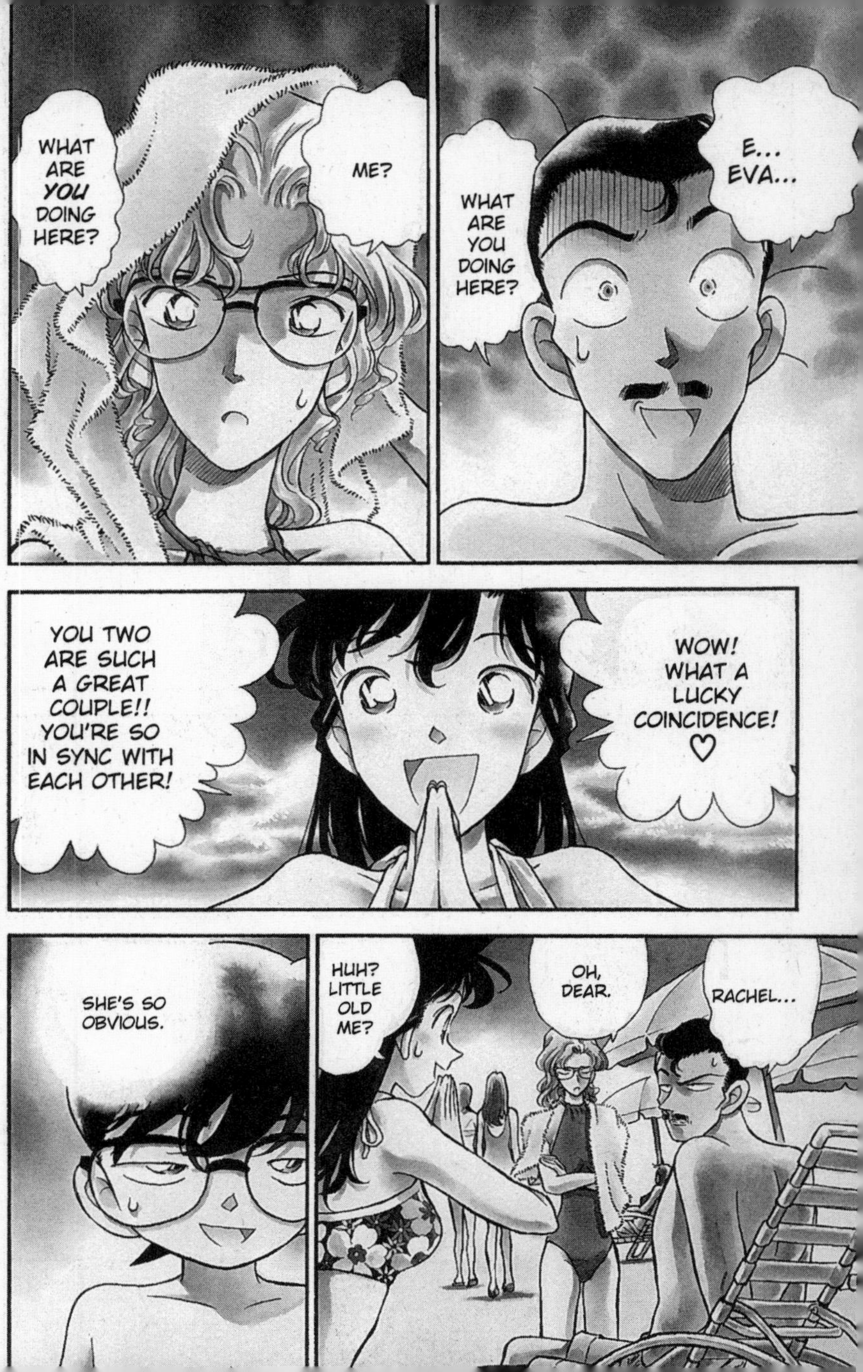
E... EVA...
WHAT ARE YOU DOING HERE?
ME?
WHAT ARE *YOU* DOING HERE?
WOW! WHAT A LUCKY COINCIDENCE! ♡
YOU TWO ARE SUCH A GREAT COUPLE!! YOU'RE SO IN SYNC WITH EACH OTHER!
RACHEL...
OH, DEAR.
HUH? LITTLE OLD ME?
SHE'S SO OBVIOUS.

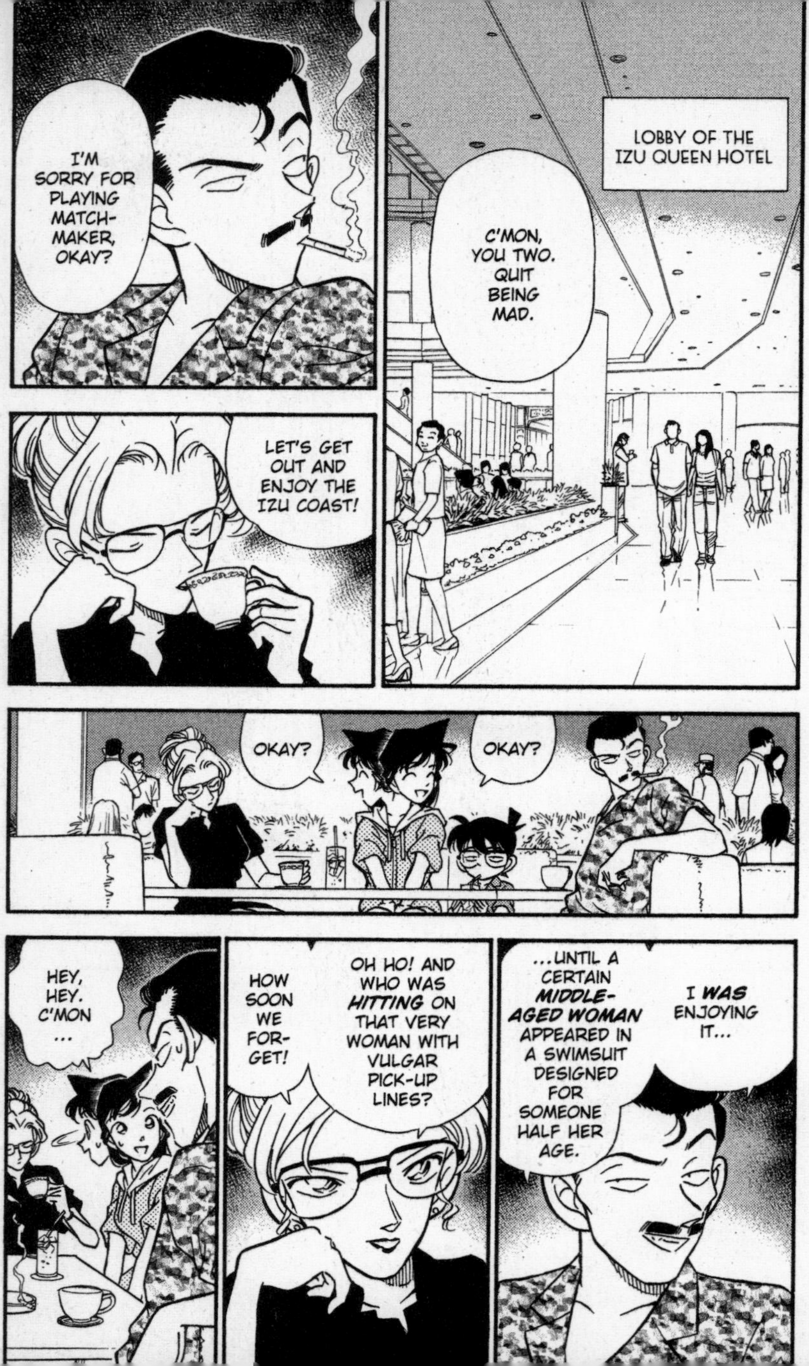
LOBBY OF THE IZU QUEEN HOTEL
C'MON, YOU TWO. QUIT BEING MAD.
I'M SORRY FOR PLAYING MATCH-MAKER, OKAY?
LET'S GET OUT AND ENJOY THE IZU COAST!
OKAY?
OKAY?
I WAS ENJOYING IT...
...UNTIL A CERTAIN MIDDLE-AGED WOMAN APPEARED IN A SWIMSUIT DESIGNED FOR SOMEONE HALF HER AGE.
OH HO! AND WHO WAS HITTING ON THAT VERY WOMAN WITH VULGAR PICK-UP LINES?
HOW SOON WE FOR-GET!
HEY, HEY. C'MON ...

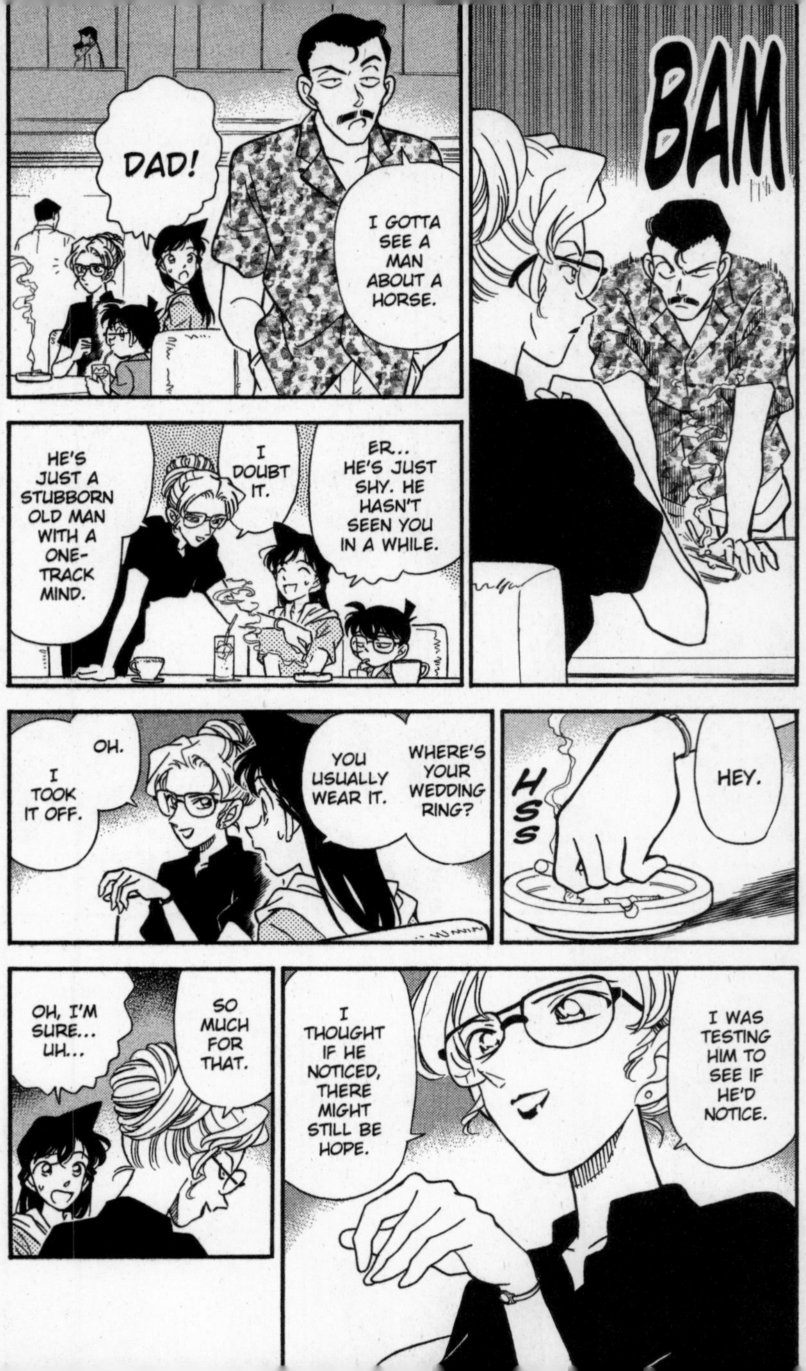
BAM
I GOTTA SEE A MAN ABOUT A HORSE.
DAD!
ER... HE'S JUST SHY. HE HASN'T SEEN YOU IN A WHILE.
I DOUBT IT.
HE'S JUST A STUBBORN OLD MAN WITH A ONE-TRACK MIND.
HSS
HEY.
WHERE'S YOUR WEDDING RING?
YOU USUALLY WEAR IT.
OH.
I TOOK IT OFF.
I WAS TESTING HIM TO SEE IF HE'D NOTICE.
I THOUGHT IF HE NOTICED, THERE MIGHT STILL BE HOPE.
SO MUCH FOR THAT.
OH, I'M SURE... UH...

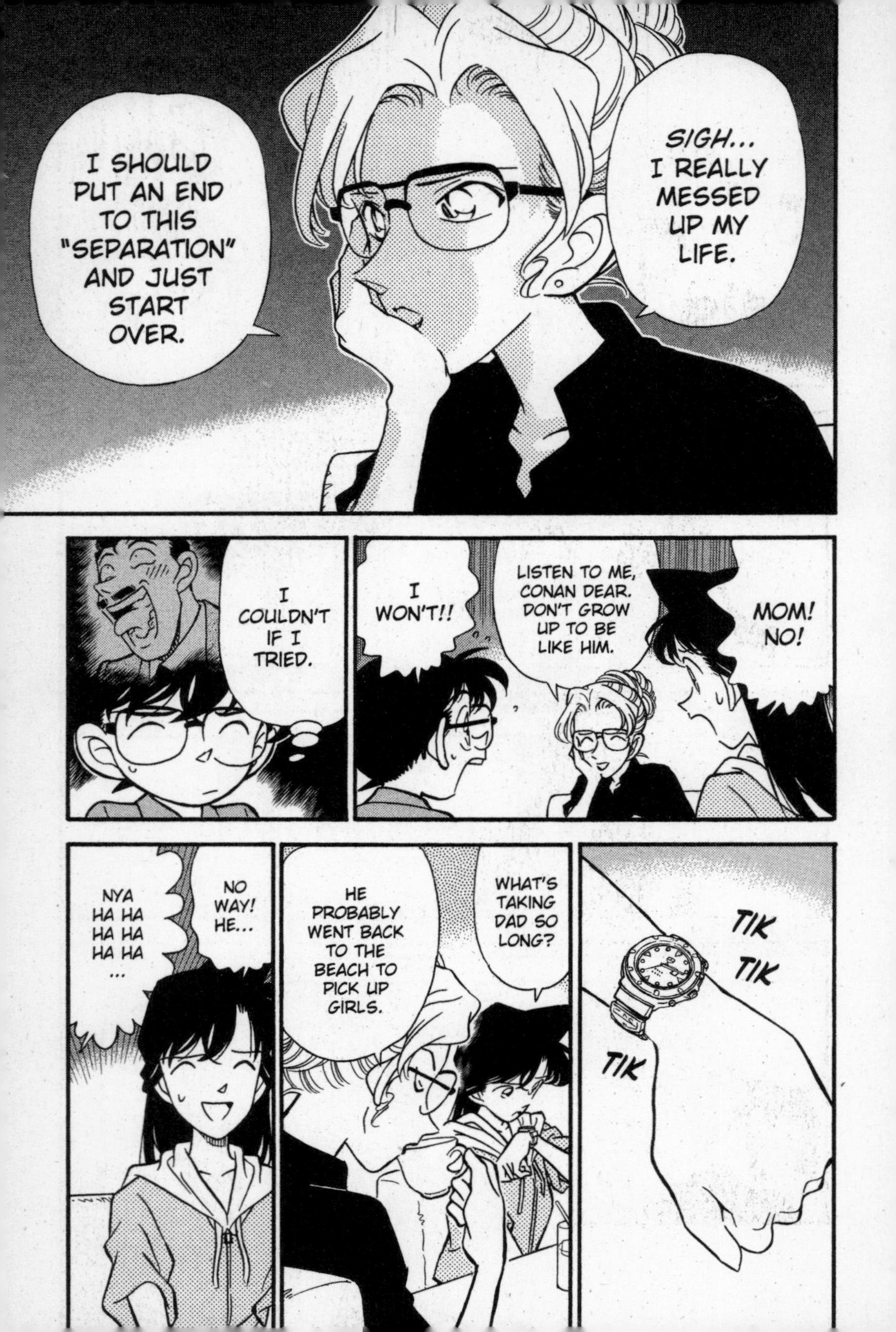
SIGH... I REALLY MESSED UP MY LIFE.
I SHOULD PUT AN END TO THIS "SEPARATION" AND JUST START OVER.
MOM! NO!
LISTEN TO ME, CONAN DEAR. DON'T GROW UP TO BE LIKE HIM.
I WON'T!!
I COULDN'T IF I TRIED.
TIK
TIK
TIK
WHAT'S TAKING DAD SO LONG?
HE PROBABLY WENT BACK TO THE BEACH TO PICK UP GIRLS.
NO WAY! HE...
NYA HA HA HA HA HA HA ...

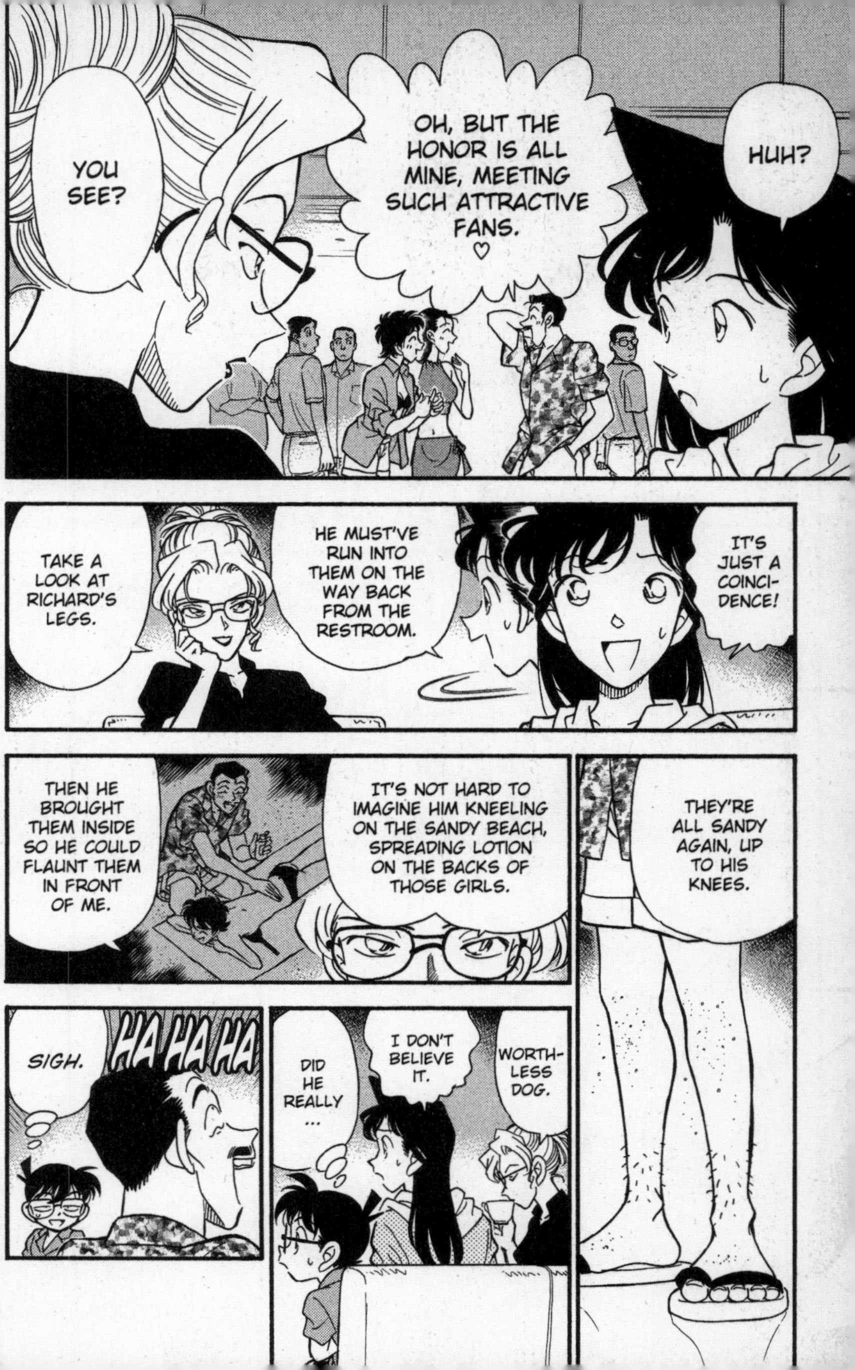
HUH?
OH, BUT THE HONOR IS ALL MINE, MEETING SUCH ATTRACTIVE FANS. ♡
YOU SEE?
IT'S JUST A COINCIDENCE!
HE MUST'VE RUN INTO THEM ON THE WAY BACK FROM THE RESTROOM.
TAKE A LOOK AT RICHARD'S LEGS.
THEY'RE ALL SANDY AGAIN, UP TO HIS KNEES.
IT'S NOT HARD TO IMAGINE HIM KNEELING ON THE SANDY BEACH, SPREADING LOTION ON THE BACKS OF THOSE GIRLS.
THEN HE BROUGHT THEM INSIDE SO HE COULD FLAUNT THEM IN FRONT OF ME.
WORTHLESS DOG.
I DON'T BELIEVE IT.
DID HE REALLY ...
HA HA HA
SIGH.

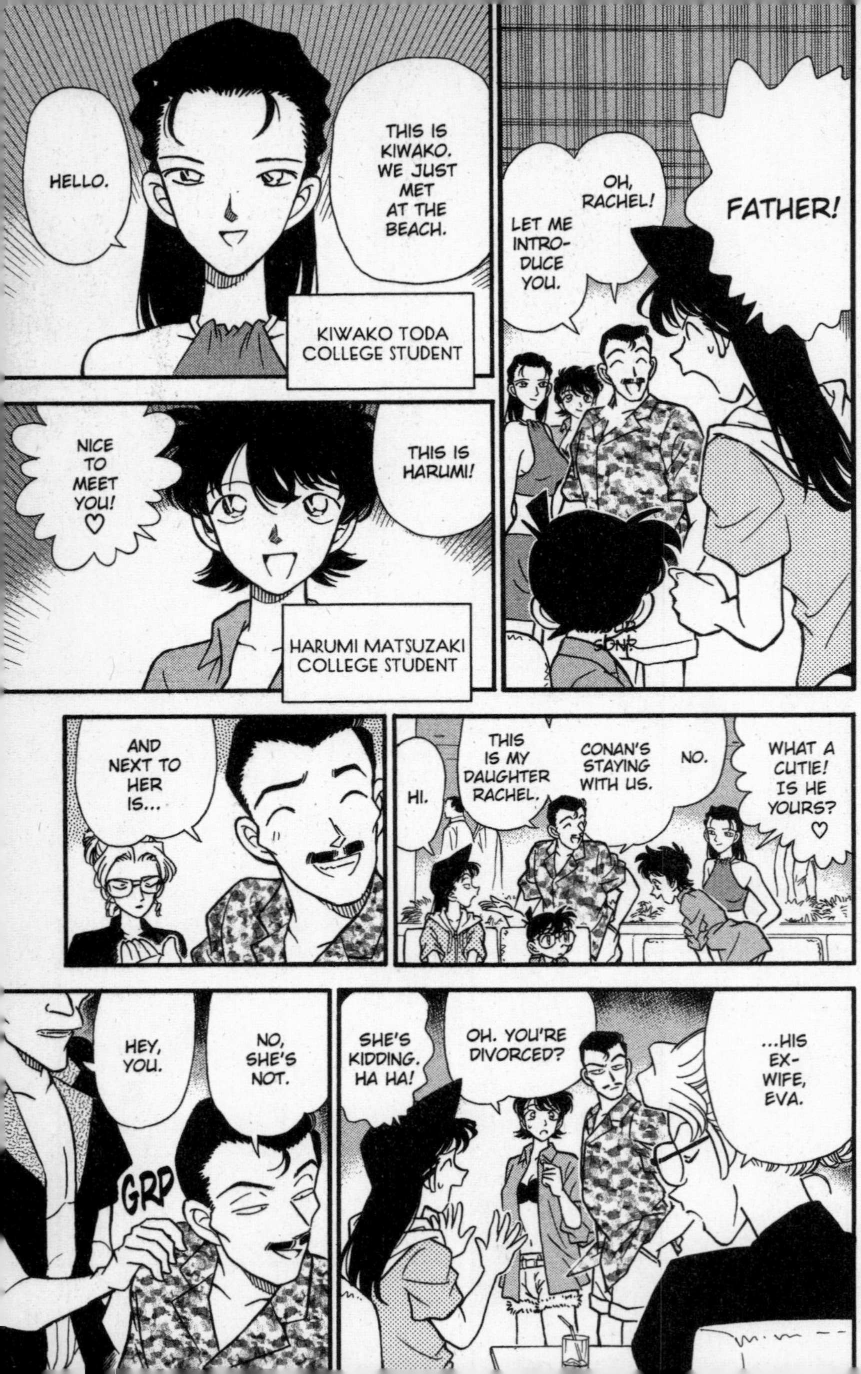
FATHER!
OH, RACHEL!
LET ME INTRODUCE YOU.
THIS IS KIWAKO. WE JUST MET AT THE BEACH.
HELLO.
KIWAKO TODA COLLEGE STUDENT
THIS IS HARUMI!
NICE TO MEET YOU! ♡
HARUMI MATSUZAKI COLLEGE STUDENT
WHAT A CUTIE! IS HE YOURS? ♡
NO.
CONAN'S STAYING WITH US.
THIS IS MY DAUGHTER RACHEL.
HI.
AND NEXT TO HER IS...
...HIS EX-WIFE, EVA.
OH. YOU'RE DIVORCED?
SHE'S KIDDING. HA HA!
NO, SHE'S NOT.
HEY, YOU.
GRP

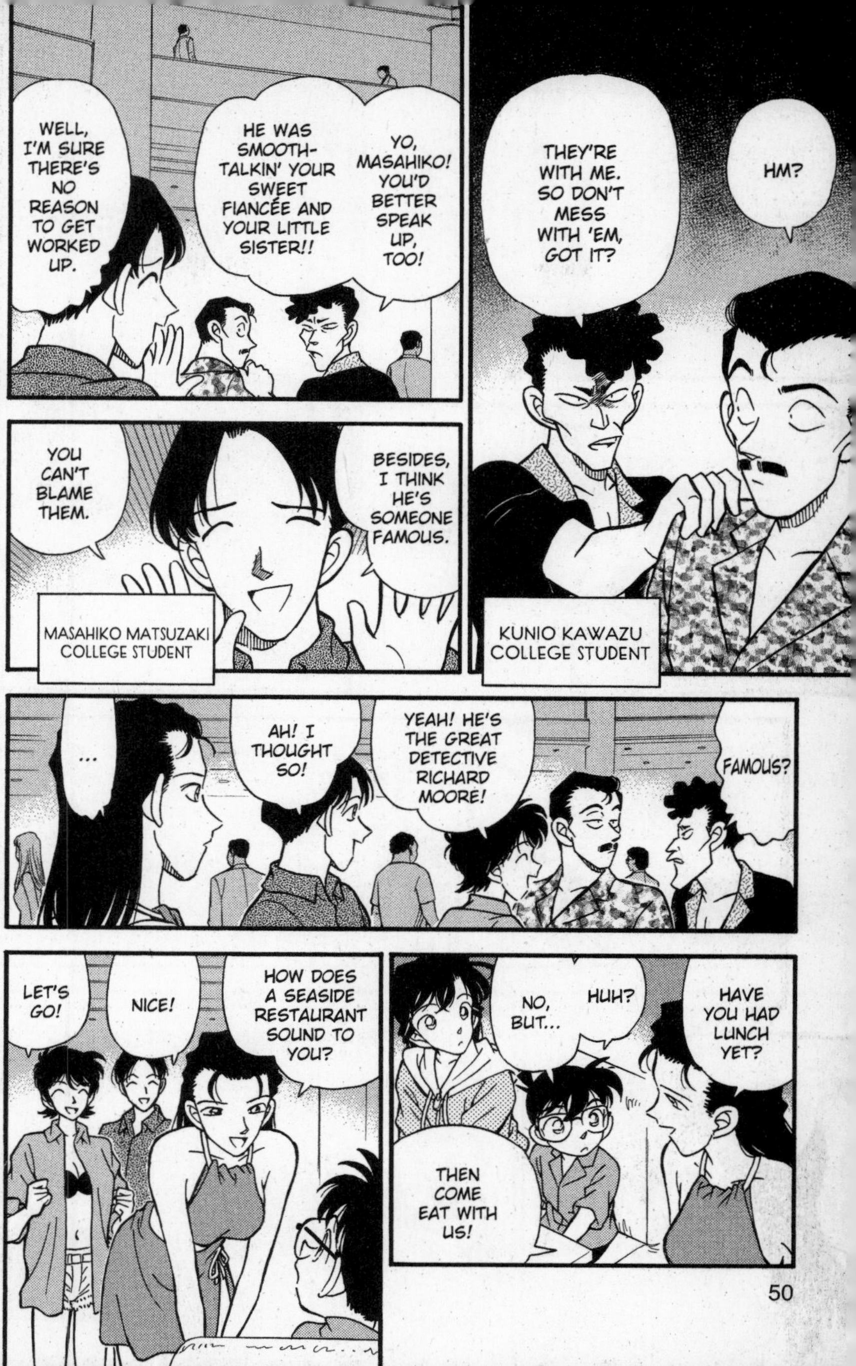
HM?
THEY'RE WITH ME. SO DON'T MESS WITH 'EM, GOT IT?
KUNIO KAWAZU COLLEGE STUDENT
YO, MASAHIKO! YOU'D BETTER SPEAK UP, TOO!
HE WAS SMOOTH-TALKIN' YOUR SWEET FIANCÉE AND YOUR LITTLE SISTER!!
WELL, I'M SURE THERE'S NO REASON TO GET WORKED UP.
BESIDES, I THINK HE'S SOMEONE FAMOUS.
YOU CAN'T BLAME THEM.
MASAHIKO MATSUZAKI COLLEGE STUDENT
FAMOUS?
YEAH! HE'S THE GREAT DETECTIVE RICHARD MOORE!
AH! I THOUGHT SO!
...
HAVE YOU HAD LUNCH YET?
HUH?
NO, BUT...
THEN COME EAT WITH US!
HOW DOES A SEASIDE RESTAURANT SOUND TO YOU?
NICE!
LET'S GO!

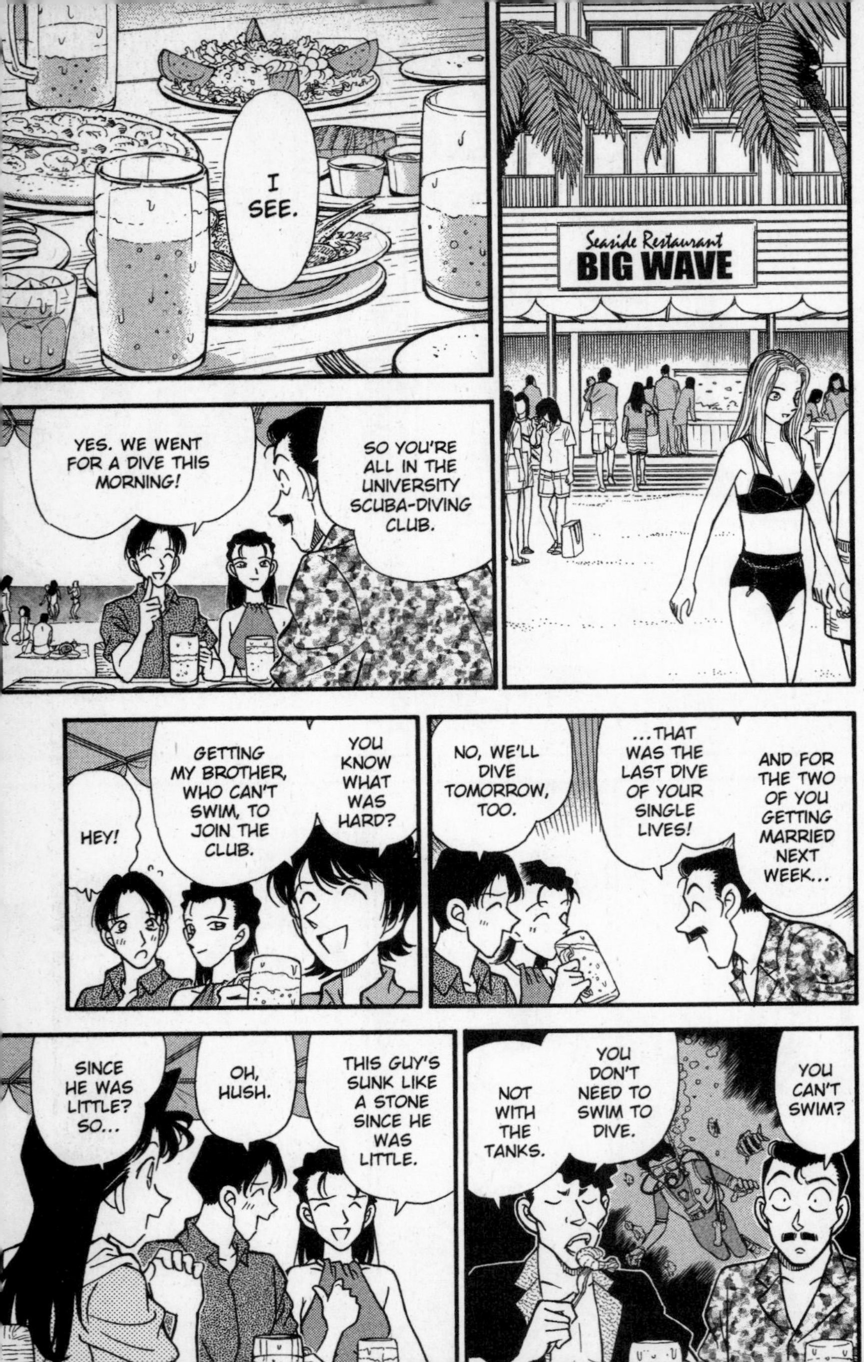
Seaside Restaurant
BIG WAVE
I SEE.
SO YOU'RE ALL IN THE UNIVERSITY SCUBA-DIVING CLUB.
YES. WE WENT FOR A DIVE THIS MORNING!
AND FOR THE TWO OF YOU GETTING MARRIED NEXT WEEK...
...THAT WAS THE LAST DIVE OF YOUR SINGLE LIVES!
NO, WE'LL DIVE TOMORROW, TOO.
YOU KNOW WHAT WAS HARD?
GETTING MY BROTHER, WHO CAN'T SWIM, TO JOIN THE CLUB.
HEY!
YOU CAN'T SWIM?
YOU DON'T NEED TO SWIM TO DIVE.
NOT WITH THE TANKS.
THIS GUY'S SUNK LIKE A STONE SINCE HE WAS LITTLE.
OH, HUSH.
SINCE HE WAS LITTLE? SO...

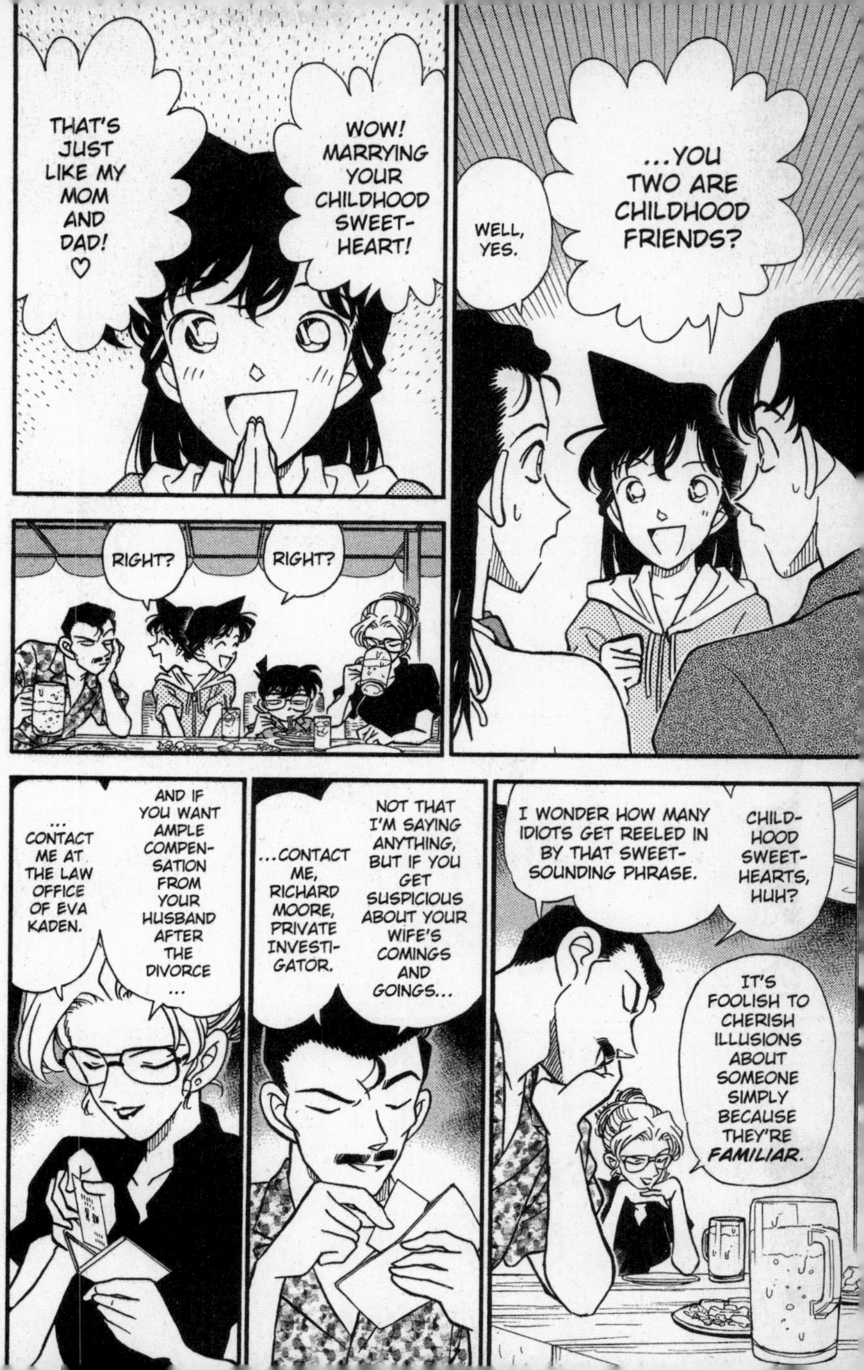
...YOU TWO ARE CHILDHOOD FRIENDS?
WELL, YES.
WOW! MARRYING YOUR CHILDHOOD SWEET-HEART!
THAT'S JUST LIKE MY MOM AND DAD! ♡
RIGHT?
RIGHT?
CHILD-HOOD SWEET-HEARTS, HUH?
I WONDER HOW MANY IDIOTS GET REELED IN BY THAT SWEET-SOUNDING PHRASE.
IT'S FOOLISH TO CHERISH ILLUSIONS ABOUT SOMEONE SIMPLY BECAUSE THEY'RE ***FAMILIAR***.
NOT THAT I'M SAYING ANYTHING, BUT IF YOU GET SUSPICIOUS ABOUT YOUR WIFE'S COMINGS AND GOINGS...
...CONTACT ME, RICHARD MOORE, PRIVATE INVESTI-GATOR.
AND IF YOU WANT AMPLE COMPEN-SATION FROM YOUR HUSBAND AFTER THE DIVORCE...
...CONTACT ME AT THE LAW OFFICE OF EVA KADEN.

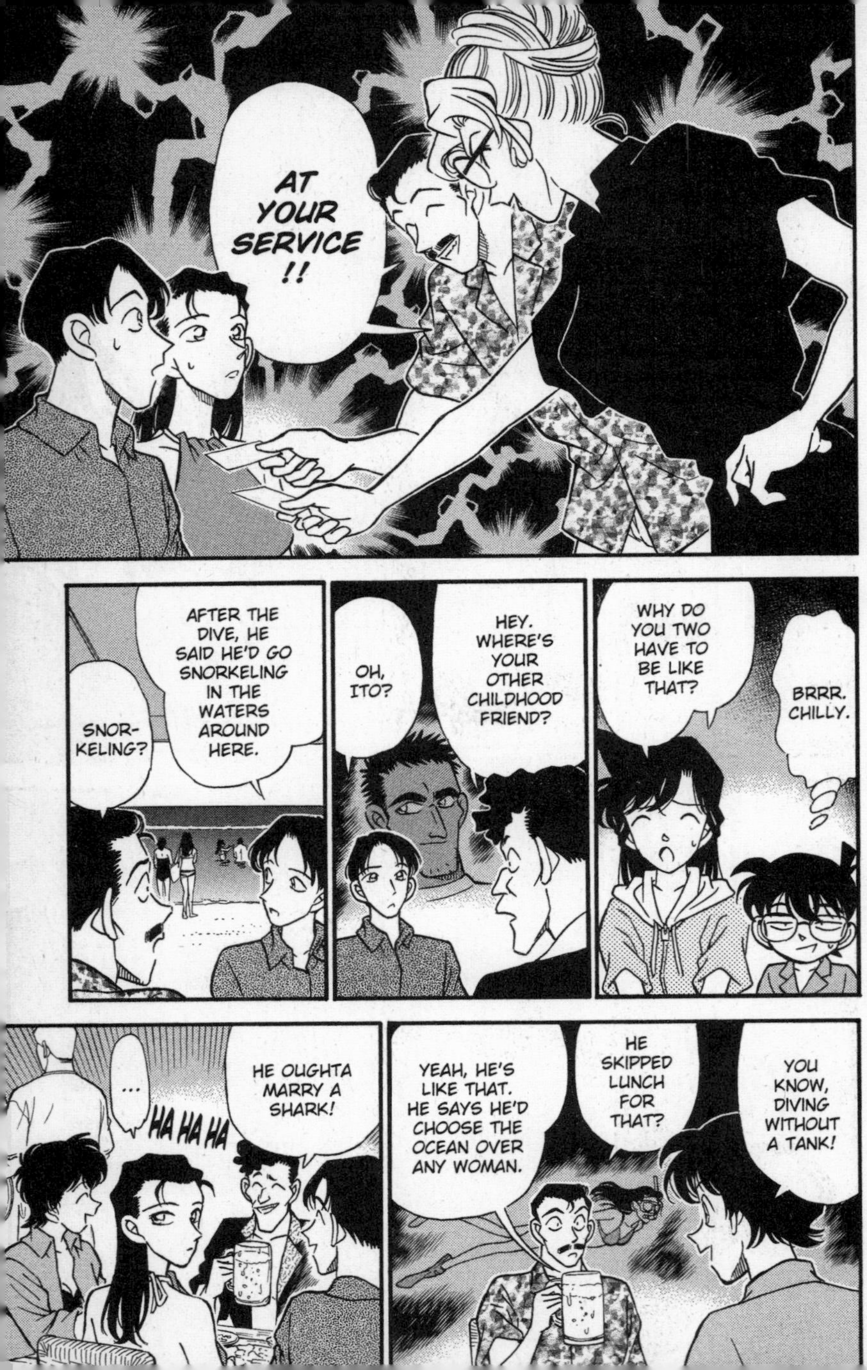
AT YOUR SERVICE !!
BRRR. CHILLY.
WHY DO YOU TWO HAVE TO BE LIKE THAT?
HEY. WHERE'S YOUR OTHER CHILDHOOD FRIEND?
OH, ITO?
AFTER THE DIVE, HE SAID HE'D GO SNORKELING IN THE WATERS AROUND HERE.
SNOR-KELING?
YOU KNOW, DIVING WITHOUT A TANK!
HE SKIPPED LUNCH FOR THAT?
YEAH, HE'S LIKE THAT. HE SAYS HE'D CHOOSE THE OCEAN OVER ANY WOMAN.
HE OUGHTA MARRY A SHARK!
HA HA HA
...

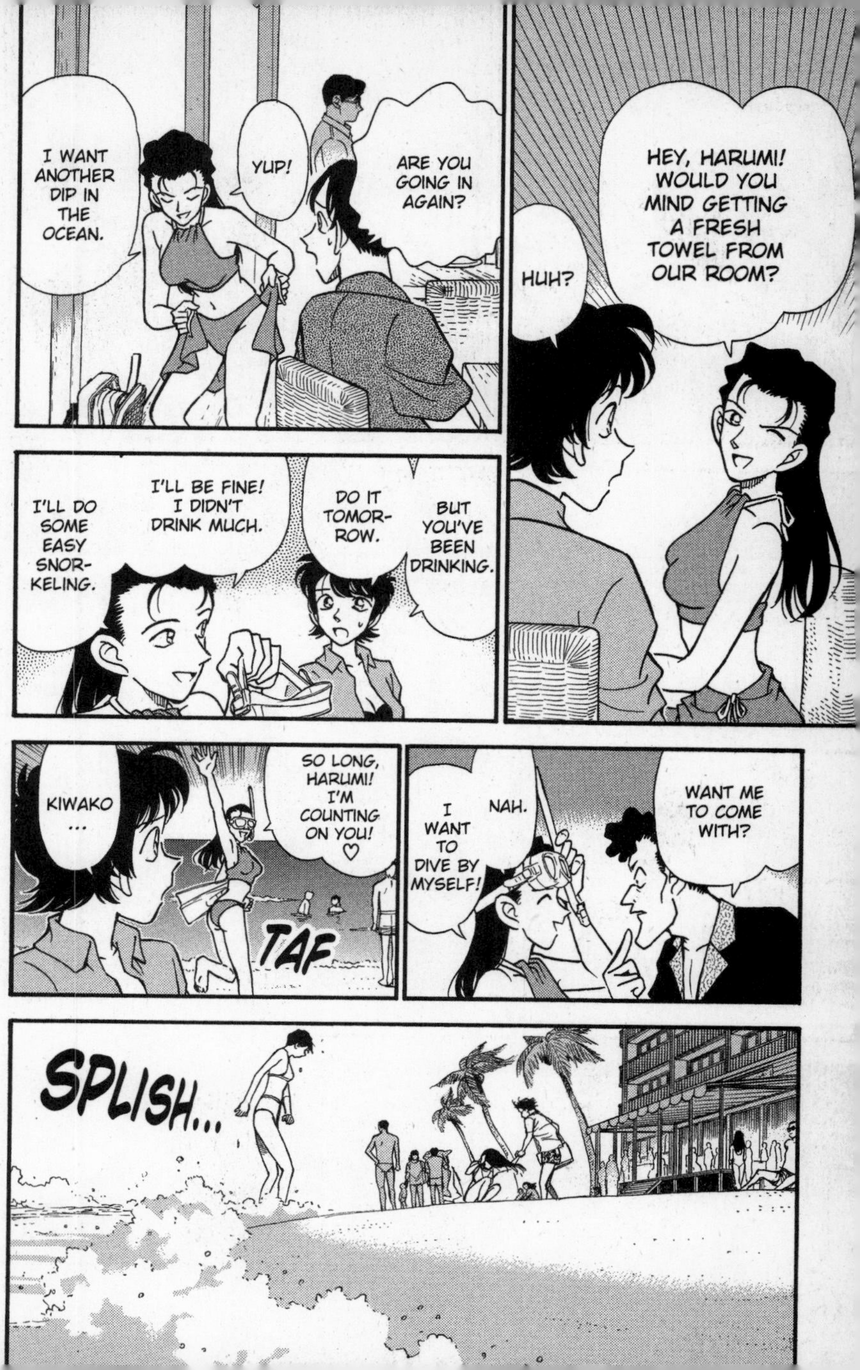
HEY, HARUMI! WOULD YOU MIND GETTING A FRESH TOWEL FROM OUR ROOM?
HUH?
ARE YOU GOING IN AGAIN?
YUP!
I WANT ANOTHER DIP IN THE OCEAN.
BUT YOU'VE BEEN DRINKING.
DO IT TOMOR-ROW.
I'LL BE FINE! I DIDN'T DRINK MUCH.
I'LL DO SOME EASY SNOR-KELING.
WANT ME TO COME WITH?
NAH.
I WANT TO DIVE BY MYSELF!
SO LONG, HARUMI! I'M COUNTING ON YOU! ♡
TAF
KIWAKO ...
SPLISH...

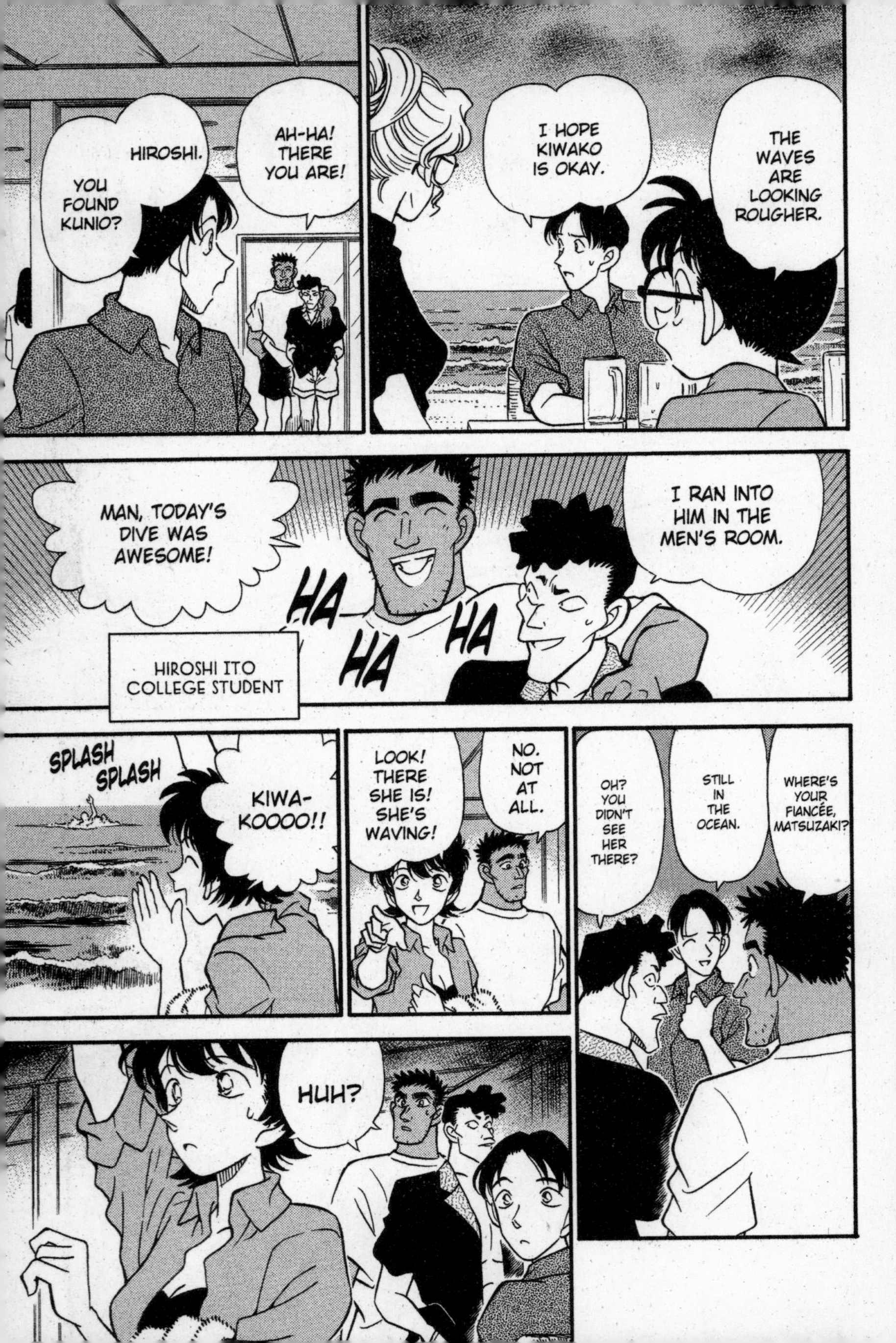
THE WAVES ARE LOOKING ROUGHER.
I HOPE KIWAKO IS OKAY.
AH-HA! THERE YOU ARE!
HIROSHI.
YOU FOUND KUNIO?
I RAN INTO HIM IN THE MEN'S ROOM.
HA HA HA HA
MAN, TODAY'S DIVE WAS AWESOME!
HIROSHI ITO COLLEGE STUDENT
WHERE'S YOUR FIANCÉE, MATSUZAKI?
STILL IN THE OCEAN.
OH? YOU DIDN'T SEE HER THERE?
NO. NOT AT ALL.
LOOK! THERE SHE IS! SHE'S WAVING!
KIWA-KOOOO!!
SPLASH SPLASH
HUH?

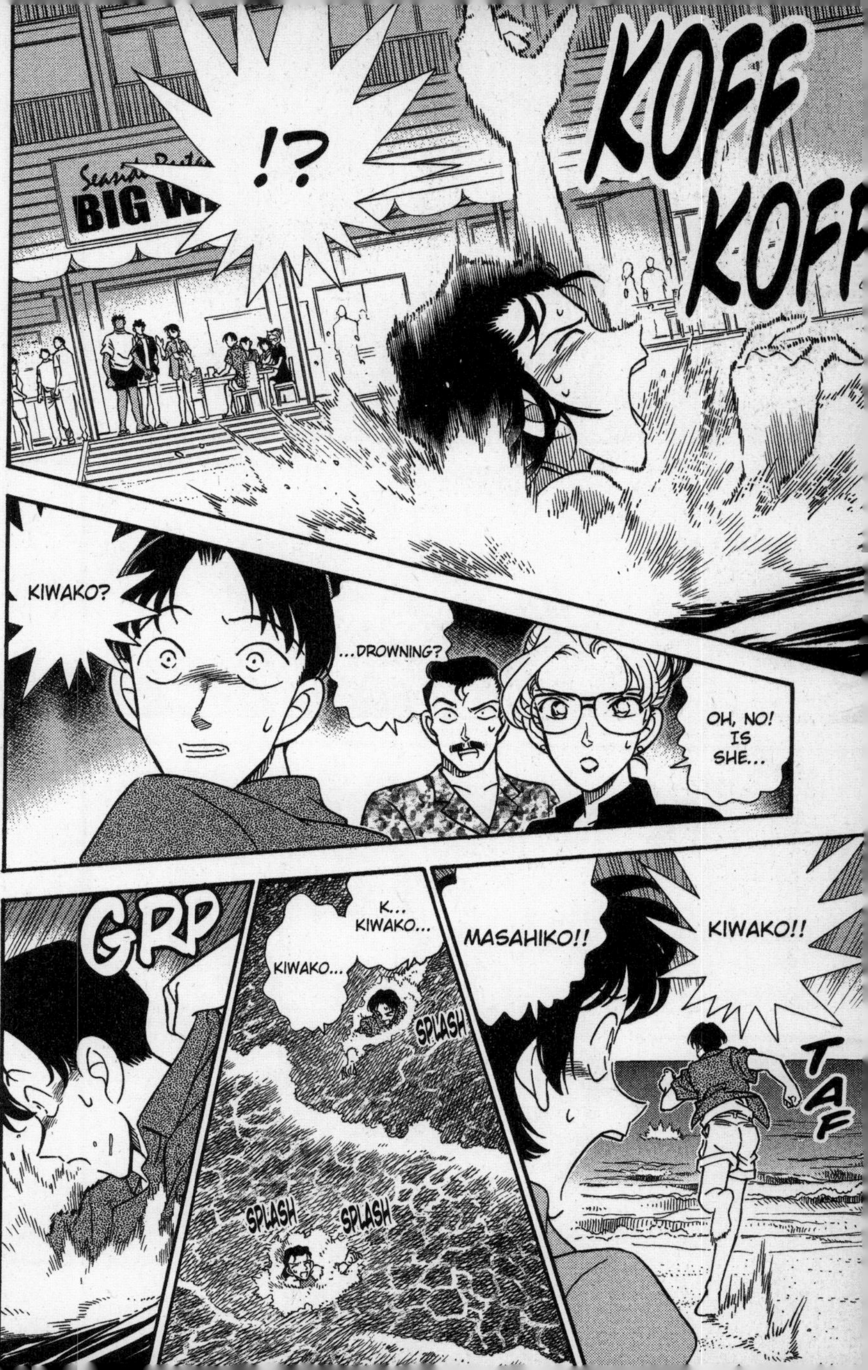
!?
KOFF KOFF
OH, NO! IS SHE...
...DROWNING?
KIWAKO?
KIWAKO!!
TAP
MASAHIKO!!
K... KIWAKO...
KIWAKO...
SPLASH
SPLASH
SPLASH
GRP

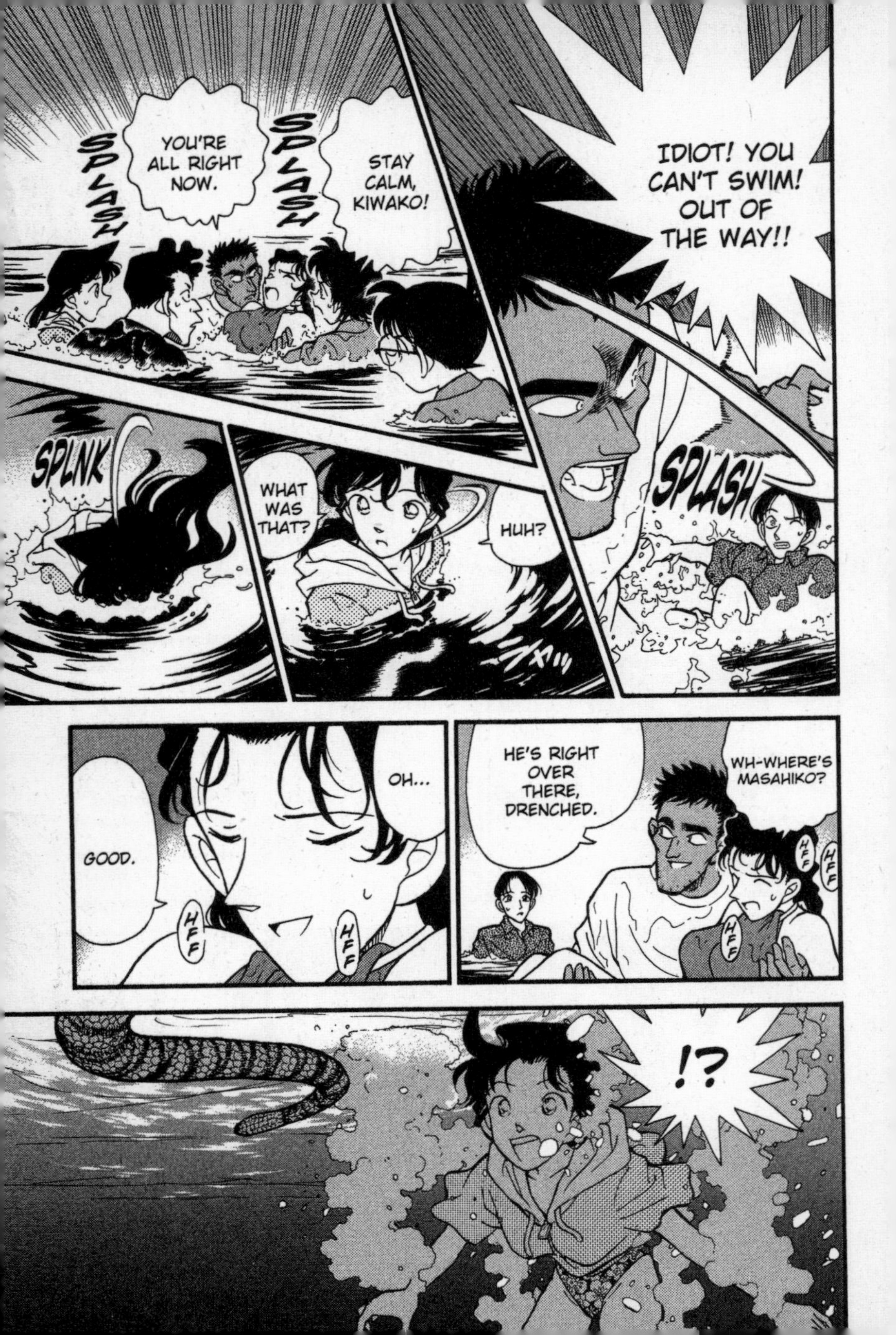
IDIOT! YOU CAN'T SWIM! OUT OF THE WAY!!
SPLASH
STAY CALM, KIWAKO!
SPLASH
YOU'RE ALL RIGHT NOW.
SPLASH
HUH?
WHAT WAS THAT?
SPLNK
WH-WHERE'S MASAHIKO?
HFF
HFF
HFF
HE'S RIGHT OVER THERE, DRENCHED.
OH...
GOOD.
HFF
HFF
!?

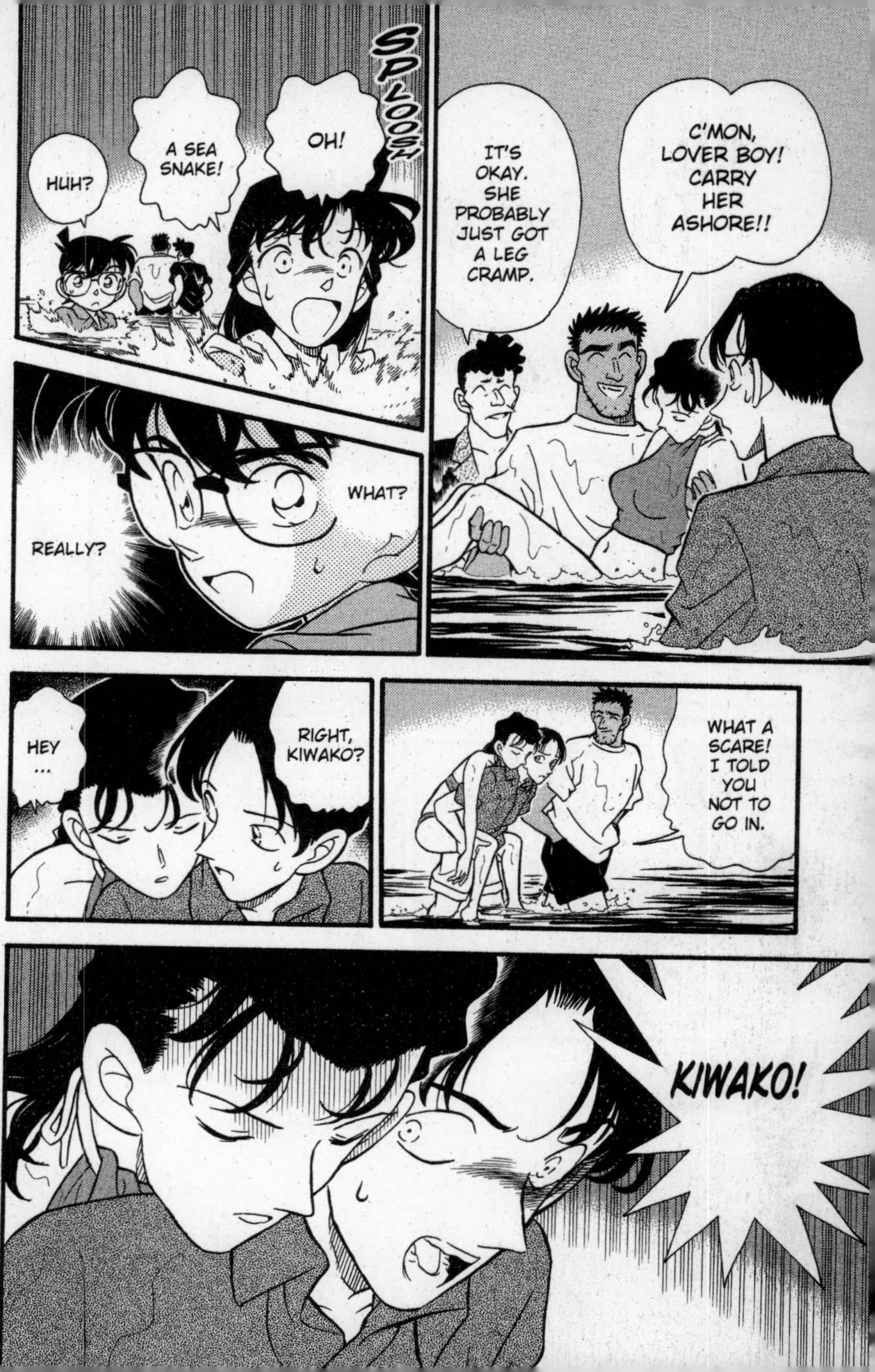
C'MON, LOVER BOY! CARRY HER ASHORE!!
IT'S OKAY. SHE PROBABLY JUST GOT A LEG CRAMP.
SPLOOSH
OH!
A SEA SNAKE!
HUH?
WHAT?
REALLY?
WHAT A SCARE! I TOLD YOU NOT TO GO IN.
RIGHT, KIWAKO?
HEY ...
KIWAKO!

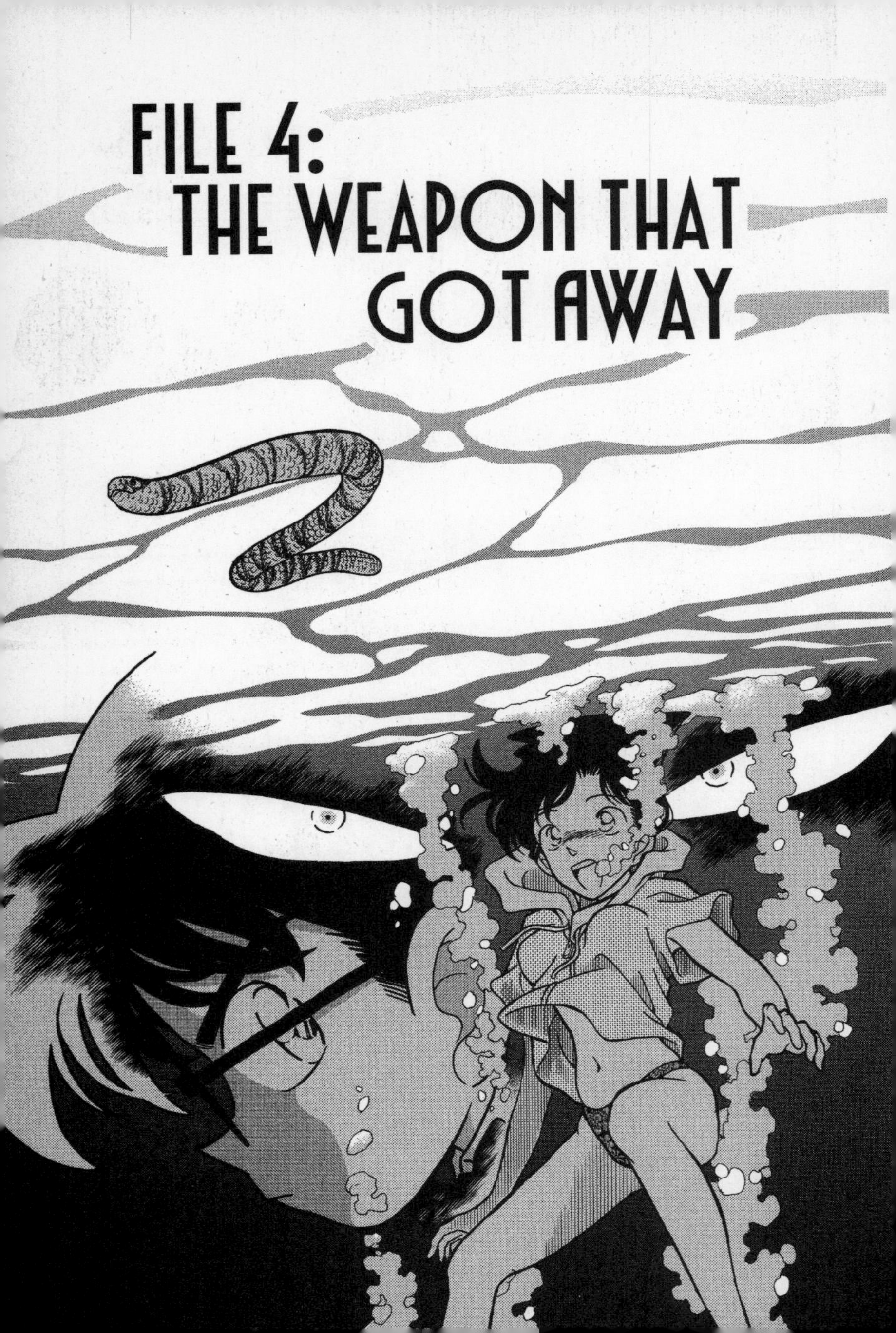
FILE 4:
THE WEAPON THAT
GOT AWAY

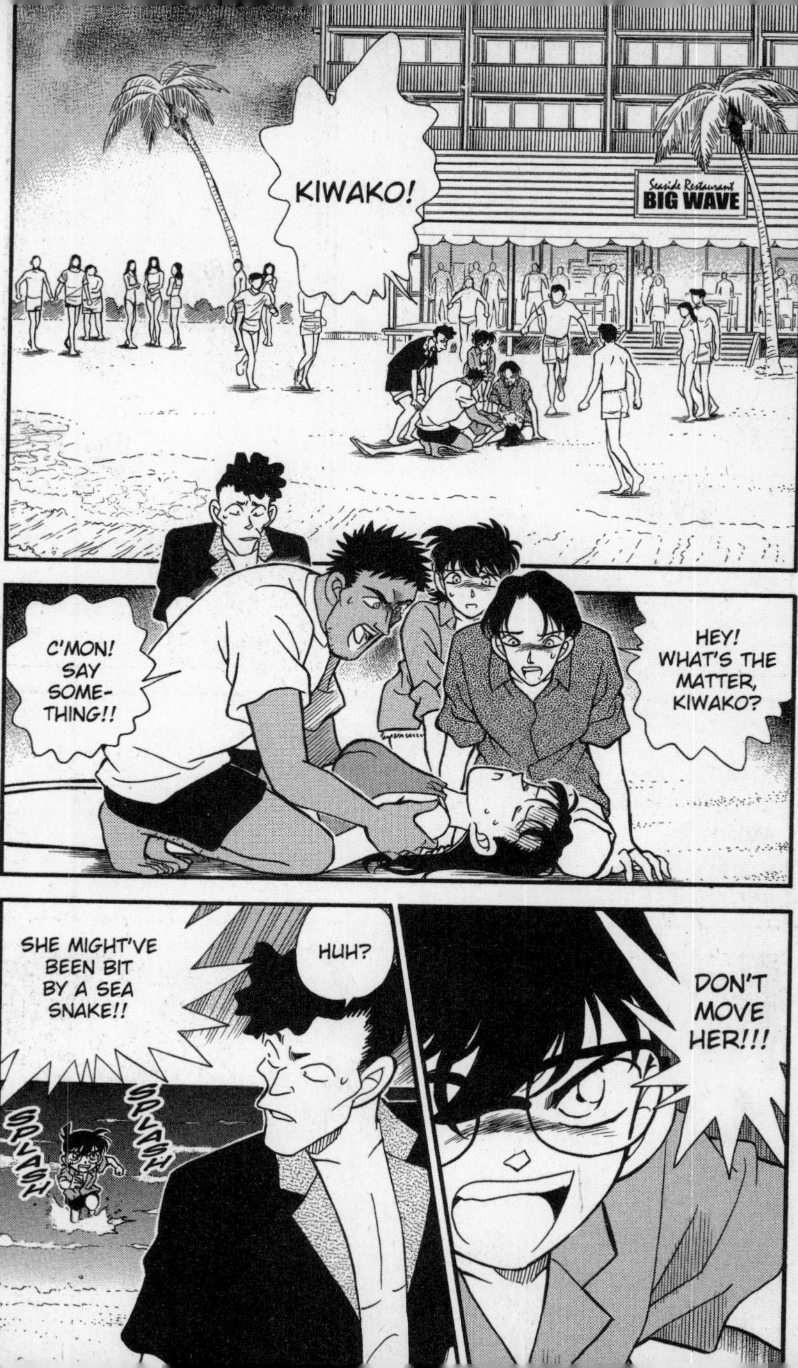
KIWAKO!
Seaside Restaurant
BIG WAVE
HEY! WHAT'S THE MATTER, KIWAKO?
C'MON! SAY SOME-THING!!
DON'T MOVE HER!!!
HUH?
SHE MIGHT'VE BEEN BIT BY A SEA SNAKE!!
SPLASH
SPLASH

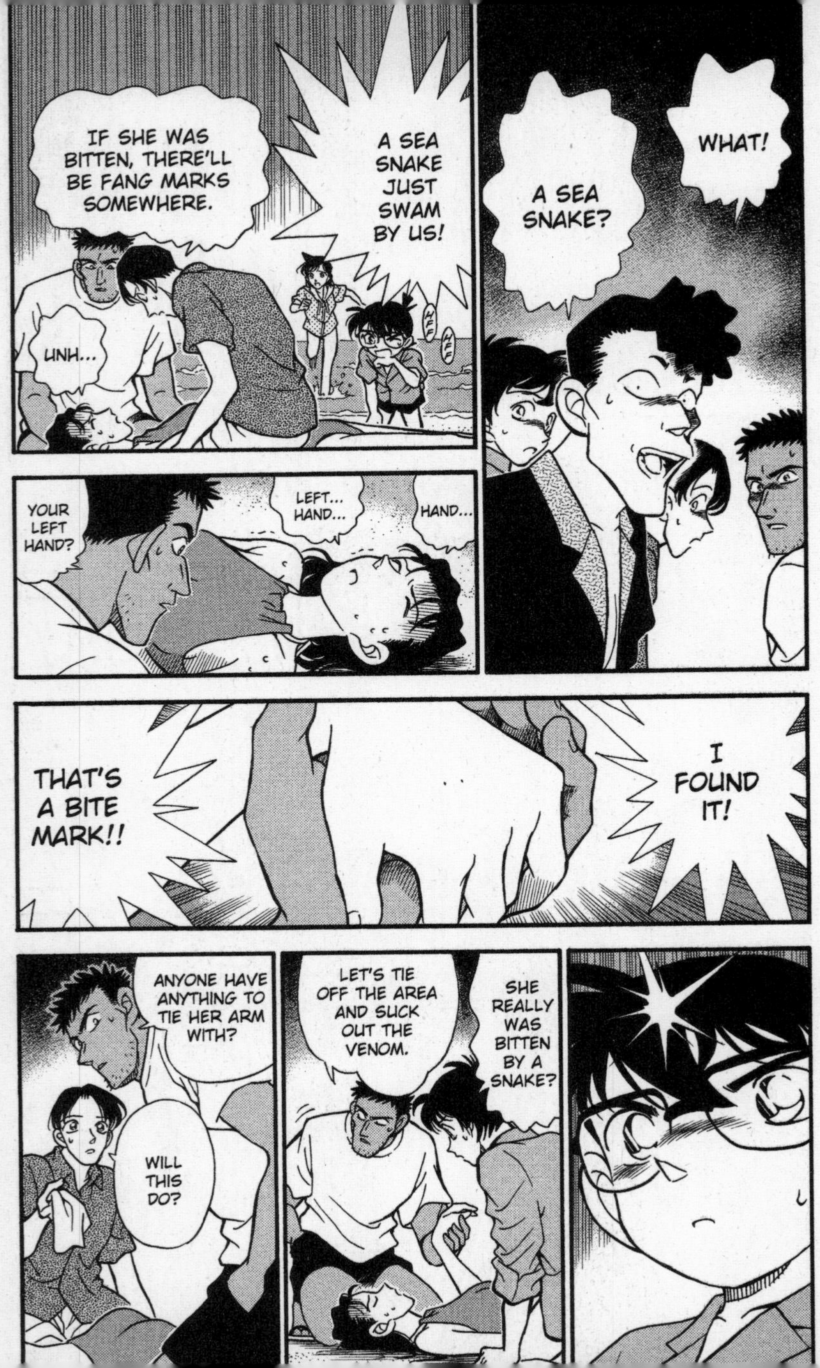
WHAT!
A SEA SNAKE?
A SEA SNAKE JUST SWAM BY US!
IF SHE WAS BITTEN, THERE'LL BE FANG MARKS SOMEWHERE.
HFF
HFF
UNH...
HAND...
LEFT... HAND...
YOUR LEFT HAND?
I FOUND IT!
THAT'S A BITE MARK!!
SHE REALLY WAS BITTEN BY A SNAKE?
LET'S TIE OFF THE AREA AND SUCK OUT THE VENOM.
ANYONE HAVE ANYTHING TO TIE HER ARM WITH?
WILL THIS DO?

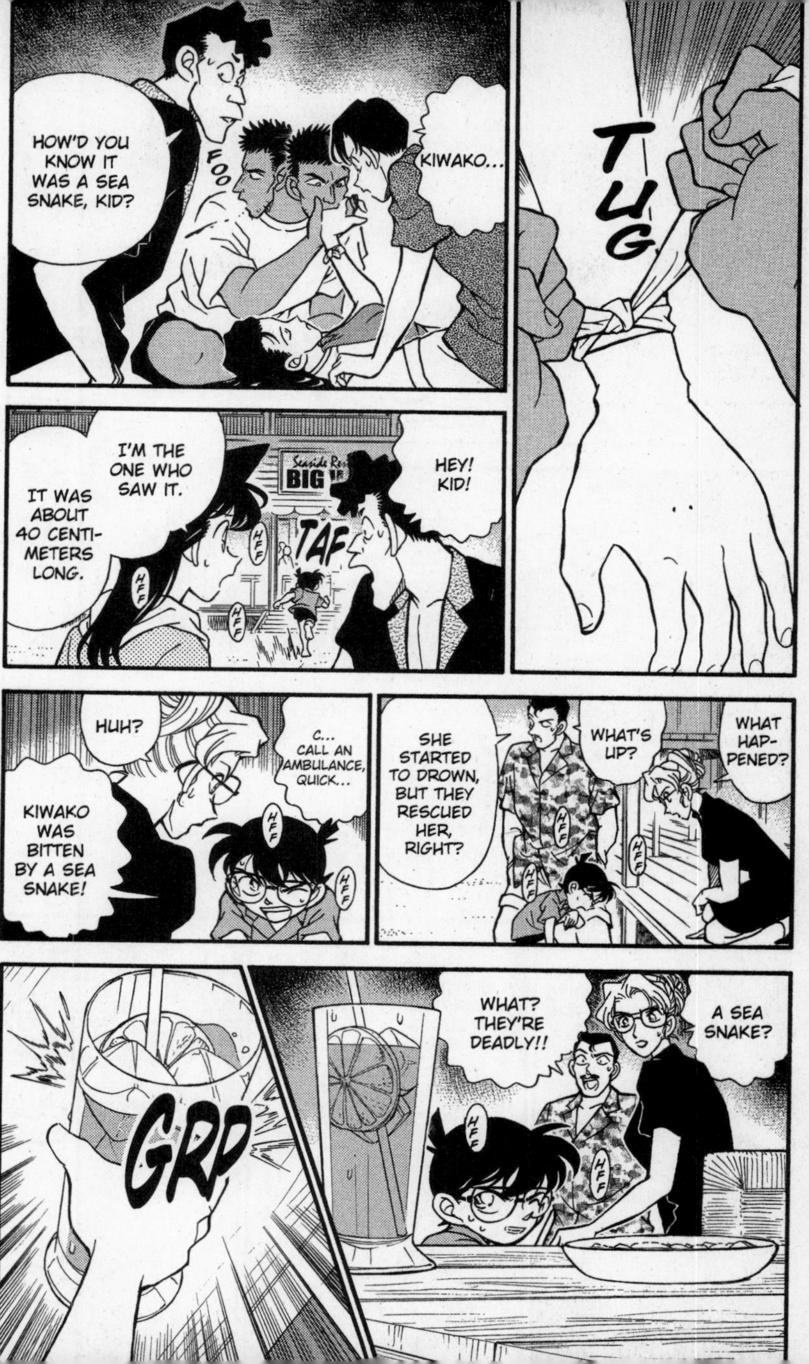
TUG
KIWAKO...
FOO
HOW'D YOU KNOW IT WAS A SEA SNAKE, KID?
HEY! KID!
TAF
HFF
HFF
HFF
I'M THE ONE WHO SAW IT.
IT WAS ABOUT 40 CENTIMETERS LONG.
WHAT HAPPENED?
WHAT'S UP?
HFF
HFF
HFF
SHE STARTED TO DROWN, BUT THEY RESCUED HER, RIGHT?
C... CALL AN AMBULANCE, QUICK...
HUH?
HFF
HFF
KIWAKO WAS BITTEN BY A SEA SNAKE!
A SEA SNAKE?
WHAT? THEY'RE DEADLY!!
HFF
HFF
GRP

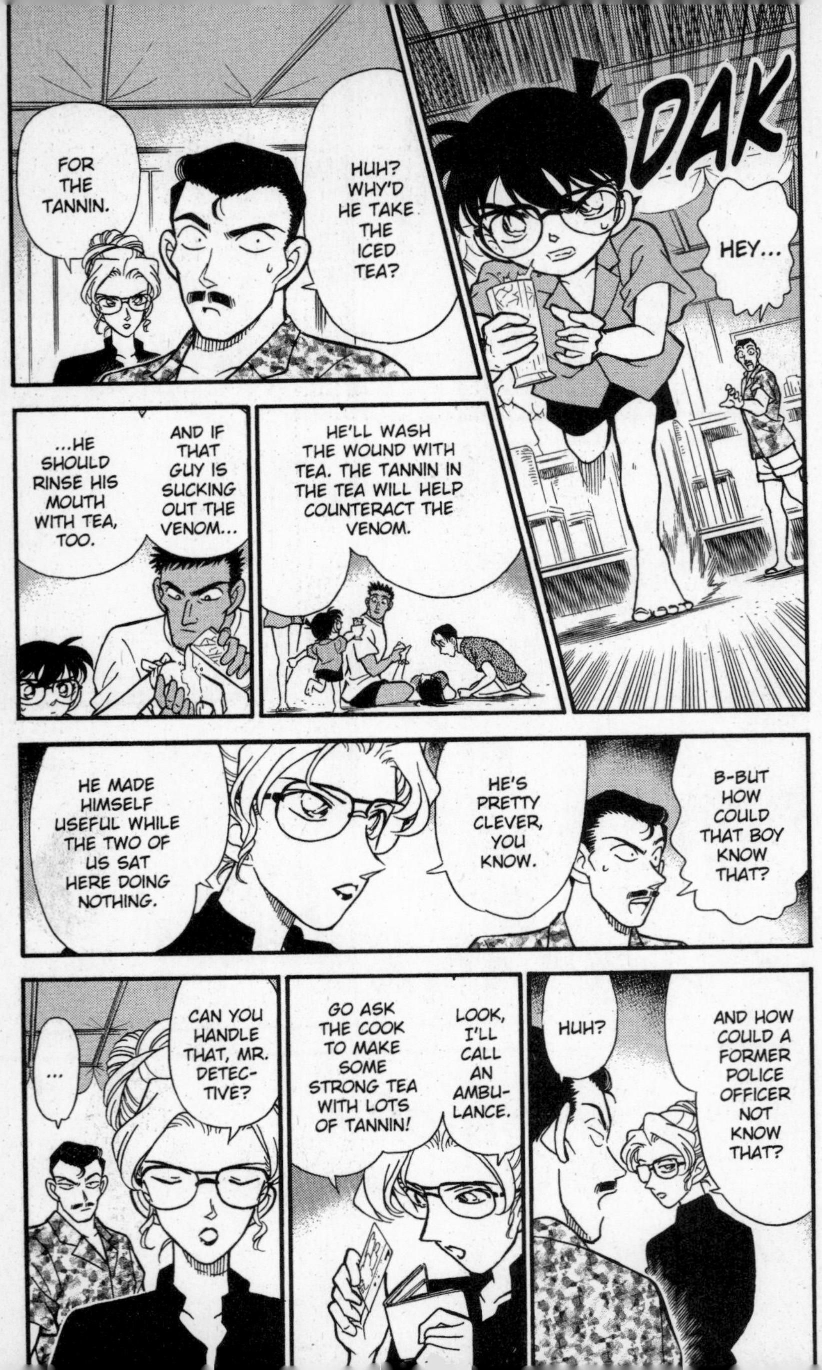
DAK
HEY...
HUH? WHY'D HE TAKE THE ICED TEA?
FOR THE TANNIN.
HE'LL WASH THE WOUND WITH TEA. THE TANNIN IN THE TEA WILL HELP COUNTERACT THE VENOM.
AND IF THAT GUY IS SUCKING OUT THE VENOM...
...HE SHOULD RINSE HIS MOUTH WITH TEA, TOO.
B-BUT HOW COULD THAT BOY KNOW THAT?
HE'S PRETTY CLEVER, YOU KNOW.
HE MADE HIMSELF USEFUL WHILE THE TWO OF US SAT HERE DOING NOTHING.
AND HOW COULD A FORMER POLICE OFFICER NOT KNOW THAT?
HUH?
LOOK, I'LL CALL AN AMBULANCE.
GO ASK THE COOK TO MAKE SOME STRONG TEA WITH LOTS OF TANNIN!
CAN YOU HANDLE THAT, MR. DETECTIVE?
...

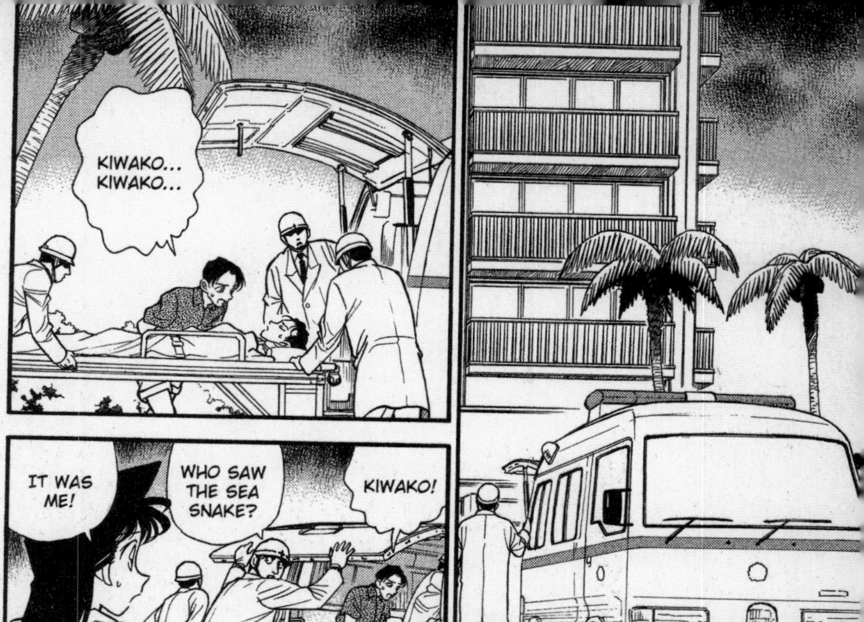
KIWAKO... KIWAKO...
KIWAKO!
WHO SAW THE SEA SNAKE?
IT WAS ME!
DO YOU KNOW WHAT TYPE IT WAS?
SLAM
WHAT TYPE?
WE HAVE AN ILLUS-TRATED GUIDE IN THE HOTEL OFFICE.
AS SOON AS YOU FIND OUT, PLEASE CALL THE HOSPITAL!!
VROOOM

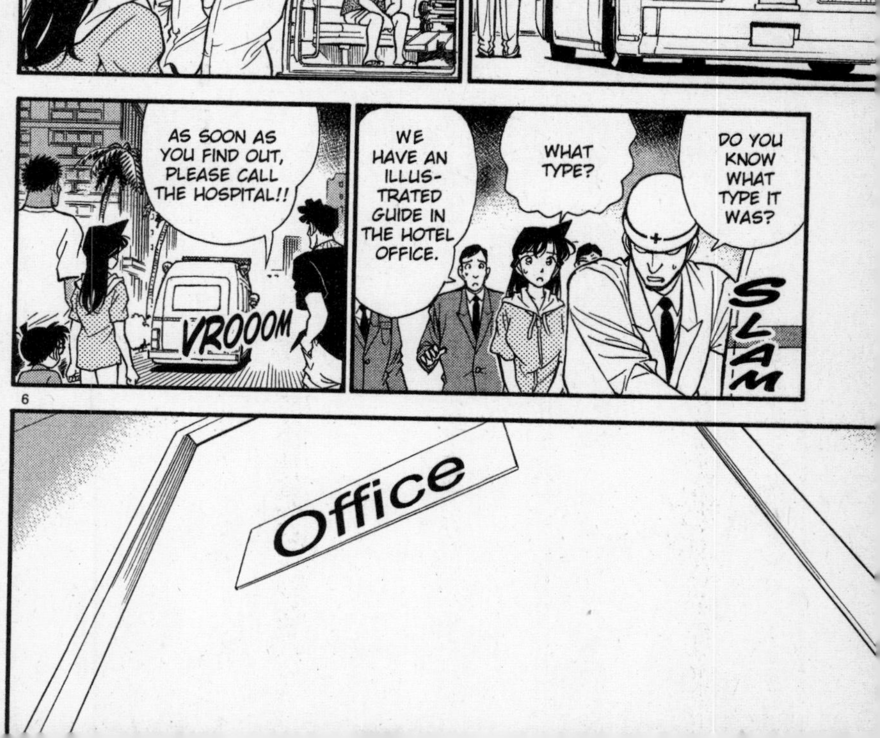
Office

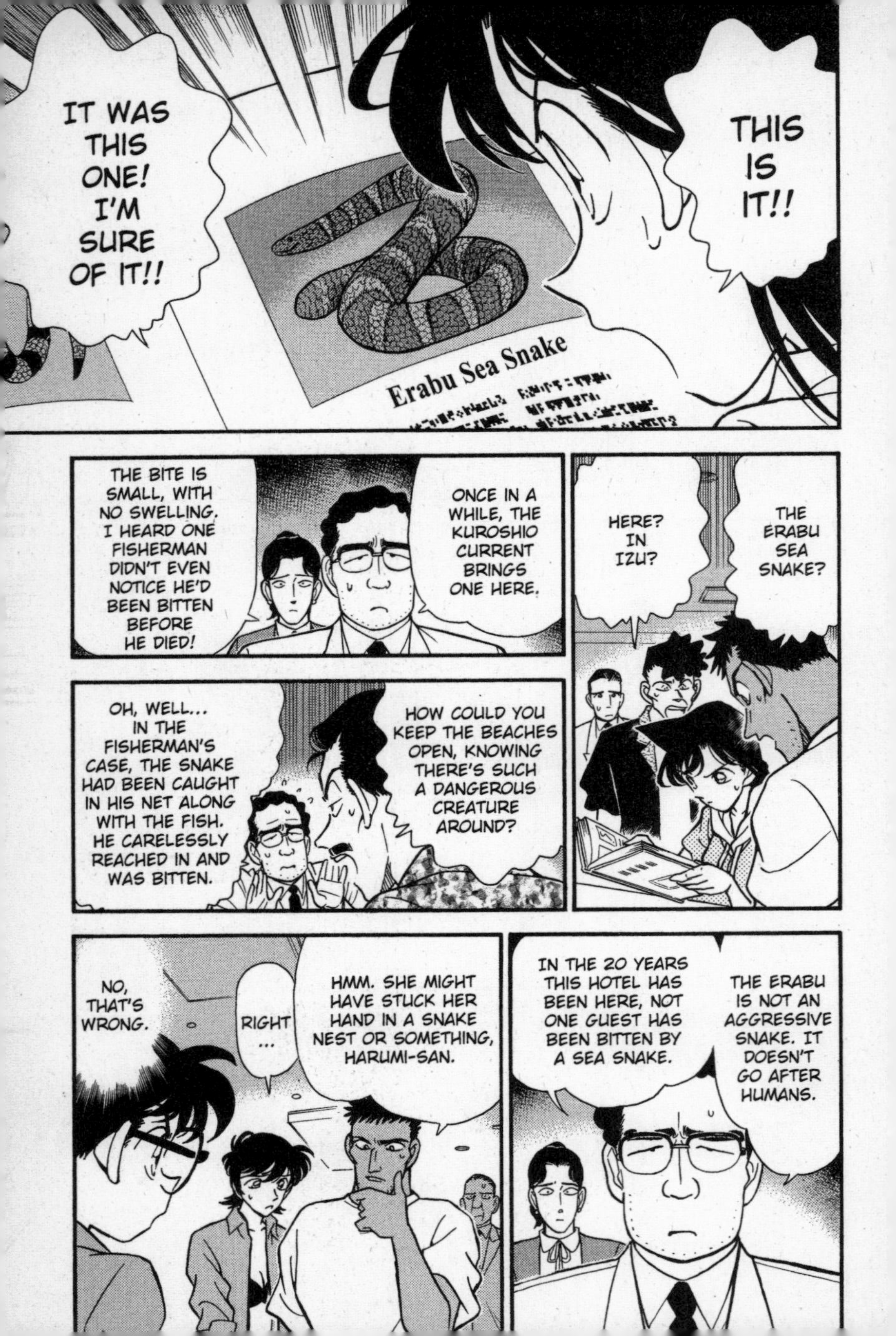
THIS IS IT!!
IT WAS THIS ONE! I'M SURE OF IT!!
Erabu Sea Snake
THE ERABU SEA SNAKE?
HERE? IN IZU?
ONCE IN A WHILE, THE KUROSHIO CURRENT BRINGS ONE HERE.
THE BITE IS SMALL, WITH NO SWELLING. I HEARD ONE FISHERMAN DIDN'T EVEN NOTICE HE'D BEEN BITTEN BEFORE HE DIED!
HOW COULD YOU KEEP THE BEACHES OPEN, KNOWING THERE'S SUCH A DANGEROUS CREATURE AROUND?
OH, WELL... IN THE FISHERMAN'S CASE, THE SNAKE HAD BEEN CAUGHT IN HIS NET ALONG WITH THE FISH. HE CARELESSLY REACHED IN AND WAS BITTEN.
THE ERABU IS NOT AN AGGRESSIVE SNAKE. IT DOESN'T GO AFTER HUMANS.
IN THE 20 YEARS THIS HOTEL HAS BEEN HERE, NOT ONE GUEST HAS BEEN BITTEN BY A SEA SNAKE.
HMM. SHE MIGHT HAVE STUCK HER HAND IN A SNAKE NEST OR SOMETHING, HARUMI-SAN.
RIGHT ...
NO, THAT'S WRONG.

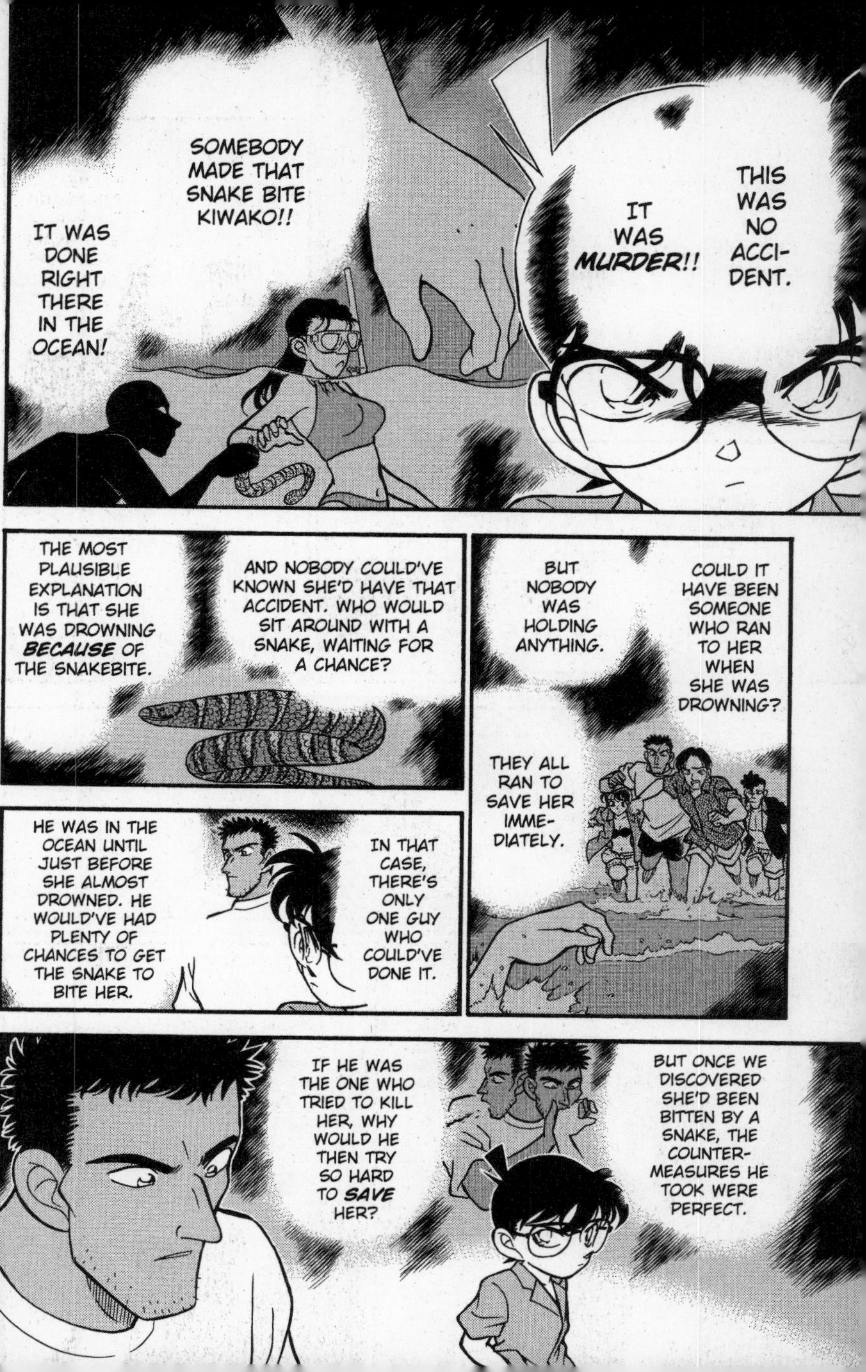
THIS WAS NO ACCIDENT.
IT WAS MURDER!!
SOMEBODY MADE THAT SNAKE BITE KIWAKO!!
IT WAS DONE RIGHT THERE IN THE OCEAN!
COULD IT HAVE BEEN SOMEONE WHO RAN TO HER WHEN SHE WAS DROWNING?
BUT NOBODY WAS HOLDING ANYTHING.
THEY ALL RAN TO SAVE HER IMMEDIATELY.
THE MOST PLAUSIBLE EXPLANATION IS THAT SHE WAS DROWNING BECAUSE OF THE SNAKEBITE.
AND NOBODY COULD'VE KNOWN SHE'D HAVE THAT ACCIDENT. WHO WOULD SIT AROUND WITH A SNAKE, WAITING FOR A CHANCE?
IN THAT CASE, THERE'S ONLY ONE GUY WHO COULD'VE DONE IT.
HE WAS IN THE OCEAN UNTIL JUST BEFORE SHE ALMOST DROWNED. HE WOULD'VE HAD PLENTY OF CHANCES TO GET THE SNAKE TO BITE HER.
BUT ONCE WE DISCOVERED SHE'D BEEN BITTEN BY A SNAKE, THE COUNTERMEASURES HE TOOK WERE PERFECT.
IF HE WAS THE ONE WHO TRIED TO KILL HER, WHY WOULD HE THEN TRY SO HARD TO SAVE HER?

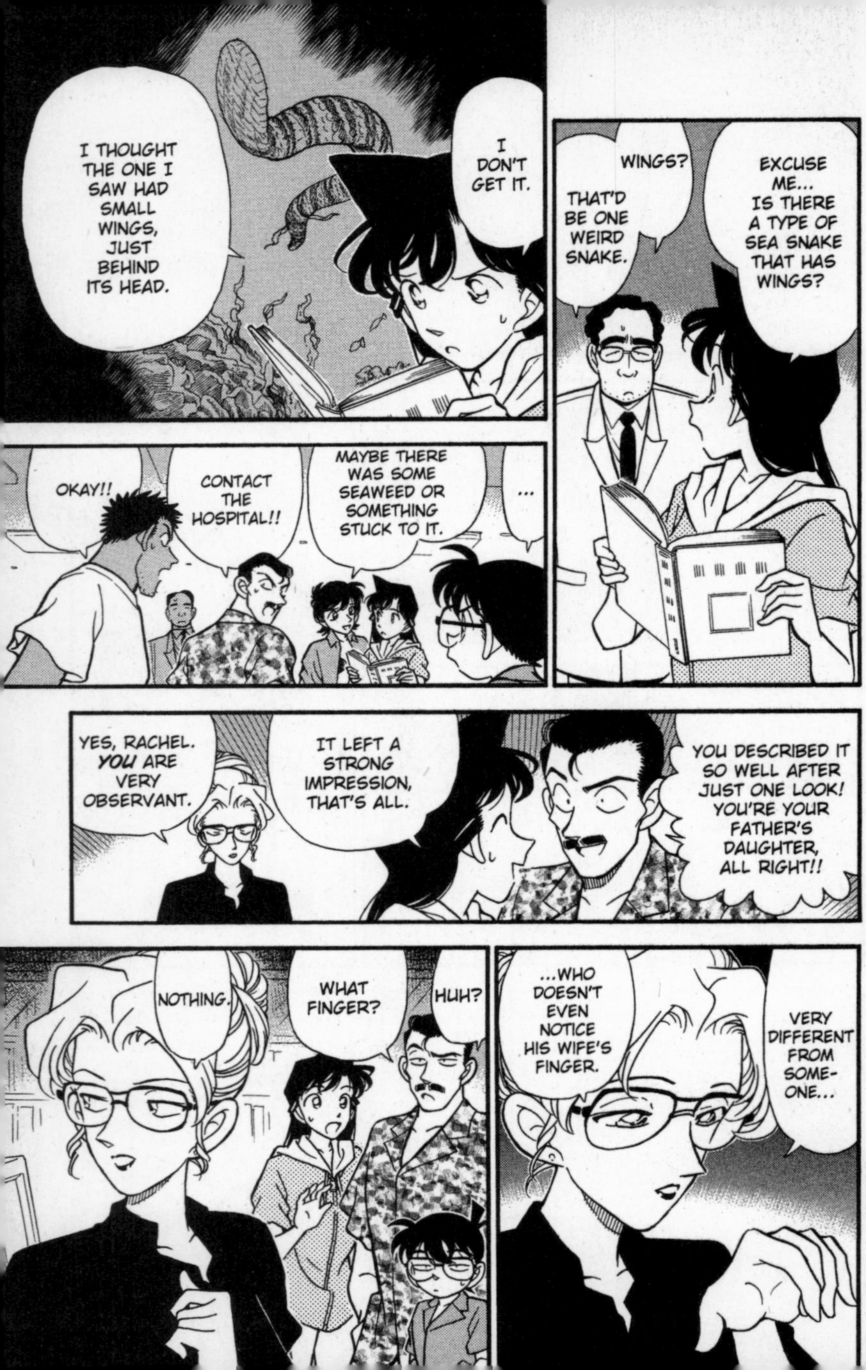
I DON'T GET IT.
I THOUGHT THE ONE I SAW HAD SMALL WINGS, JUST BEHIND ITS HEAD.
EXCUSE ME... IS THERE A TYPE OF SEA SNAKE THAT HAS WINGS?
WINGS?
THAT'D BE ONE WEIRD SNAKE.
...
MAYBE THERE WAS SOME SEAWEED OR SOMETHING STUCK TO IT.
CONTACT THE HOSPITAL!!
OKAY!!
YOU DESCRIBED IT SO WELL AFTER JUST ONE LOOK! YOU'RE YOUR FATHER'S DAUGHTER, ALL RIGHT!!
IT LEFT A STRONG IMPRESSION, THAT'S ALL.
YES, RACHEL. *YOU* ARE VERY OBSERVANT.
VERY DIFFERENT FROM SOME-ONE...
...WHO DOESN'T EVEN NOTICE HIS WIFE'S FINGER.
HUH?
WHAT FINGER?
NOTHING.

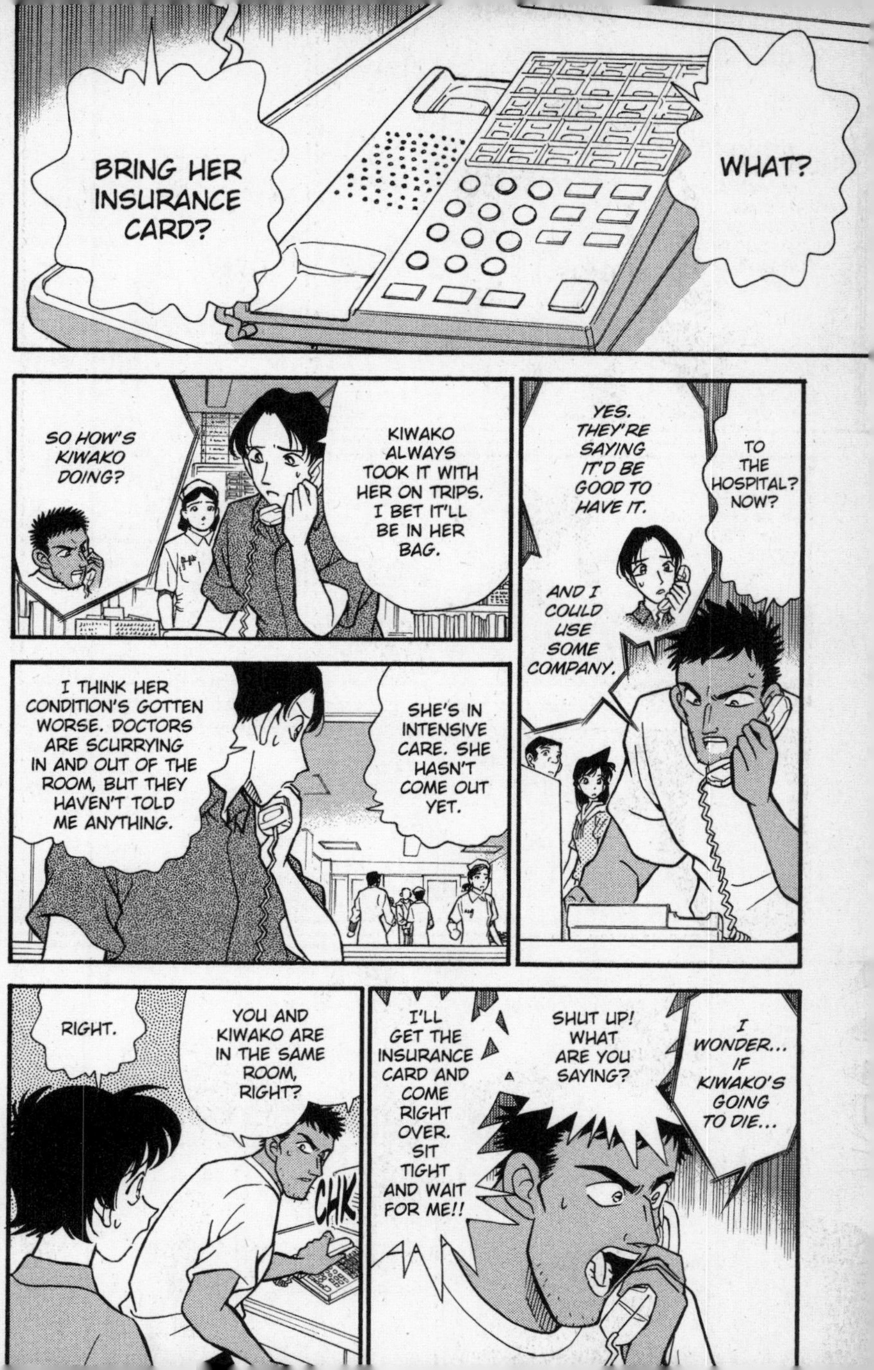
WHAT?
BRING HER INSURANCE CARD?
TO THE HOSPITAL? NOW?
YES. THEY'RE SAYING IT'D BE GOOD TO HAVE IT.
AND I COULD USE SOME COMPANY.
KIWAKO ALWAYS TOOK IT WITH HER ON TRIPS. I BET IT'LL BE IN HER BAG.
SO HOW'S KIWAKO DOING?
SHE'S IN INTENSIVE CARE. SHE HASN'T COME OUT YET.
I THINK HER CONDITION'S GOTTEN WORSE. DOCTORS ARE SCURRYING IN AND OUT OF THE ROOM, BUT THEY HAVEN'T TOLD ME ANYTHING.
I WONDER... IF KIWAKO'S GOING TO DIE...
SHUT UP! WHAT ARE YOU SAYING?
I'LL GET THE INSURANCE CARD AND COME RIGHT OVER. SIT TIGHT AND WAIT FOR ME!!
YOU AND KIWAKO ARE IN THE SAME ROOM, RIGHT?
RIGHT.
CHK

IT MUST'VE BEEN WHEN KIWAKO ASKED ME TO GET A TOWEL FOR HER.

I LEFT MY KEY CARD INSIDE.

OH, NO.

406

GUESS WE'LL HAVE TO CALL THE FRONT DESK FROM OUR ROOM AND GET THEM TO BRING UP ANOTHER KEY.

WHAT SHOULD I DO? THE DOOR LOCKS AUTO- MATICALLY.

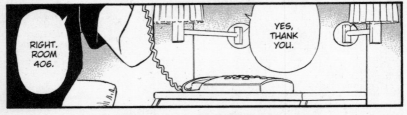

RIGHT. ROOM 406.

YES, THANK YOU.

ARGH!

HEY!

WHEW.

CHK

SORRY TO TROUBLE YOU.

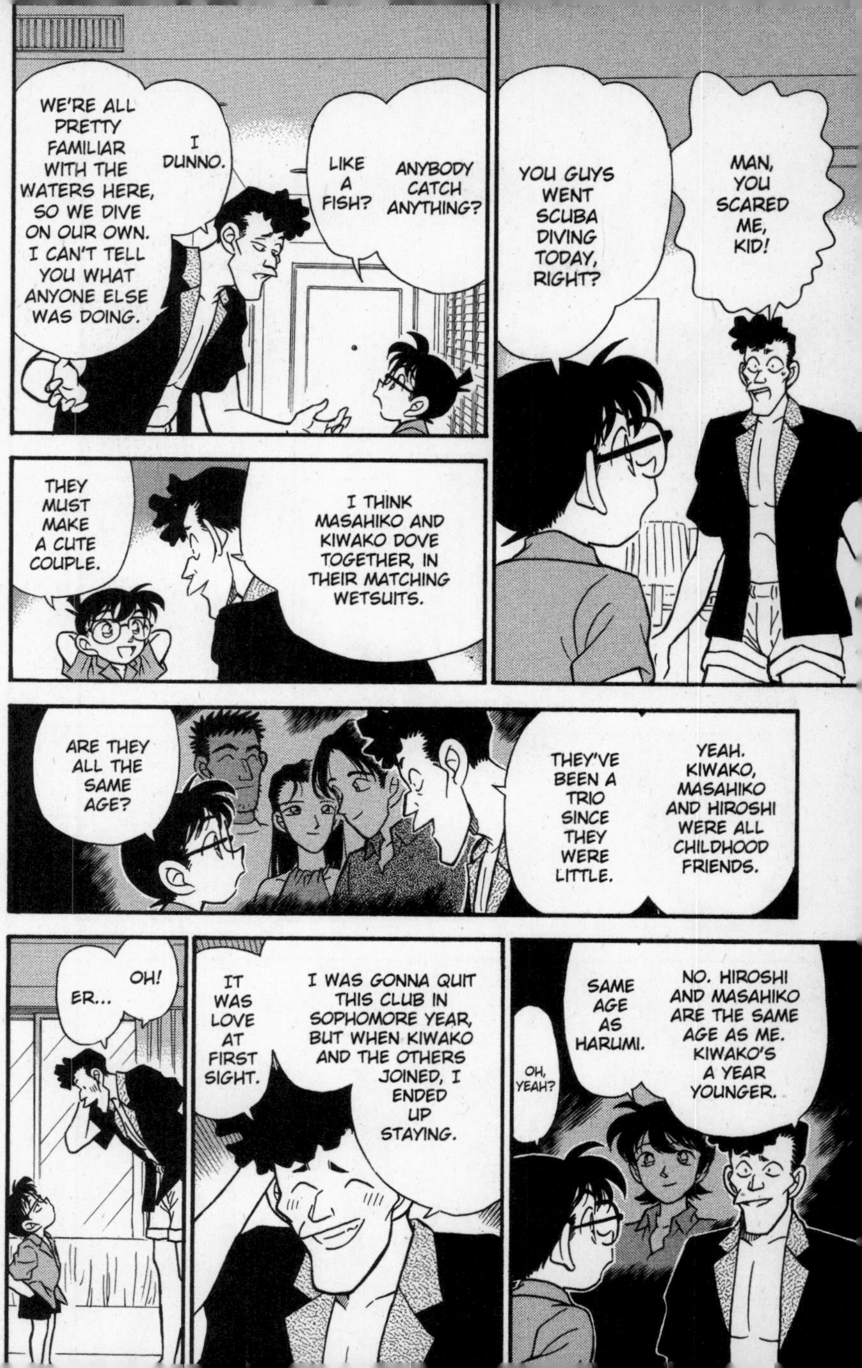
MAN, YOU SCARED ME, KID!
YOU GUYS WENT SCUBA DIVING TODAY, RIGHT?
ANYBODY CATCH ANYTHING?
LIKE A FISH?
I DUNNO.
WE'RE ALL PRETTY FAMILIAR WITH THE WATERS HERE, SO WE DIVE ON OUR OWN. I CAN'T TELL YOU WHAT ANYONE ELSE WAS DOING.
I THINK MASAHIKO AND KIWAKO DOVE TOGETHER, IN THEIR MATCHING WETSUITS.
THEY MUST MAKE A CUTE COUPLE.
YEAH. KIWAKO, MASAHIKO AND HIROSHI WERE ALL CHILDHOOD FRIENDS.
THEY'VE BEEN A TRIO SINCE THEY WERE LITTLE.
ARE THEY ALL THE SAME AGE?
NO. HIROSHI AND MASAHIKO ARE THE SAME AGE AS ME. KIWAKO'S A YEAR YOUNGER.
SAME AGE AS HARUMI.
OH, YEAH?
I WAS GONNA QUIT THIS CLUB IN SOPHOMORE YEAR, BUT WHEN KIWAKO AND THE OTHERS JOINED, I ENDED UP STAYING.
IT WAS LOVE AT FIRST SIGHT.
OH!
ER...

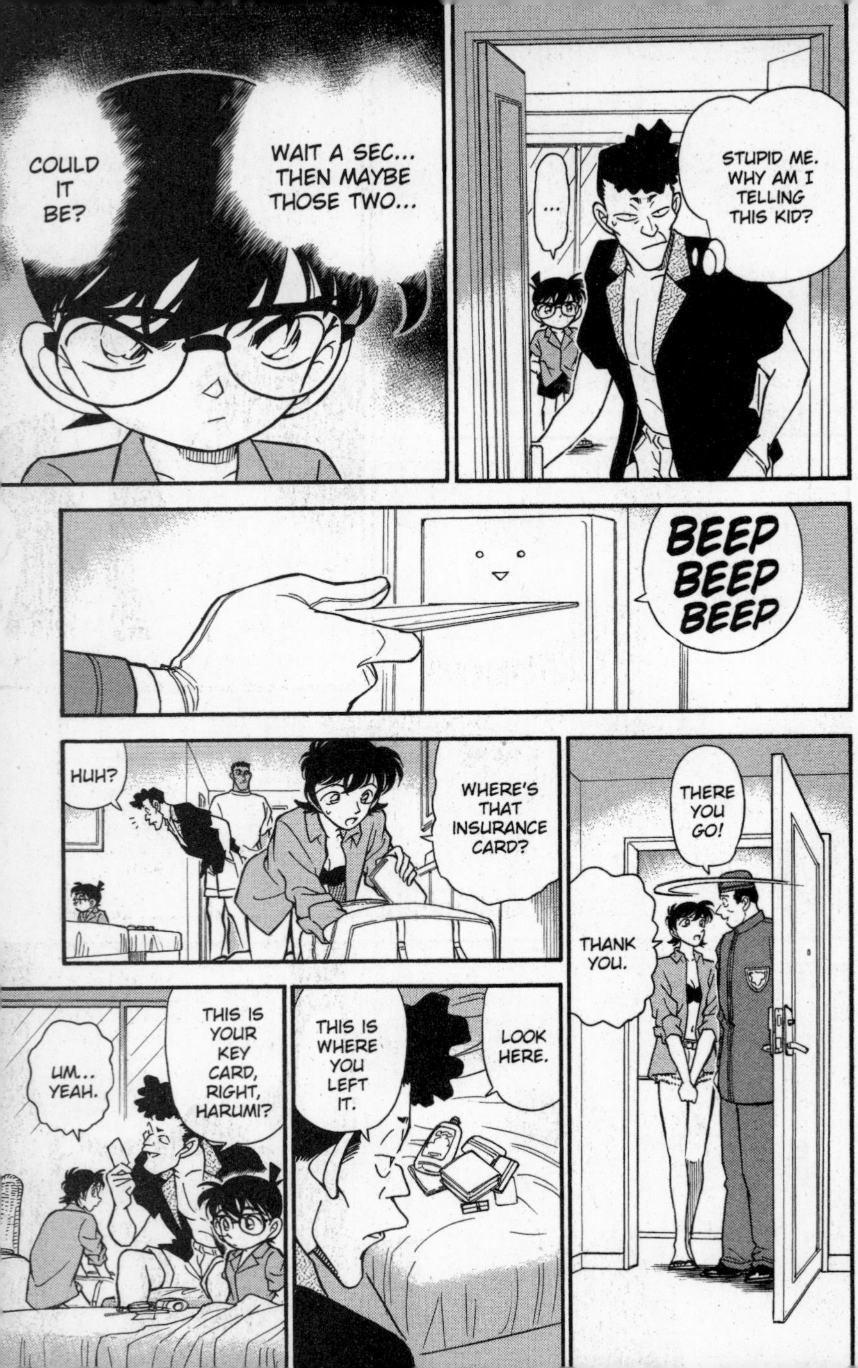
STUPID ME. WHY AM I TELLING THIS KID?
...
WAIT A SEC... THEN MAYBE THOSE TWO...
COULD IT BE?
BEEP BEEP BEEP
THERE YOU GO!
THANK YOU.
WHERE'S THAT INSURANCE CARD?
HUH?
LOOK HERE.
THIS IS WHERE YOU LEFT IT.
THIS IS YOUR KEY CARD, RIGHT, HARUMI?
UM... YEAH.

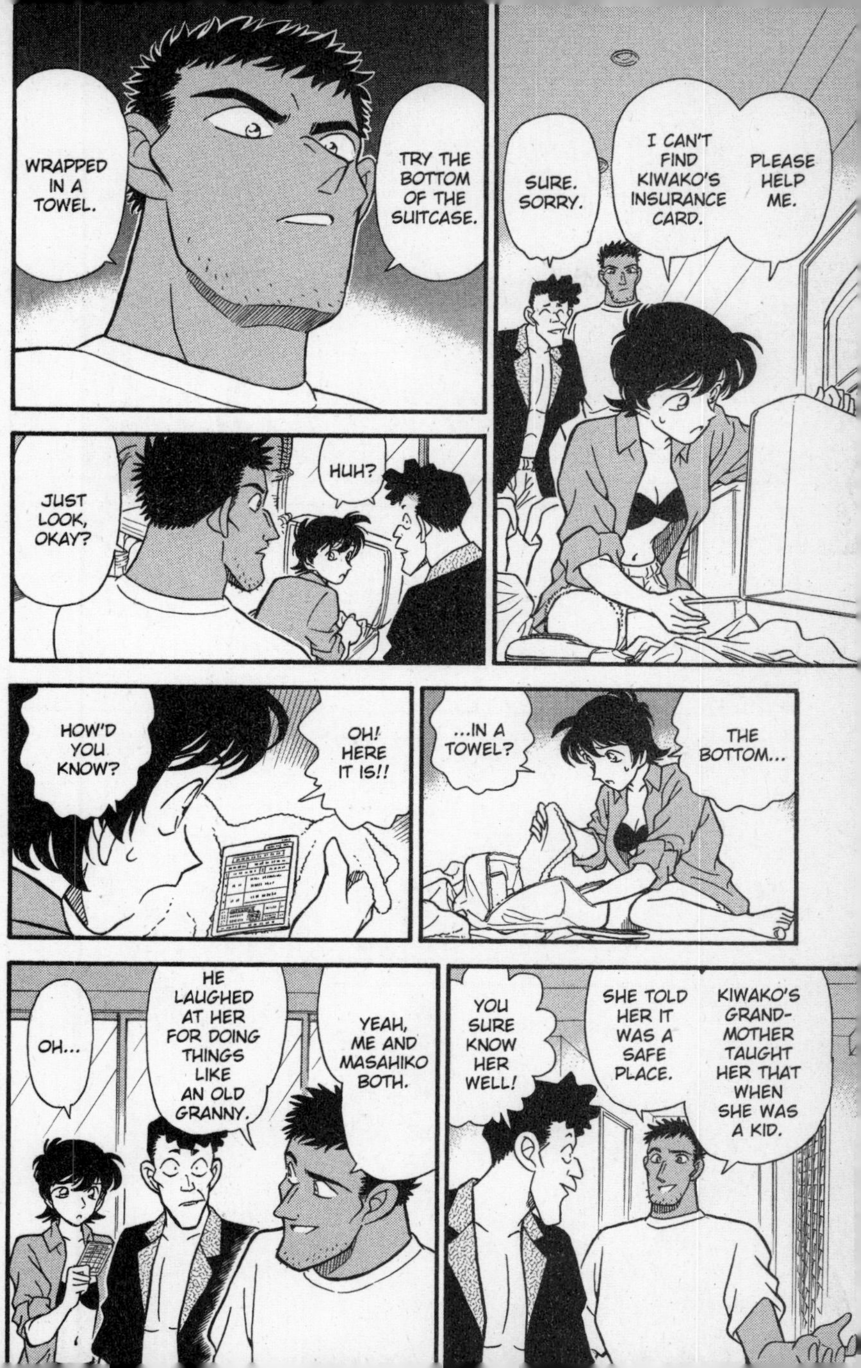
PLEASE HELP ME.
I CAN'T FIND KIWAKO'S INSURANCE CARD.
SURE. SORRY.
TRY THE BOTTOM OF THE SUITCASE.
WRAPPED IN A TOWEL.
HUH?
JUST LOOK, OKAY?
THE BOTTOM...
...IN A TOWEL?
OH! HERE IT IS!!
HOW'D YOU KNOW?
KIWAKO'S GRAND-MOTHER TAUGHT HER THAT WHEN SHE WAS A KID.
SHE TOLD HER IT WAS A SAFE PLACE.
YOU SURE KNOW HER WELL!
YEAH, ME AND MASAHIKO BOTH.
HE LAUGHED AT HER FOR DOING THINGS LIKE AN OLD GRANNY.
OH...

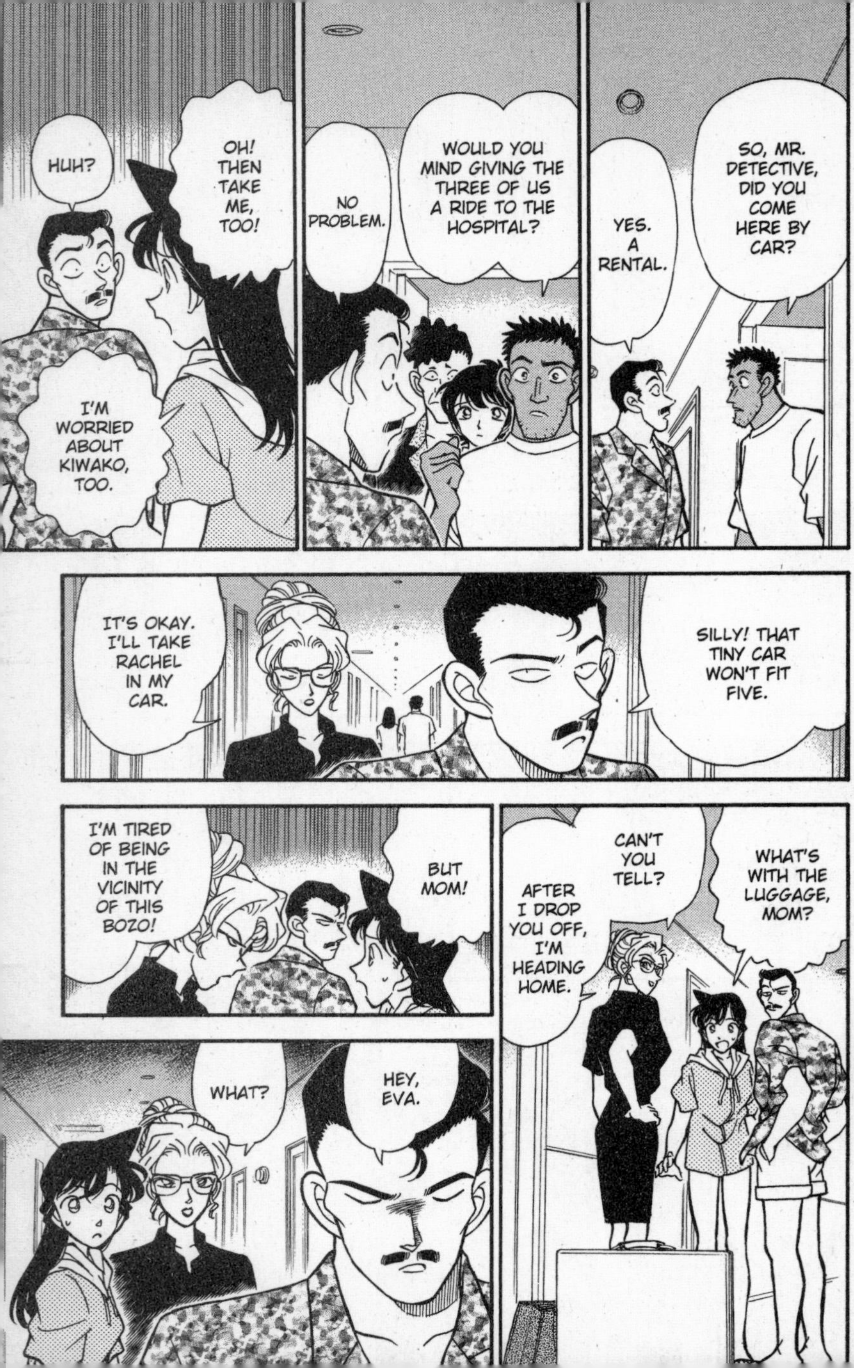
SO, MR. DETECTIVE, DID YOU COME HERE BY CAR?
YES. A RENTAL.
WOULD YOU MIND GIVING THE THREE OF US A RIDE TO THE HOSPITAL?
NO PROBLEM.
OH! THEN TAKE ME, TOO!
HUH?
I'M WORRIED ABOUT KIWAKO, TOO.
SILLY! THAT TINY CAR WON'T FIT FIVE.
IT'S OKAY. I'LL TAKE RACHEL IN MY CAR.
WHAT'S WITH THE LUGGAGE, MOM?
CAN'T YOU TELL?
AFTER I DROP YOU OFF, I'M HEADING HOME.
BUT MOM!
I'M TIRED OF BEING IN THE VICINITY OF THIS BOZO!
HEY, EVA.
WHAT?

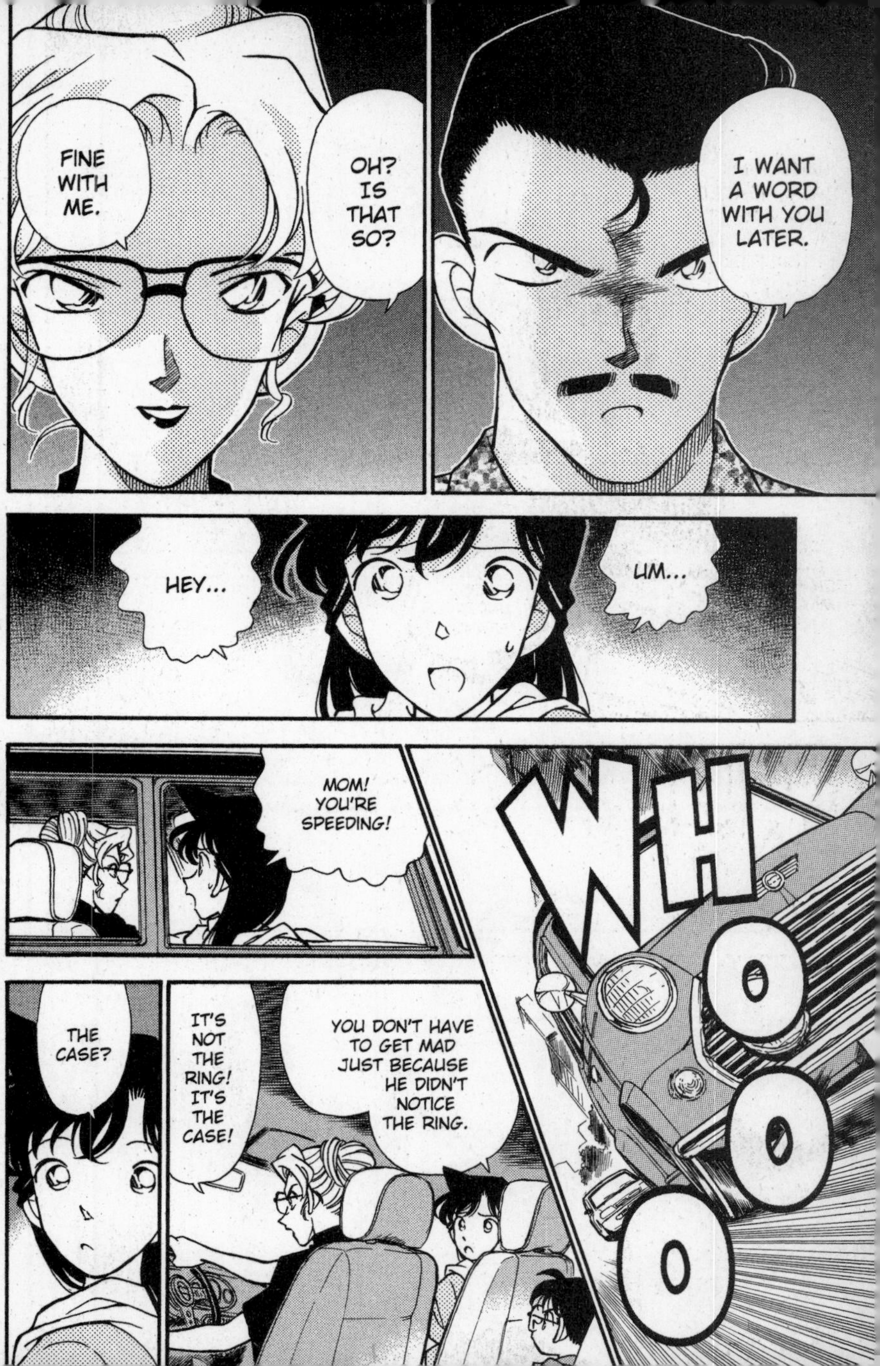
I WANT A WORD WITH YOU LATER.
OH? IS THAT SO?
FINE WITH ME.
UM...
HEY...
WHOOOO
MOM! YOU'RE SPEEDING!
YOU DON'T HAVE TO GET MAD JUST BECAUSE HE DIDN'T NOTICE THE RING.
IT'S NOT THE RING! IT'S THE CASE!
THE CASE?

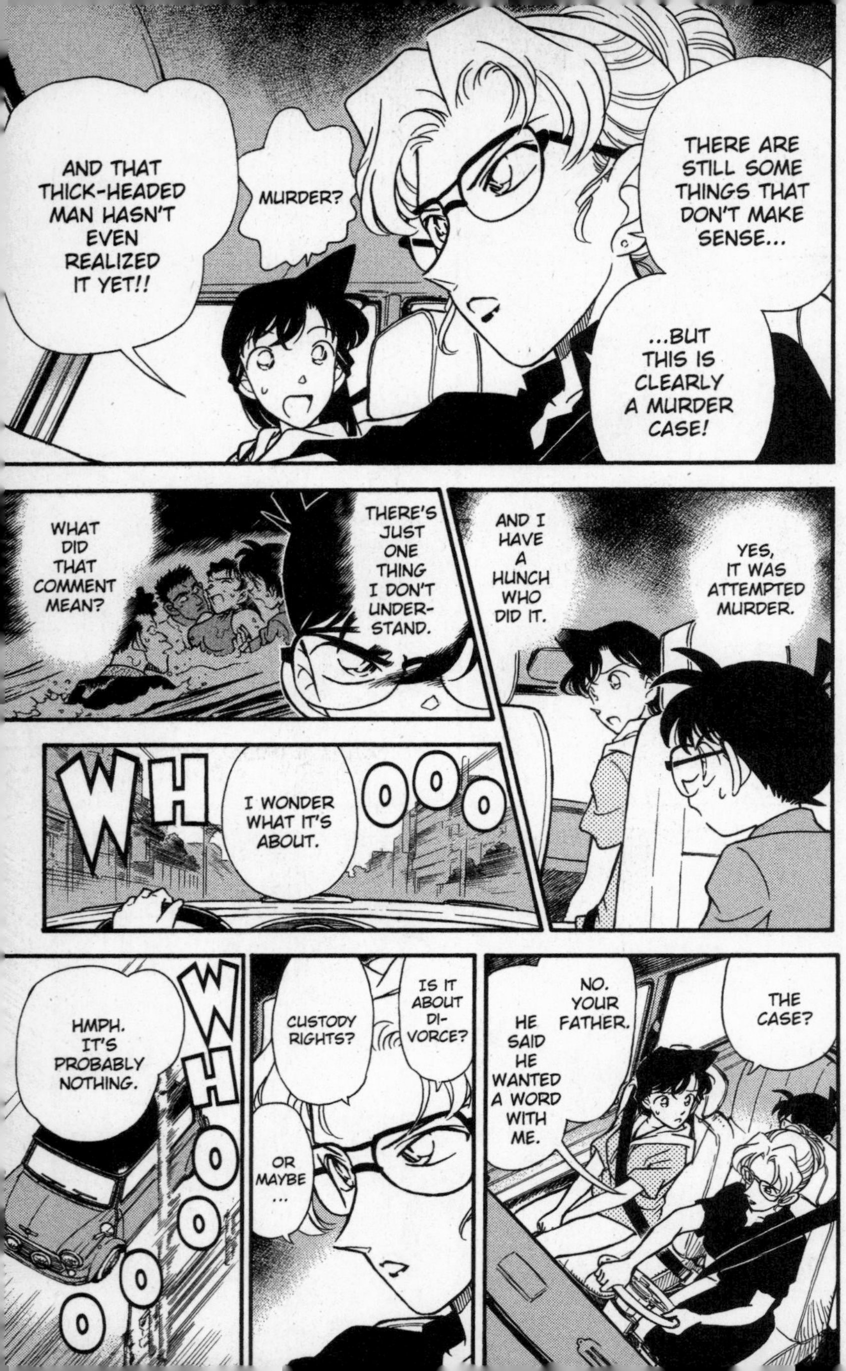
THERE ARE STILL SOME THINGS THAT DON'T MAKE SENSE...
...BUT THIS IS CLEARLY A MURDER CASE!
MURDER?
AND THAT THICK-HEADED MAN HASN'T EVEN REALIZED IT YET!!
YES, IT WAS ATTEMPTED MURDER.
AND I HAVE A HUNCH WHO DID IT.
THERE'S JUST ONE THING I DON'T UNDER-STAND.
WHAT DID THAT COMMENT MEAN?
WHOOO
I WONDER WHAT IT'S ABOUT.
THE CASE?
NO. YOUR FATHER.
HE SAID HE WANTED A WORD WITH ME.
IS IT ABOUT DI-VORCE?
CUSTODY RIGHTS?
OR MAYBE ...
WHOOOO
HMPH. IT'S PROBABLY NOTHING.

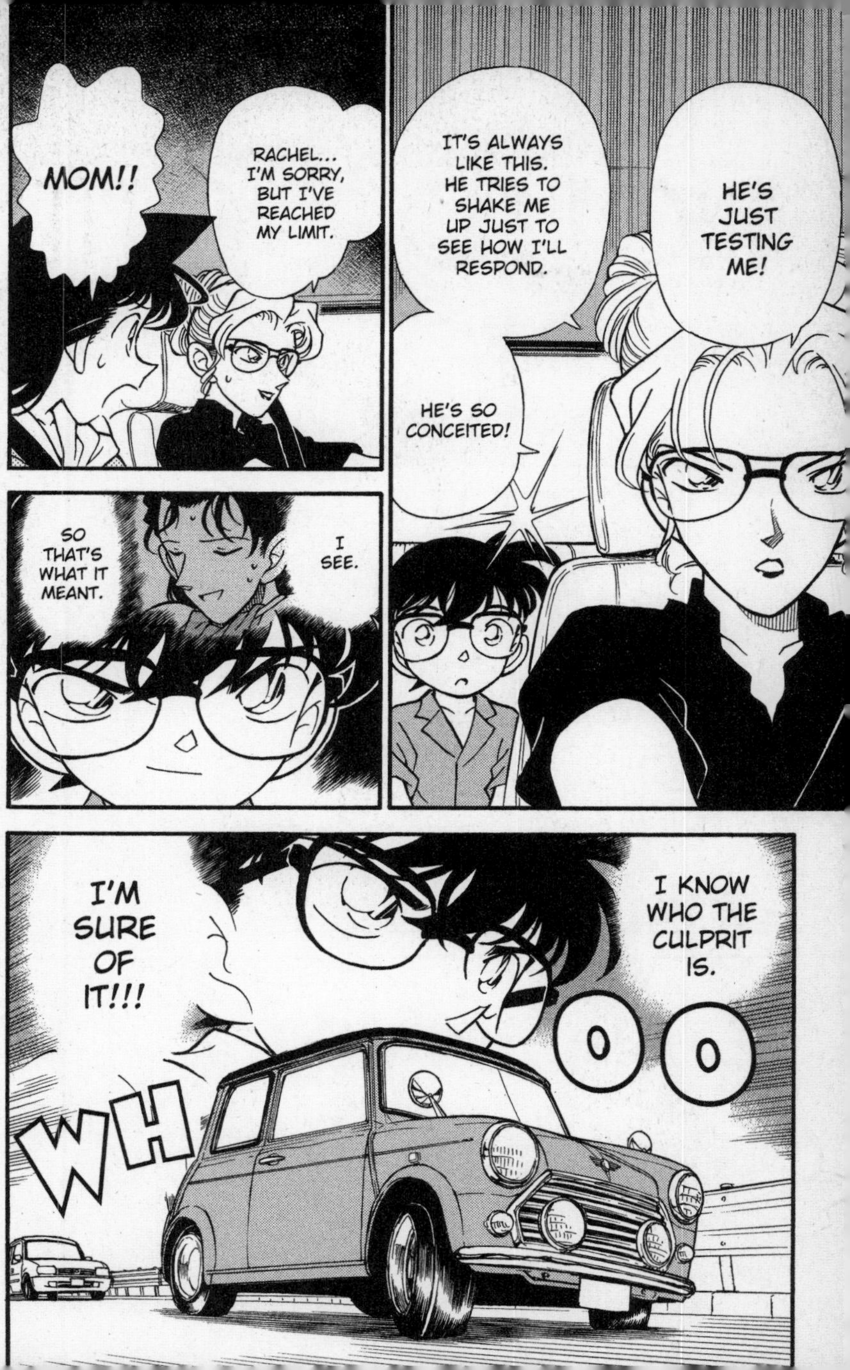
HE'S JUST TESTING ME!
IT'S ALWAYS LIKE THIS. HE TRIES TO SHAKE ME UP JUST TO SEE HOW I'LL RESPOND.
HE'S SO CONCEITED!
RACHEL... I'M SORRY, BUT I'VE REACHED MY LIMIT.
MOM!!
I SEE.
SO THAT'S WHAT IT MEANT.
I KNOW WHO THE CULPRIT IS.
I'M SURE OF IT!!!
WH
OO

NOT FORGOTTEN

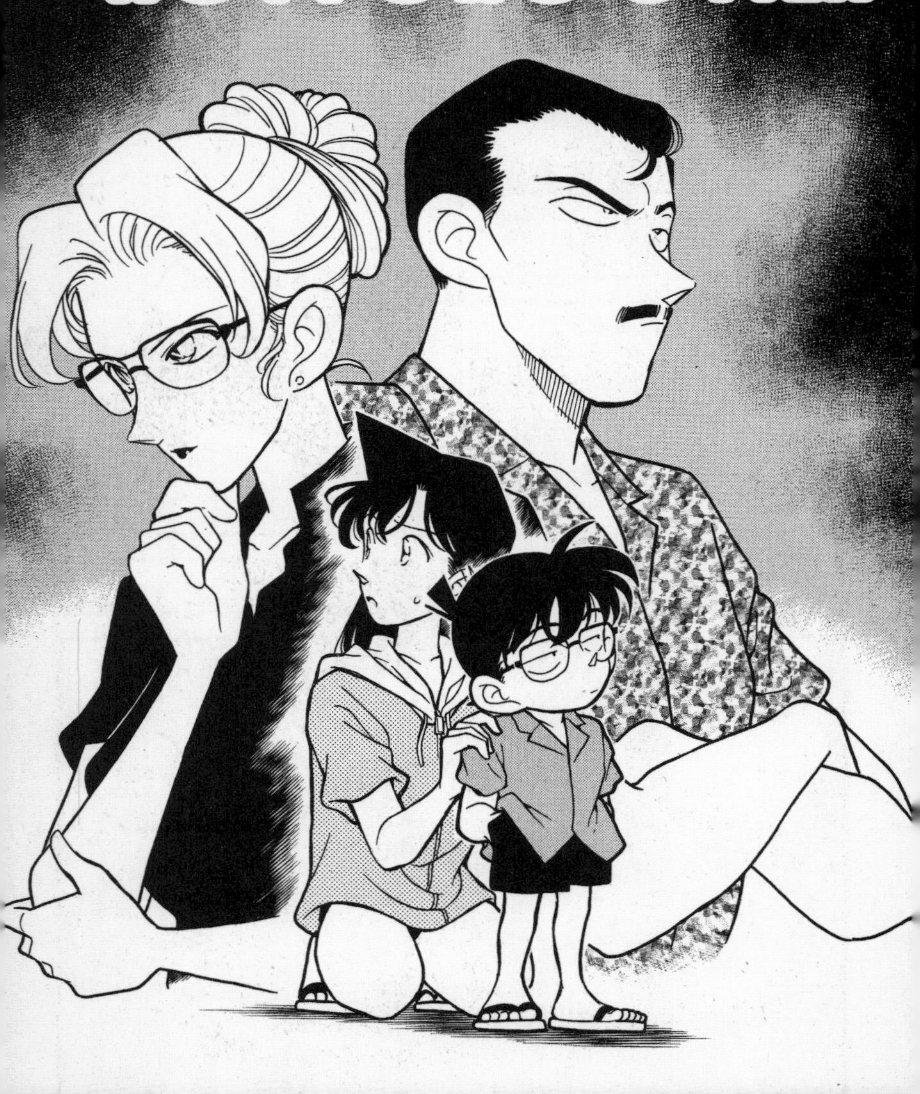

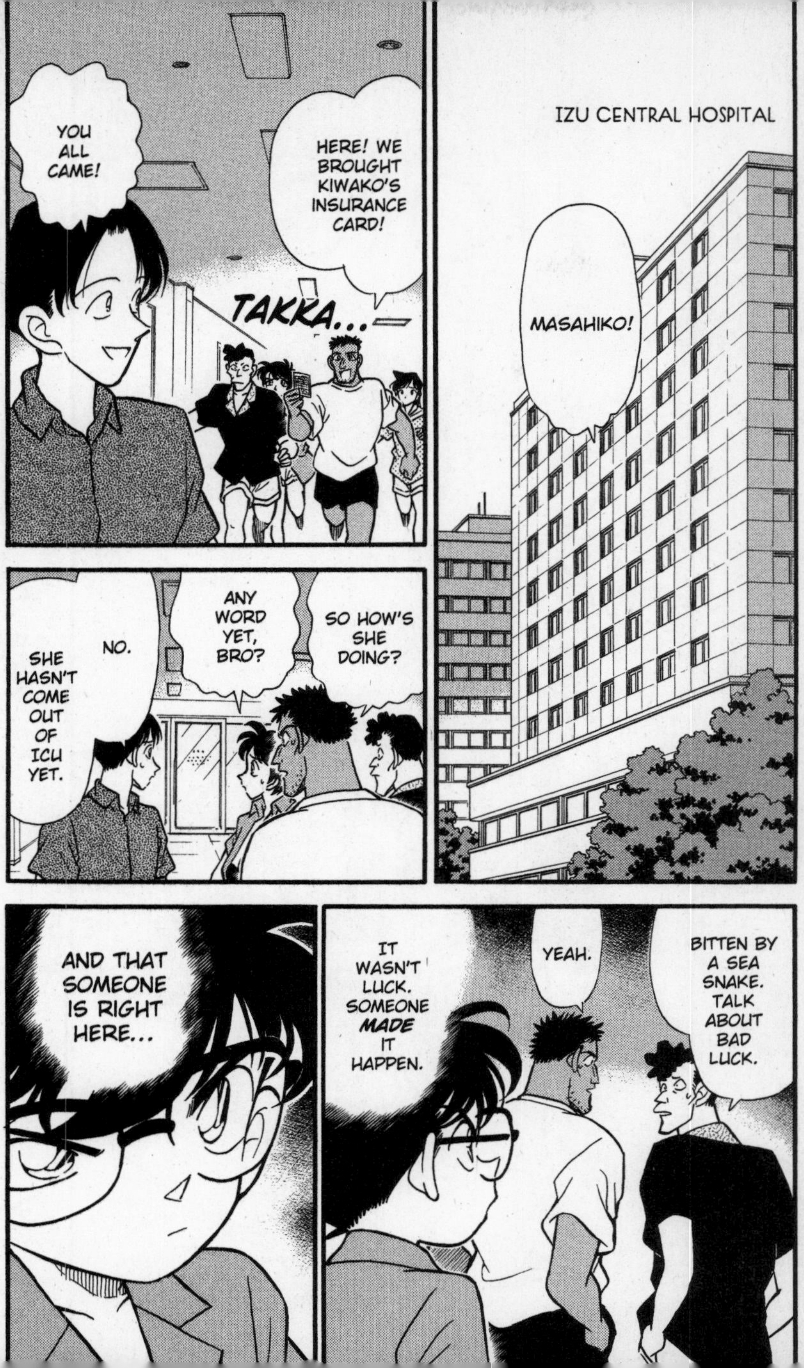
IZU CENTRAL HOSPITAL
MASAHIKO!
HERE! WE BROUGHT KIWAKO'S INSURANCE CARD!
TAKKA...
YOU ALL CAME!
SO HOW'S SHE DOING?
ANY WORD YET, BRO?
NO.
SHE HASN'T COME OUT OF ICU YET.
BITTEN BY A SEA SNAKE. TALK ABOUT BAD LUCK.
YEAH.
IT WASN'T LUCK. SOMEONE *MADE* IT HAPPEN.
AND THAT SOMEONE IS RIGHT HERE...

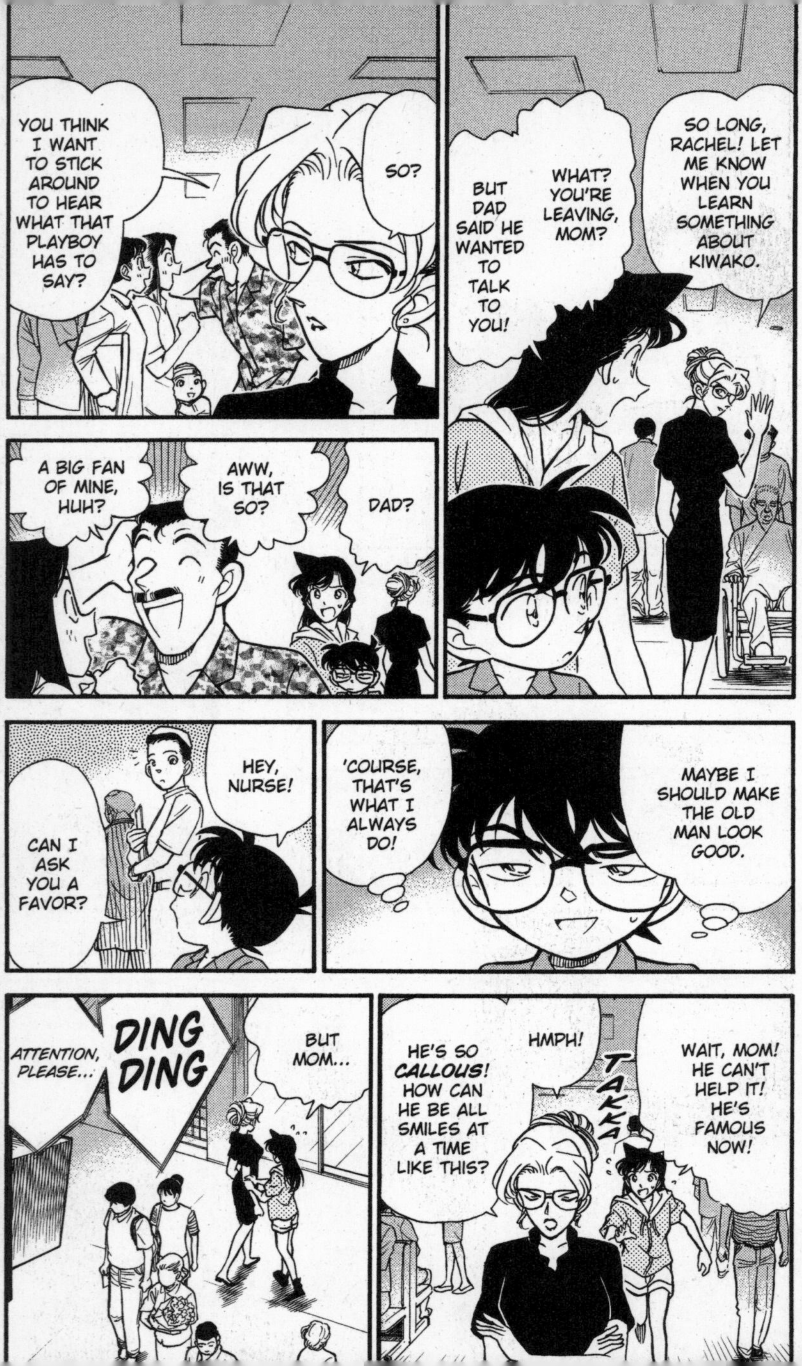
SO LONG, RACHEL! LET ME KNOW WHEN YOU LEARN SOMETHING ABOUT KIWAKO.
WHAT? YOU'RE LEAVING, MOM?
BUT DAD SAID HE WANTED TO TALK TO YOU!
SO?
YOU THINK I WANT TO STICK AROUND TO HEAR WHAT THAT PLAYBOY HAS TO SAY?
DAD?
AWW, IS THAT SO?
A BIG FAN OF MINE, HUH?
MAYBE I SHOULD MAKE THE OLD MAN LOOK GOOD.
'COURSE, THAT'S WHAT I ALWAYS DO!
HEY, NURSE!
CAN I ASK YOU A FAVOR?
WAIT, MOM! HE CAN'T HELP IT! HE'S FAMOUS NOW!
TAKKA
HMPH!
HE'S SO CALLOUS! HOW CAN HE BE ALL SMILES AT A TIME LIKE THIS?
BUT MOM...
DING DING
ATTENTION, PLEASE...

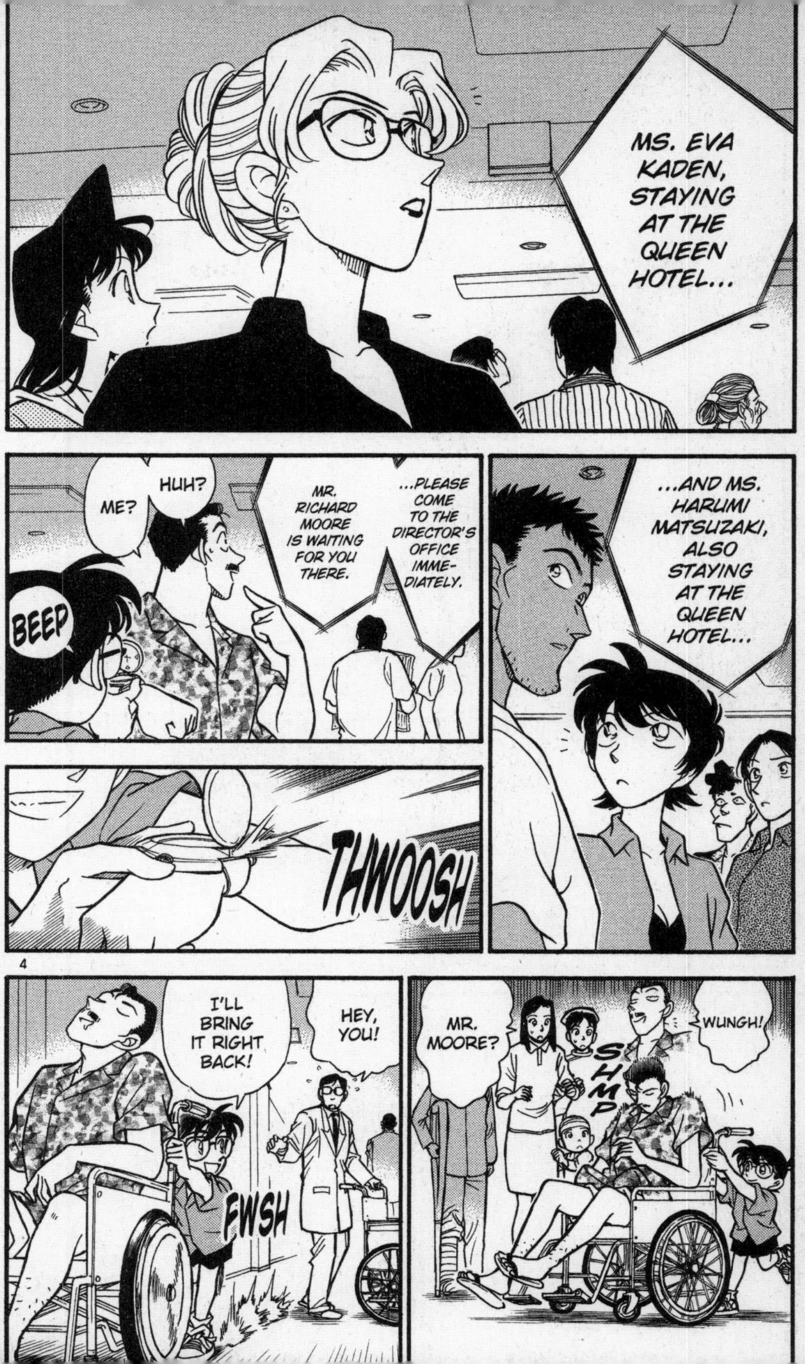
MS. EVA KADEN, STAYING AT THE QUEEN HOTEL...
ME?
HUH?
BEEP
MR. RICHARD MOORE IS WAITING FOR YOU THERE.
...PLEASE COME TO THE DIRECTOR'S OFFICE IMMEDIATELY.
...AND MS. HARUMI MATSUZAKI, ALSO STAYING AT THE QUEEN HOTEL...
THWOOSH
I'LL BRING IT RIGHT BACK!
HEY, YOU!
FWSH
MR. MOORE?
WUNGH!
SHMP

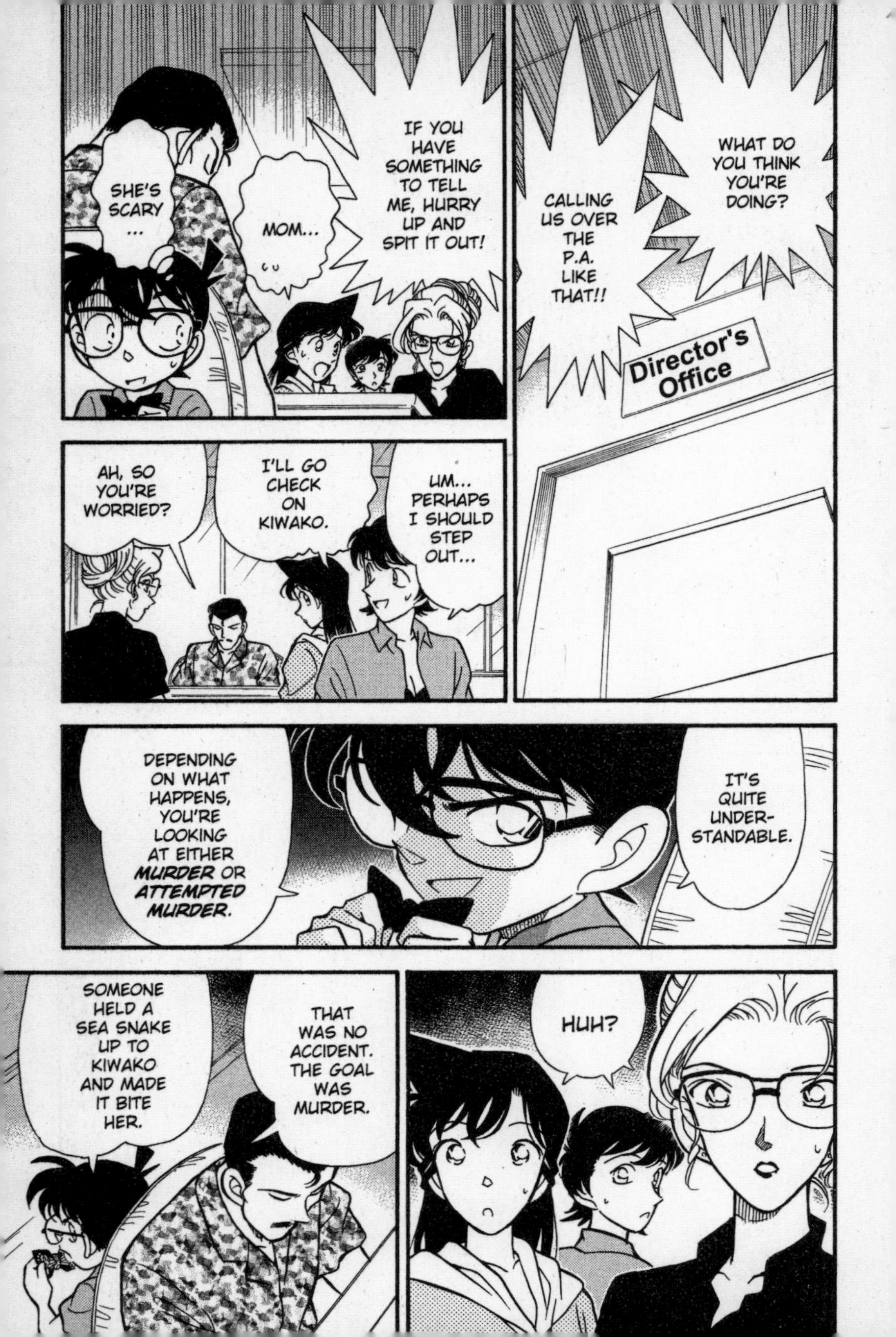
WHAT DO YOU THINK YOU'RE DOING?
CALLING US OVER THE P.A. LIKE THAT!!
Director's Office
IF YOU HAVE SOMETHING TO TELL ME, HURRY UP AND SPIT IT OUT!
MOM...
SHE'S SCARY ...
UM... PERHAPS I SHOULD STEP OUT...
I'LL GO CHECK ON KIWAKO.
AH, SO YOU'RE WORRIED?
IT'S QUITE UNDER-STANDABLE.
DEPENDING ON WHAT HAPPENS, YOU'RE LOOKING AT EITHER MURDER OR ATTEMPTED MURDER.
HUH?
THAT WAS NO ACCIDENT. THE GOAL WAS MURDER.
SOMEONE HELD A SEA SNAKE UP TO KIWAKO AND MADE IT BITE HER.

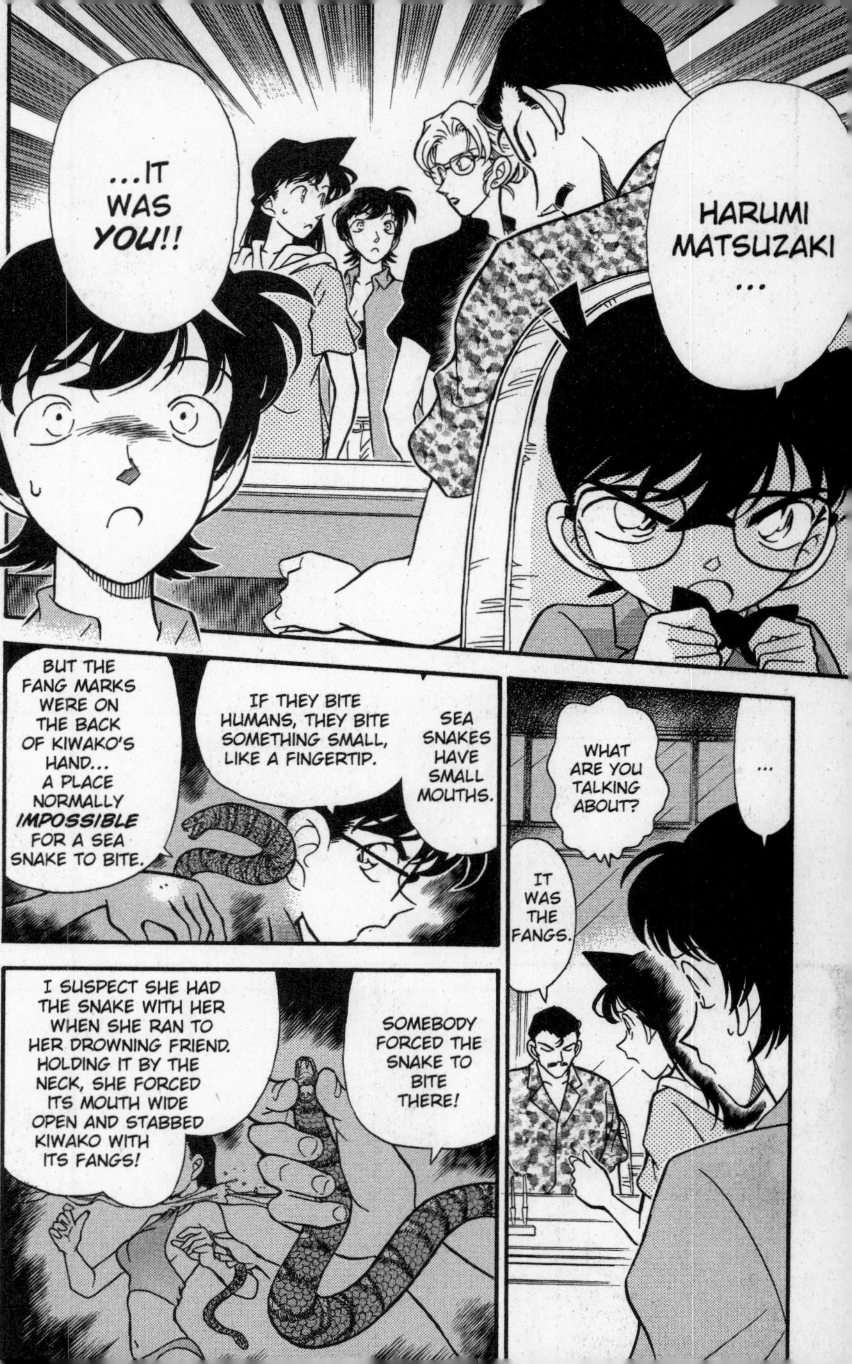
HARUMI MATSUZAKI ...
...IT WAS YOU!!
...
WHAT ARE YOU TALKING ABOUT?
IT WAS THE FANGS.
SEA SNAKES HAVE SMALL MOUTHS.
IF THEY BITE HUMANS, THEY BITE SOMETHING SMALL, LIKE A FINGERTIP.
BUT THE FANG MARKS WERE ON THE BACK OF KIWAKO'S HAND... A PLACE NORMALLY IMPOSSIBLE FOR A SEA SNAKE TO BITE.
SOMEBODY FORCED THE SNAKE TO BITE THERE!
I SUSPECT SHE HAD THE SNAKE WITH HER WHEN SHE RAN TO HER DROWNING FRIEND. HOLDING IT BY THE NECK, SHE FORCED ITS MOUTH WIDE OPEN AND STABBED KIWAKO WITH ITS FANGS!

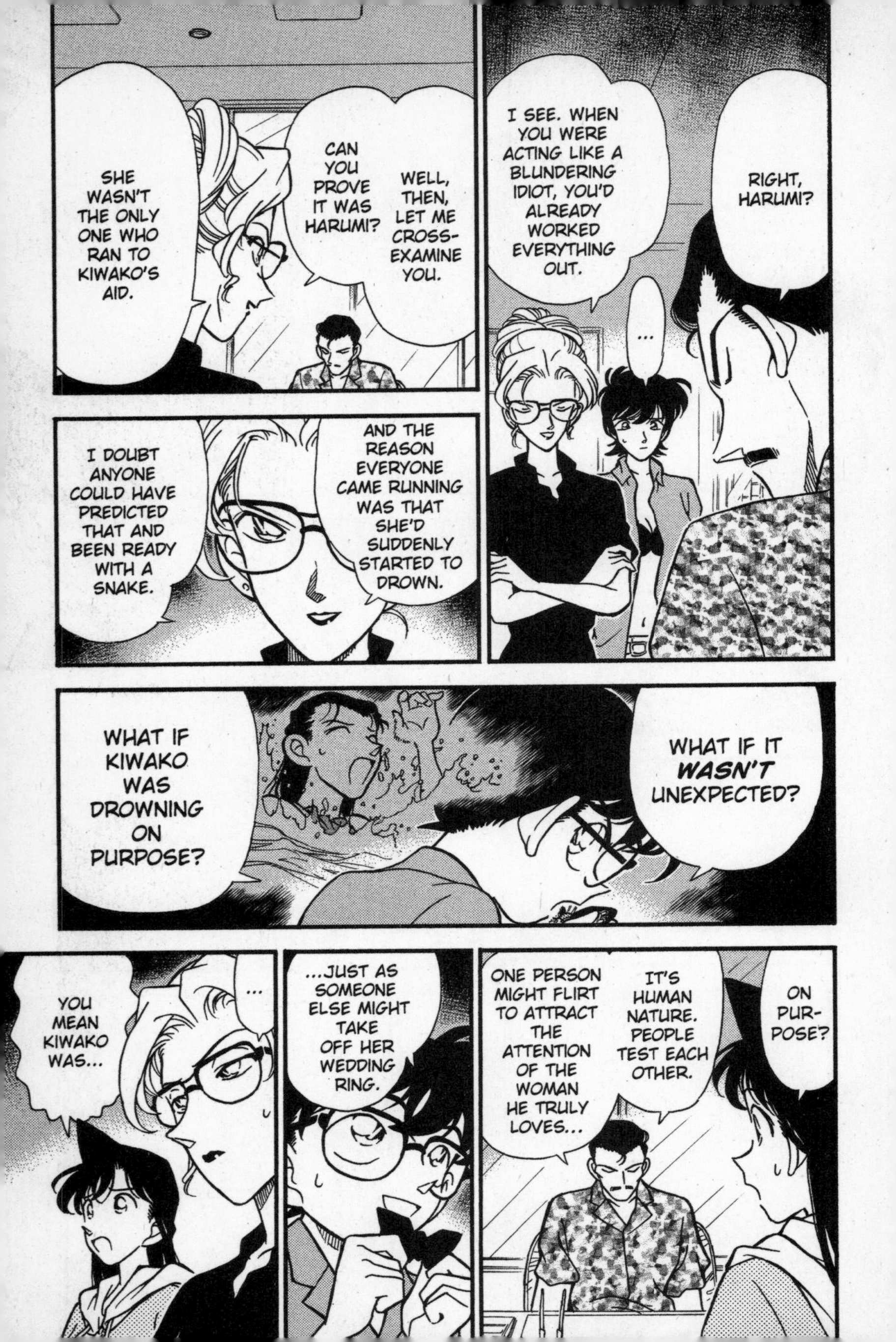

RIGHT, HARUMI?
I SEE. WHEN YOU WERE ACTING LIKE A BLUNDERING IDIOT, YOU'D ALREADY WORKED EVERYTHING OUT.
...
CAN YOU PROVE IT WAS HARUMI? WELL, THEN, LET ME CROSS-EXAMINE YOU.
SHE WASN'T THE ONLY ONE WHO RAN TO KIWAKO'S AID.
AND THE REASON EVERYONE CAME RUNNING WAS THAT SHE'D SUDDENLY STARTED TO DROWN.
I DOUBT ANYONE COULD HAVE PREDICTED THAT AND BEEN READY WITH A SNAKE.
WHAT IF IT *WASN'T* UNEXPECTED?
WHAT IF KIWAKO WAS DROWNING ON PURPOSE?
ON PUR-POSE?
IT'S HUMAN NATURE. PEOPLE TEST EACH OTHER.
ONE PERSON MIGHT FLIRT TO ATTRACT THE ATTENTION OF THE WOMAN HE TRULY LOVES...
...JUST AS SOMEONE ELSE MIGHT TAKE OFF HER WEDDING RING.
...
YOU MEAN KIWAKO WAS...

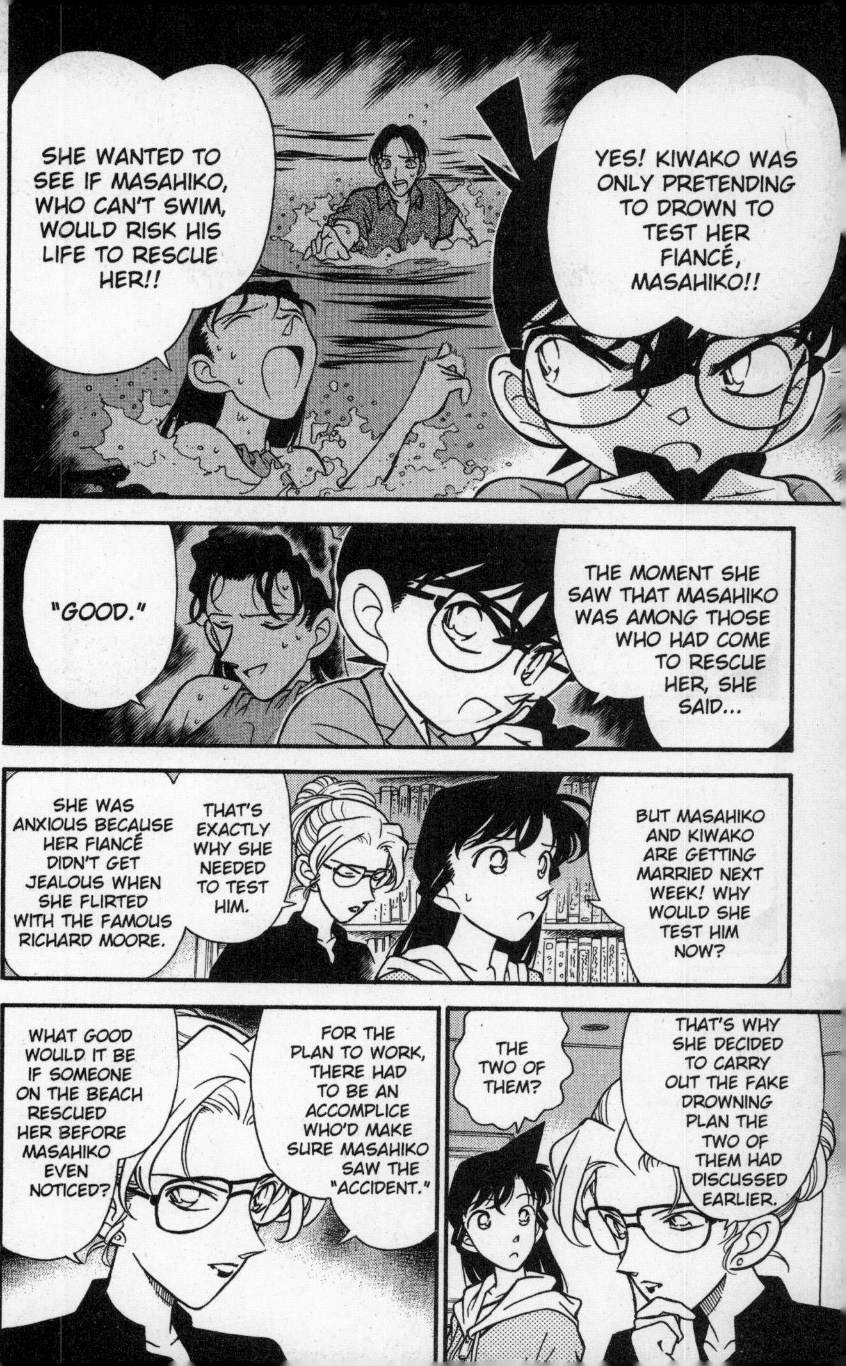
YES! KIWAKO WAS ONLY PRETENDING TO DROWN TO TEST HER FIANCÉ, MASAHIKO!!
SHE WANTED TO SEE IF MASAHIKO, WHO CAN'T SWIM, WOULD RISK HIS LIFE TO RESCUE HER!!
THE MOMENT SHE SAW THAT MASAHIKO WAS AMONG THOSE WHO HAD COME TO RESCUE HER, SHE SAID...
"GOOD."
BUT MASAHIKO AND KIWAKO ARE GETTING MARRIED NEXT WEEK! WHY WOULD SHE TEST HIM NOW?
THAT'S EXACTLY WHY SHE NEEDED TO TEST HIM.
SHE WAS ANXIOUS BECAUSE HER FIANCÉ DIDN'T GET JEALOUS WHEN SHE FLIRTED WITH THE FAMOUS RICHARD MOORE.
THAT'S WHY SHE DECIDED TO CARRY OUT THE FAKE DROWNING PLAN THE TWO OF THEM HAD DISCUSSED EARLIER.
THE TWO OF THEM?
FOR THE PLAN TO WORK, THERE HAD TO BE AN ACCOMPLICE WHO'D MAKE SURE MASAHIKO SAW THE "ACCIDENT."
WHAT GOOD WOULD IT BE IF SOMEONE ON THE BEACH RESCUED HER BEFORE MASAHIKO EVEN NOTICED?

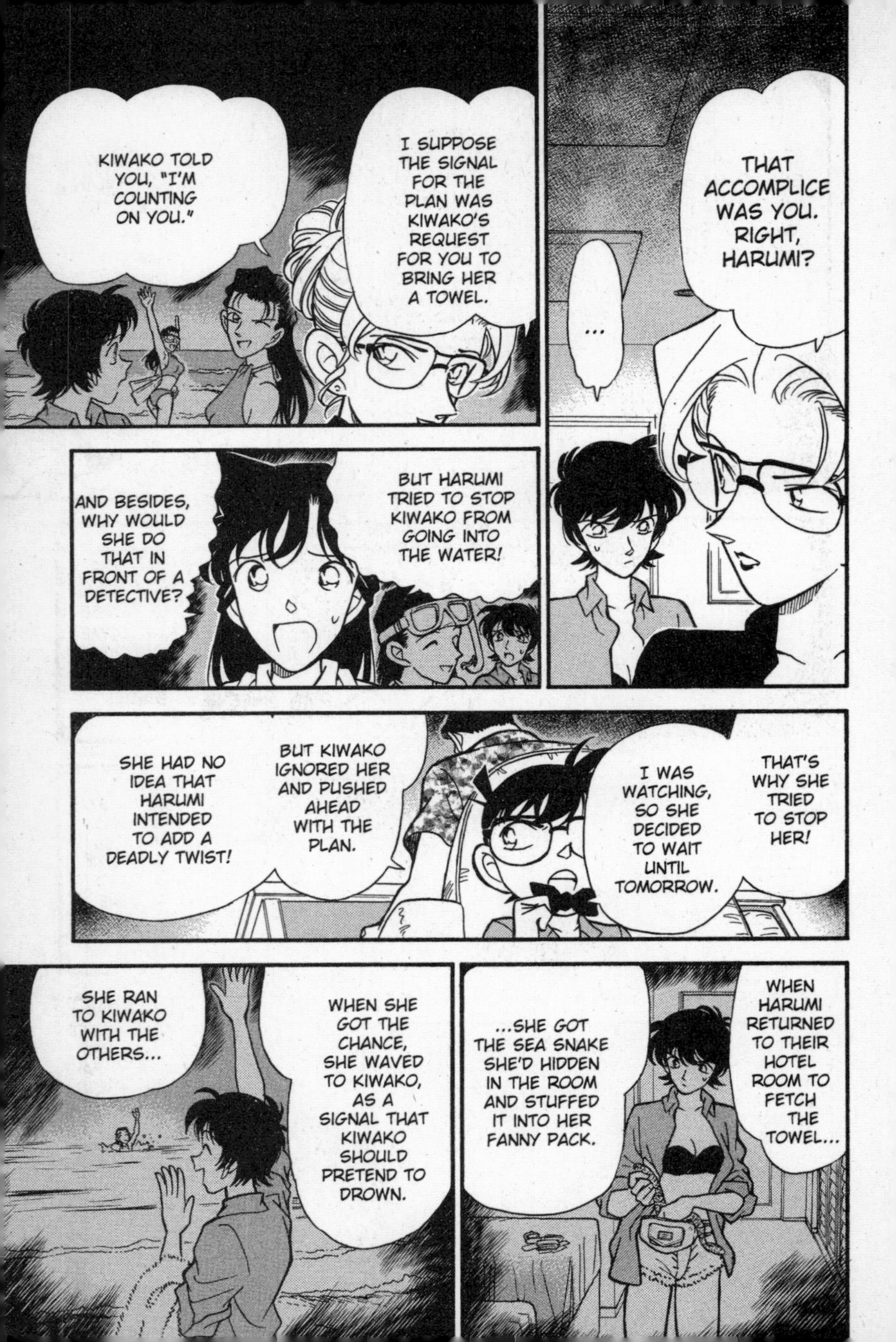
THAT ACCOMPLICE WAS YOU. RIGHT, HARUMI?
...
I SUPPOSE THE SIGNAL FOR THE PLAN WAS KIWAKO'S REQUEST FOR YOU TO BRING HER A TOWEL.
KIWAKO TOLD YOU, "I'M COUNTING ON YOU."
BUT HARUMI TRIED TO STOP KIWAKO FROM GOING INTO THE WATER!
AND BESIDES, WHY WOULD SHE DO THAT IN FRONT OF A DETECTIVE?
THAT'S WHY SHE TRIED TO STOP HER!
I WAS WATCHING, SO SHE DECIDED TO WAIT UNTIL TOMORROW.
BUT KIWAKO IGNORED HER AND PUSHED AHEAD WITH THE PLAN.
SHE HAD NO IDEA THAT HARUMI INTENDED TO ADD A DEADLY TWIST!
WHEN HARUMI RETURNED TO THEIR HOTEL ROOM TO FETCH THE TOWEL...
...SHE GOT THE SEA SNAKE SHE'D HIDDEN IN THE ROOM AND STUFFED IT INTO HER FANNY PACK.
SHE RAN TO KIWAKO WITH THE OTHERS...
WHEN SHE GOT THE CHANCE, SHE WAVED TO KIWAKO, AS A SIGNAL THAT KIWAKO SHOULD PRETEND TO DROWN.

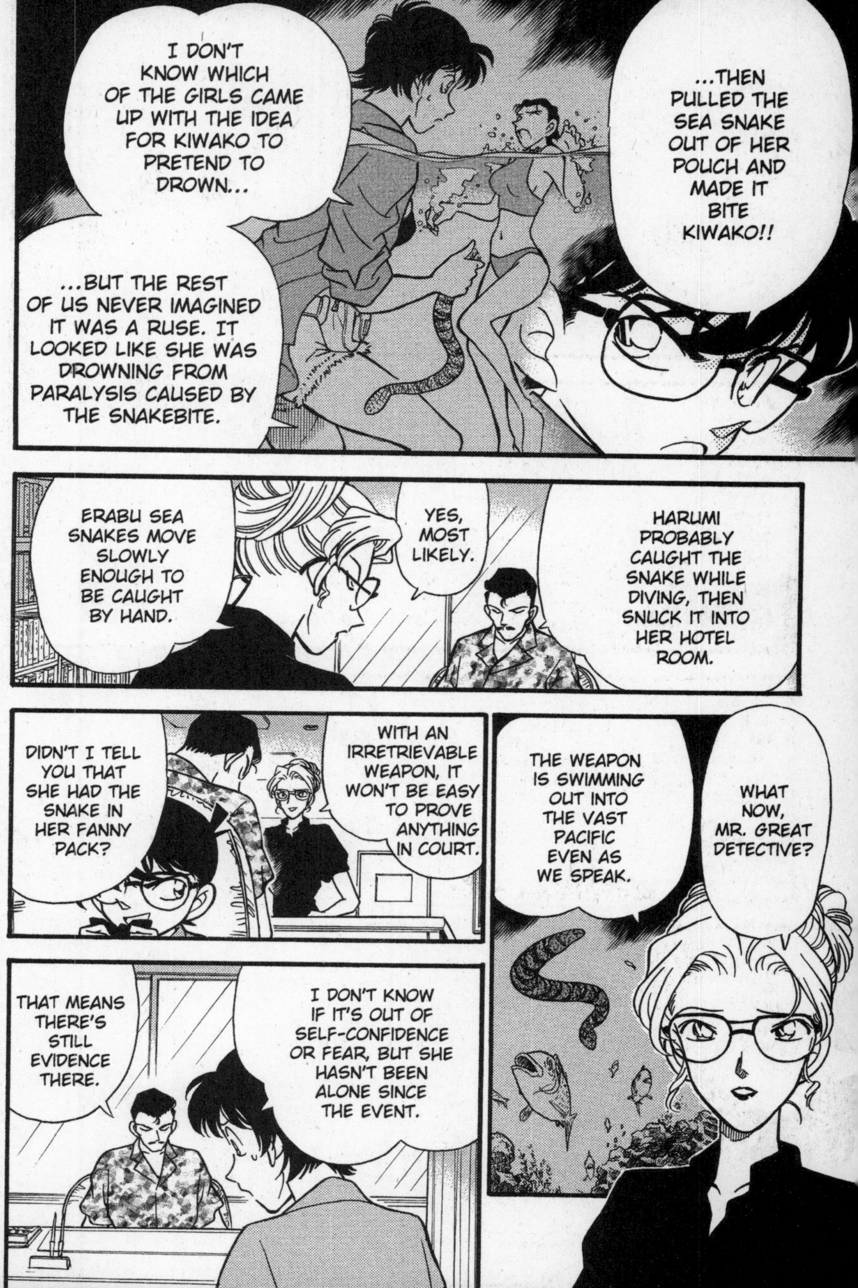
...THEN PULLED THE SEA SNAKE OUT OF HER POUCH AND MADE IT BITE KIWAKO!!
I DON'T KNOW WHICH OF THE GIRLS CAME UP WITH THE IDEA FOR KIWAKO TO PRETEND TO DROWN...
...BUT THE REST OF US NEVER IMAGINED IT WAS A RUSE. IT LOOKED LIKE SHE WAS DROWNING FROM PARALYSIS CAUSED BY THE SNAKEBITE.
HARUMI PROBABLY CAUGHT THE SNAKE WHILE DIVING, THEN SNUCK IT INTO HER HOTEL ROOM.
YES, MOST LIKELY.
ERABU SEA SNAKES MOVE SLOWLY ENOUGH TO BE CAUGHT BY HAND.
WHAT NOW, MR. GREAT DETECTIVE?
THE WEAPON IS SWIMMING OUT INTO THE VAST PACIFIC EVEN AS WE SPEAK.
WITH AN IRRETRIEVABLE WEAPON, IT WON'T BE EASY TO PROVE ANYTHING IN COURT.
DIDN'T I TELL YOU THAT SHE HAD THE SNAKE IN HER FANNY PACK?
I DON'T KNOW IF IT'S OUT OF SELF-CONFIDENCE OR FEAR, BUT SHE HASN'T BEEN ALONE SINCE THE EVENT.
THAT MEANS THERE'S STILL EVIDENCE THERE.

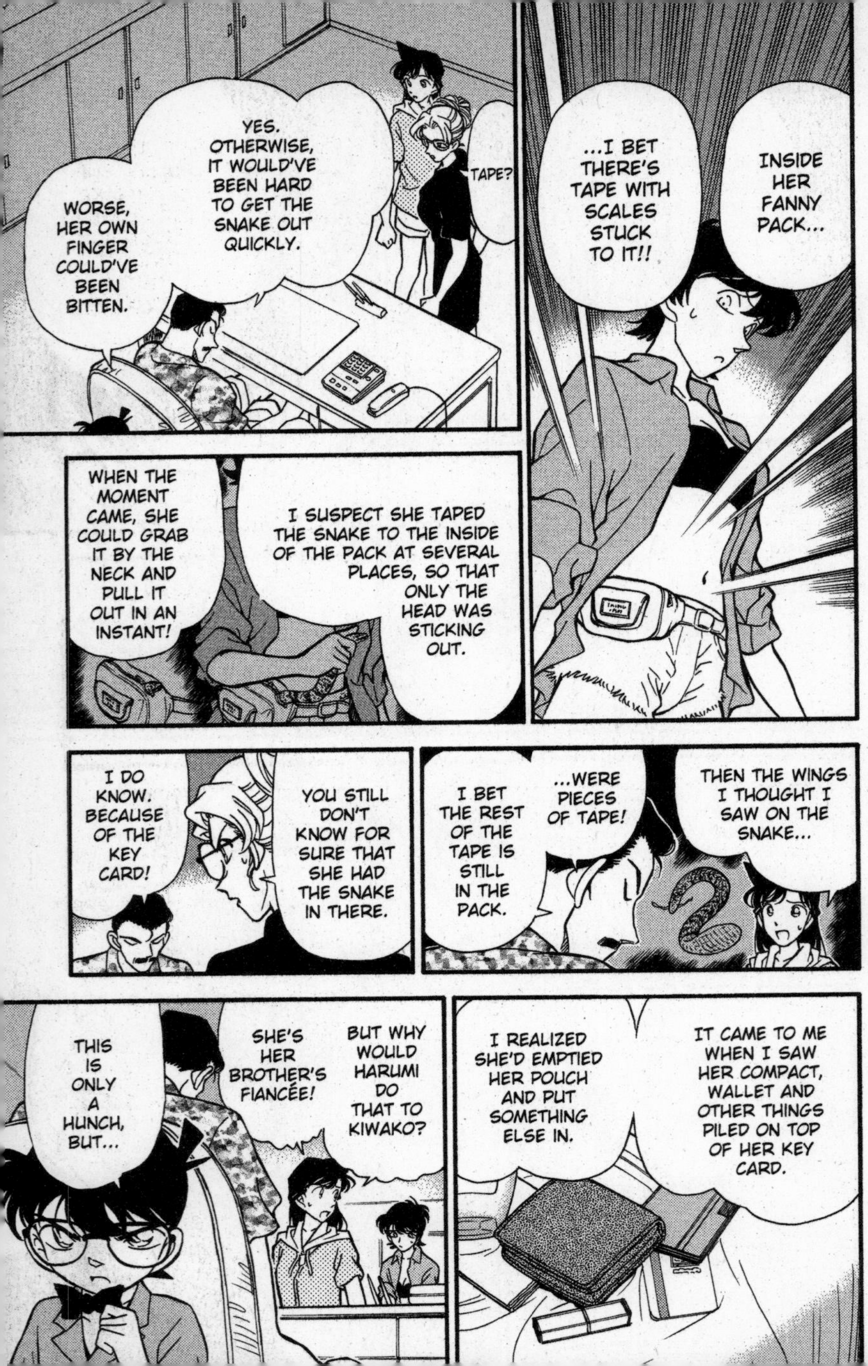
INSIDE HER FANNY PACK...
...I BET THERE'S TAPE WITH SCALES STUCK TO IT!!
TAPE?
YES. OTHERWISE, IT WOULD'VE BEEN HARD TO GET THE SNAKE OUT QUICKLY.
WORSE, HER OWN FINGER COULD'VE BEEN BITTEN.
I SUSPECT SHE TAPED THE SNAKE TO THE INSIDE OF THE PACK AT SEVERAL PLACES, SO THAT ONLY THE HEAD WAS STICKING OUT.
WHEN THE MOMENT CAME, SHE COULD GRAB IT BY THE NECK AND PULL IT OUT IN AN INSTANT!
THEN THE WINGS I THOUGHT I SAW ON THE SNAKE...
...WERE PIECES OF TAPE!
I BET THE REST OF THE TAPE IS STILL IN THE PACK.
YOU STILL DON'T KNOW FOR SURE THAT SHE HAD THE SNAKE IN THERE.
I DO KNOW. BECAUSE OF THE KEY CARD!
IT CAME TO ME WHEN I SAW HER COMPACT, WALLET AND OTHER THINGS PILED ON TOP OF HER KEY CARD.
I REALIZED SHE'D EMPTIED HER POUCH AND PUT SOMETHING ELSE IN.
BUT WHY WOULD HARUMI DO THAT TO KIWAKO?
SHE'S HER BROTHER'S FIANCÉE!
THIS IS ONLY A HUNCH, BUT...

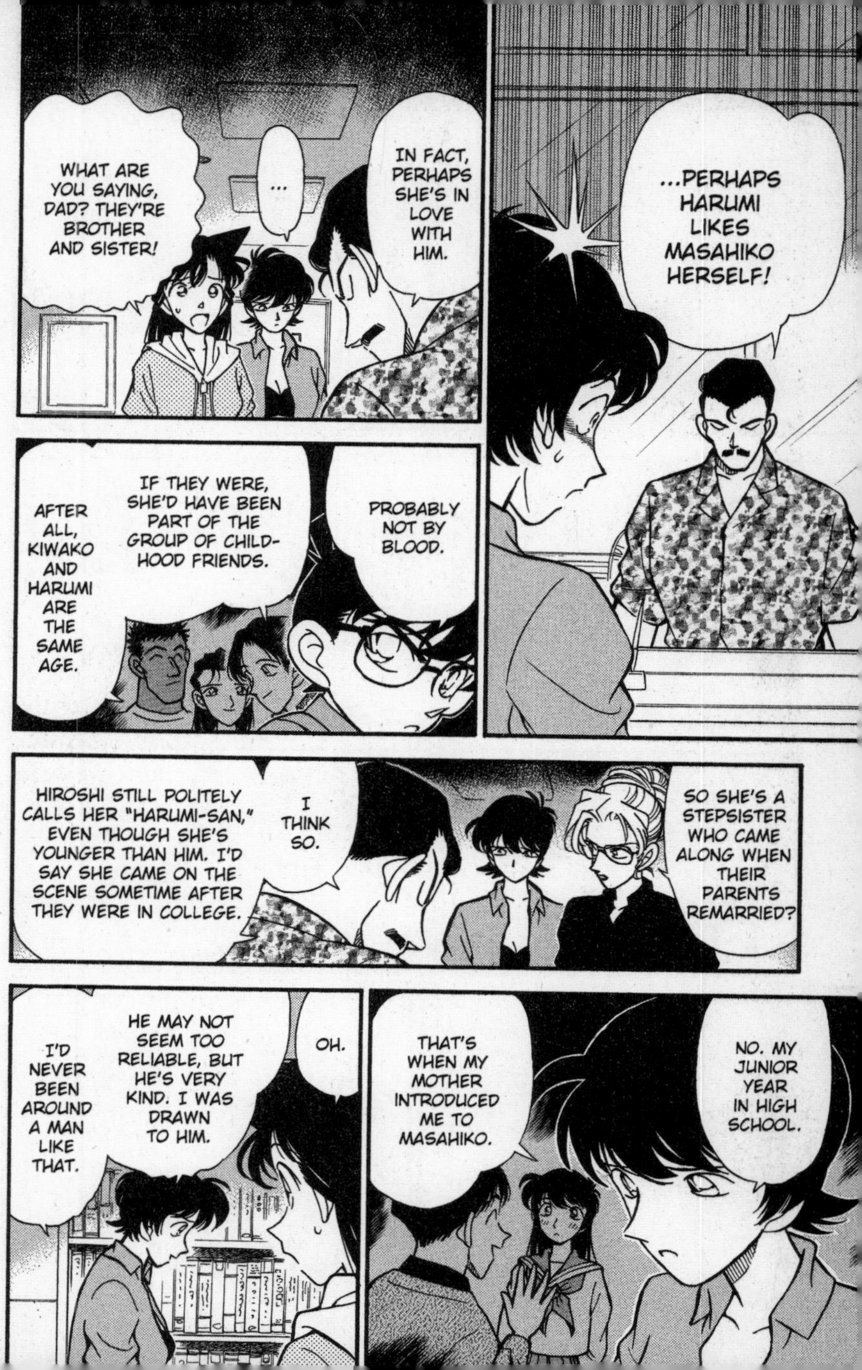
...PERHAPS HARUMI LIKES MASAHIKO HERSELF!
IN FACT, PERHAPS SHE'S IN LOVE WITH HIM.
...
WHAT ARE YOU SAYING, DAD? THEY'RE BROTHER AND SISTER!
PROBABLY NOT BY BLOOD.
IF THEY WERE, SHE'D HAVE BEEN PART OF THE GROUP OF CHILDHOOD FRIENDS.
AFTER ALL, KIWAKO AND HARUMI ARE THE SAME AGE.
SO SHE'S A STEPSISTER WHO CAME ALONG WHEN THEIR PARENTS REMARRIED?
I THINK SO.
HIROSHI STILL POLITELY CALLS HER "HARUMI-SAN," EVEN THOUGH SHE'S YOUNGER THAN HIM. I'D SAY SHE CAME ON THE SCENE SOMETIME AFTER THEY WERE IN COLLEGE.
NO. MY JUNIOR YEAR IN HIGH SCHOOL.
THAT'S WHEN MY MOTHER INTRODUCED ME TO MASAHIKO.
OH.
HE MAY NOT SEEM TOO RELIABLE, BUT HE'S VERY KIND. I WAS DRAWN TO HIM.
I'D NEVER BEEN AROUND A MAN LIKE THAT.

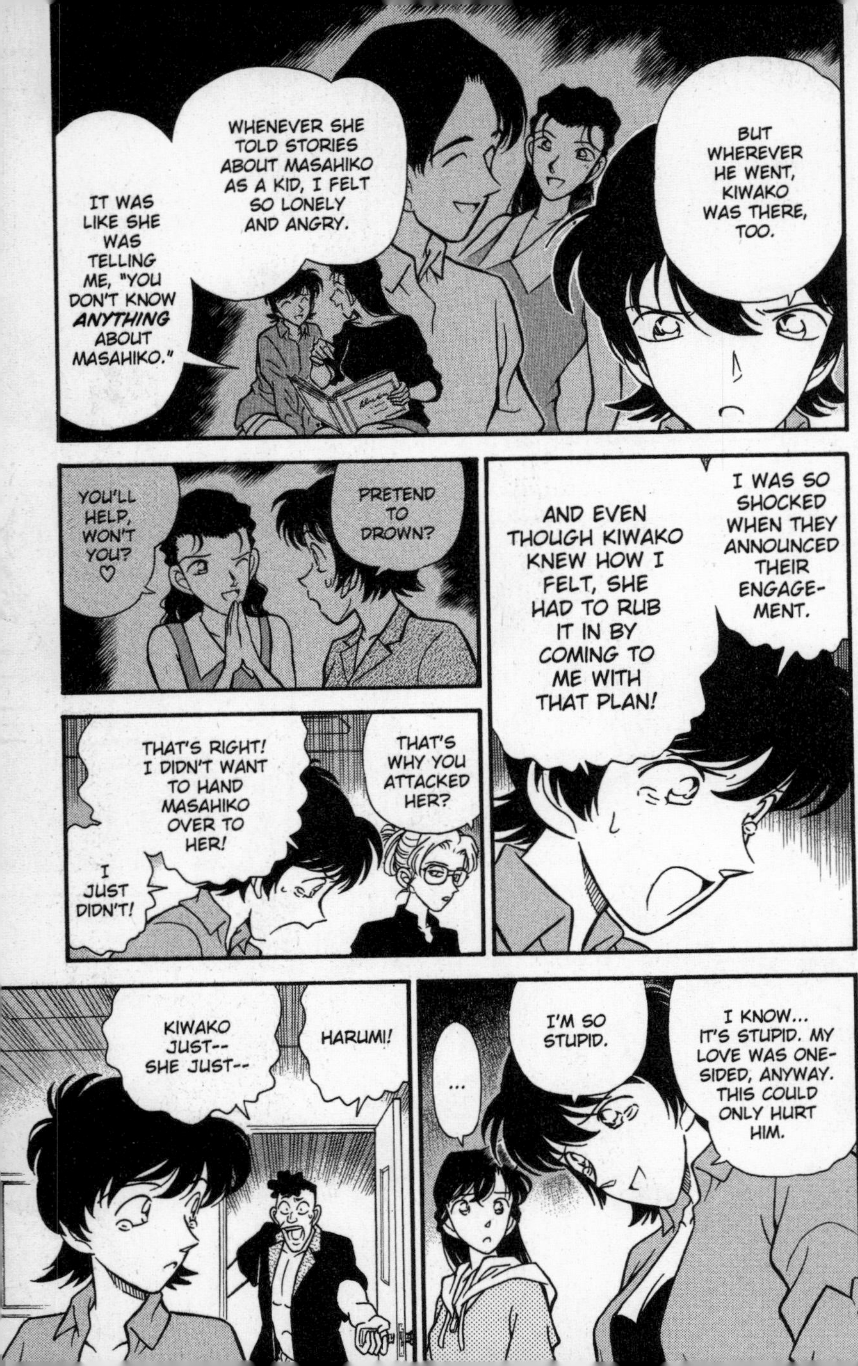
BUT WHEREVER HE WENT, KIWAKO WAS THERE, TOO.
WHENEVER SHE TOLD STORIES ABOUT MASAHIKO AS A KID, I FELT SO LONELY AND ANGRY.
IT WAS LIKE SHE WAS TELLING ME, "YOU DON'T KNOW *ANYTHING* ABOUT MASAHIKO."
I WAS SO SHOCKED WHEN THEY ANNOUNCED THEIR ENGAGEMENT.
AND EVEN THOUGH KIWAKO KNEW HOW I FELT, SHE HAD TO RUB IT IN BY COMING TO ME WITH THAT PLAN!
PRETEND TO DROWN?
YOU'LL HELP, WON'T YOU? ♡
THAT'S WHY YOU ATTACKED HER?
THAT'S RIGHT! I DIDN'T WANT TO HAND MASAHIKO OVER TO HER!
I JUST DIDN'T!
I KNOW... IT'S STUPID. MY LOVE WAS ONE-SIDED, ANYWAY. THIS COULD ONLY HURT HIM.
I'M SO STUPID.
...
HARUMI!
KIWAKO JUST-- SHE JUST--

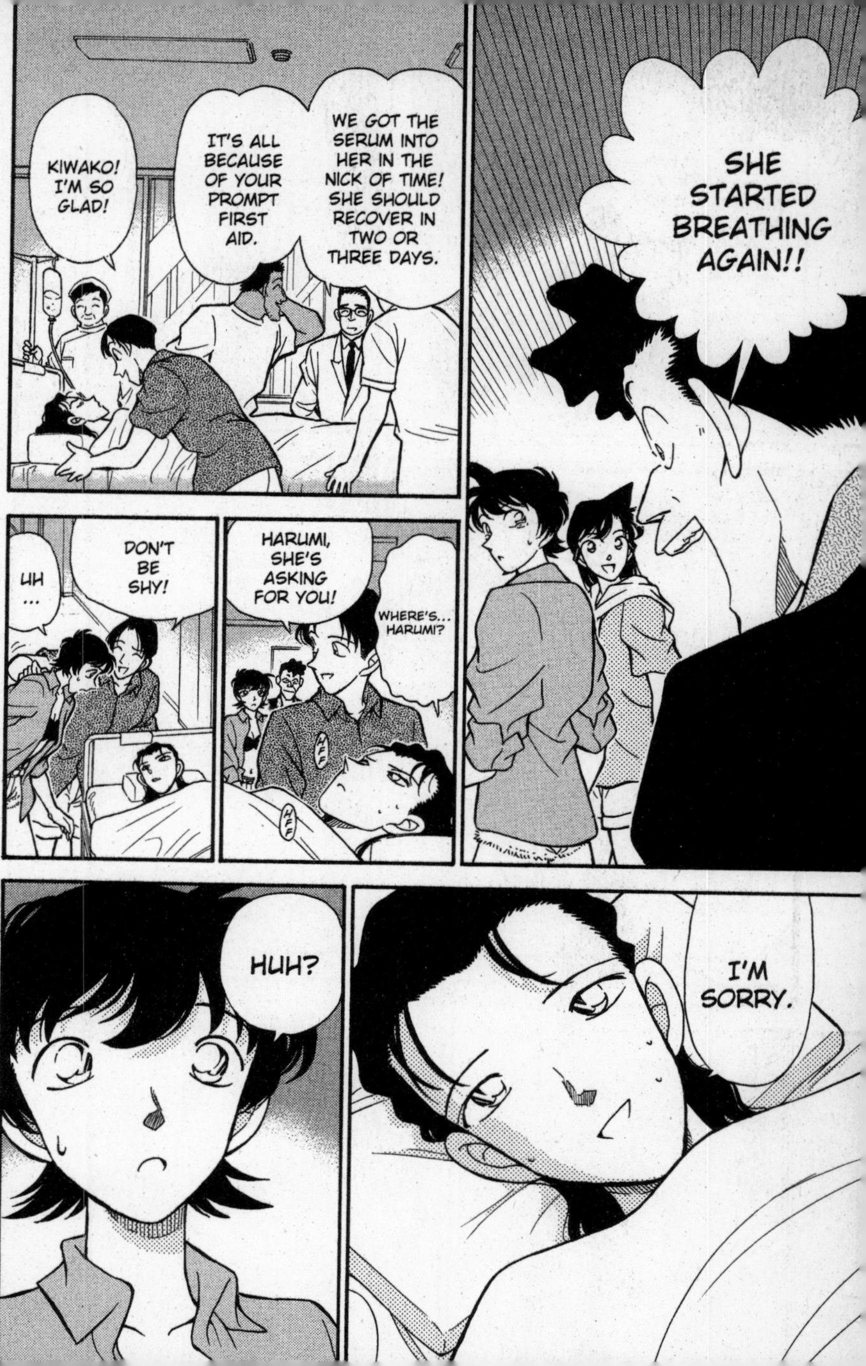
SHE STARTED BREATHING AGAIN!!
WE GOT THE SERUM INTO HER IN THE NICK OF TIME! SHE SHOULD RECOVER IN TWO OR THREE DAYS.
IT'S ALL BECAUSE OF YOUR PROMPT FIRST AID.
KIWAKO! I'M SO GLAD!
WHERE'S... HARUMI?
HFF
HFF
HARUMI, SHE'S ASKING FOR YOU!
DON'T BE SHY!
UH ...
I'M SORRY.
HUH?

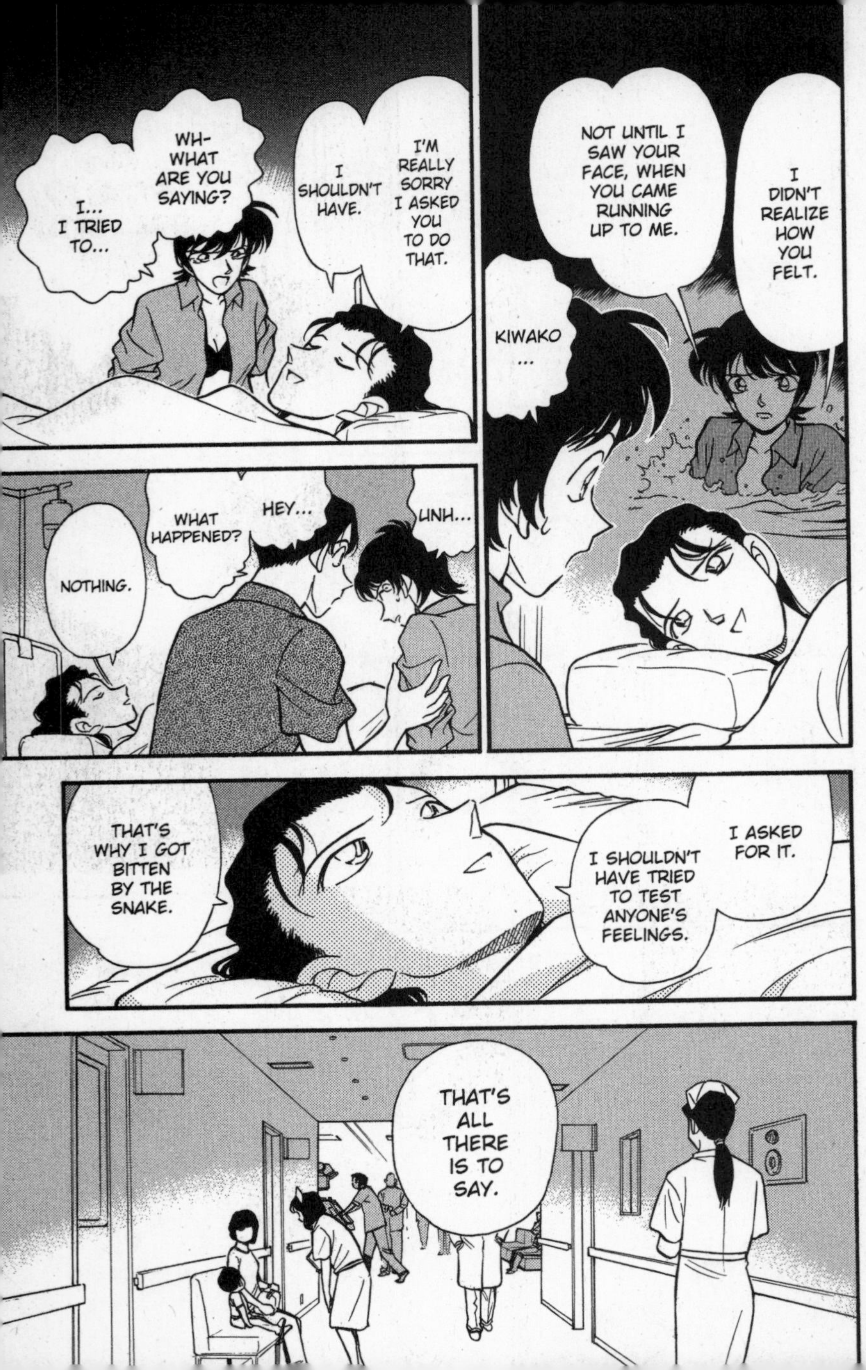
I DIDN'T REALIZE HOW YOU FELT.
NOT UNTIL I SAW YOUR FACE, WHEN YOU CAME RUNNING UP TO ME.
KIWAKO ...
I'M REALLY SORRY I ASKED YOU TO DO THAT.
I SHOULDN'T HAVE.
WH- WHAT ARE YOU SAYING?
I... I TRIED TO...
UNH...
HEY...
WHAT HAPPENED?
NOTHING.
I ASKED FOR IT.
I SHOULDN'T HAVE TRIED TO TEST ANYONE'S FEELINGS.
THAT'S WHY I GOT BITTEN BY THE SNAKE.
THAT'S ALL THERE IS TO SAY.

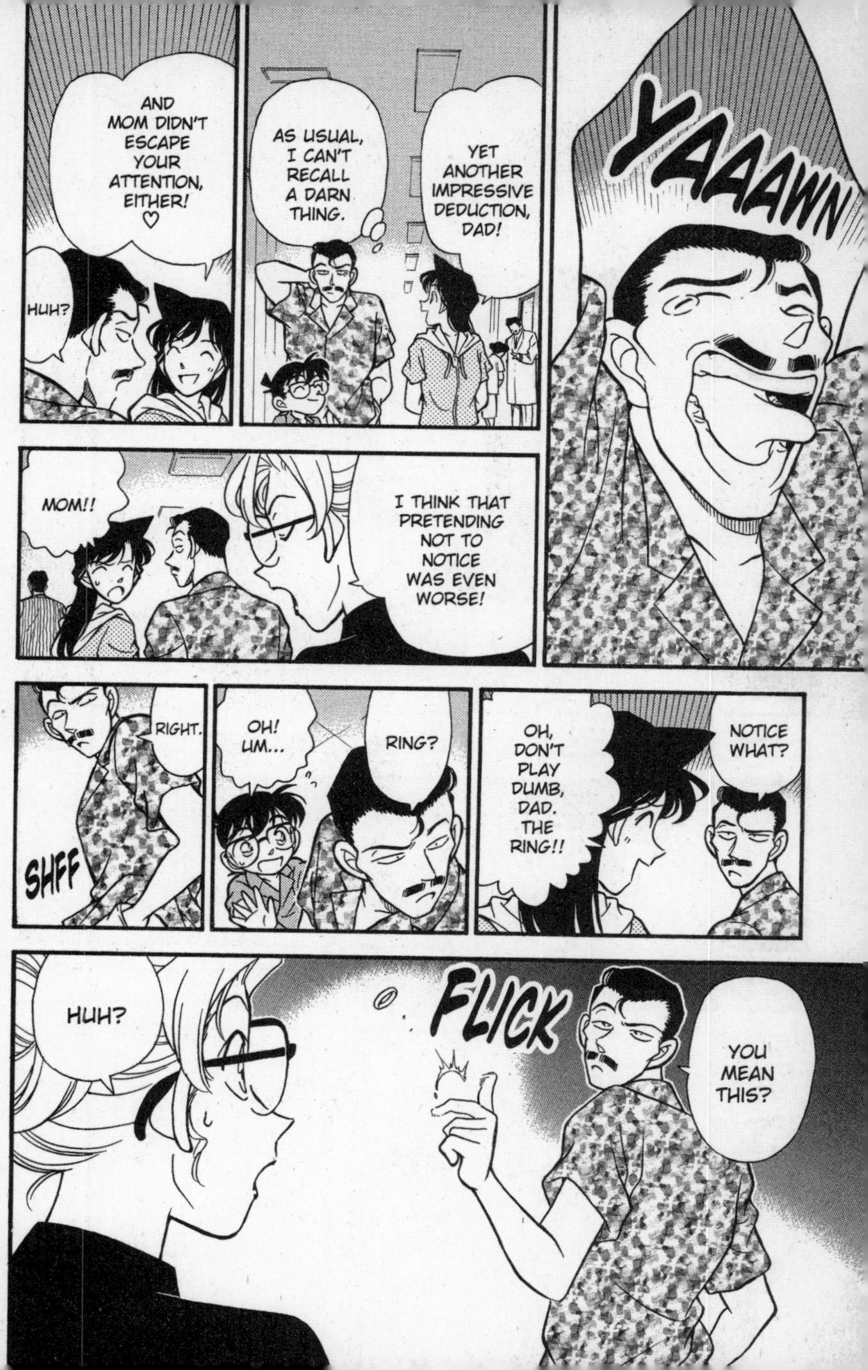
YAAAWN
YET ANOTHER IMPRESSIVE DEDUCTION, DAD!
AS USUAL, I CAN'T RECALL A DARN THING.
AND MOM DIDN'T ESCAPE YOUR ATTENTION, EITHER! ♡
HUH?
I THINK THAT PRETENDING NOT TO NOTICE WAS EVEN WORSE!
MOM!!
NOTICE WHAT?
OH, DON'T PLAY DUMB, DAD. THE RING!!
RING?
OH! UM...
RIGHT.
SHFF
YOU MEAN THIS?
FLICK
HUH?

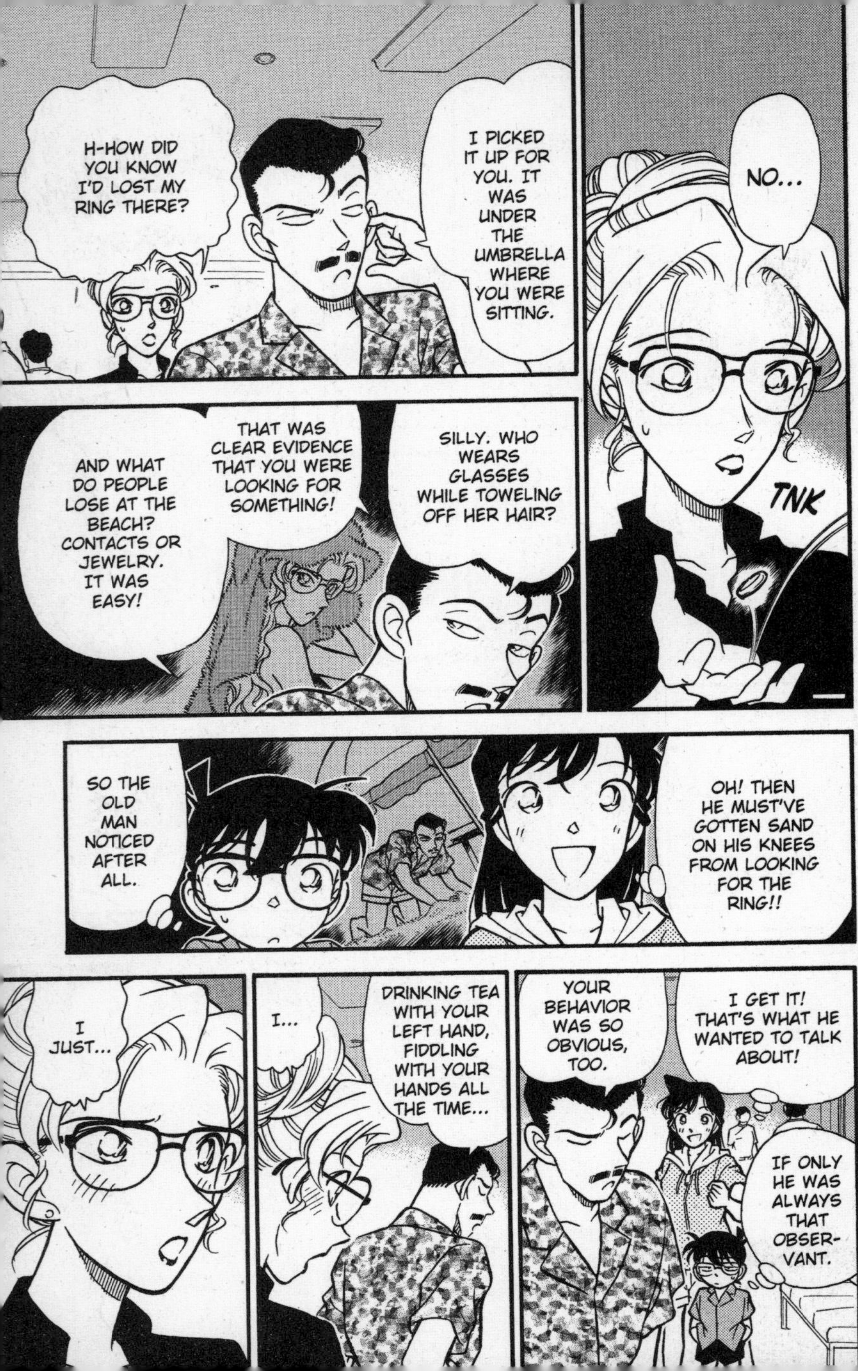
NO...
TNK
I PICKED IT UP FOR YOU. IT WAS UNDER THE UMBRELLA WHERE YOU WERE SITTING.
H-HOW DID YOU KNOW I'D LOST MY RING THERE?
SILLY. WHO WEARS GLASSES WHILE TOWELING OFF HER HAIR?
THAT WAS CLEAR EVIDENCE THAT YOU WERE LOOKING FOR SOMETHING!
AND WHAT DO PEOPLE LOSE AT THE BEACH? CONTACTS OR JEWELRY. IT WAS EASY!
OH! THEN HE MUST'VE GOTTEN SAND ON HIS KNEES FROM LOOKING FOR THE RING!!
SO THE OLD MAN NOTICED AFTER ALL.
I GET IT! THAT'S WHAT HE WANTED TO TALK ABOUT!
YOUR BEHAVIOR WAS SO OBVIOUS, TOO.
IF ONLY HE WAS ALWAYS THAT OBSERVANT.
DRINKING TEA WITH YOUR LEFT HAND, FIDDLING WITH YOUR HANDS ALL THE TIME...
I...
I JUST...

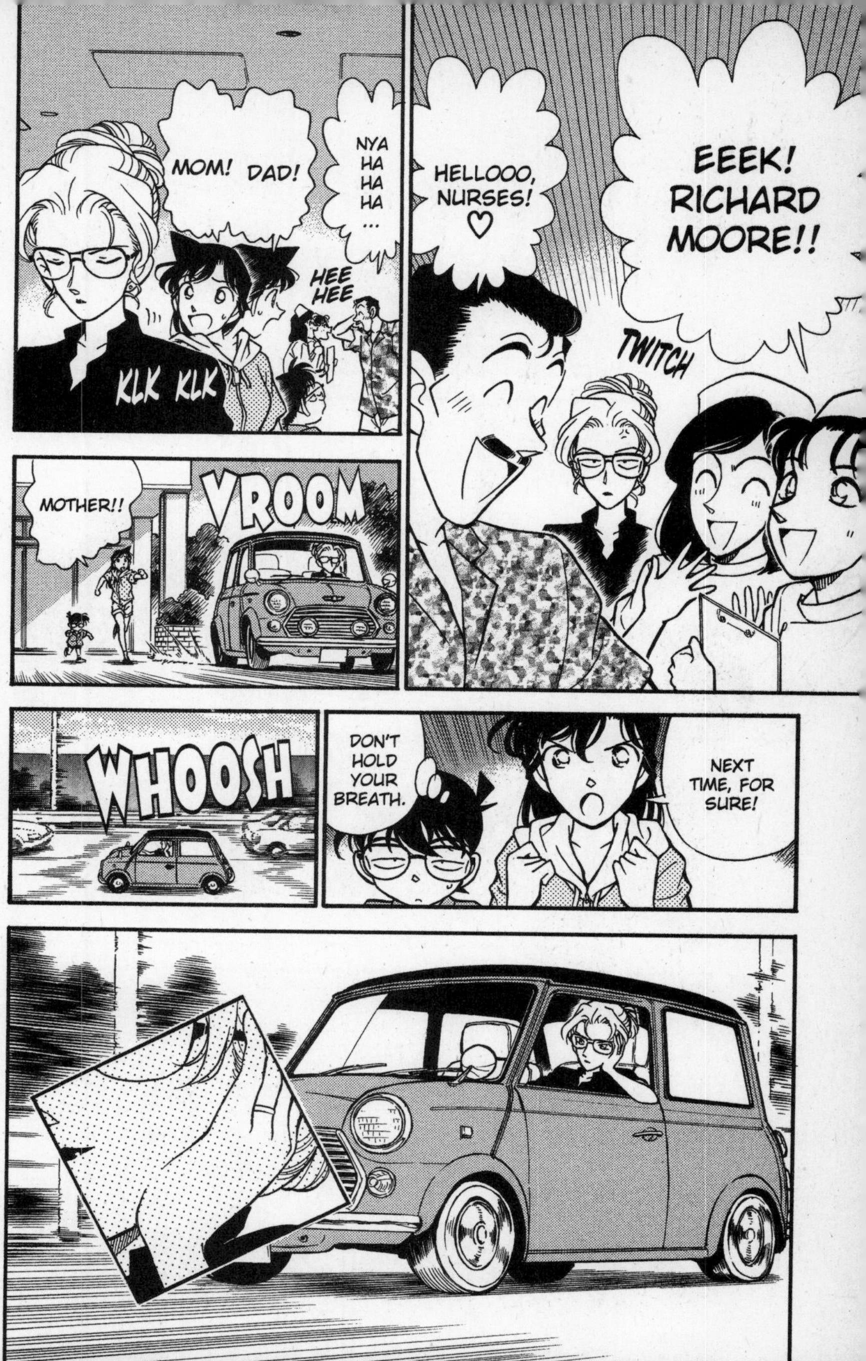
EEEK! RICHARD MOORE!!
HELLOOO, NURSES! ♡
TWITCH
NYA HA HA HA ...
MOM! DAD!
HEE HEE
KLK KLK
VROOM
MOTHER!!
NEXT TIME, FOR SURE!
DON'T HOLD YOUR BREATH.
WHOOSH

FILE 6: WHAT TO DO?

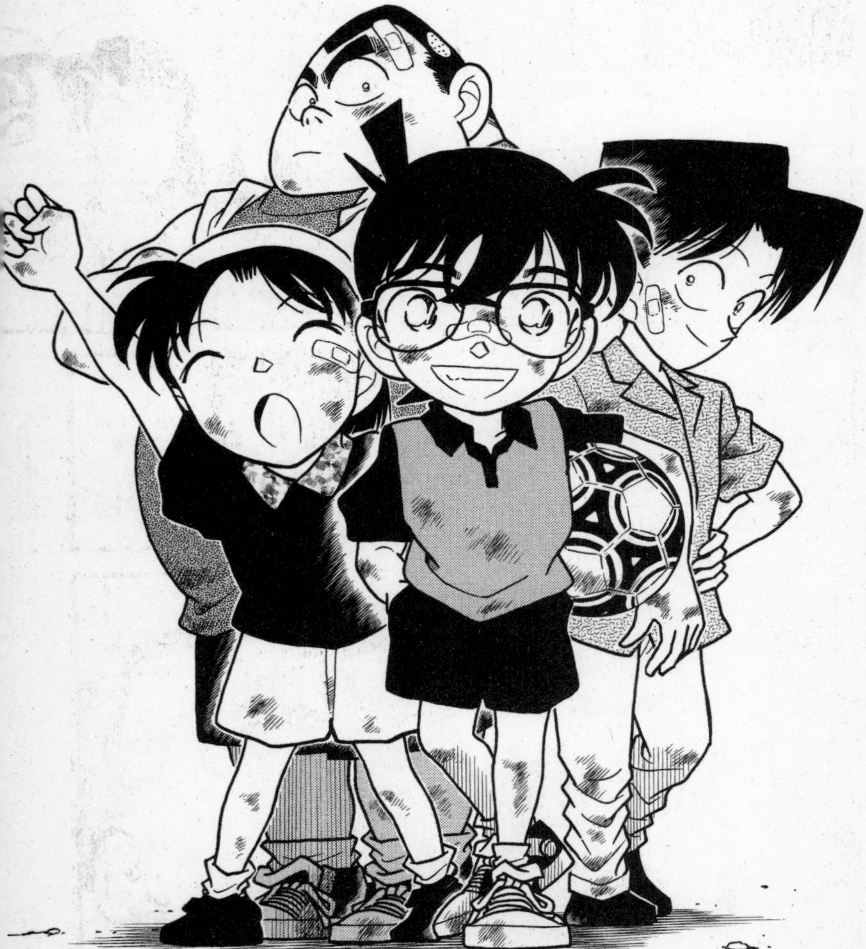

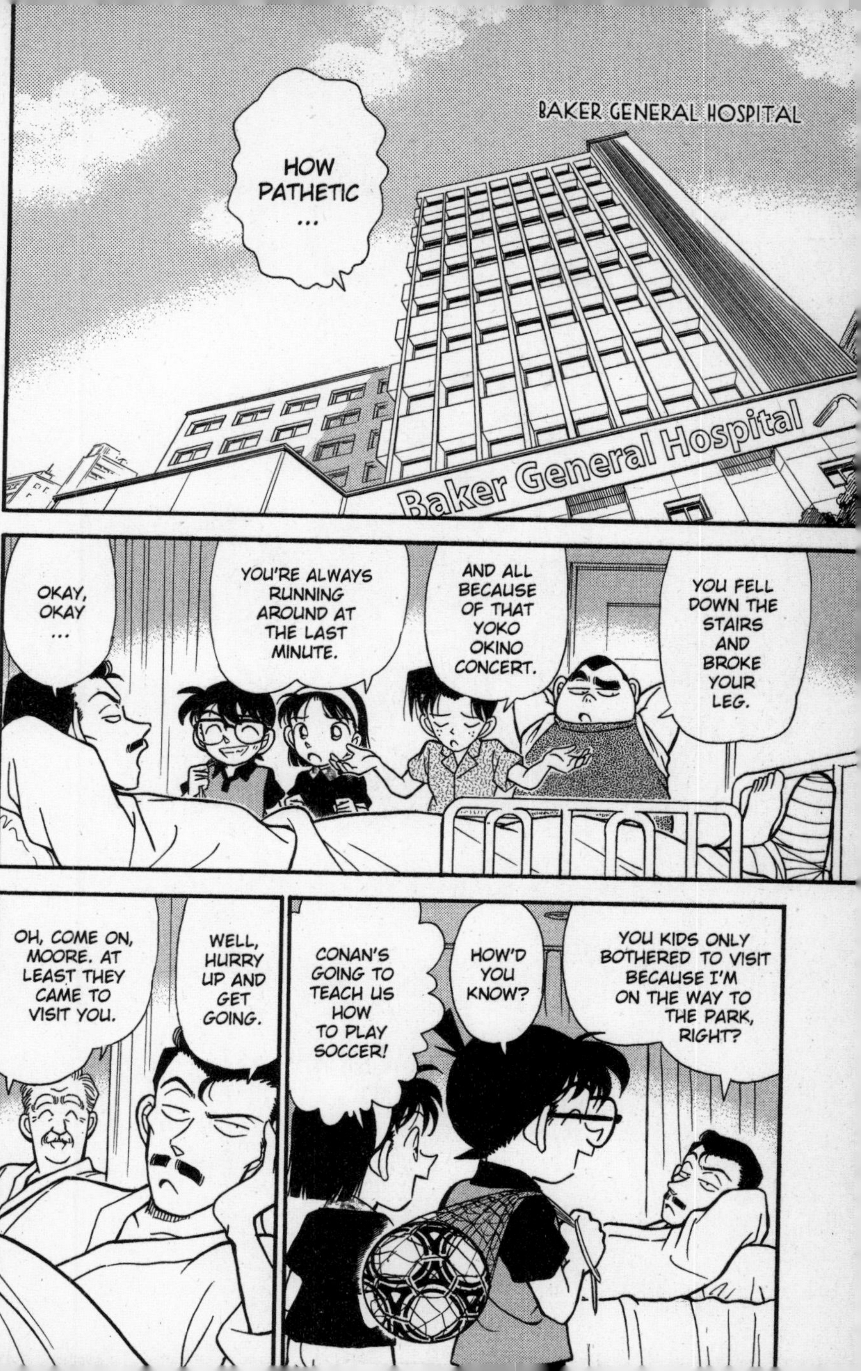
BAKER GENERAL HOSPITAL
HOW PATHETIC ...
Baker General Hospital
YOU FELL DOWN THE STAIRS AND BROKE YOUR LEG.
AND ALL BECAUSE OF THAT YOKO OKINO CONCERT.
YOU'RE ALWAYS RUNNING AROUND AT THE LAST MINUTE.
OKAY, OKAY ...
YOU KIDS ONLY BOTHERED TO VISIT BECAUSE I'M ON THE WAY TO THE PARK, RIGHT?
HOW'D YOU KNOW?
CONAN'S GOING TO TEACH US HOW TO PLAY SOCCER!
WELL, HURRY UP AND GET GOING.
OH, COME ON, MOORE. AT LEAST THEY CAME TO VISIT YOU.

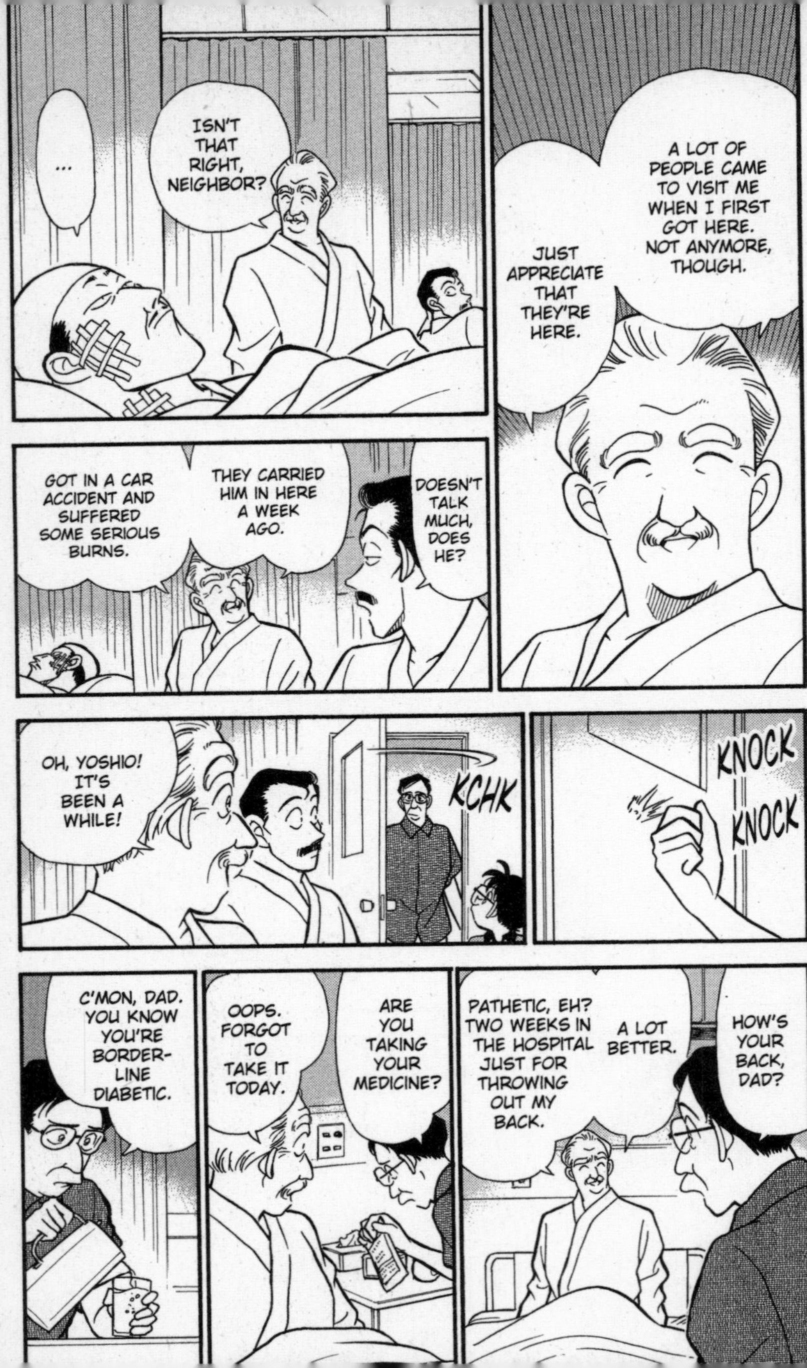
A LOT OF PEOPLE CAME TO VISIT ME WHEN I FIRST GOT HERE. NOT ANYMORE, THOUGH.
JUST APPRECIATE THAT THEY'RE HERE.
ISN'T THAT RIGHT, NEIGHBOR?
...
DOESN'T TALK MUCH, DOES HE?
THEY CARRIED HIM IN HERE A WEEK AGO.
GOT IN A CAR ACCIDENT AND SUFFERED SOME SERIOUS BURNS.
KNOCK
KNOCK
KCHK
OH, YOSHIO! IT'S BEEN A WHILE!
HOW'S YOUR BACK, DAD?
A LOT BETTER.
PATHETIC, EH? TWO WEEKS IN THE HOSPITAL JUST FOR THROWING OUT MY BACK.
ARE YOU TAKING YOUR MEDICINE?
OOPS. FORGOT TO TAKE IT TODAY.
C'MON, DAD. YOU KNOW YOU'RE BORDER-LINE DIABETIC.

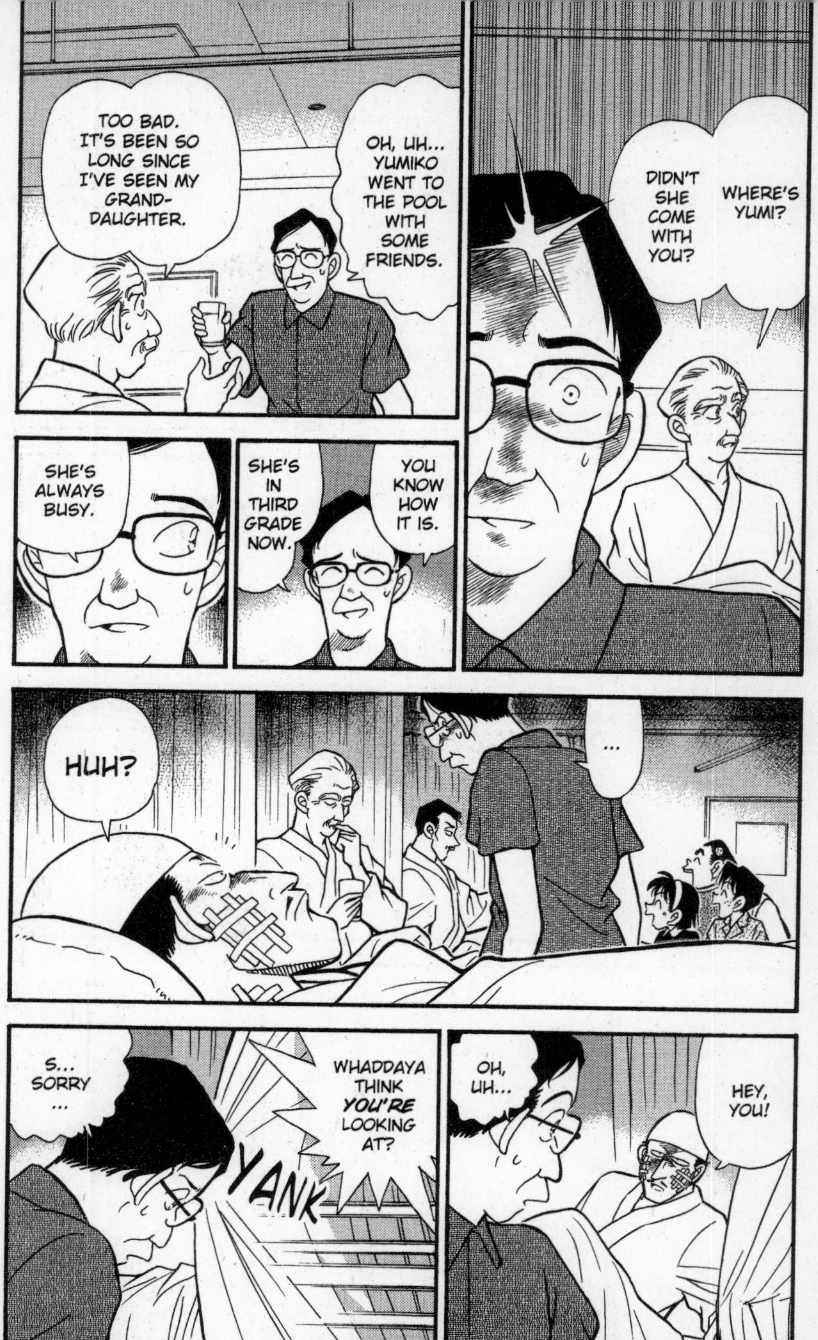
WHERE'S YUMI?
DIDN'T SHE COME WITH YOU?
OH, UH... YUMIKO WENT TO THE POOL WITH SOME FRIENDS.
TOO BAD. IT'S BEEN SO LONG SINCE I'VE SEEN MY GRAND-DAUGHTER.
YOU KNOW HOW IT IS.
SHE'S IN THIRD GRADE NOW.
SHE'S ALWAYS BUSY.
...
HUH?
HEY, YOU!
OH, UH...
WHADDAYA THINK *YOU'RE* LOOKING AT?
YANK
S... SORRY ...

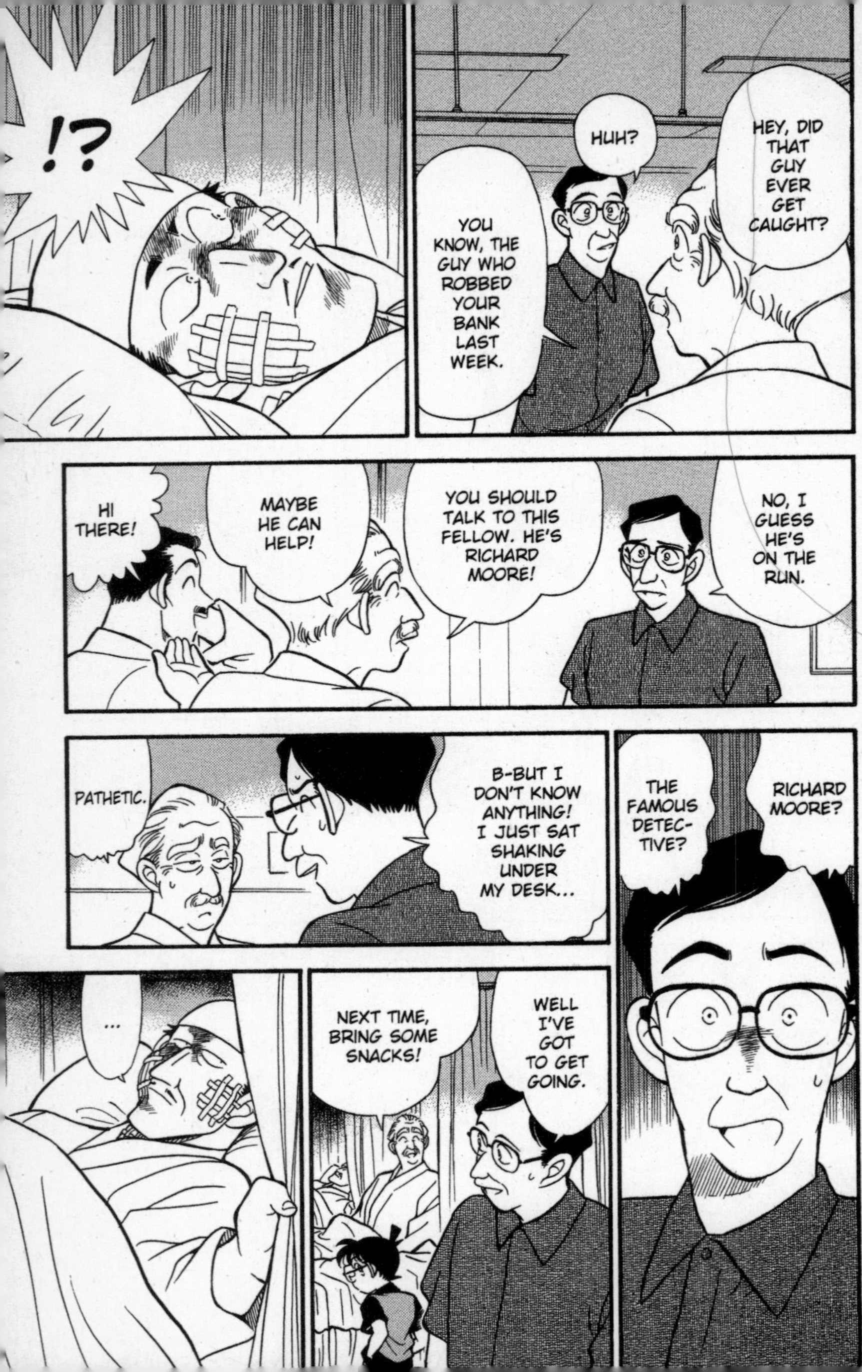
HEY, DID THAT GUY EVER GET CAUGHT?
HUH?
YOU KNOW, THE GUY WHO ROBBED YOUR BANK LAST WEEK.
!?
NO, I GUESS HE'S ON THE RUN.
YOU SHOULD TALK TO THIS FELLOW. HE'S RICHARD MOORE!
MAYBE HE CAN HELP!
HI THERE!
RICHARD MOORE?
THE FAMOUS DETECTIVE?
B-BUT I DON'T KNOW ANYTHING! I JUST SAT SHAKING UNDER MY DESK...
PATHETIC.
WELL I'VE GOT TO GET GOING.
NEXT TIME, BRING SOME SNACKS!
...

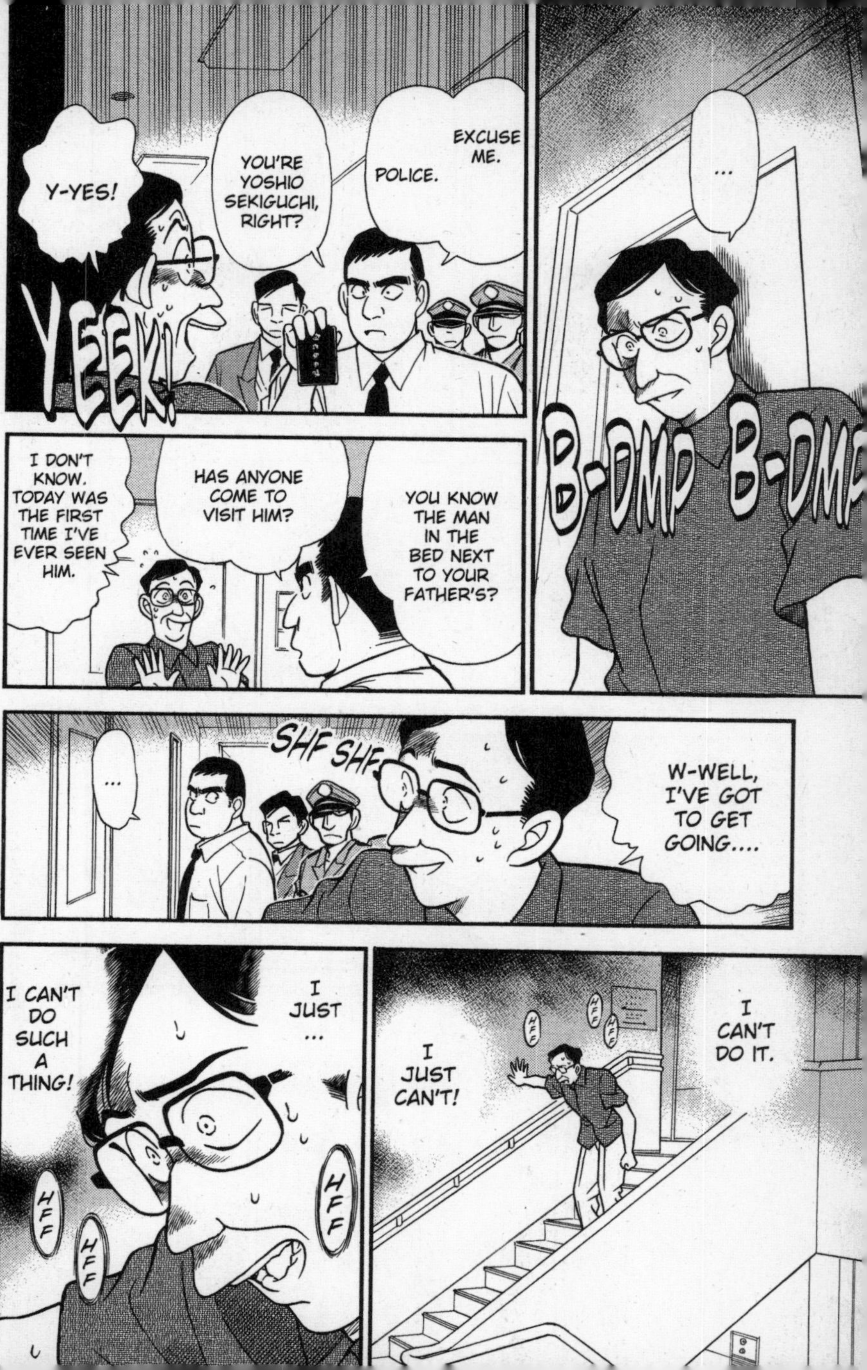
...
B-DMP B-DMP
EXCUSE ME. POLICE.
YOU'RE YOSHIO SEKIGUCHI, RIGHT?
Y-YES!
YEEK!
YOU KNOW THE MAN IN THE BED NEXT TO YOUR FATHER'S?
HAS ANYONE COME TO VISIT HIM?
I DON'T KNOW. TODAY WAS THE FIRST TIME I'VE EVER SEEN HIM.
W-WELL, I'VE GOT TO GET GOING....
SHF SHF
...
I CAN'T DO IT.
HFF
HFF
HFF
I JUST CAN'T!
I JUST...
I CAN'T DO SUCH A THING!
HFF
HFF
HFF

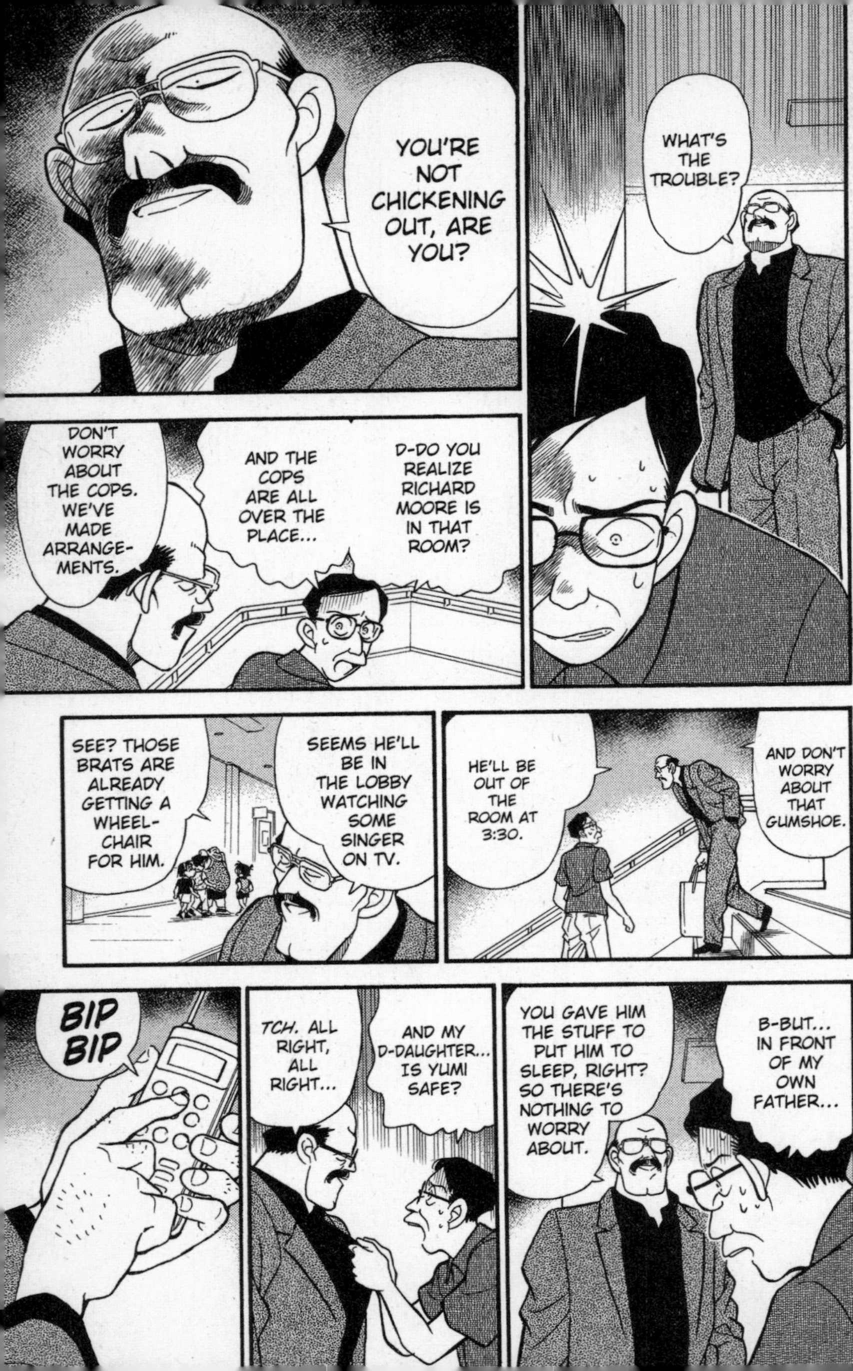
WHAT'S THE TROUBLE?
YOU'RE NOT CHICKENING OUT, ARE YOU?
D-DO YOU REALIZE RICHARD MOORE IS IN THAT ROOM?
AND THE COPS ARE ALL OVER THE PLACE...
DON'T WORRY ABOUT THE COPS. WE'VE MADE ARRANGE-MENTS.
AND DON'T WORRY ABOUT THAT GUMSHOE.
HE'LL BE OUT OF THE ROOM AT 3:30.
SEEMS HE'LL BE IN THE LOBBY WATCHING SOME SINGER ON TV.
SEE? THOSE BRATS ARE ALREADY GETTING A WHEEL-CHAIR FOR HIM.
B-BUT... IN FRONT OF MY OWN FATHER...
YOU GAVE HIM THE STUFF TO PUT HIM TO SLEEP, RIGHT? SO THERE'S NOTHING TO WORRY ABOUT.
AND MY D-DAUGHTER... IS YUMI SAFE?
TCH. ALL RIGHT, ALL RIGHT...
BIP BIP

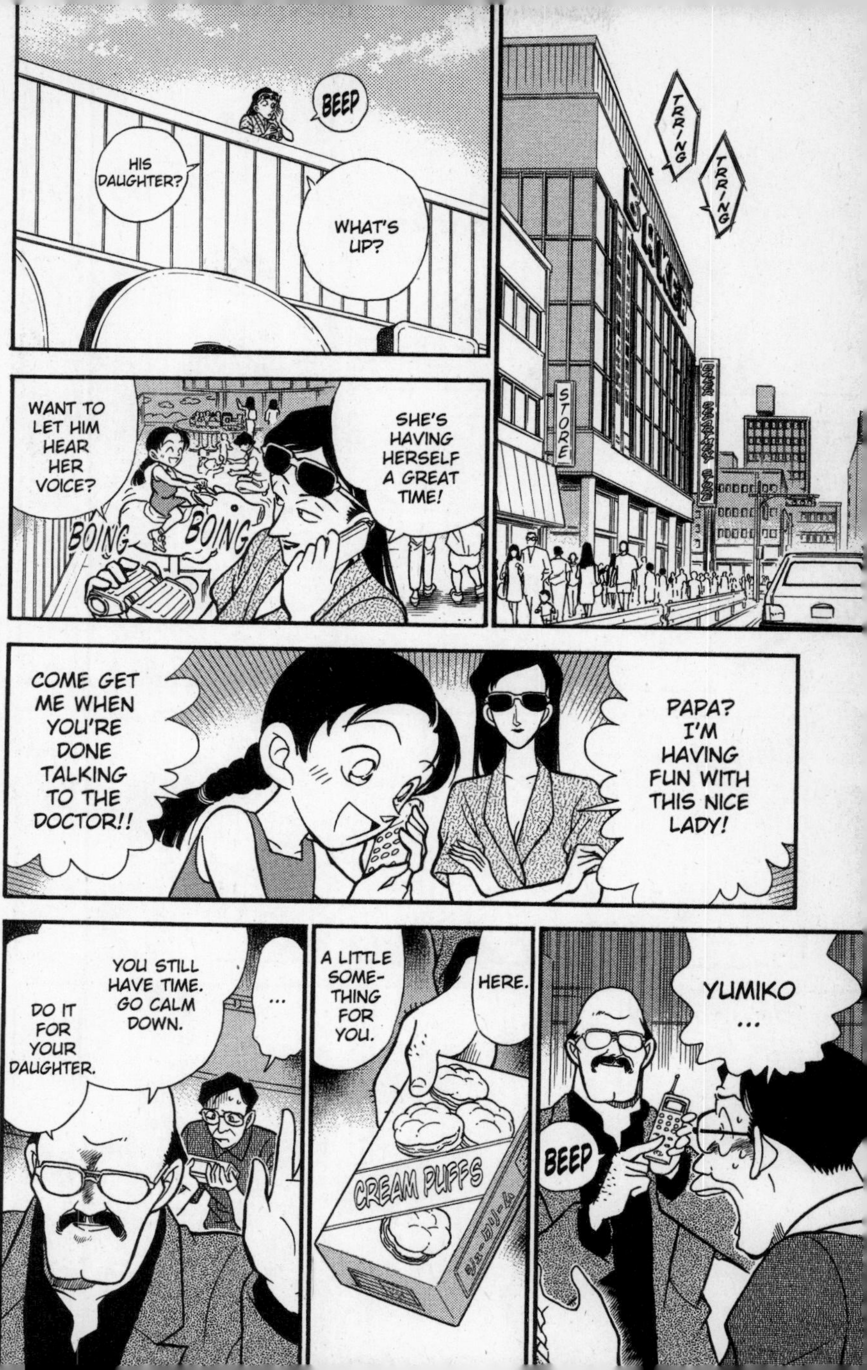
TRRING
TRRING
STORE
BEEP
WHAT'S UP?
HIS DAUGHTER?
SHE'S HAVING HERSELF A GREAT TIME!
WANT TO LET HIM HEAR HER VOICE?
BOING
BOING
PAPA? I'M HAVING FUN WITH THIS NICE LADY!
COME GET ME WHEN YOU'RE DONE TALKING TO THE DOCTOR!!
YUMIKO ...
BEEP
HERE.
A LITTLE SOME-THING FOR YOU.
CREAM PUFFS
...
YOU STILL HAVE TIME. GO CALM DOWN.
DO IT FOR YOUR DAUGHTER.

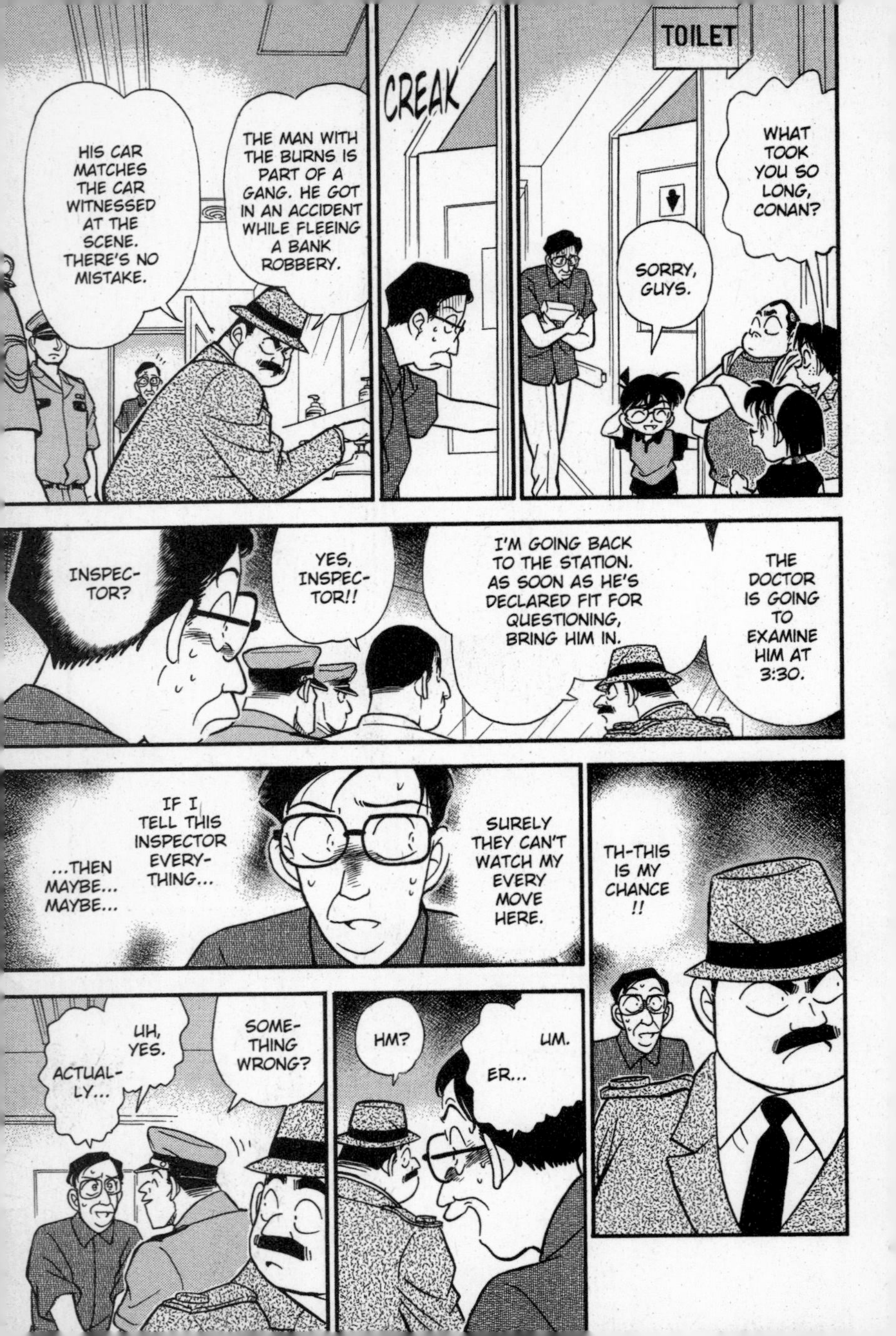
TOILET
WHAT TOOK YOU SO LONG, CONAN?
SORRY, GUYS.
CREAK
THE MAN WITH THE BURNS IS PART OF A GANG. HE GOT IN AN ACCIDENT WHILE FLEEING A BANK ROBBERY.
HIS CAR MATCHES THE CAR WITNESSED AT THE SCENE. THERE'S NO MISTAKE.
THE DOCTOR IS GOING TO EXAMINE HIM AT 3:30.
I'M GOING BACK TO THE STATION. AS SOON AS HE'S DECLARED FIT FOR QUESTIONING, BRING HIM IN.
YES, INSPECTOR!!
INSPECTOR?
TH-THIS IS MY CHANCE!!
SURELY THEY CAN'T WATCH MY EVERY MOVE HERE.
IF I TELL THIS INSPECTOR EVERYTHING...
...THEN MAYBE... MAYBE...
UM.
ER...
HM?
SOMETHING WRONG?
UH, YES.
ACTUALLY...

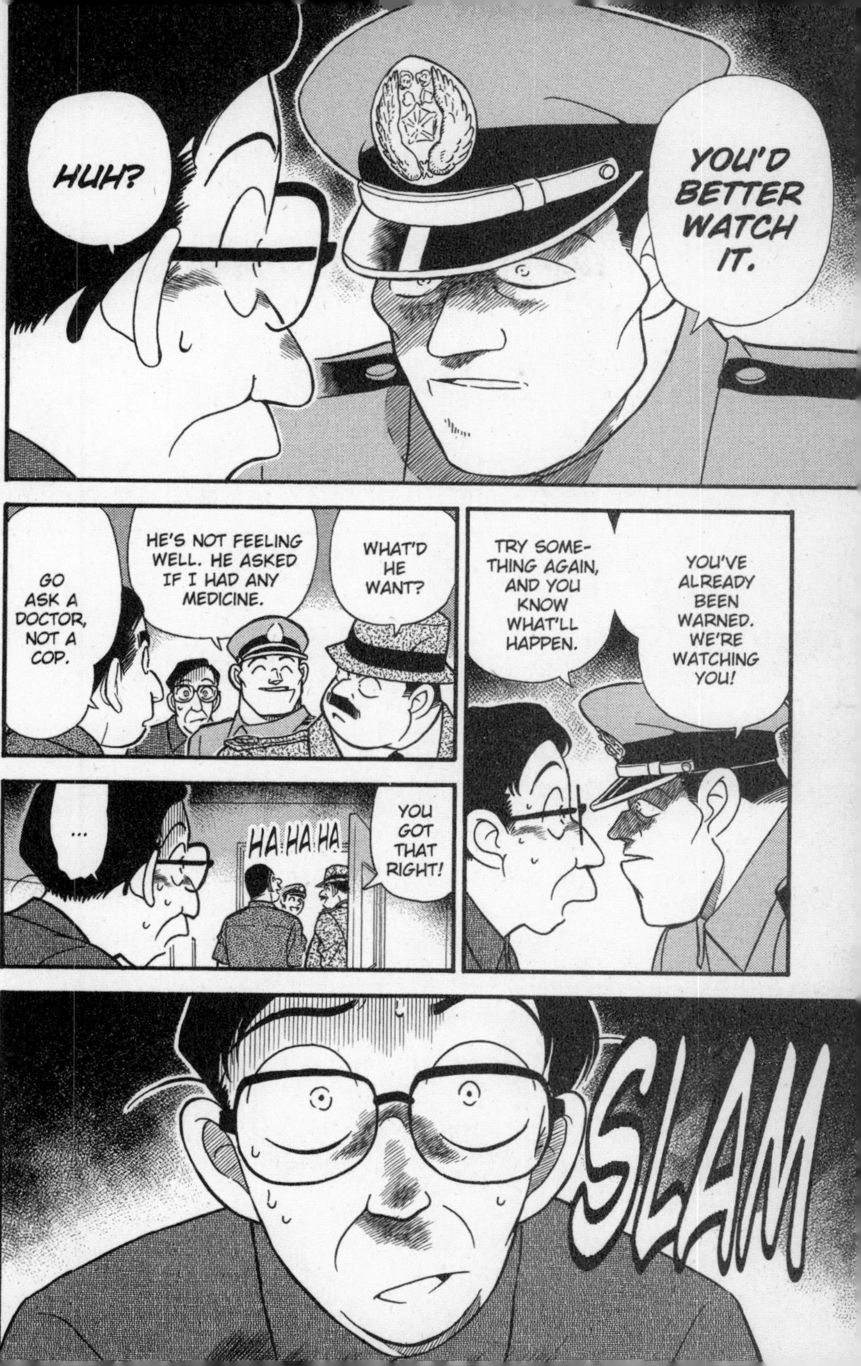
YOU'D BETTER WATCH IT.
HUH?
YOU'VE ALREADY BEEN WARNED. WE'RE WATCHING YOU!
TRY SOME-THING AGAIN, AND YOU KNOW WHAT'LL HAPPEN.
WHAT'D HE WANT?
HE'S NOT FEELING WELL. HE ASKED IF I HAD ANY MEDICINE.
GO ASK A DOCTOR, NOT A COP.
YOU GOT THAT RIGHT!
HA HA HA
...
SLAM

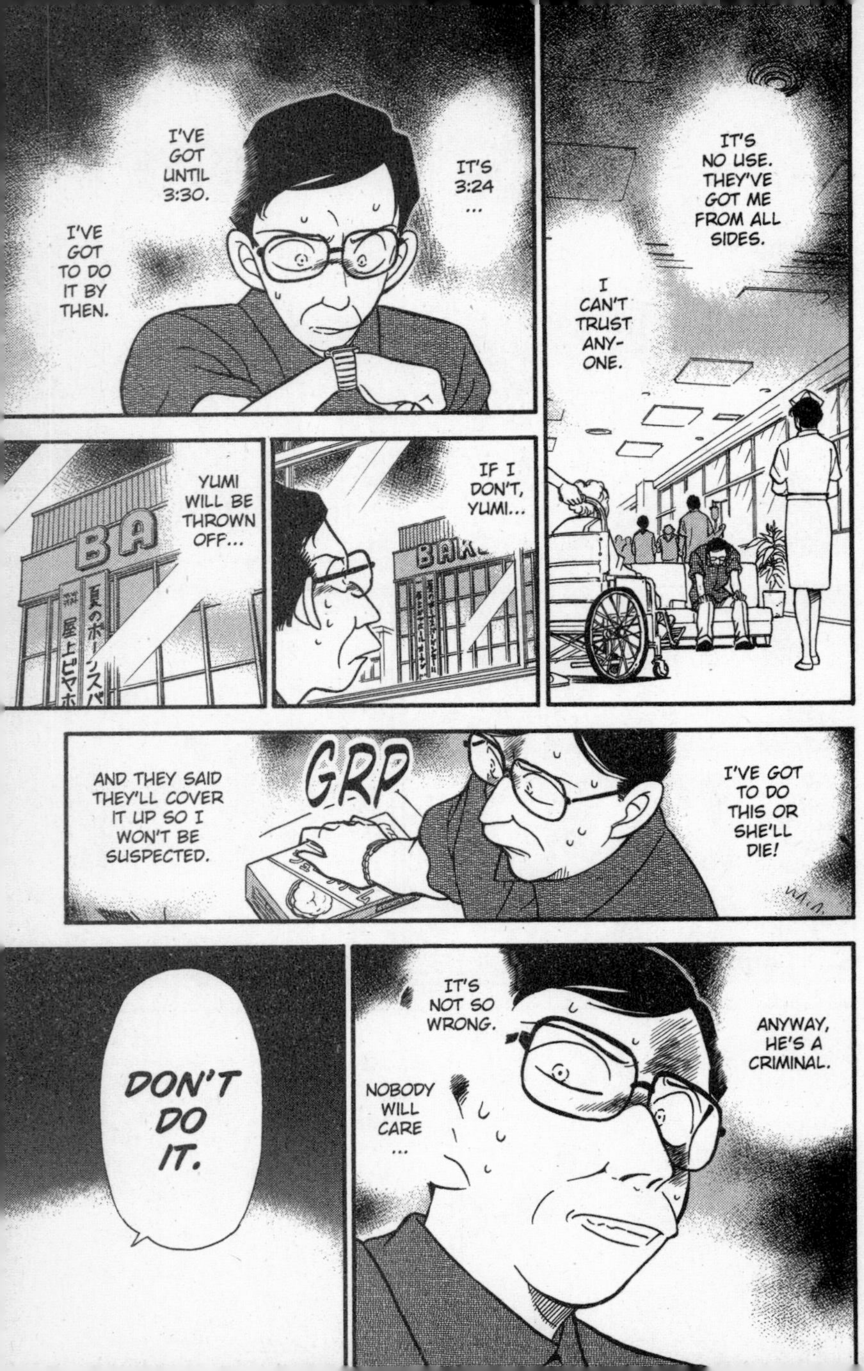
IT'S NO USE. THEY'VE GOT ME FROM ALL SIDES.
I CAN'T TRUST ANY-ONE.
IT'S 3:24 ...
I'VE GOT UNTIL 3:30.
I'VE GOT TO DO IT BY THEN.
IF I DON'T, YUMI...
YUMI WILL BE THROWN OFF...
I'VE GOT TO DO THIS OR SHE'LL DIE!
GRP
AND THEY SAID THEY'LL COVER IT UP SO I WON'T BE SUSPECTED.
ANYWAY, HE'S A CRIMINAL.
IT'S NOT SO WRONG.
NOBODY WILL CARE ...
DON'T DO IT.

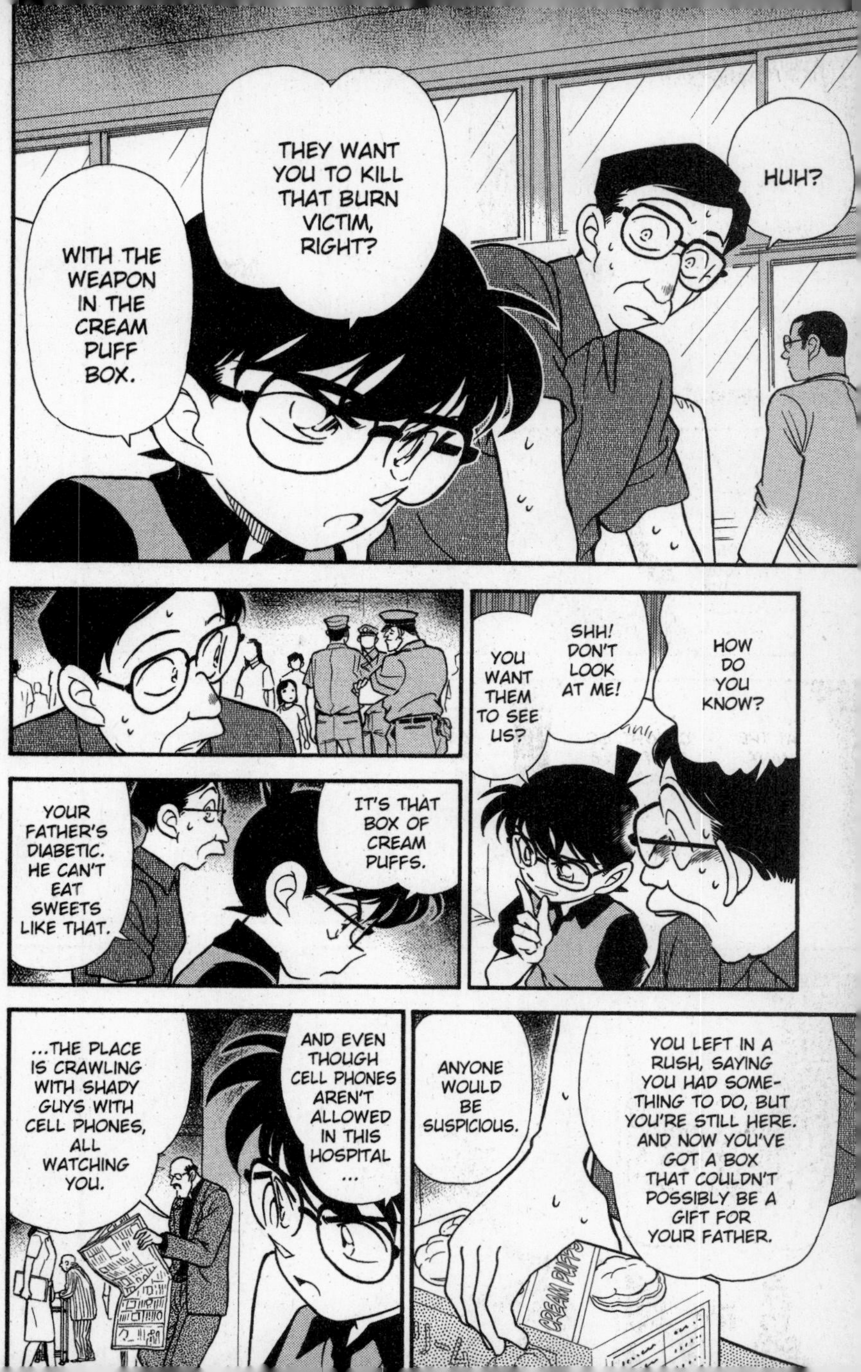
THEY WANT YOU TO KILL THAT BURN VICTIM, RIGHT?
WITH THE WEAPON IN THE CREAM PUFF BOX.
HUH?
HOW DO YOU KNOW?
SHH! DON'T LOOK AT ME!
YOU WANT THEM TO SEE US?
IT'S THAT BOX OF CREAM PUFFS.
YOUR FATHER'S DIABETIC. HE CAN'T EAT SWEETS LIKE THAT.
YOU LEFT IN A RUSH, SAYING YOU HAD SOME-THING TO DO, BUT YOU'RE STILL HERE. AND NOW YOU'VE GOT A BOX THAT COULDN'T POSSIBLY BE A GIFT FOR YOUR FATHER.
CREAM PUFFS
ANYONE WOULD BE SUSPICIOUS.
AND EVEN THOUGH CELL PHONES AREN'T ALLOWED IN THIS HOSPITAL ...
...THE PLACE IS CRAWLING WITH SHADY GUYS WITH CELL PHONES, ALL WATCHING YOU.

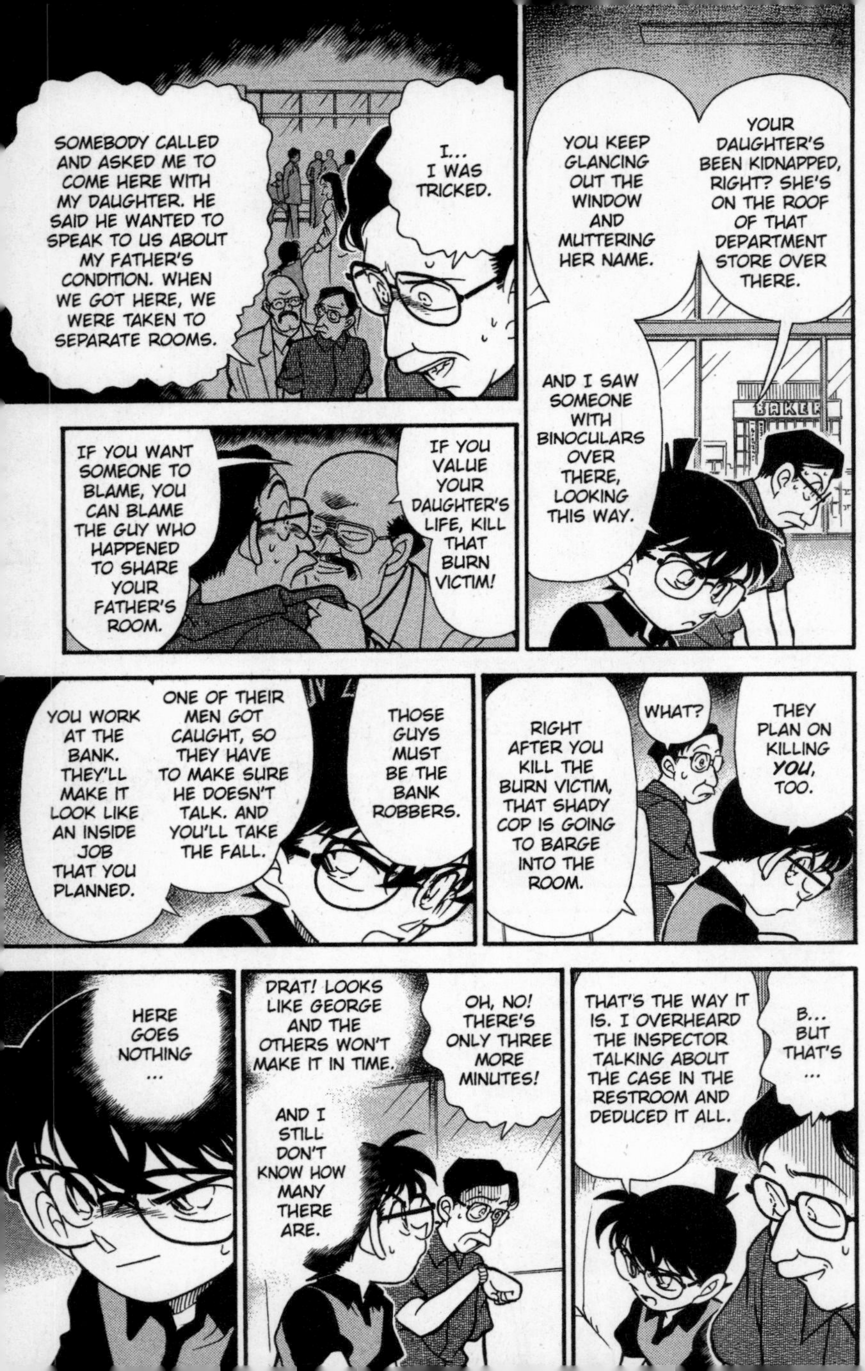
YOUR DAUGHTER'S BEEN KIDNAPPED, RIGHT? SHE'S ON THE ROOF OF THAT DEPARTMENT STORE OVER THERE.
YOU KEEP GLANCING OUT THE WINDOW AND MUTTERING HER NAME.
AND I SAW SOMEONE WITH BINOCULARS OVER THERE, LOOKING THIS WAY.
BAKER
I... I WAS TRICKED.
SOMEBODY CALLED AND ASKED ME TO COME HERE WITH MY DAUGHTER. HE SAID HE WANTED TO SPEAK TO US ABOUT MY FATHER'S CONDITION. WHEN WE GOT HERE, WE WERE TAKEN TO SEPARATE ROOMS.
IF YOU VALUE YOUR DAUGHTER'S LIFE, KILL THAT BURN VICTIM!
IF YOU WANT SOMEONE TO BLAME, YOU CAN BLAME THE GUY WHO HAPPENED TO SHARE YOUR FATHER'S ROOM.
THEY PLAN ON KILLING *YOU*, TOO.
WHAT?
RIGHT AFTER YOU KILL THE BURN VICTIM, THAT SHADY COP IS GOING TO BARGE INTO THE ROOM.
THOSE GUYS MUST BE THE BANK ROBBERS.
ONE OF THEIR MEN GOT CAUGHT, SO THEY HAVE TO MAKE SURE HE DOESN'T TALK. AND YOU'LL TAKE THE FALL.
YOU WORK AT THE BANK. THEY'LL MAKE IT LOOK LIKE AN INSIDE JOB THAT YOU PLANNED.
B... BUT THAT'S ...
THAT'S THE WAY IT IS. I OVERHEARD THE INSPECTOR TALKING ABOUT THE CASE IN THE RESTROOM AND DEDUCED IT ALL.
OH, NO! THERE'S ONLY THREE MORE MINUTES!
DRAT! LOOKS LIKE GEORGE AND THE OTHERS WON'T MAKE IT IN TIME.
AND I STILL DON'T KNOW HOW MANY THERE ARE.
HERE GOES NOTHING ...

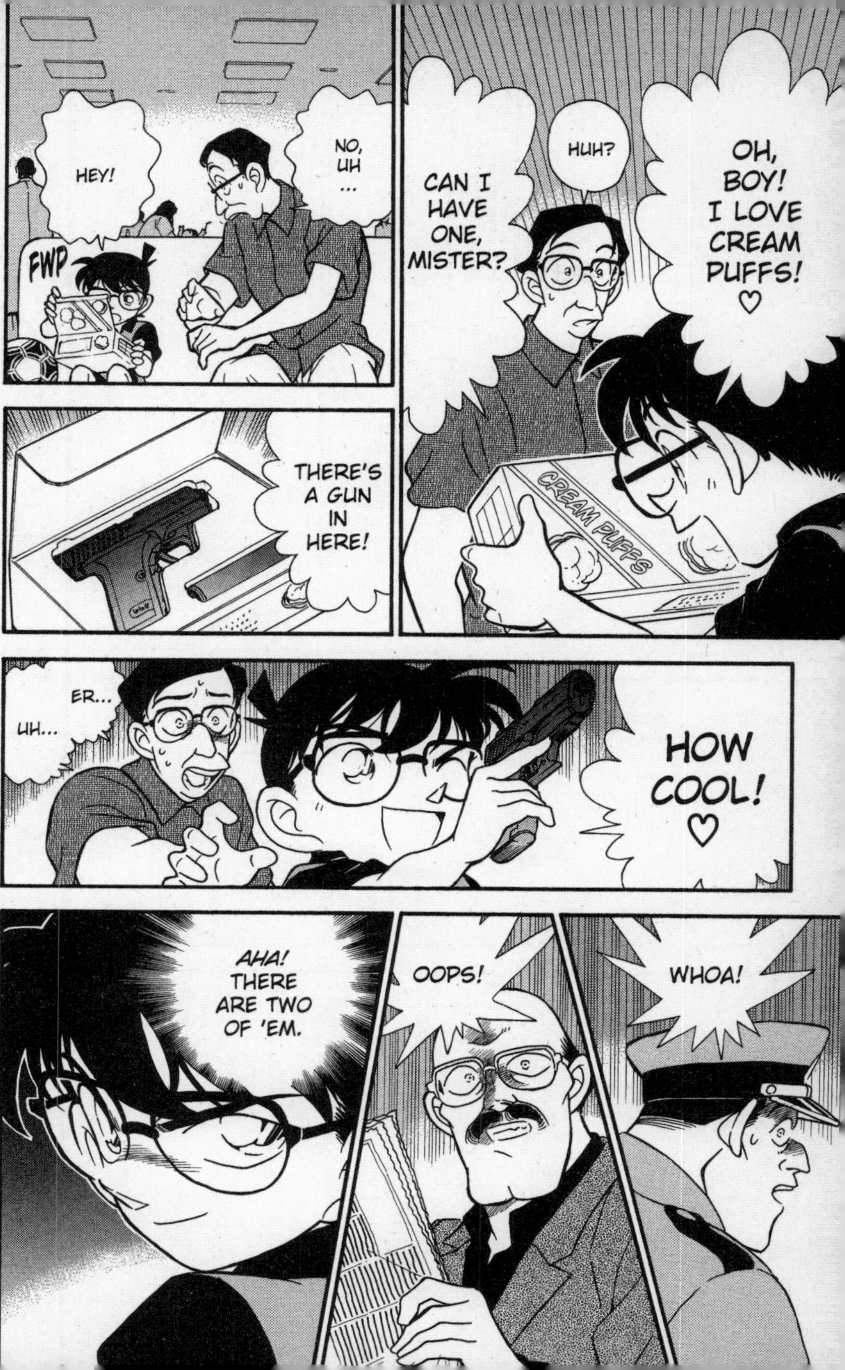
OH, BOY! I LOVE CREAM PUFFS! ♡
HUH?
CAN I HAVE ONE, MISTER?
CREAM PUFFS
NO, UH ...
HEY!
FWP
THERE'S A GUN IN HERE!
HOW COOL! ♡
ER...
UH...
WHOA!
OOPS!
AHA! THERE ARE TWO OF 'EM.

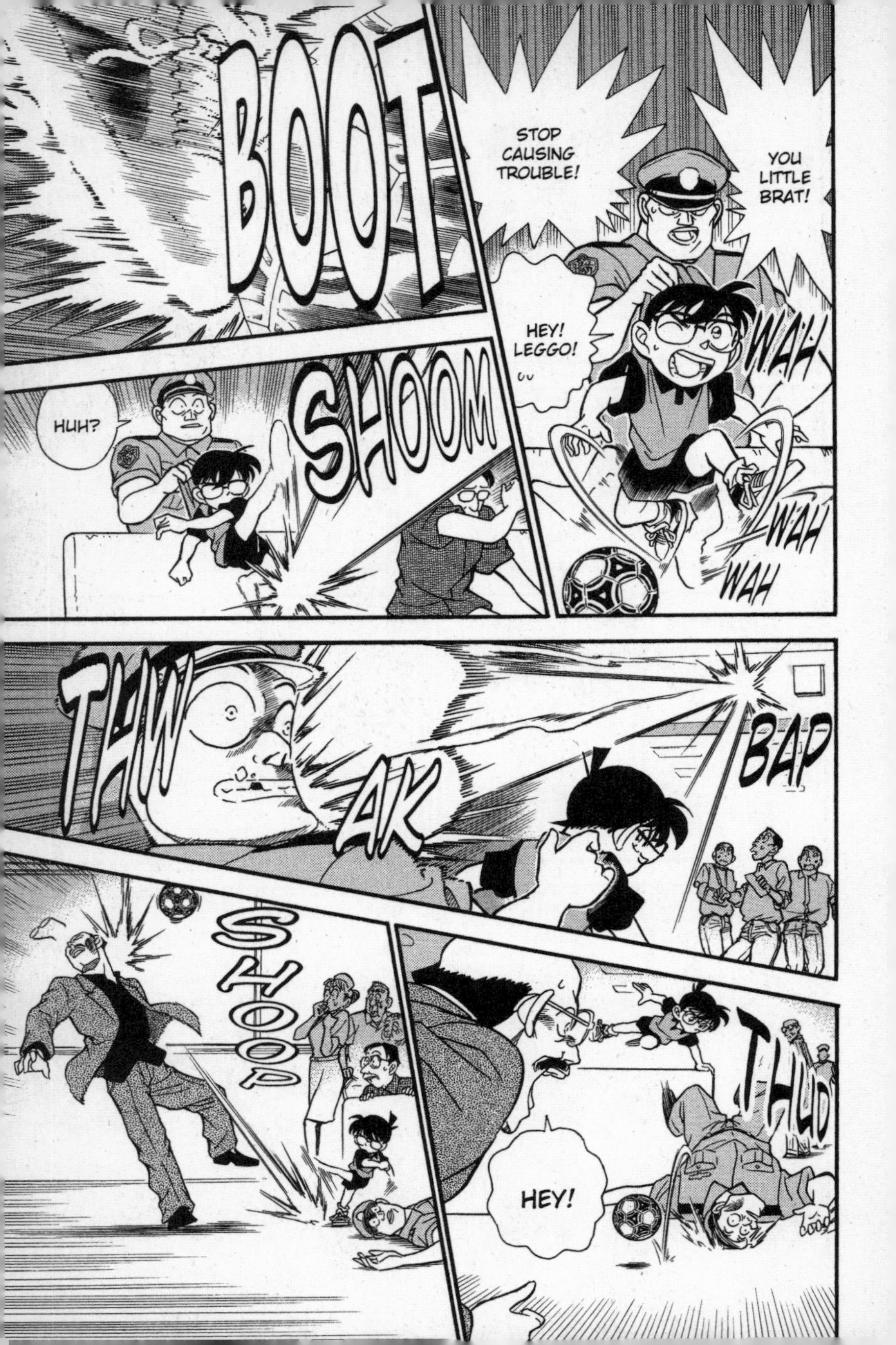
STOP CAUSING TROUBLE!
YOU LITTLE BRAT!
WAH
HEY! LEGGO!
WAH
WAH
BOOT
SHOOM
HUH?
BAP
THWAK
THUD
HEY!
SHOOP

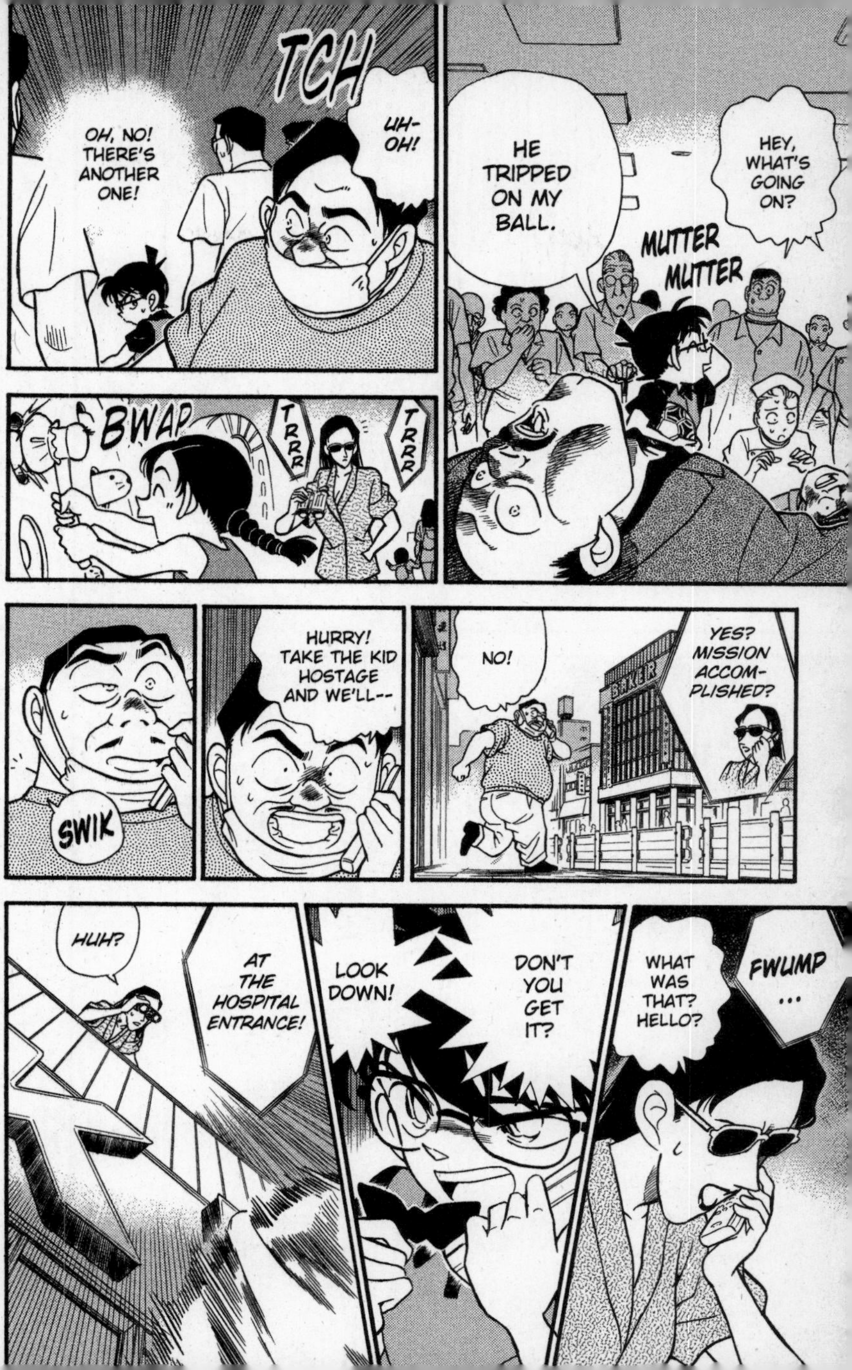
HEY, WHAT'S GOING ON?
HE TRIPPED ON MY BALL.
MUTTER MUTTER
TCH
UH-OH!
OH, NO! THERE'S ANOTHER ONE!
TRRR
TRRR
BWAP
YES? MISSION ACCOM-PLISHED?
NO!
HURRY! TAKE THE KID HOSTAGE AND WE'LL--
SWIK
FWUMP...
WHAT WAS THAT? HELLO?
DON'T YOU GET IT?
LOOK DOWN!
AT THE HOSPITAL ENTRANCE!
HUH?

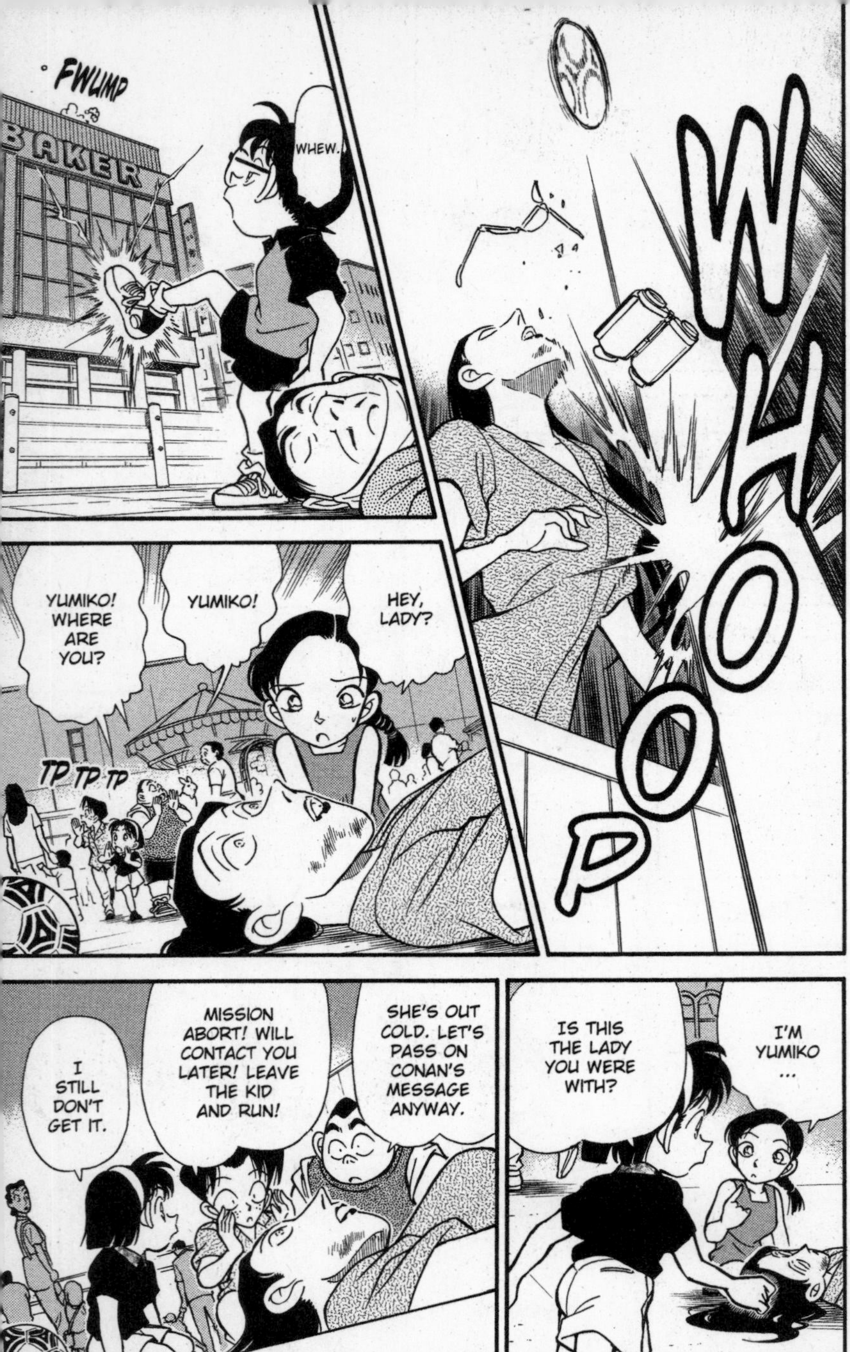
WHOOOP
FWUMP
WHEW.
HEY, LADY?
YUMIKO!
YUMIKO! WHERE ARE YOU?
TP TP TP
I'M YUMIKO...
IS THIS THE LADY YOU WERE WITH?
SHE'S OUT COLD. LET'S PASS ON CONAN'S MESSAGE ANYWAY.
MISSION ABORT! WILL CONTACT YOU LATER! LEAVE THE KID AND RUN!
I STILL DON'T GET IT.

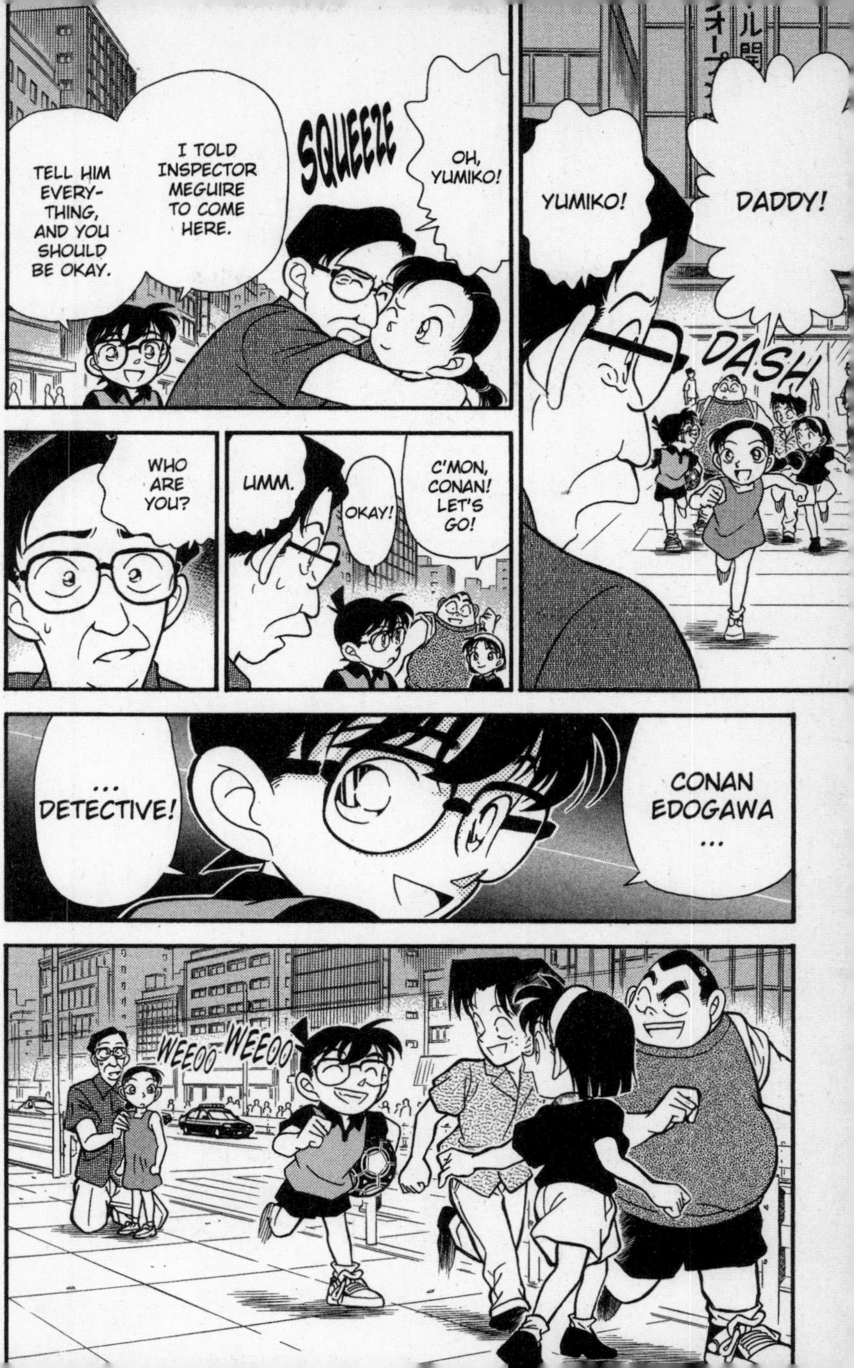
DADDY!
YUMIKO!
DASH
OH, YUMIKO!
SQUEEZE
I TOLD INSPECTOR MEGUIRE TO COME HERE.
TELL HIM EVERYTHING, AND YOU SHOULD BE OKAY.
C'MON, CONAN! LET'S GO!
OKAY!
UMM.
WHO ARE YOU?
CONAN EDOGAWA ...
... DETECTIVE!
WEEOO WEEOO

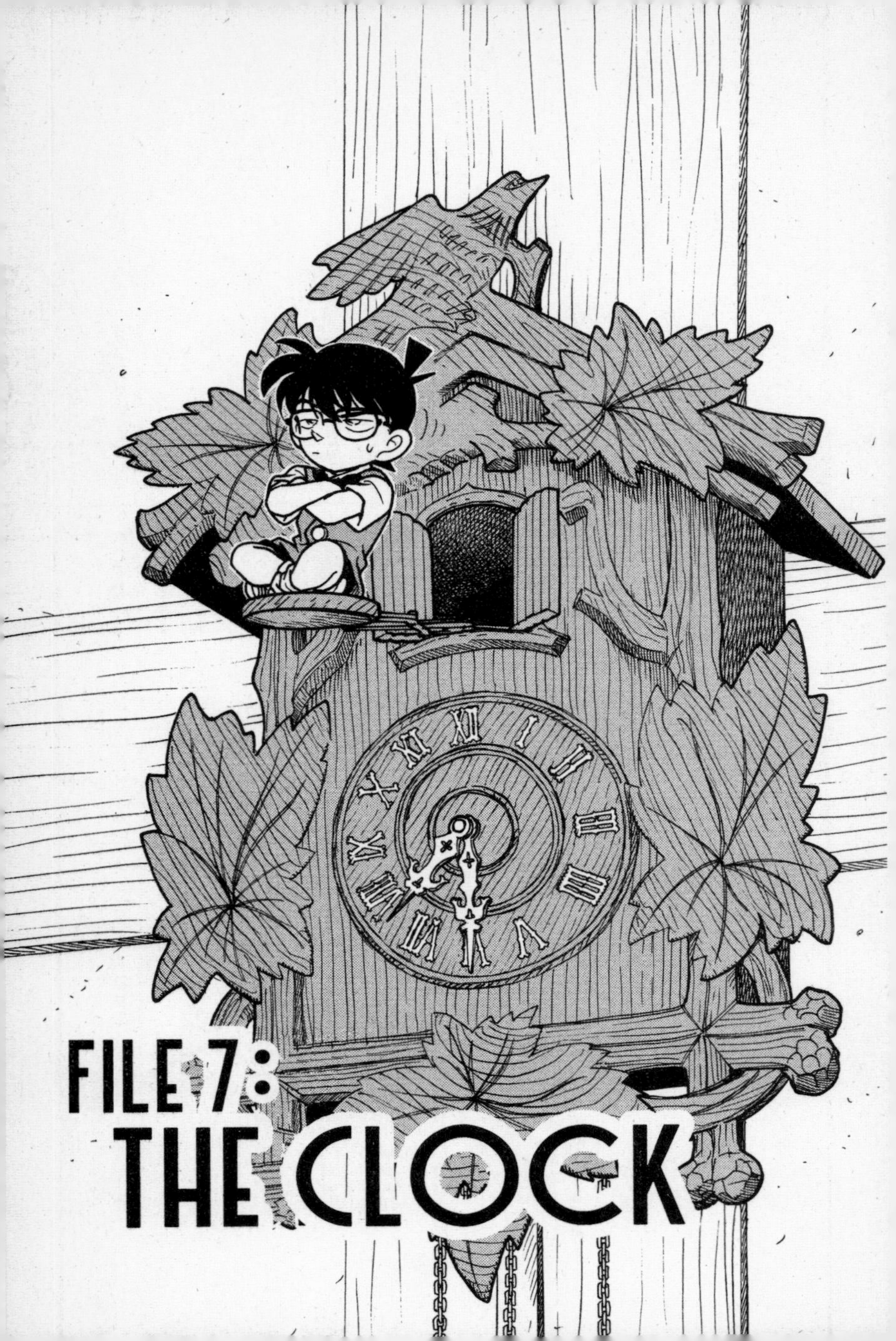
FILE 7:
THE CLOCK

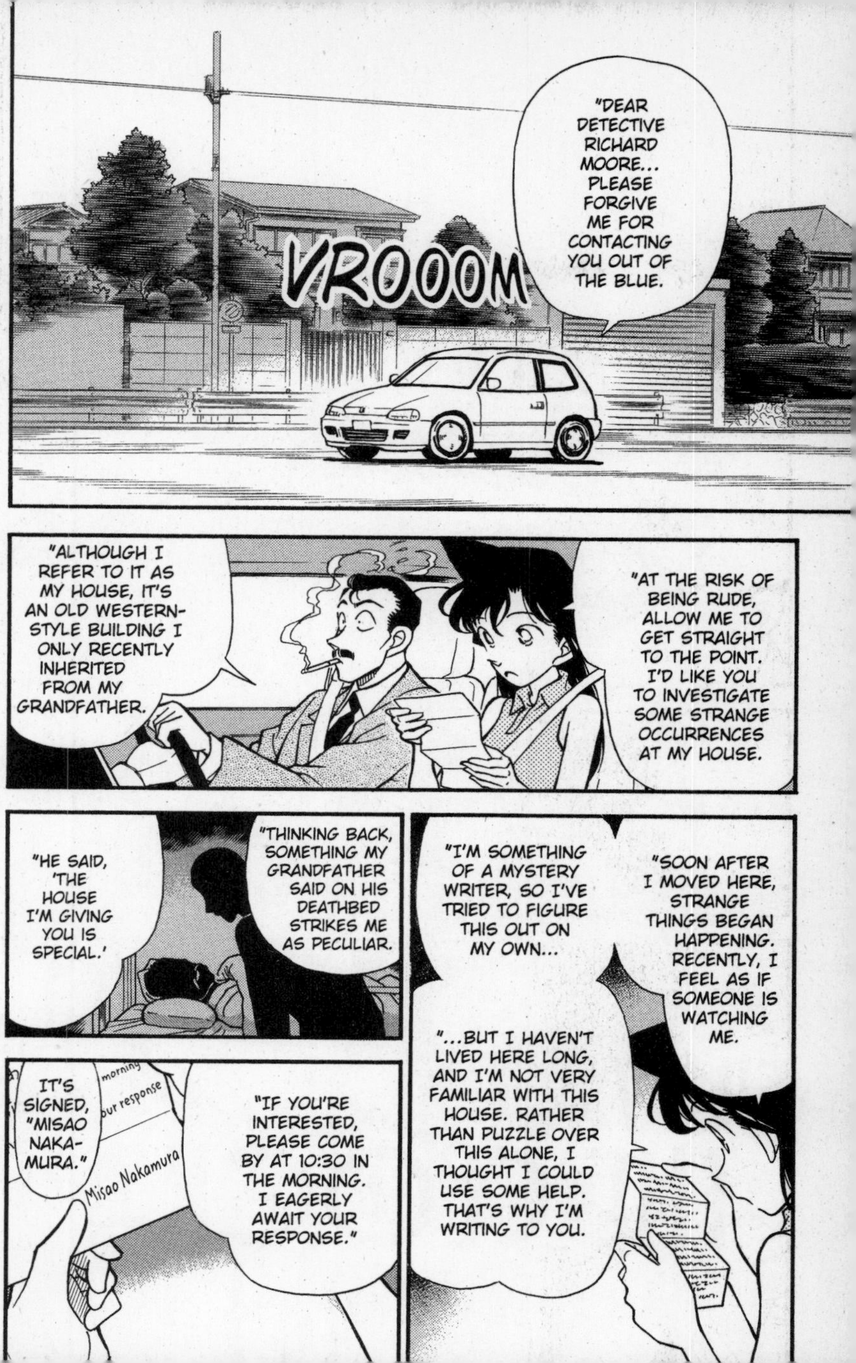
VROOOM
"DEAR DETECTIVE RICHARD MOORE... PLEASE FORGIVE ME FOR CONTACTING YOU OUT OF THE BLUE.
"AT THE RISK OF BEING RUDE, ALLOW ME TO GET STRAIGHT TO THE POINT. I'D LIKE YOU TO INVESTIGATE SOME STRANGE OCCURRENCES AT MY HOUSE.
"ALTHOUGH I REFER TO IT AS MY HOUSE, IT'S AN OLD WESTERN-STYLE BUILDING I ONLY RECENTLY INHERITED FROM MY GRANDFATHER.
"SOON AFTER I MOVED HERE, STRANGE THINGS BEGAN HAPPENING. RECENTLY, I FEEL AS IF SOMEONE IS WATCHING ME.
"I'M SOMETHING OF A MYSTERY WRITER, SO I'VE TRIED TO FIGURE THIS OUT ON MY OWN...
"...BUT I HAVEN'T LIVED HERE LONG, AND I'M NOT VERY FAMILIAR WITH THIS HOUSE. RATHER THAN PUZZLE OVER THIS ALONE, I THOUGHT I COULD USE SOME HELP. THAT'S WHY I'M WRITING TO YOU.
"THINKING BACK, SOMETHING MY GRANDFATHER SAID ON HIS DEATHBED STRIKES ME AS PECULIAR.
"HE SAID, 'THE HOUSE I'M GIVING YOU IS SPECIAL.'
"IF YOU'RE INTERESTED, PLEASE COME BY AT 10:30 IN THE MORNING. I EAGERLY AWAIT YOUR RESPONSE."
morning
our response
Misao Nakamura
IT'S SIGNED, "MISAO NAKA-MURA."

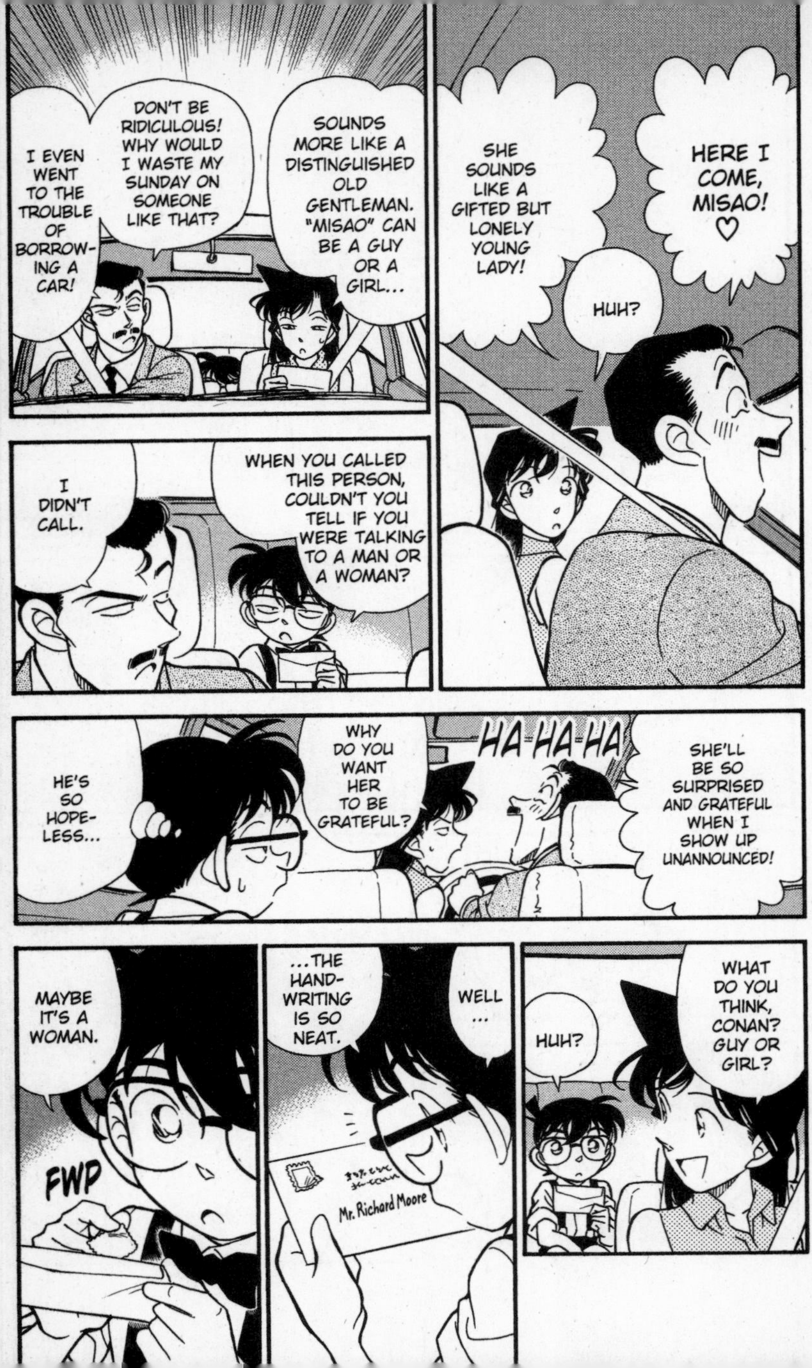
HERE I COME, MISAO! ♡
HUH?
SHE SOUNDS LIKE A GIFTED BUT LONELY YOUNG LADY!
SOUNDS MORE LIKE A DISTINGUISHED OLD GENTLEMAN. "MISAO" CAN BE A GUY OR A GIRL...
DON'T BE RIDICULOUS! WHY WOULD I WASTE MY SUNDAY ON SOMEONE LIKE THAT?
I EVEN WENT TO THE TROUBLE OF BORROWING A CAR!
WHEN YOU CALLED THIS PERSON, COULDN'T YOU TELL IF YOU WERE TALKING TO A MAN OR A WOMAN?
I DIDN'T CALL.
SHE'LL BE SO SURPRISED AND GRATEFUL WHEN I SHOW UP UNANNOUNCED!
HA-HA-HA
WHY DO YOU WANT HER TO BE GRATEFUL?
HE'S SO HOPELESS...
WHAT DO YOU THINK, CONAN? GUY OR GIRL?
HUH?
WELL...
...THE HANDWRITING IS SO NEAT.
Mr. Richard Moore
MAYBE IT'S A WOMAN.
FWP

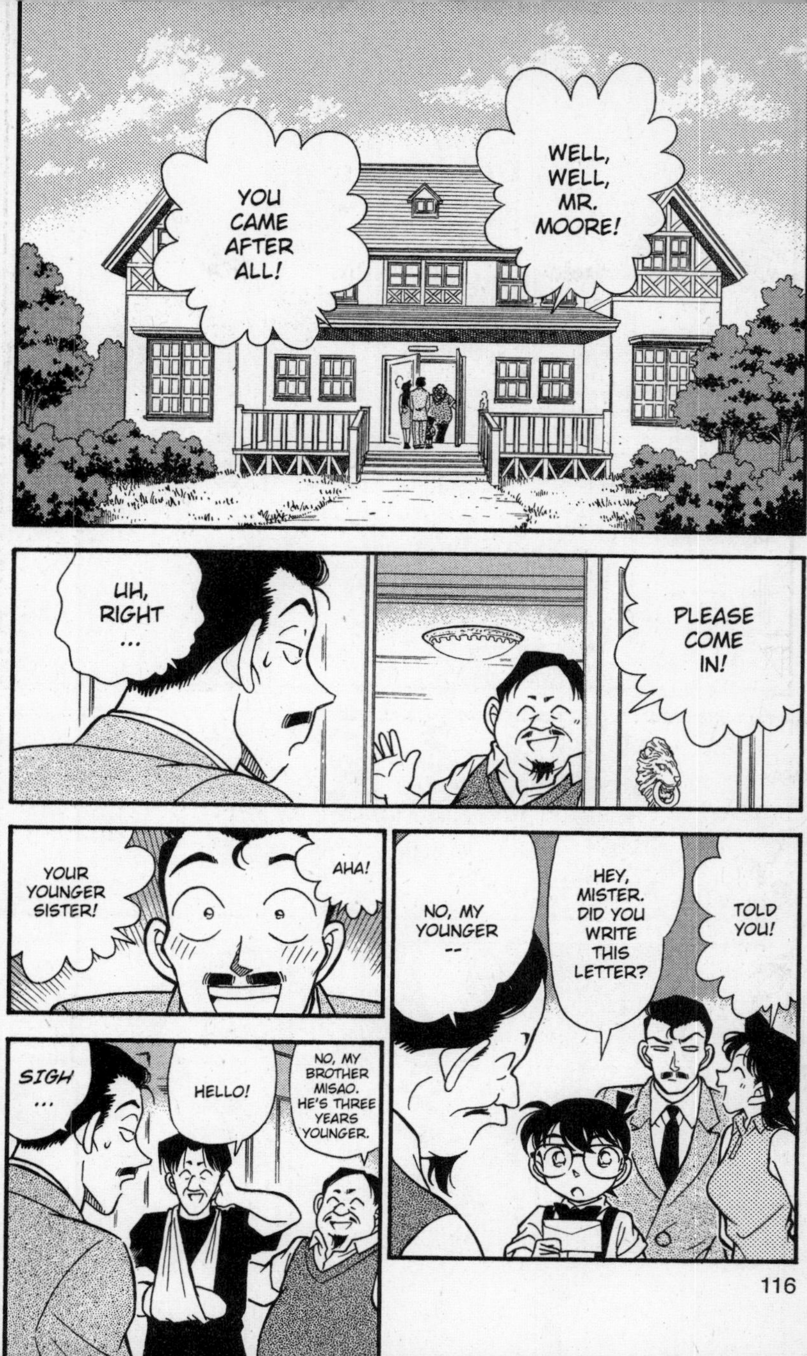
WELL, WELL, MR. MOORE!
YOU CAME AFTER ALL!
PLEASE COME IN!
UH, RIGHT ...
TOLD YOU!
HEY, MISTER. DID YOU WRITE THIS LETTER?
NO, MY YOUNGER --
AHA!
YOUR YOUNGER SISTER!
NO, MY BROTHER MISAO. HE'S THREE YEARS YOUNGER.
HELLO!
SIGH ...

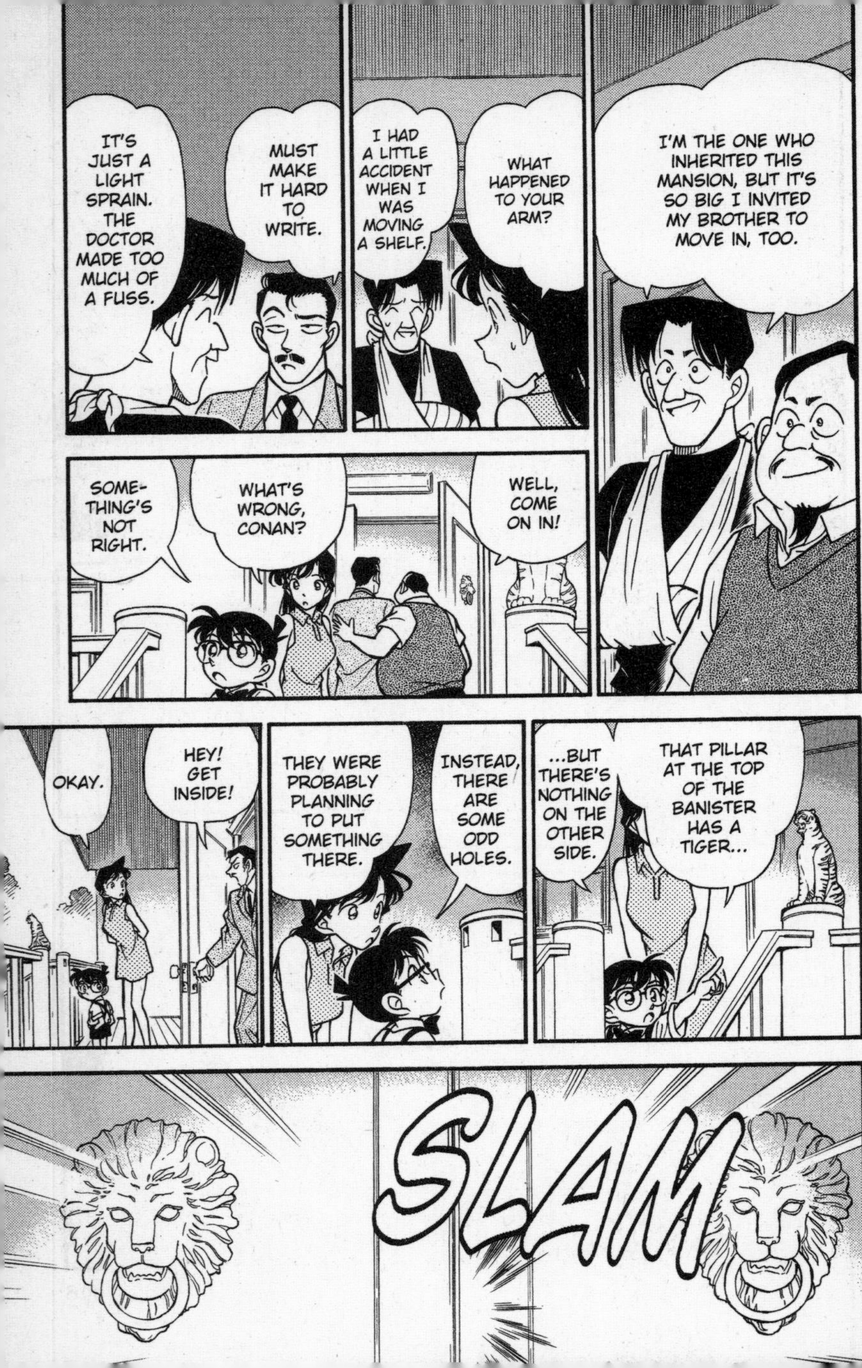
I'M THE ONE WHO INHERITED THIS MANSION, BUT IT'S SO BIG I INVITED MY BROTHER TO MOVE IN, TOO.
WHAT HAPPENED TO YOUR ARM?
I HAD A LITTLE ACCIDENT WHEN I WAS MOVING A SHELF.
MUST MAKE IT HARD TO WRITE.
IT'S JUST A LIGHT SPRAIN. THE DOCTOR MADE TOO MUCH OF A FUSS.
WELL, COME ON IN!
WHAT'S WRONG, CONAN?
SOME-THING'S NOT RIGHT.
THAT PILLAR AT THE TOP OF THE BANISTER HAS A TIGER...
...BUT THERE'S NOTHING ON THE OTHER SIDE.
INSTEAD, THERE ARE SOME ODD HOLES.
THEY WERE PROBABLY PLANNING TO PUT SOMETHING THERE.
HEY! GET INSIDE!
OKAY.
SLAM

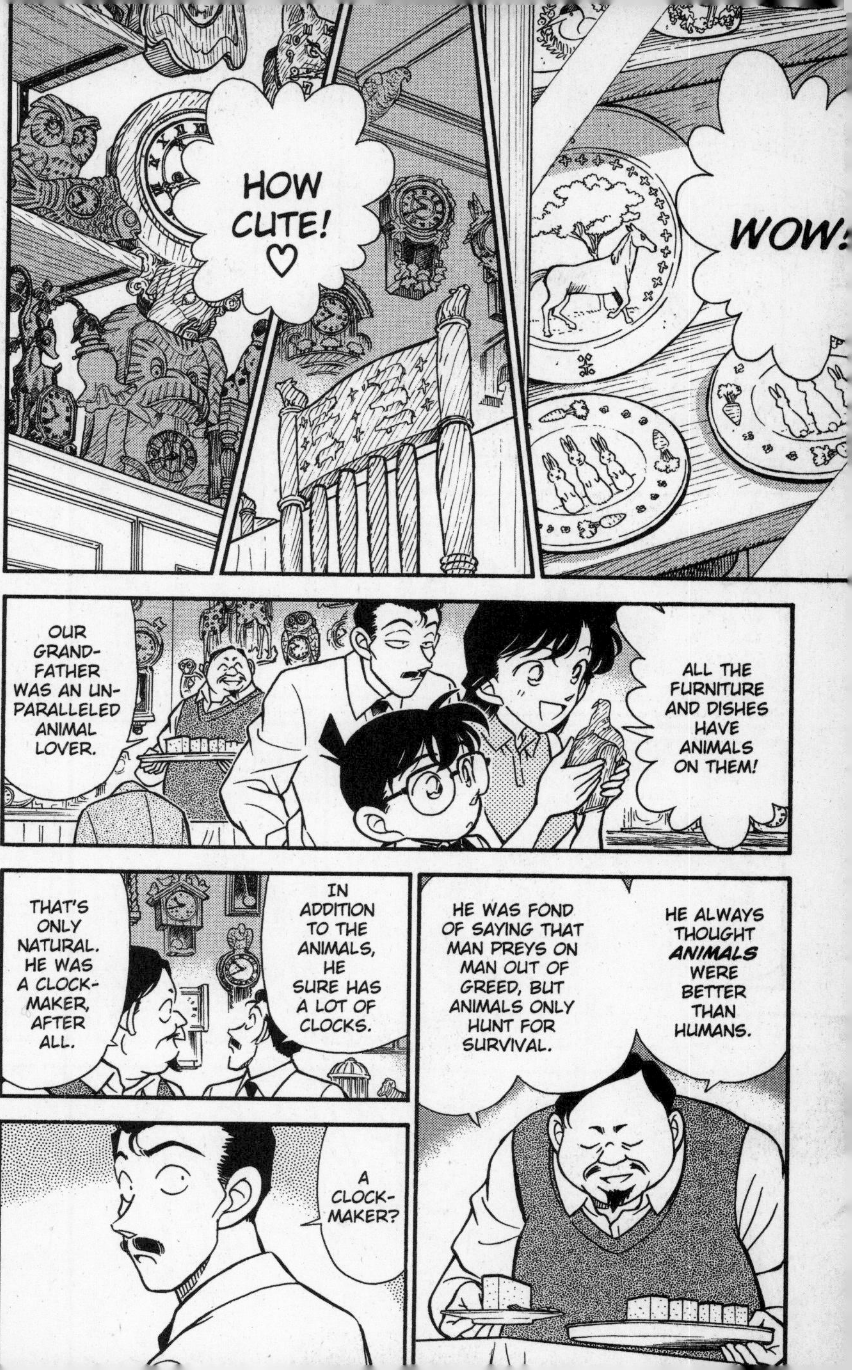

WOW!
HOW CUTE! ♡
ALL THE FURNITURE AND DISHES HAVE ANIMALS ON THEM!
OUR GRANDFATHER WAS AN UNPARALLELED ANIMAL LOVER.
HE ALWAYS THOUGHT *ANIMALS* WERE BETTER THAN HUMANS.
HE WAS FOND OF SAYING THAT MAN PREYS ON MAN OUT OF GREED, BUT ANIMALS ONLY HUNT FOR SURVIVAL.
IN ADDITION TO THE ANIMALS, HE SURE HAS A LOT OF CLOCKS.
THAT'S ONLY NATURAL. HE WAS A CLOCKMAKER, AFTER ALL.
A CLOCKMAKER?

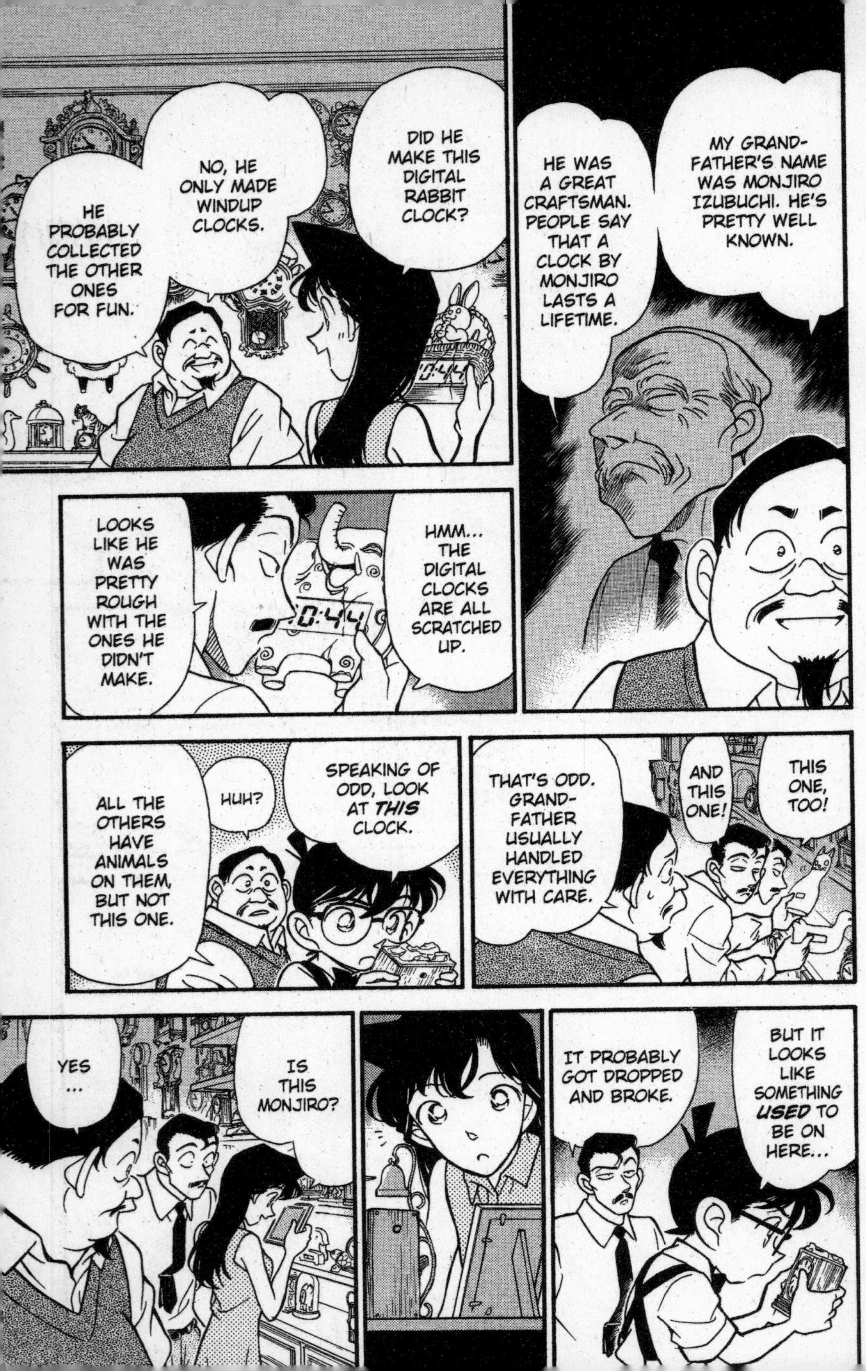
MY GRAND-FATHER'S NAME WAS MONJIRO IZUBUCHI. HE'S PRETTY WELL KNOWN.
HE WAS A GREAT CRAFTSMAN. PEOPLE SAY THAT A CLOCK BY MONJIRO LASTS A LIFETIME.
DID HE MAKE THIS DIGITAL RABBIT CLOCK?
NO, HE ONLY MADE WINDUP CLOCKS.
HE PROBABLY COLLECTED THE OTHER ONES FOR FUN.
HMM... THE DIGITAL CLOCKS ARE ALL SCRATCHED UP.
LOOKS LIKE HE WAS PRETTY ROUGH WITH THE ONES HE DIDN'T MAKE.
THIS ONE, TOO!
AND THIS ONE!
THAT'S ODD. GRAND-FATHER USUALLY HANDLED EVERYTHING WITH CARE.
SPEAKING OF ODD, LOOK AT *THIS* CLOCK.
HUH?
ALL THE OTHERS HAVE ANIMALS ON THEM, BUT NOT THIS ONE.
BUT IT LOOKS LIKE SOMETHING ***USED*** TO BE ON HERE...
IT PROBABLY GOT DROPPED AND BROKE.
IS THIS MONJIRO?
YES ...

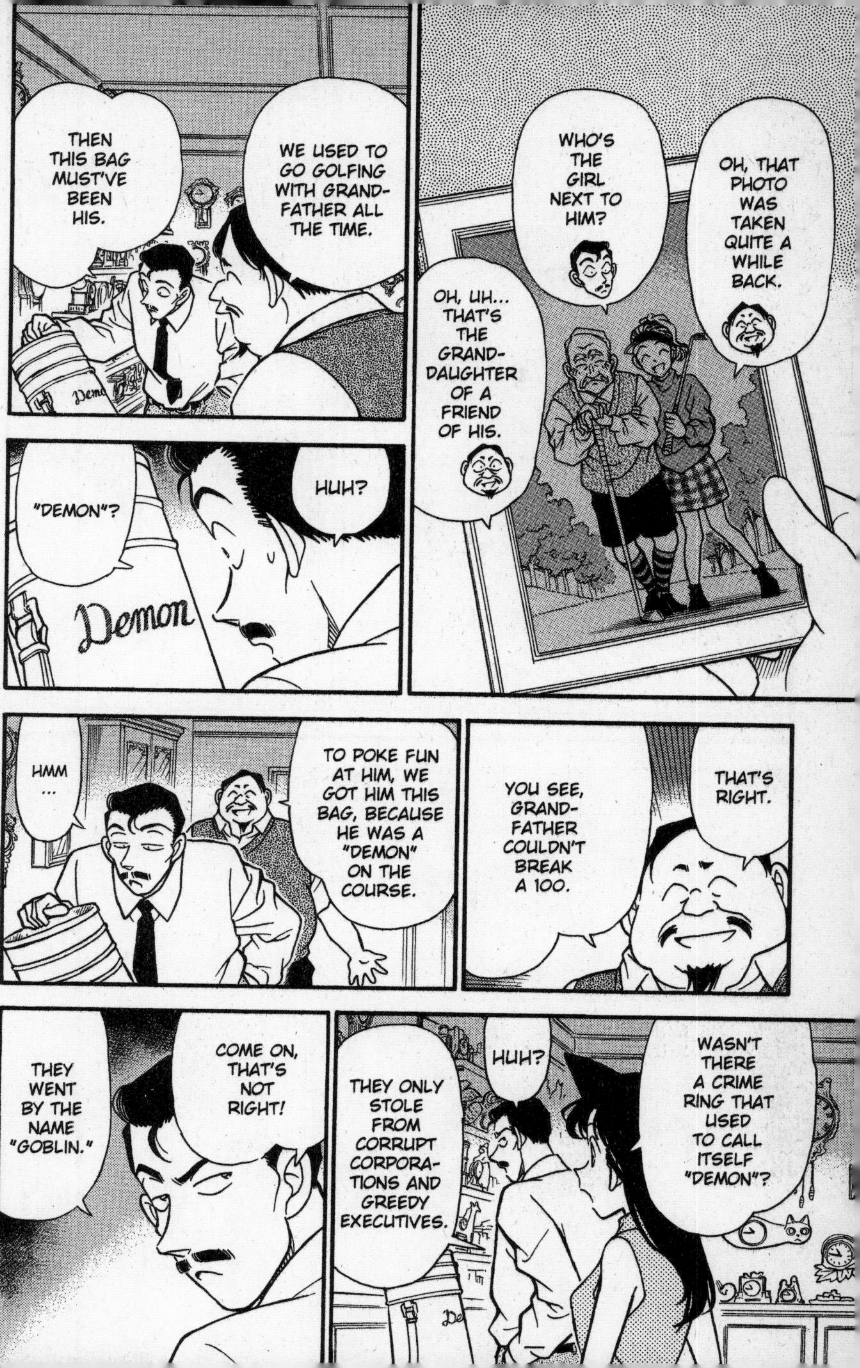
OH, THAT PHOTO WAS TAKEN QUITE A WHILE BACK.
WHO'S THE GIRL NEXT TO HIM?
OH, UH... THAT'S THE GRANDDAUGHTER OF A FRIEND OF HIS.
WE USED TO GO GOLFING WITH GRANDFATHER ALL THE TIME.
THEN THIS BAG MUST'VE BEEN HIS.
HUH?
"DEMON"?
Demon
THAT'S RIGHT.
YOU SEE, GRANDFATHER COULDN'T BREAK A 100.
TO POKE FUN AT HIM, WE GOT HIM THIS BAG, BECAUSE HE WAS A "DEMON" ON THE COURSE.
HMM ...
WASN'T THERE A CRIME RING THAT USED TO CALL ITSELF "DEMON"?
HUH?
THEY ONLY STOLE FROM CORRUPT CORPORATIONS AND GREEDY EXECUTIVES.
COME ON, THAT'S NOT RIGHT!
THEY WENT BY THE NAME "GOBLIN."

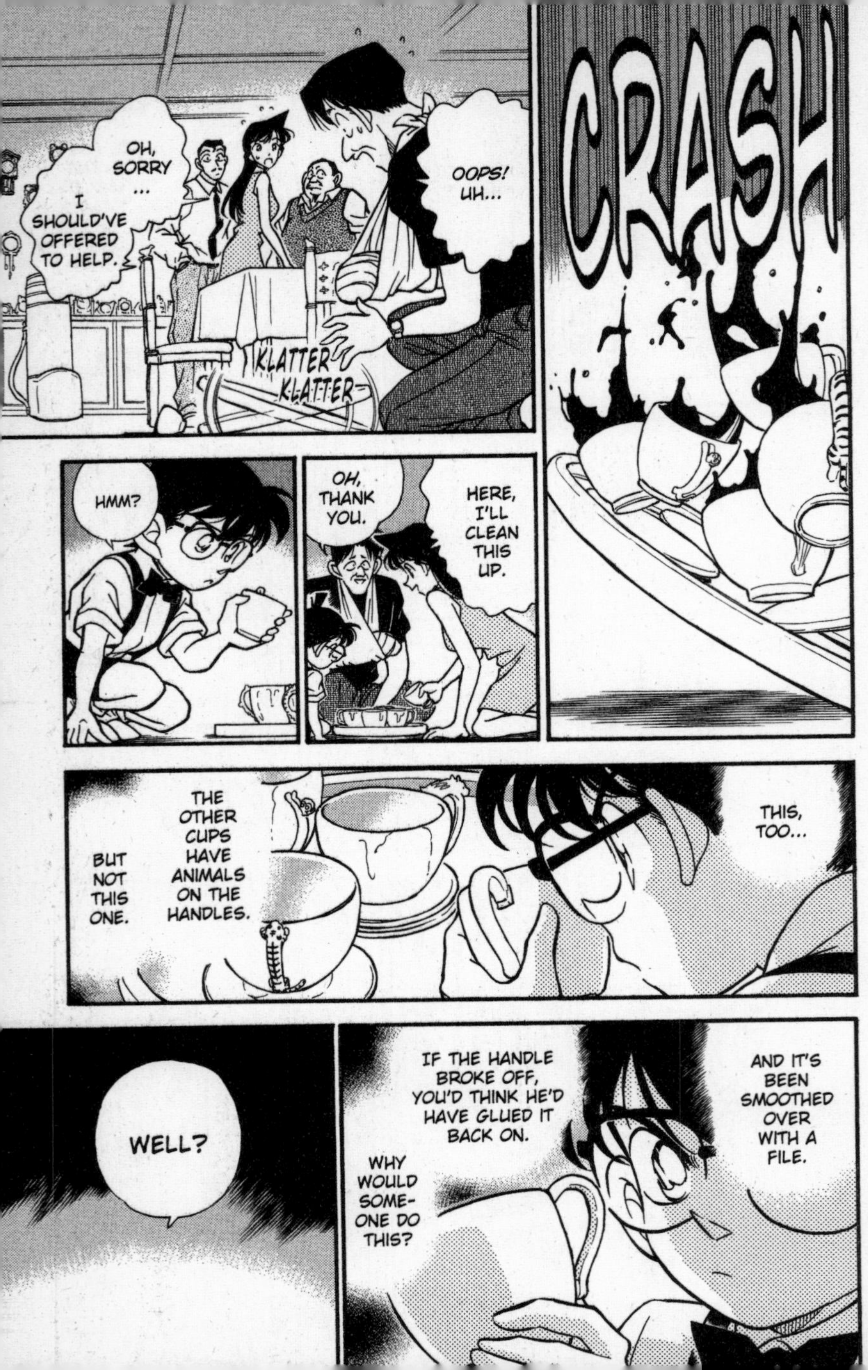
CRASH
OOPS! UH...
OH, SORRY ... I SHOULD'VE OFFERED TO HELP.
KLATTER KLATTER
HERE, I'LL CLEAN THIS UP.
OH, THANK YOU.
HMM?
THIS, TOO...
THE OTHER CUPS HAVE ANIMALS ON THE HANDLES.
BUT NOT THIS ONE.
AND IT'S BEEN SMOOTHED OVER WITH A FILE.
IF THE HANDLE BROKE OFF, YOU'D THINK HE'D HAVE GLUED IT BACK ON.
WHY WOULD SOME-ONE DO THIS?
WELL?

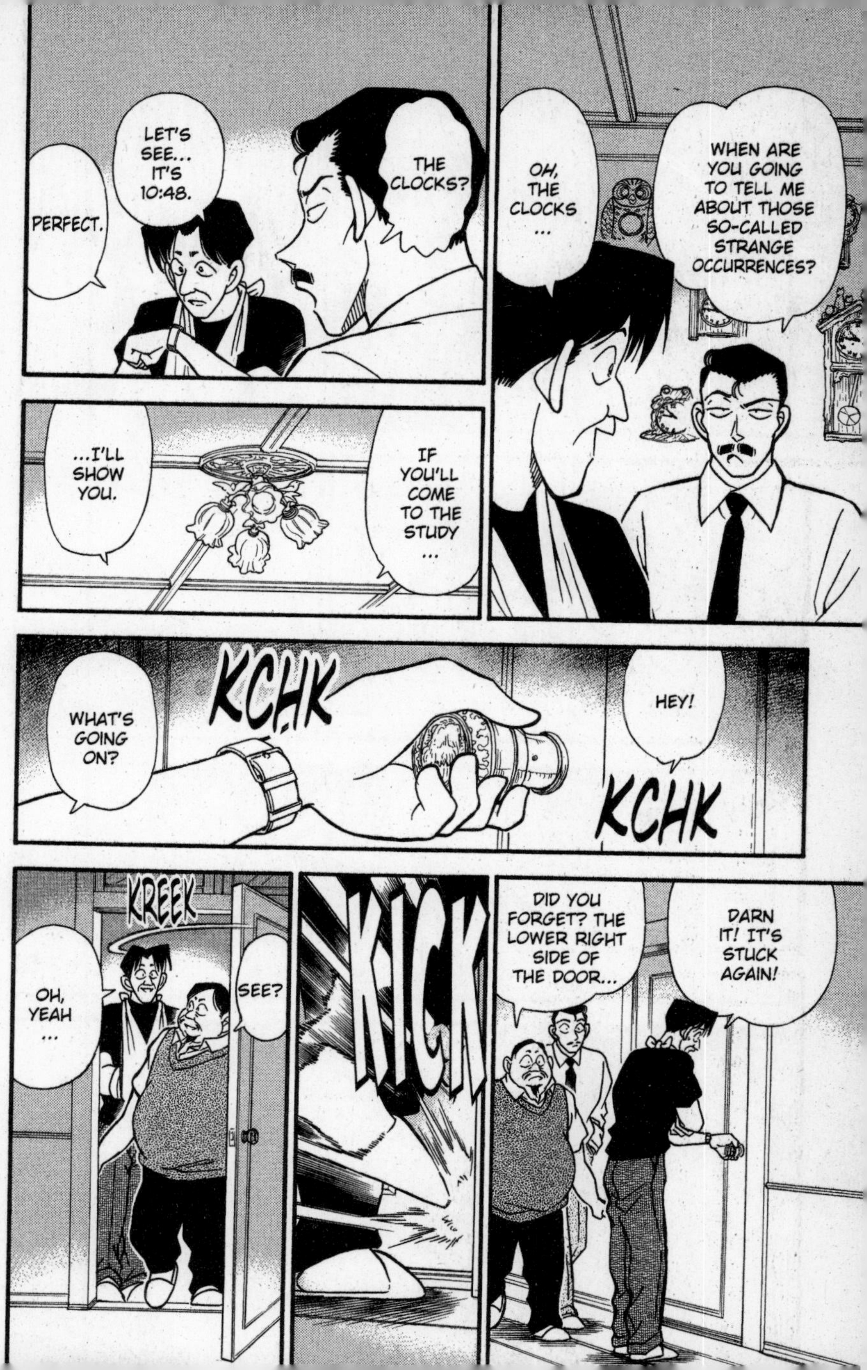
WHEN ARE YOU GOING TO TELL ME ABOUT THOSE SO-CALLED STRANGE OCCURRENCES?
OH, THE CLOCKS ...
THE CLOCKS?
LET'S SEE... IT'S 10:48.
PERFECT.
IF YOU'LL COME TO THE STUDY ...
...I'LL SHOW YOU.
HEY!
KCHK
WHAT'S GOING ON?
KCHK
DARN IT! IT'S STUCK AGAIN!
DID YOU FORGET? THE LOWER RIGHT SIDE OF THE DOOR...
KICK
KREEK
SEE?
OH, YEAH ...

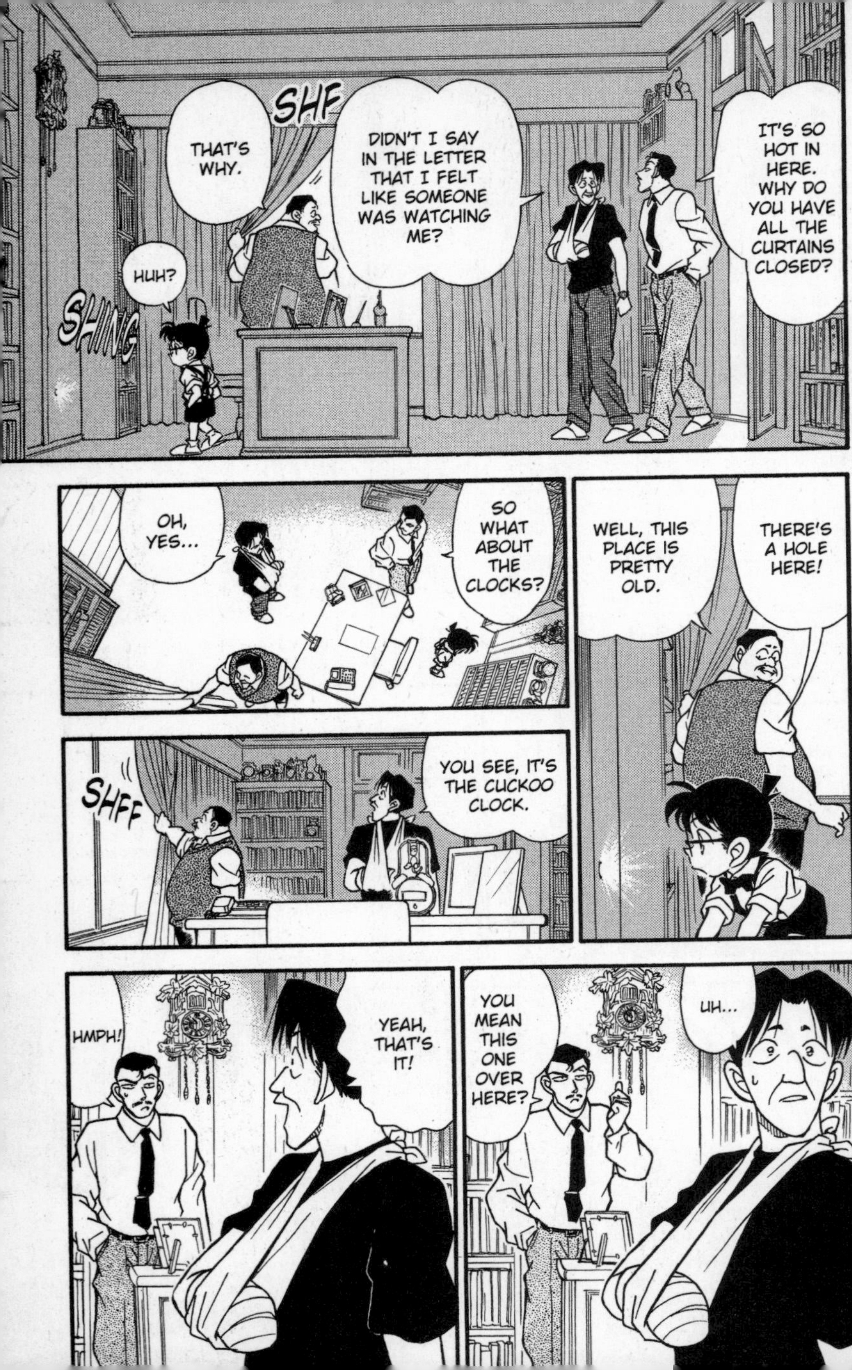

IT'S SO HOT IN HERE. WHY DO YOU HAVE ALL THE CURTAINS CLOSED?
SHF
DIDN'T I SAY IN THE LETTER THAT I FELT LIKE SOMEONE WAS WATCHING ME?
THAT'S WHY.
HUH?
SHING
THERE'S A HOLE HERE!
WELL, THIS PLACE IS PRETTY OLD.
SO WHAT ABOUT THE CLOCKS?
OH, YES...
YOU SEE, IT'S THE CUCKOO CLOCK.
SHFF
UH...
YOU MEAN THIS ONE OVER HERE?
YEAH, THAT'S IT!
HMPH!

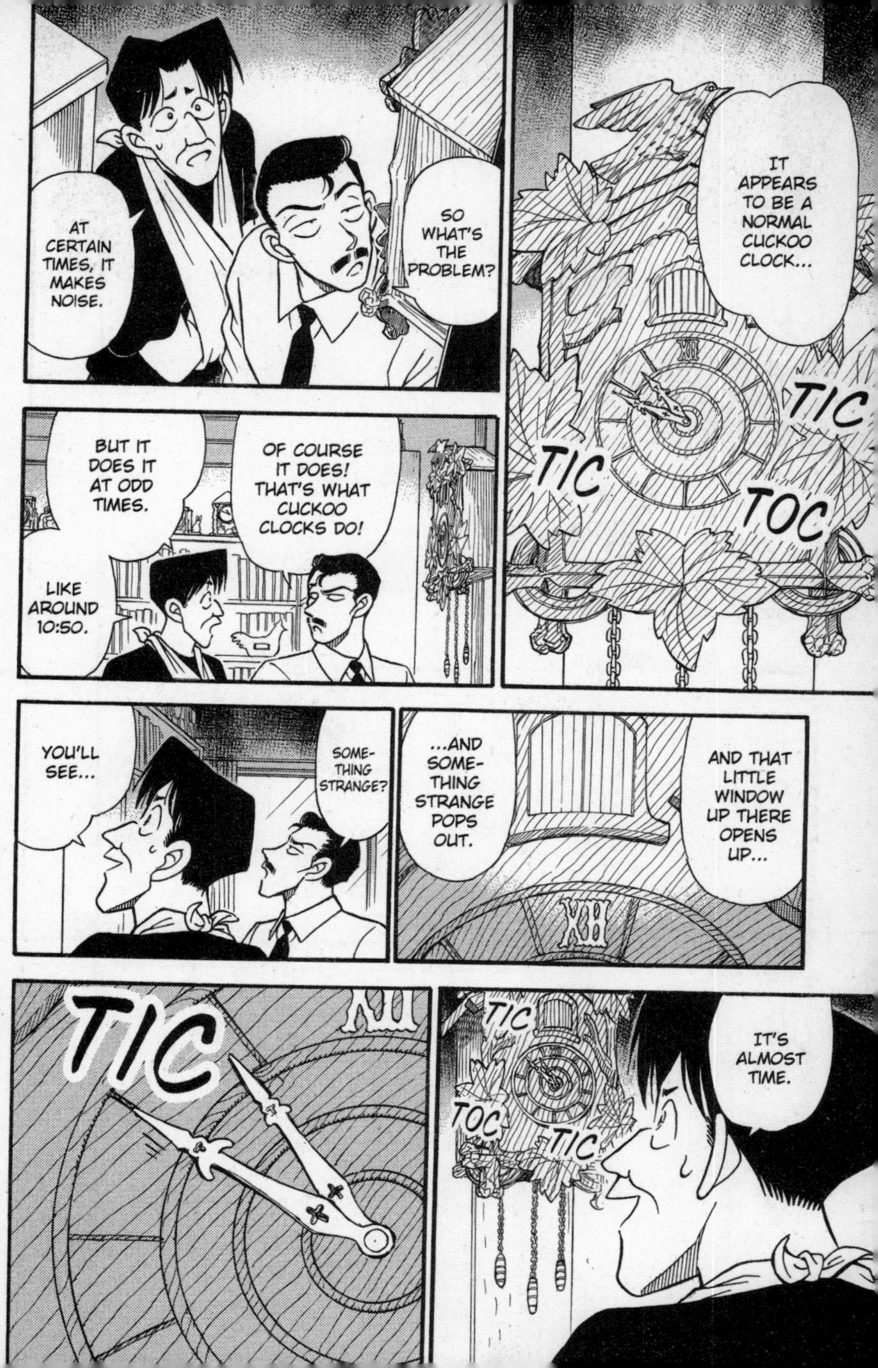
IT APPEARS TO BE A NORMAL CUCKOO CLOCK...
TIC
TIC
TOC
SO WHAT'S THE PROBLEM?
AT CERTAIN TIMES, IT MAKES NOISE.
OF COURSE IT DOES! THAT'S WHAT CUCKOO CLOCKS DO!
BUT IT DOES IT AT ODD TIMES.
LIKE AROUND 10:50.
AND THAT LITTLE WINDOW UP THERE OPENS UP...
...AND SOMETHING STRANGE POPS OUT.
SOMETHING STRANGE?
YOU'LL SEE...
IT'S ALMOST TIME.
TIC
TOC
TIC
TIC

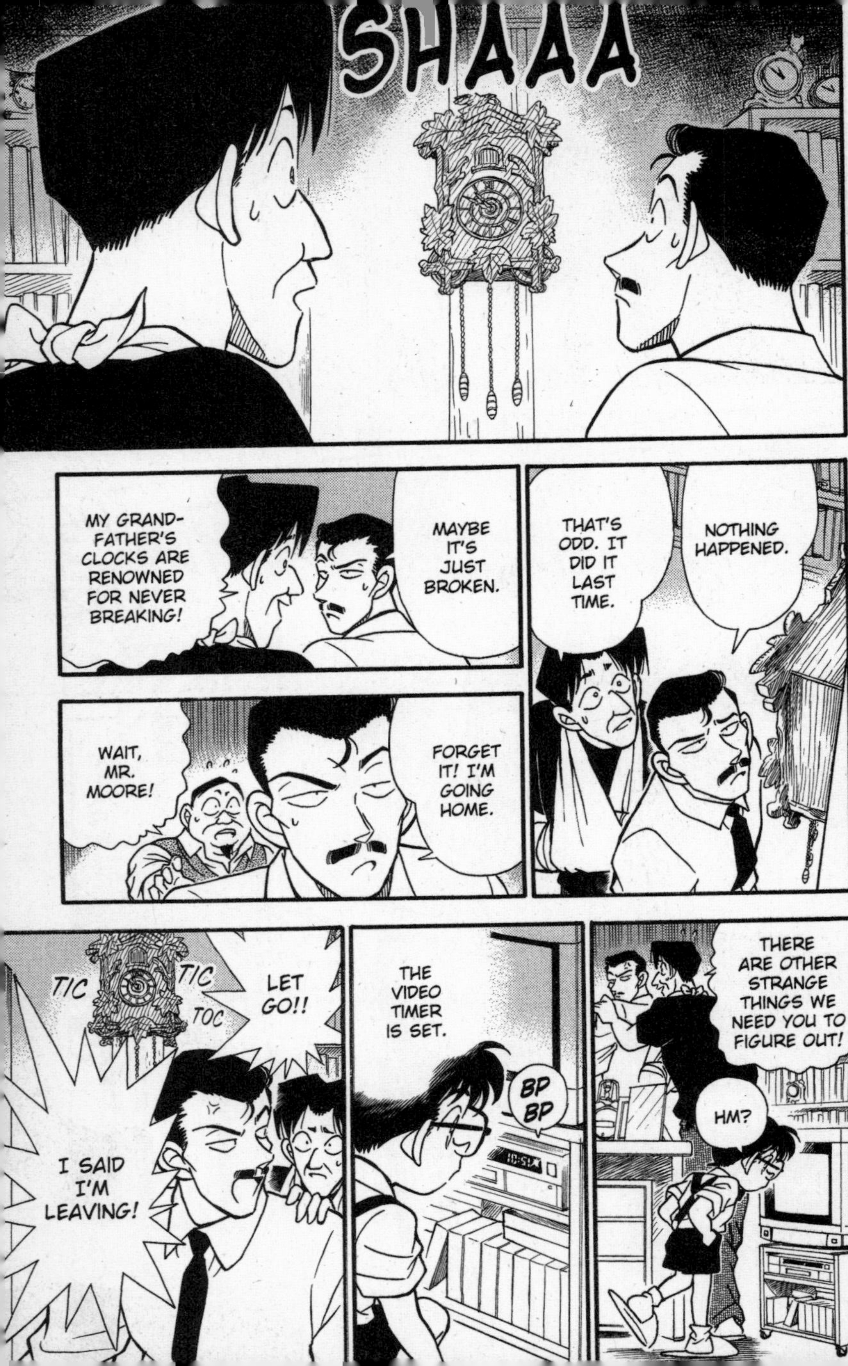
SHAAA
NOTHING HAPPENED.
THAT'S ODD. IT DID IT LAST TIME.
MAYBE IT'S JUST BROKEN.
MY GRAND-FATHER'S CLOCKS ARE RENOWNED FOR NEVER BREAKING!
FORGET IT! I'M GOING HOME.
WAIT, MR. MOORE!
THERE ARE OTHER STRANGE THINGS WE NEED YOU TO FIGURE OUT!
HM?
THE VIDEO TIMER IS SET.
BP BP
TIC
TIC
TOC
LET GO!!
I SAID I'M LEAVING!

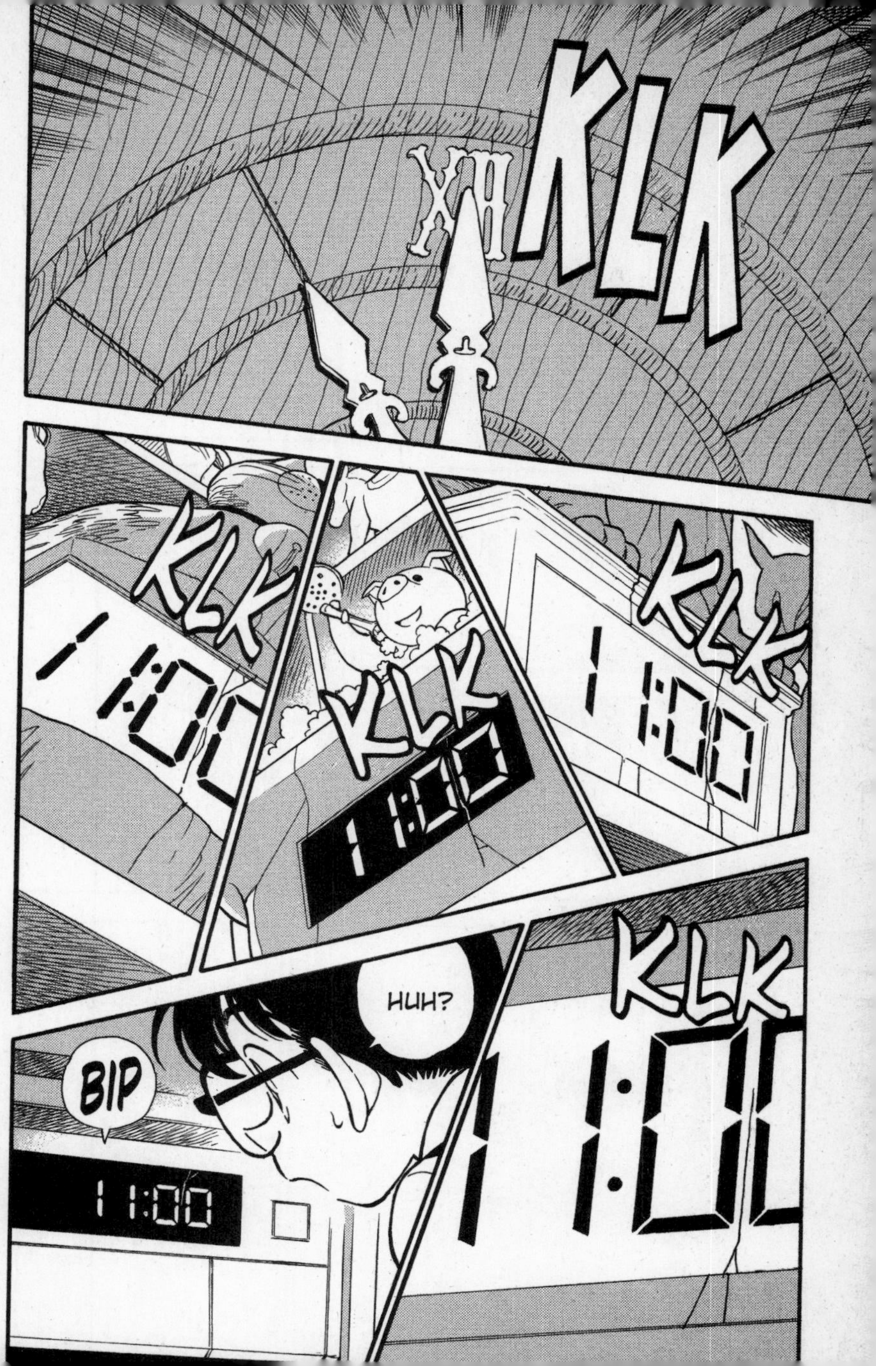
XII
KLK
KLK
11:00
KLK
11:00
KLK
KLK
HUH?
BIP
11:00

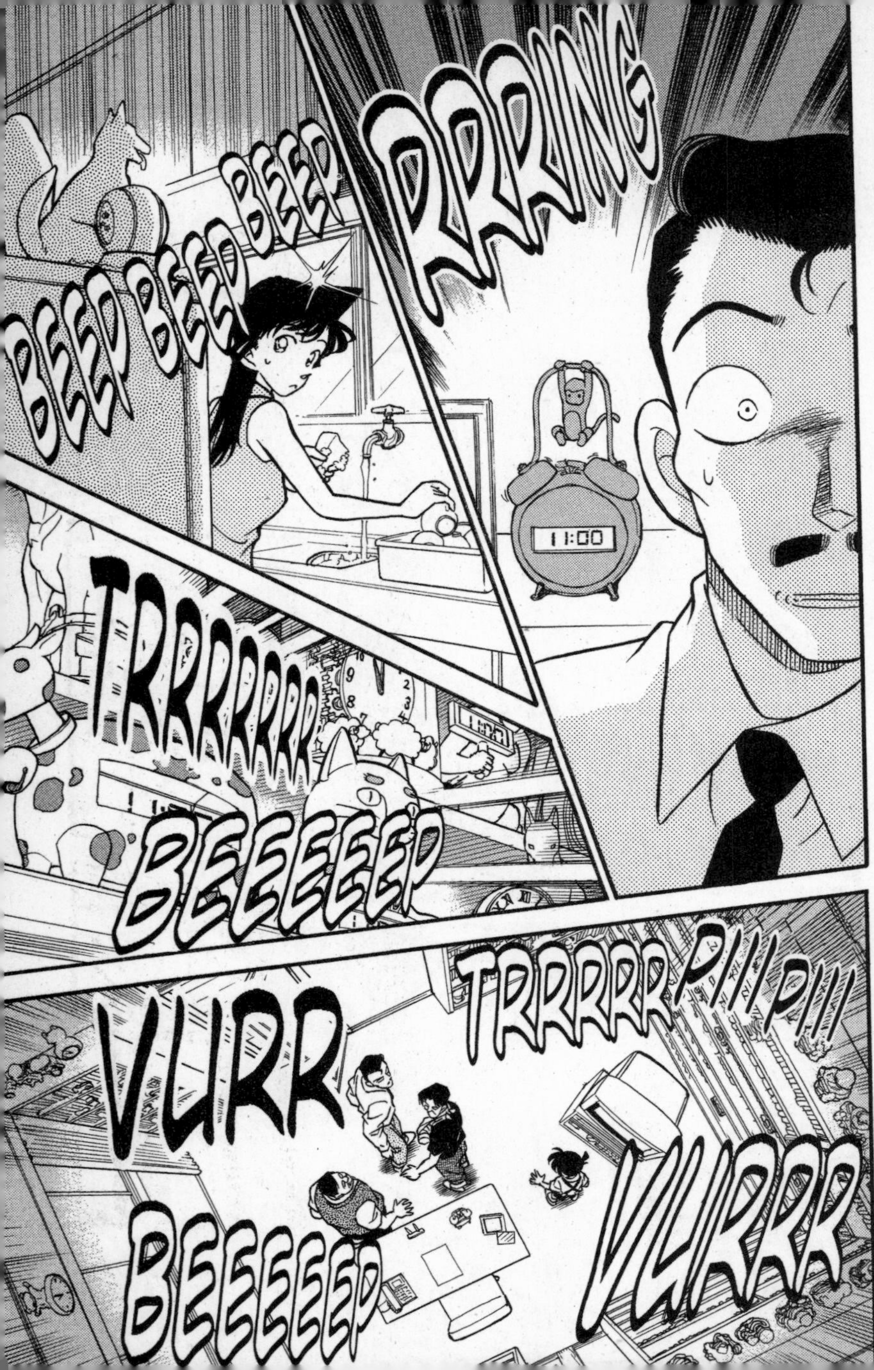
RRRING
11:00
BEEP BEEP BEEP
TRRRRRRR
BEEEEEEP
TRRRRR PIII PIII
VURRRR
VURR
BEEEEEEP

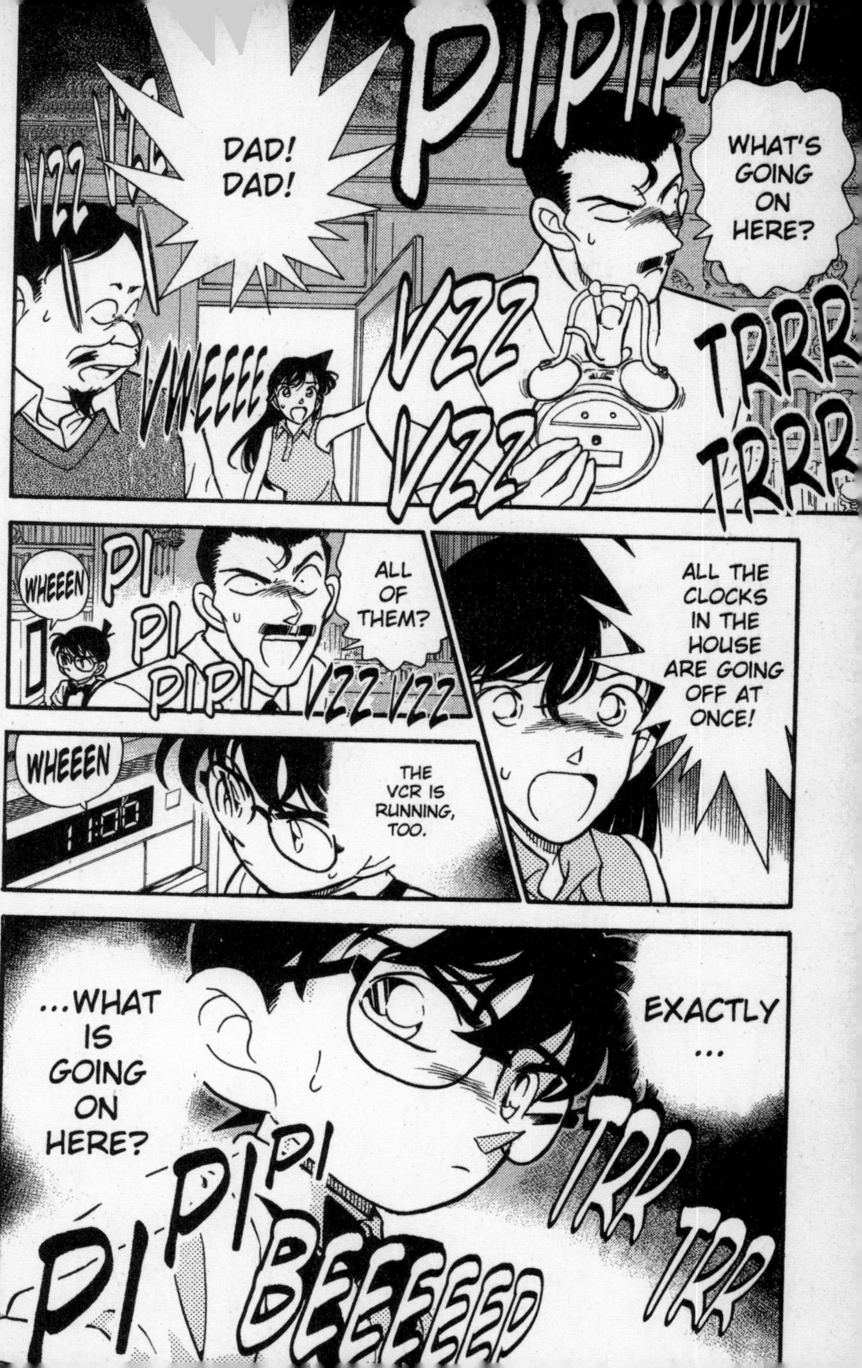
PIPIPIPIPIPI
WHAT'S GOING ON HERE?
TRRR TRRR
VZZ VZZ
DAD! DAD!
VWEEEE
VZZ VZZ
ALL THE CLOCKS IN THE HOUSE ARE GOING OFF AT ONCE!
ALL OF THEM?
WHEEEN
PI PI PIPI
VZZ VZZ
THE VCR IS RUNNING, TOO.
WHEEEN
11:00
EXACTLY ...
...WHAT IS GOING ON HERE?
TRR TRR
BEEEEEP
PI PI PI PI

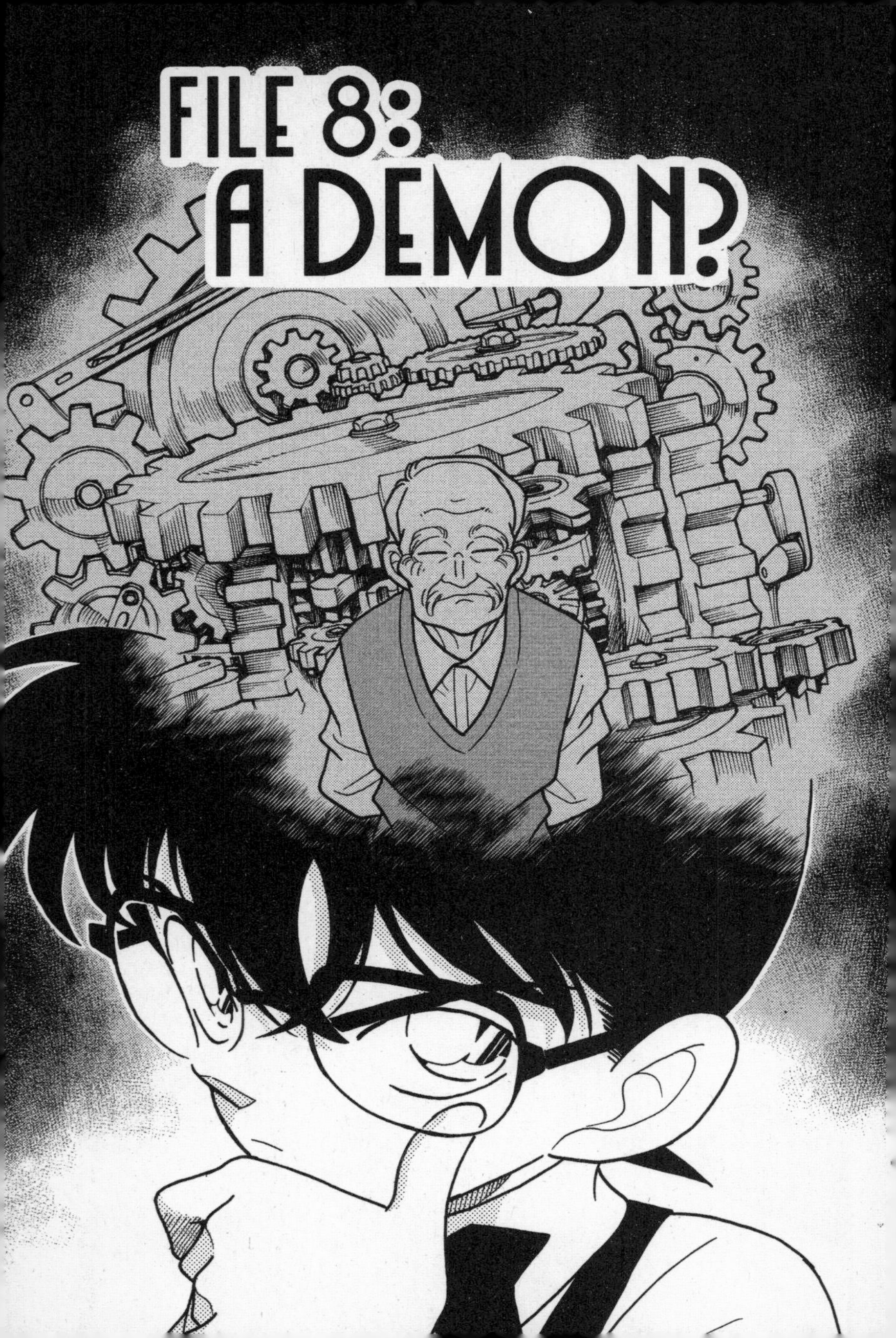
FILE 8:
A DEMON?

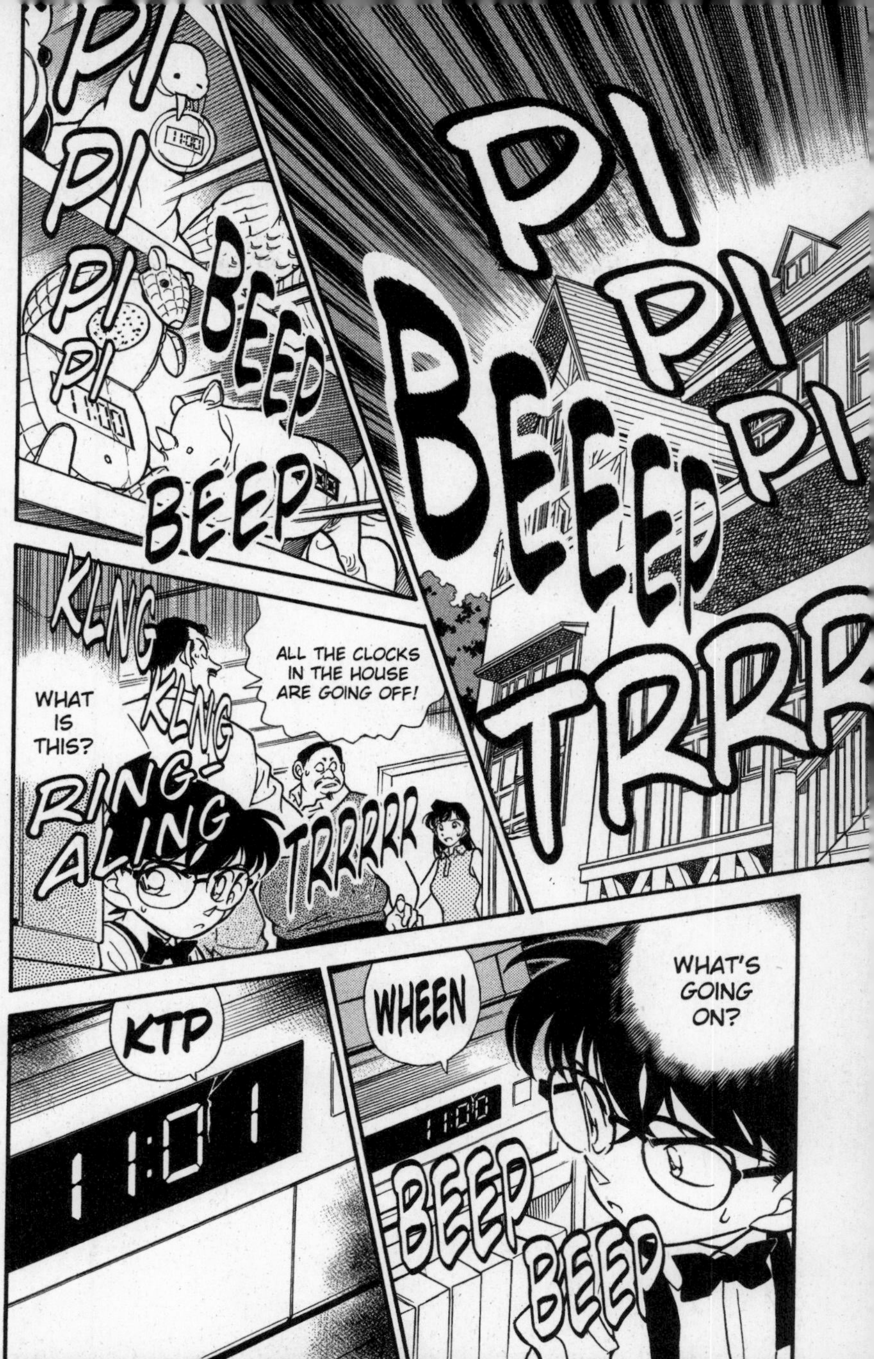
PI
PI
BEEEEP
PI
PI
TRRR
PI
PI
PI
PI
BEEP
BEEP
ALL THE CLOCKS IN THE HOUSE ARE GOING OFF!
WHAT IS THIS?
KLNG
KLNG
TRRRRR
RING-A-LING
WHAT'S GOING ON?
WHEEN
BEEP
BEEP
KTP
11:01

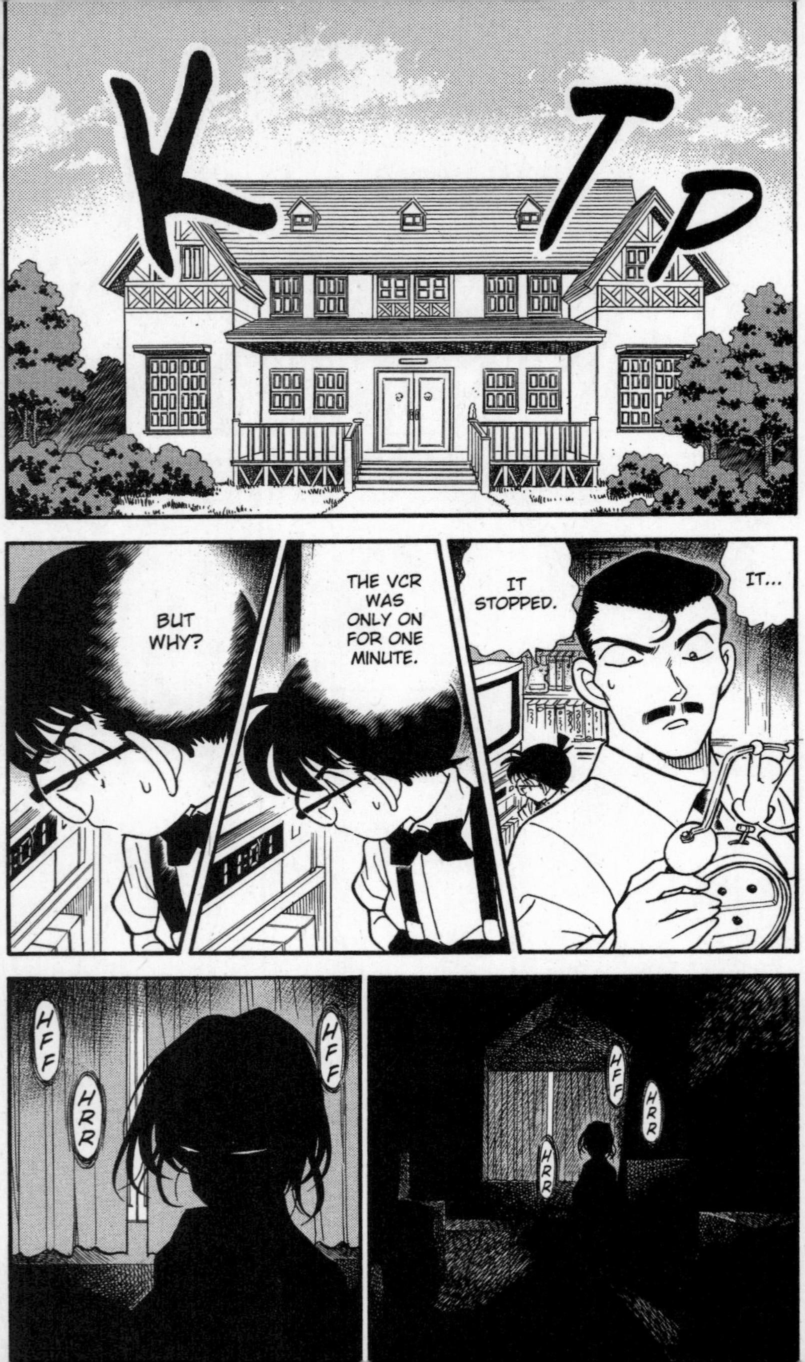
IT...
IT STOPPED.
THE VCR WAS ONLY ON FOR ONE MINUTE.
BUT WHY?
HFF
HRR
HRR
HFF
HRR
HFF

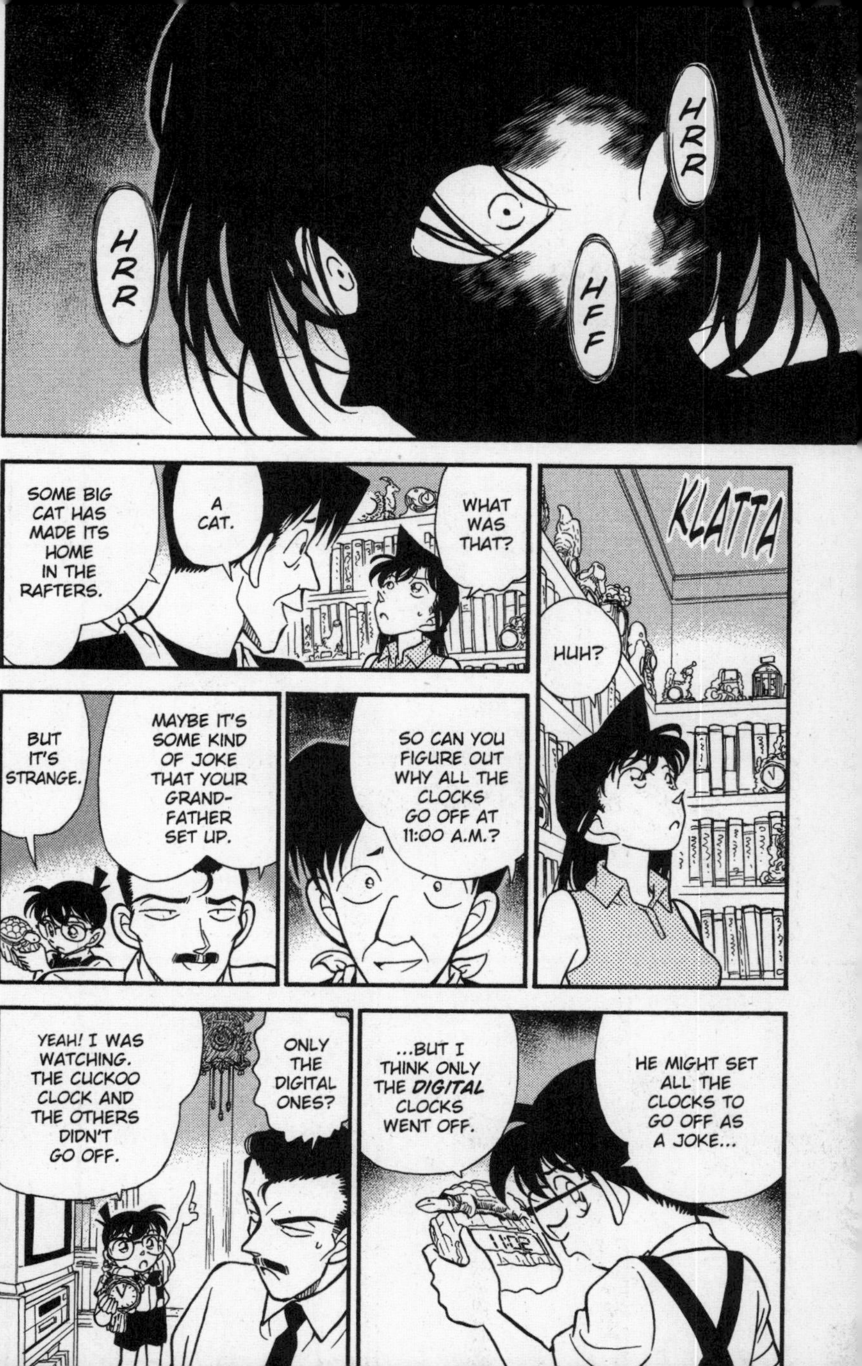
HRR
HFF
HRR
KLATTA
HUH?
WHAT WAS THAT?
A CAT.
SOME BIG CAT HAS MADE ITS HOME IN THE RAFTERS.
SO CAN YOU FIGURE OUT WHY ALL THE CLOCKS GO OFF AT 11:00 A.M.?
MAYBE IT'S SOME KIND OF JOKE THAT YOUR GRAND-FATHER SET UP.
BUT IT'S STRANGE.
HE MIGHT SET ALL THE CLOCKS TO GO OFF AS A JOKE...
...BUT I THINK ONLY THE *DIGITAL* CLOCKS WENT OFF.
ONLY THE DIGITAL ONES?
YEAH! I WAS WATCHING. THE CUCKOO CLOCK AND THE OTHERS DIDN'T GO OFF.

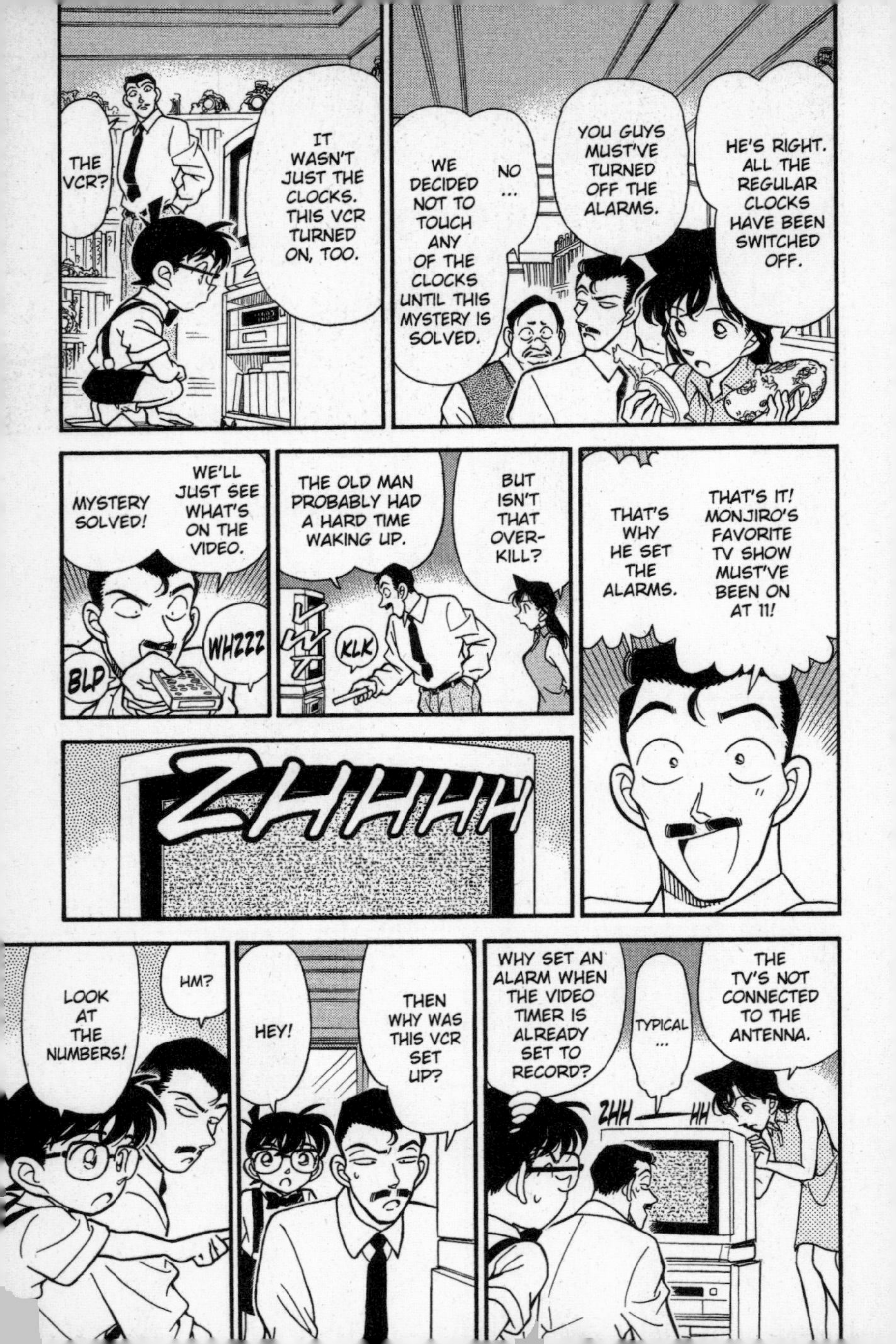

HE'S RIGHT. ALL THE REGULAR CLOCKS HAVE BEEN SWITCHED OFF.
YOU GUYS MUST'VE TURNED OFF THE ALARMS.
NO ...
WE DECIDED NOT TO TOUCH ANY OF THE CLOCKS UNTIL THIS MYSTERY IS SOLVED.
IT WASN'T JUST THE CLOCKS. THIS VCR TURNED ON, TOO.
THE VCR?
THAT'S IT! MONJIRO'S FAVORITE TV SHOW MUST'VE BEEN ON AT 11!
THAT'S WHY HE SET THE ALARMS.
BUT ISN'T THAT OVER-KILL?
THE OLD MAN PROBABLY HAD A HARD TIME WAKING UP.
KLK
WE'LL JUST SEE WHAT'S ON THE VIDEO.
MYSTERY SOLVED!
WHZZZ
BLP
ZHHHH
THE TV'S NOT CONNECTED TO THE ANTENNA.
TYPICAL ...
WHY SET AN ALARM WHEN THE VIDEO TIMER IS ALREADY SET TO RECORD?
ZHH—HH
THEN WHY WAS THIS VCR SET UP?
HEY!
HM?
LOOK AT THE NUMBERS!

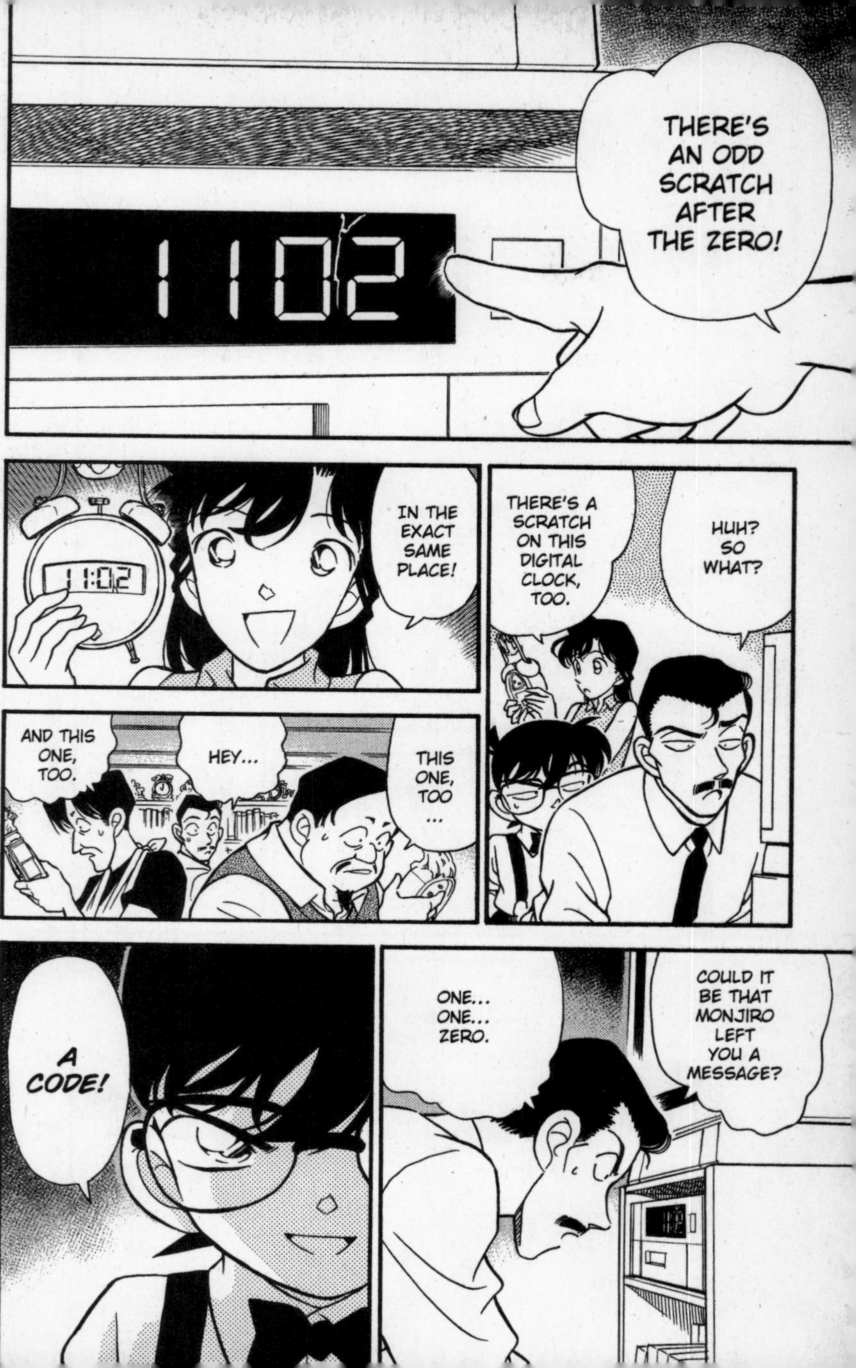
THERE'S AN ODD SCRATCH AFTER THE ZERO!
HUH? SO WHAT?
THERE'S A SCRATCH ON THIS DIGITAL CLOCK, TOO.
IN THE EXACT SAME PLACE!
THIS ONE, TOO ...
HEY...
AND THIS ONE, TOO.
COULD IT BE THAT MONJIRO LEFT YOU A MESSAGE?
ONE... ONE... ZERO.
A CODE!

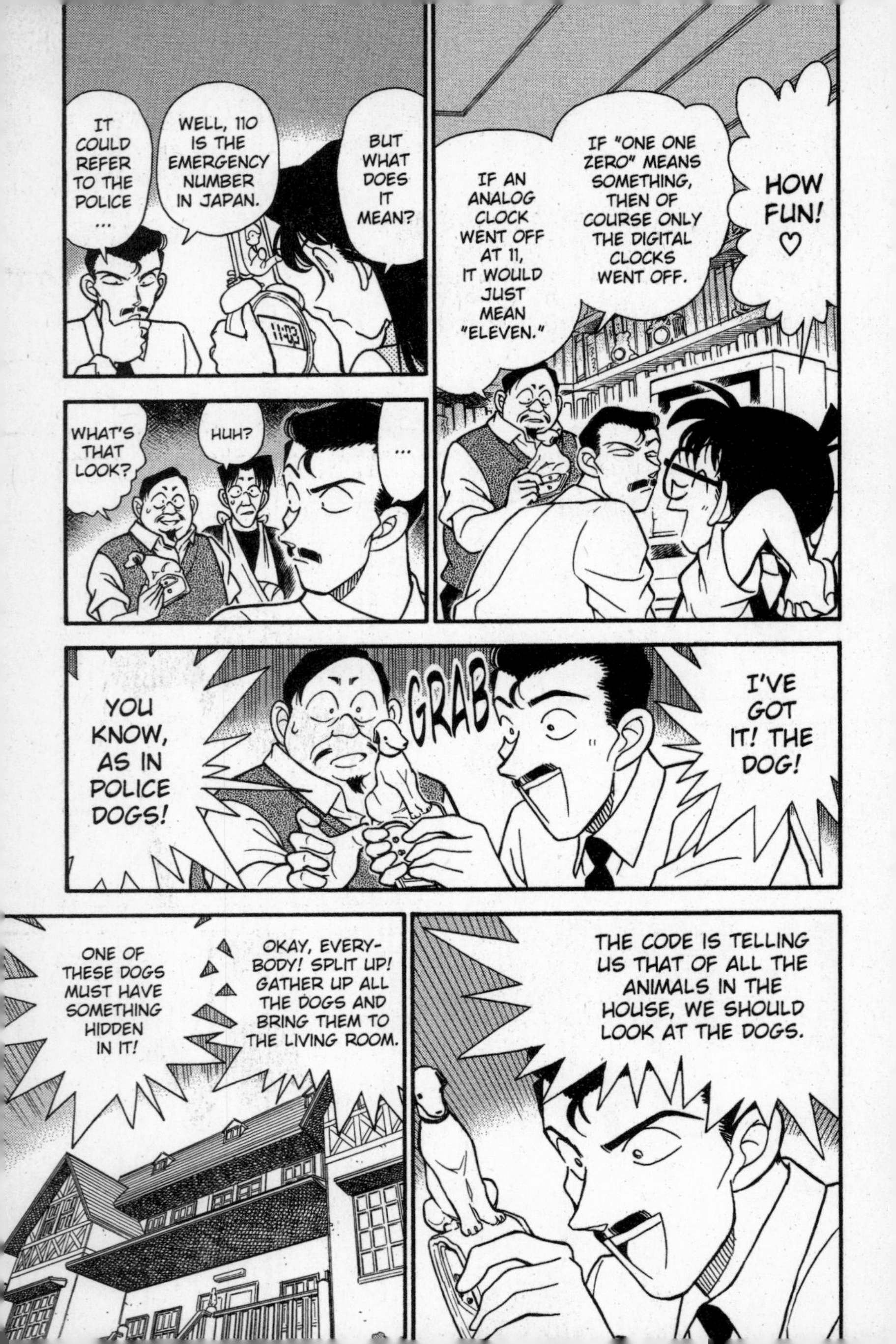
HOW FUN! ♡
IF "ONE ONE ZERO" MEANS SOMETHING, THEN OF COURSE ONLY THE DIGITAL CLOCKS WENT OFF.
IF AN ANALOG CLOCK WENT OFF AT 11, IT WOULD JUST MEAN "ELEVEN."
BUT WHAT DOES IT MEAN?
WELL, 110 IS THE EMERGENCY NUMBER IN JAPAN.
IT COULD REFER TO THE POLICE ...
...
HUH?
WHAT'S THAT LOOK?
I'VE GOT IT! THE DOG!
GRAB
YOU KNOW, AS IN POLICE DOGS!
THE CODE IS TELLING US THAT OF ALL THE ANIMALS IN THE HOUSE, WE SHOULD LOOK AT THE DOGS.
OKAY, EVERYBODY! SPLIT UP! GATHER UP ALL THE DOGS AND BRING THEM TO THE LIVING ROOM.
ONE OF THESE DOGS MUST HAVE SOMETHING HIDDEN IN IT!

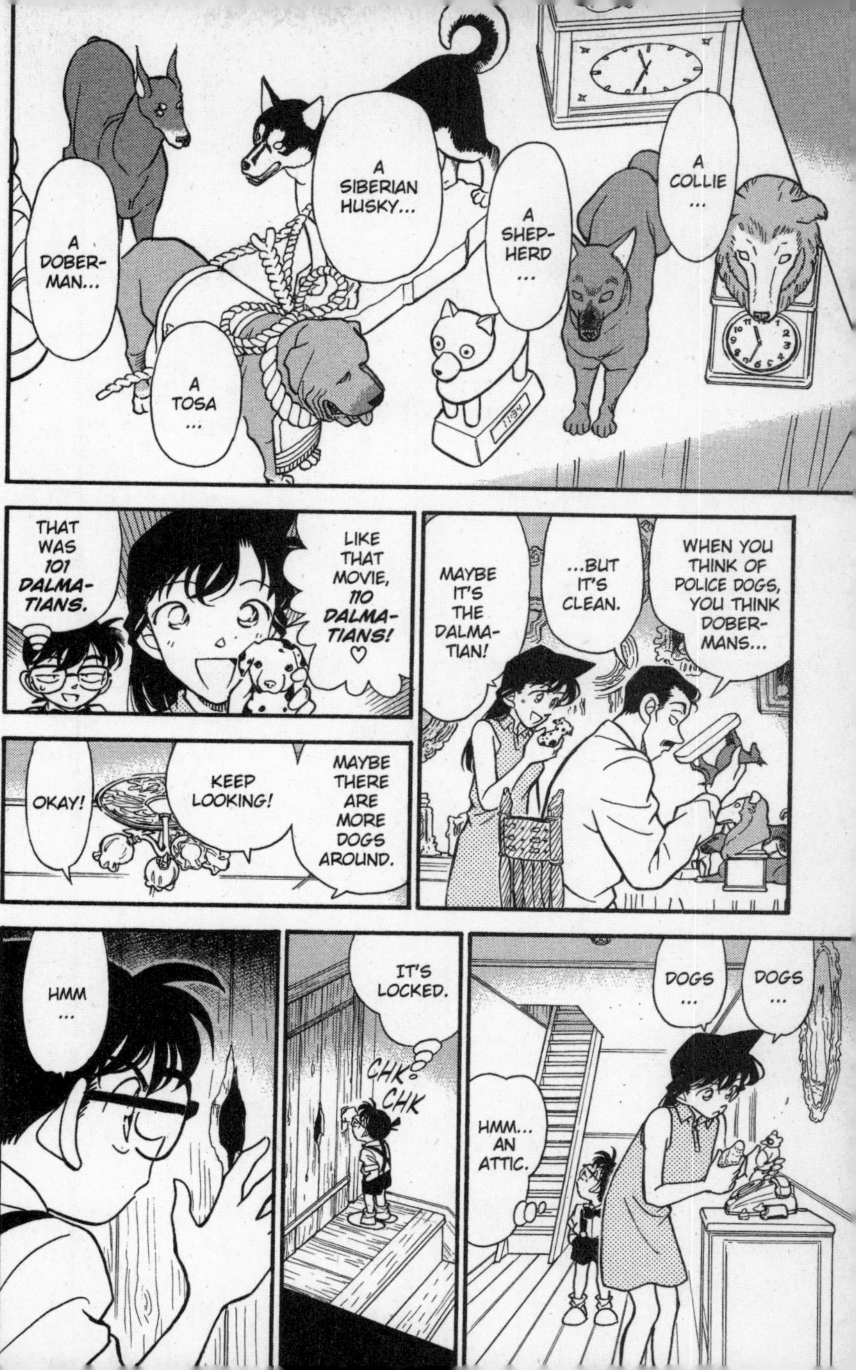

A COLLIE...
A SHEPHERD...
A SIBERIAN HUSKY...
A DOBERMAN...
A TOSA...
WHEN YOU THINK OF POLICE DOGS, YOU THINK DOBERMANS...
...BUT IT'S CLEAN.
MAYBE IT'S THE DALMATIAN!
LIKE THAT MOVIE, *110 DALMATIANS!* ♡
THAT WAS *101 DALMATIANS.*
MAYBE THERE ARE MORE DOGS AROUND.
KEEP LOOKING!
OKAY!
DOGS...
DOGS...
HMM... AN ATTIC.
IT'S LOCKED.
CHK CHK
HMM...

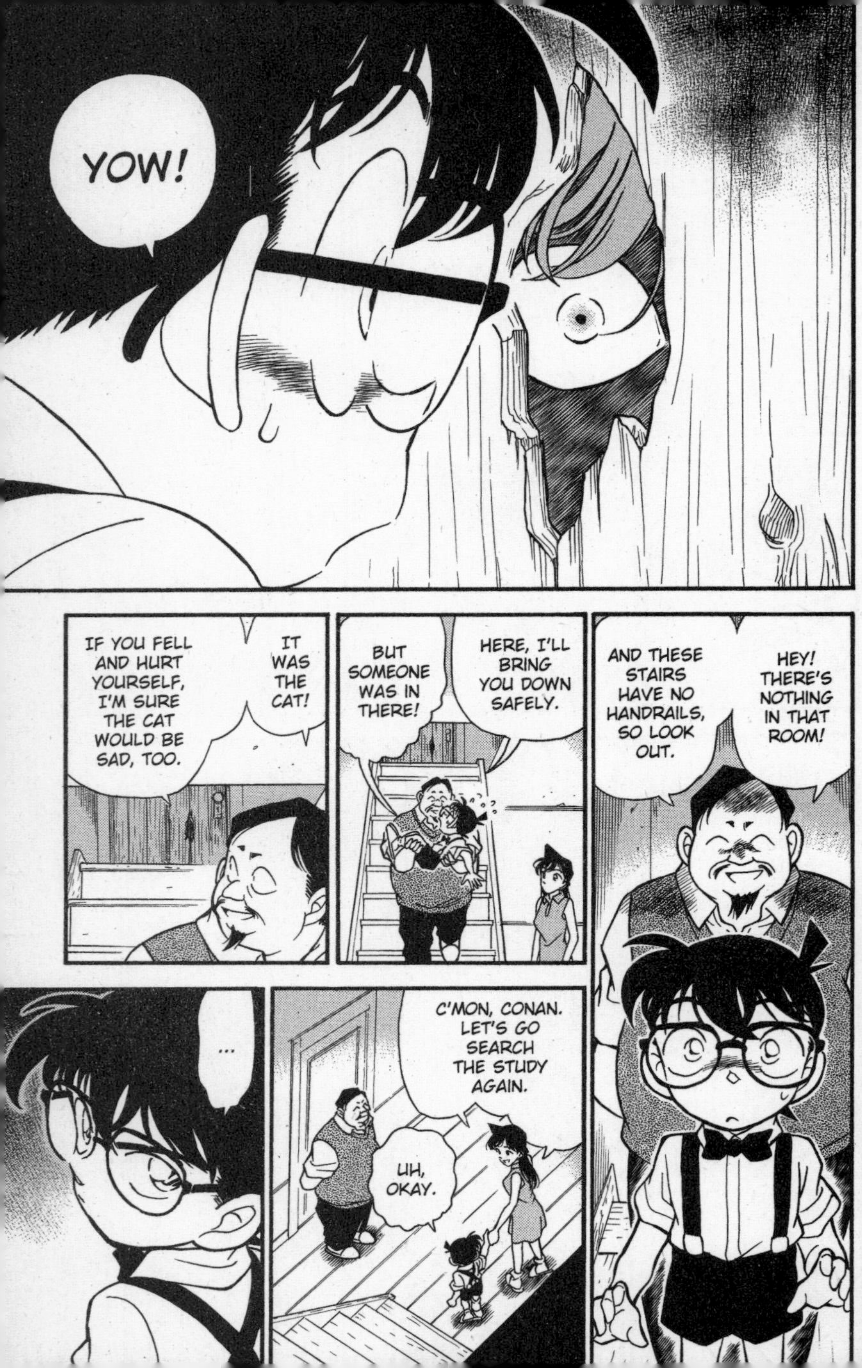
YOW!
HEY! THERE'S NOTHING IN THAT ROOM!
AND THESE STAIRS HAVE NO HANDRAILS, SO LOOK OUT.
HERE, I'LL BRING YOU DOWN SAFELY.
BUT SOMEONE WAS IN THERE!
IT WAS THE CAT!
IF YOU FELL AND HURT YOURSELF, I'M SURE THE CAT WOULD BE SAD, TOO.
C'MON, CONAN. LET'S GO SEARCH THE STUDY AGAIN.
UH, OKAY.
...

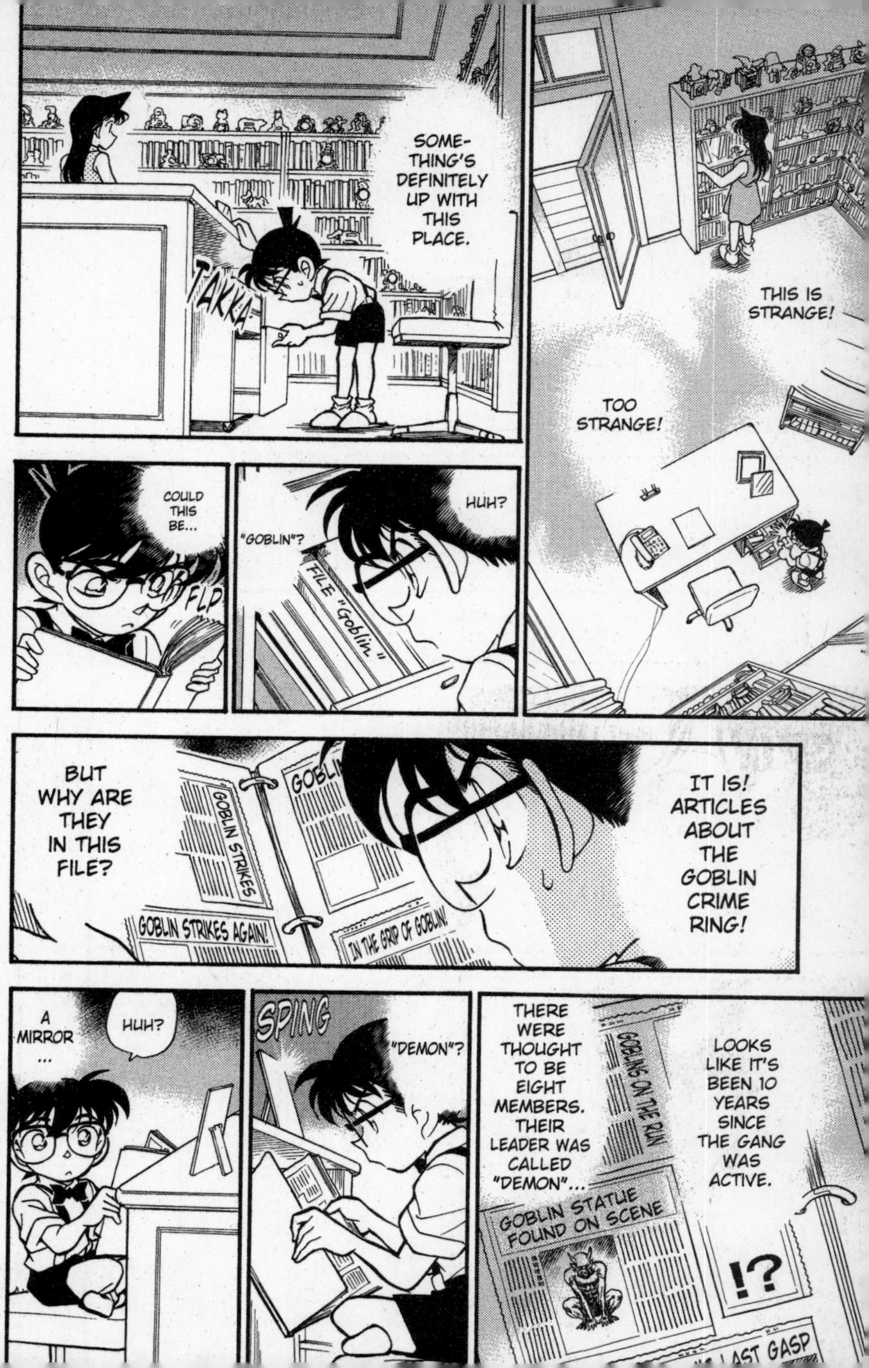
THIS IS STRANGE!
TOO STRANGE!
SOME-THING'S DEFINITELY UP WITH THIS PLACE.
TAKKA
HUH?
"GOBLIN"?
FILE "Goblin"
COULD THIS BE...
FLP
IT IS! ARTICLES ABOUT THE GOBLIN CRIME RING!
GOBLIN STRIKES
GOBLIN STRIKES AGAIN!
IN THE GRIP OF GOBLIN!
BUT WHY ARE THEY IN THIS FILE?
LOOKS LIKE IT'S BEEN 10 YEARS SINCE THE GANG WAS ACTIVE.
THERE WERE THOUGHT TO BE EIGHT MEMBERS. THEIR LEADER WAS CALLED "DEMON"...
GOBLINS ON THE RUN
GOBLIN STATUE FOUND ON SCENE
LAST GASP
!?
SPING
"DEMON"?
HUH?
A MIRROR ...

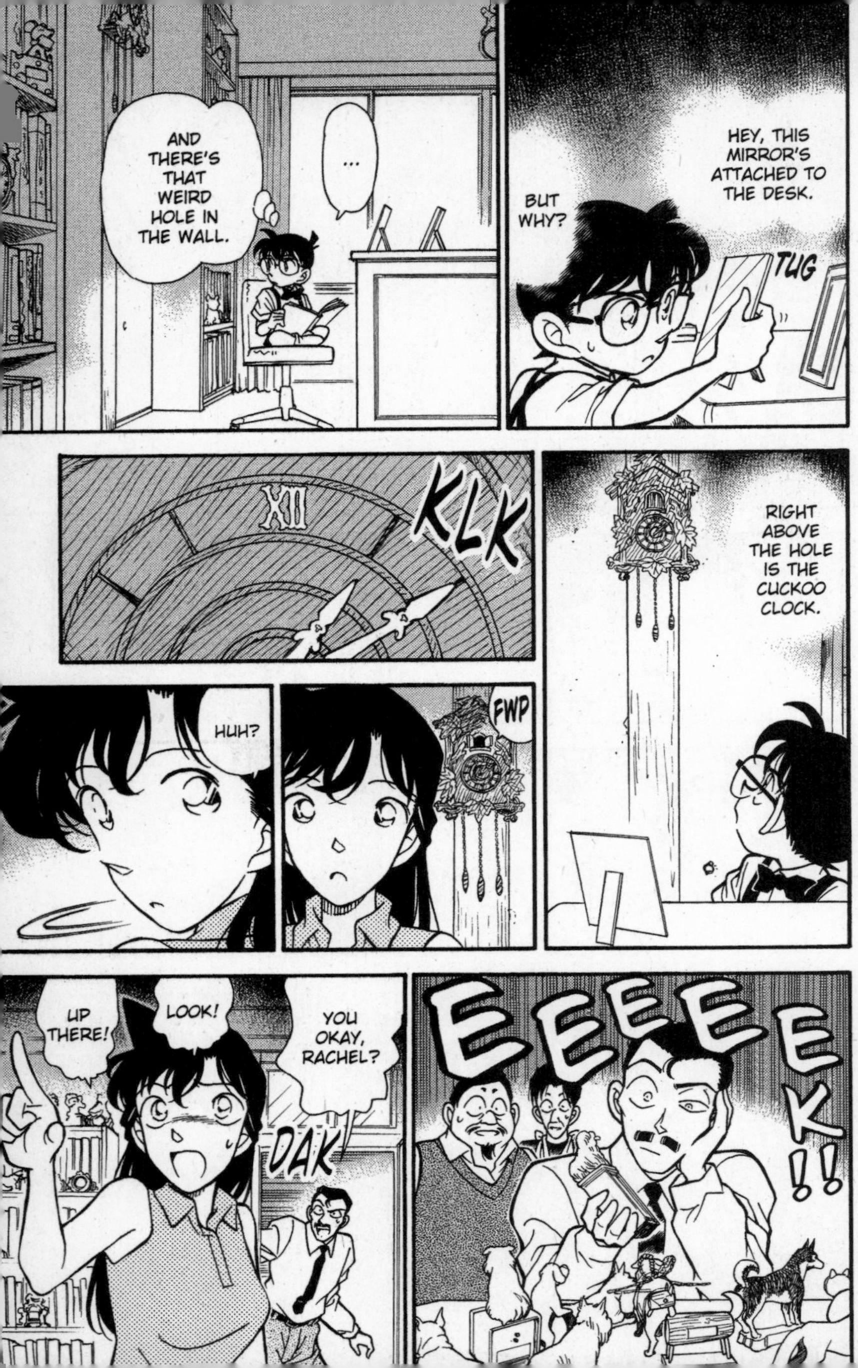
HEY, THIS MIRROR'S ATTACHED TO THE DESK.
BUT WHY?
TUG
...
AND THERE'S THAT WEIRD HOLE IN THE WALL.
RIGHT ABOVE THE HOLE IS THE CUCKOO CLOCK.
KLK
FWP
HUH?
EEEEEK!!
YOU OKAY, RACHEL?
LOOK!
UP THERE!
DAK

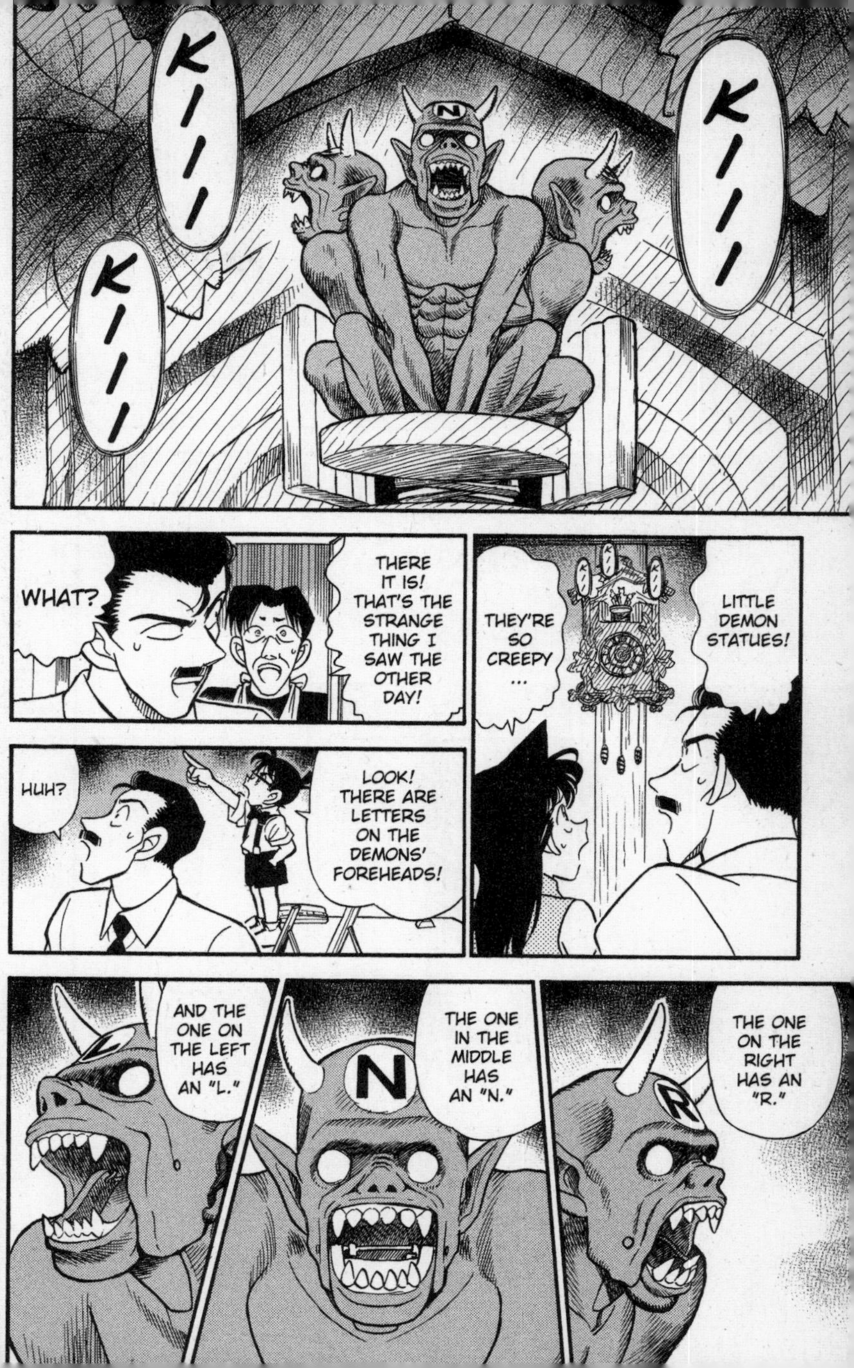
KIIII
KIIII
KIII
LITTLE DEMON STATUES!
THEY'RE SO CREEPY ...
THERE IT IS! THAT'S THE STRANGE THING I SAW THE OTHER DAY!
WHAT?
LOOK! THERE ARE LETTERS ON THE DEMONS' FOREHEADS!
HUH?
THE ONE ON THE RIGHT HAS AN "R."
THE ONE IN THE MIDDLE HAS AN "N."
AND THE ONE ON THE LEFT HAS AN "L."

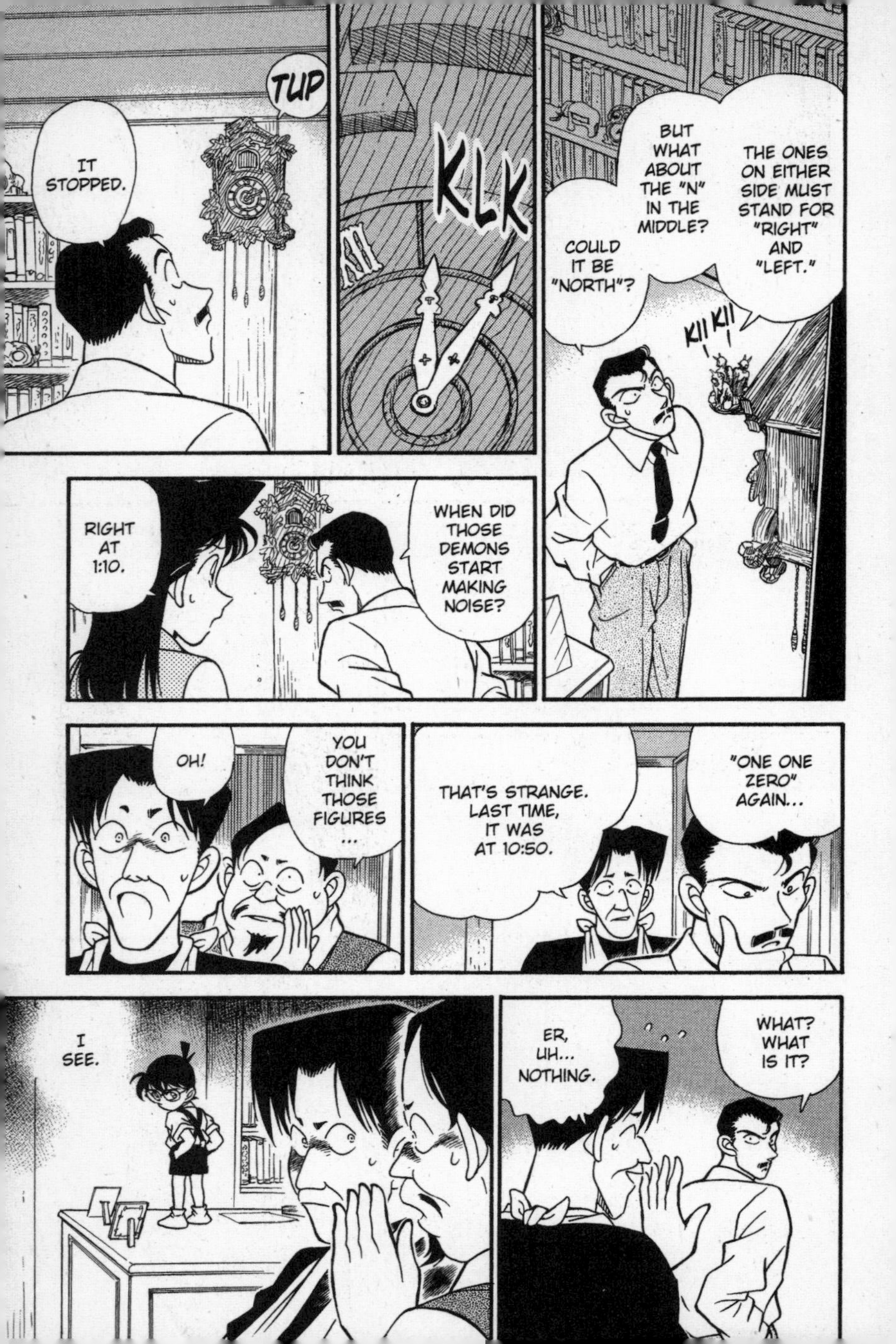

THE ONES ON EITHER SIDE MUST STAND FOR "RIGHT" AND "LEFT."
BUT WHAT ABOUT THE "N" IN THE MIDDLE?
COULD IT BE "NORTH"?
KII KII
KLK
TUP
IT STOPPED.
WHEN DID THOSE DEMONS START MAKING NOISE?
RIGHT AT 1:10.
"ONE ONE ZERO" AGAIN...
THAT'S STRANGE. LAST TIME, IT WAS AT 10:50.
YOU DON'T THINK THOSE FIGURES...
OH!
WHAT? WHAT IS IT?
ER, UH... NOTHING.
I SEE.

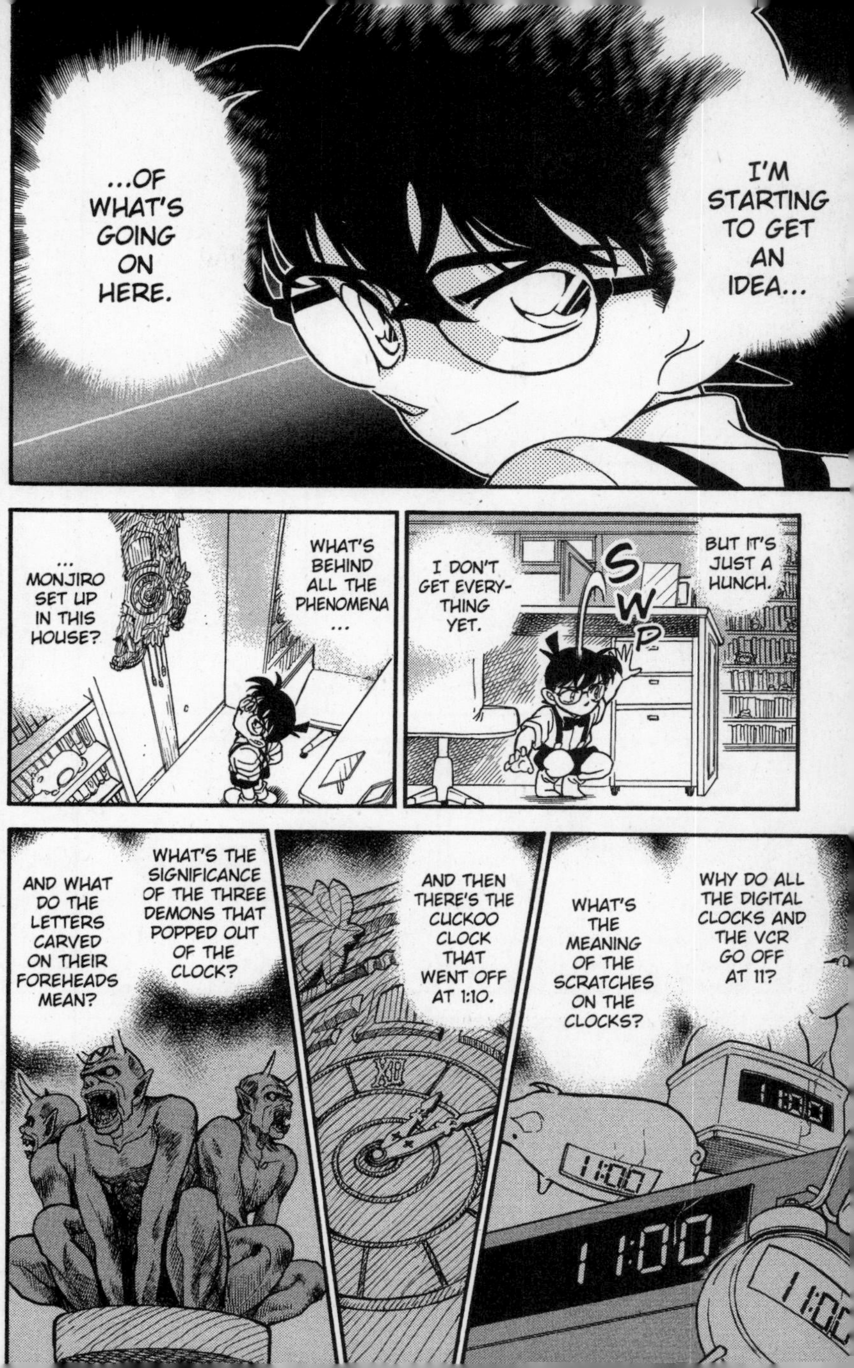
I'M STARTING TO GET AN IDEA...
...OF WHAT'S GOING ON HERE.
BUT IT'S JUST A HUNCH.
SWP
I DON'T GET EVERY-THING YET.
WHAT'S BEHIND ALL THE PHENOMENA ...
... MONJIRO SET UP IN THIS HOUSE?
WHY DO ALL THE DIGITAL CLOCKS AND THE VCR GO OFF AT 11?
WHAT'S THE MEANING OF THE SCRATCHES ON THE CLOCKS?
AND THEN THERE'S THE CUCKOO CLOCK THAT WENT OFF AT 1:10.
WHAT'S THE SIGNIFICANCE OF THE THREE DEMONS THAT POPPED OUT OF THE CLOCK?
AND WHAT DO THE LETTERS CARVED ON THEIR FOREHEADS MEAN?

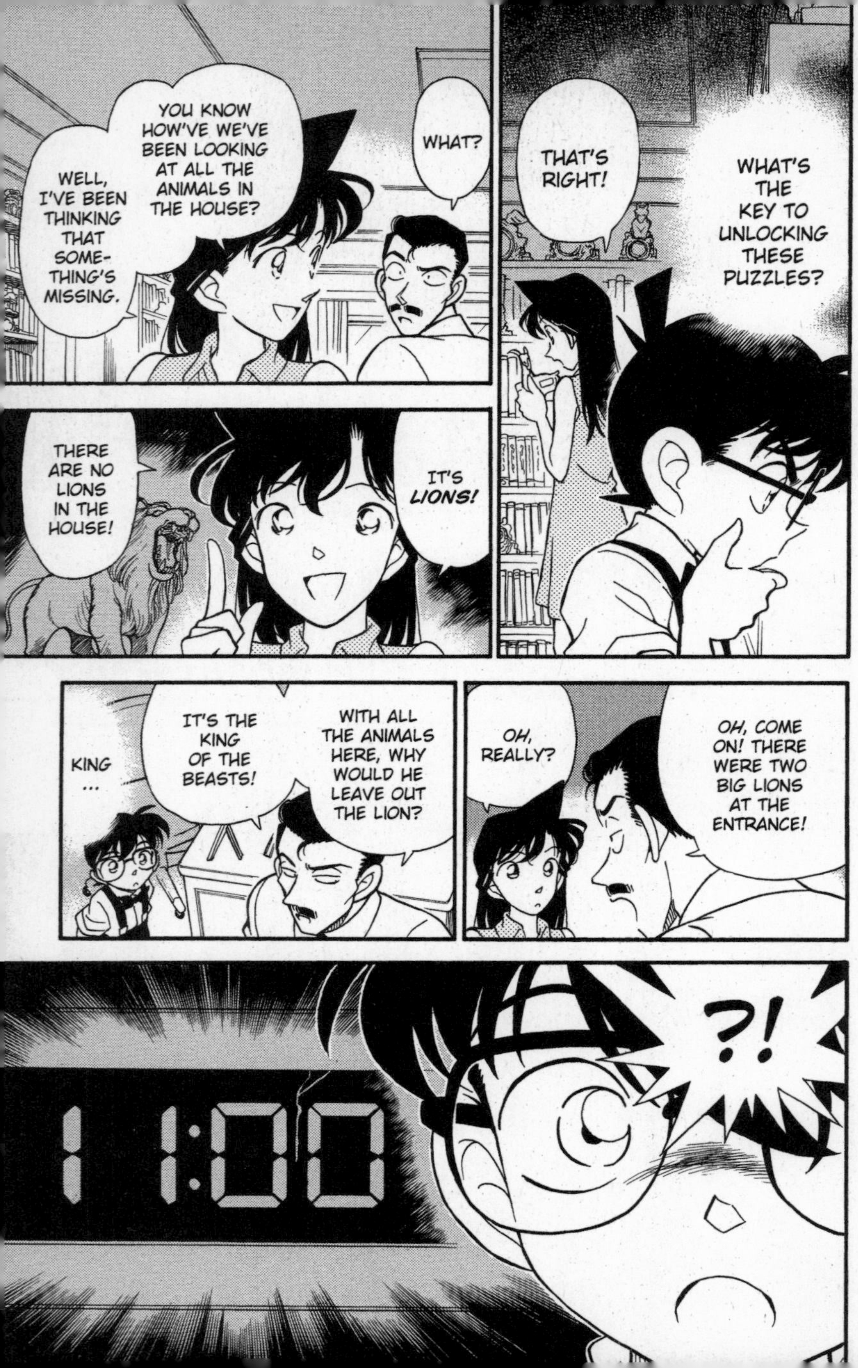
WHAT'S THE KEY TO UNLOCKING THESE PUZZLES?
THAT'S RIGHT!
YOU KNOW HOW'VE WE'VE BEEN LOOKING AT ALL THE ANIMALS IN THE HOUSE?
WHAT?
WELL, I'VE BEEN THINKING THAT SOME-THING'S MISSING.
IT'S *LIONS!*
THERE ARE NO LIONS IN THE HOUSE!
OH, COME ON! THERE WERE TWO BIG LIONS AT THE ENTRANCE!
OH, REALLY?
WITH ALL THE ANIMALS HERE, WHY WOULD HE LEAVE OUT THE LION?
IT'S THE KING OF THE BEASTS!
KING ...
?!
11:00

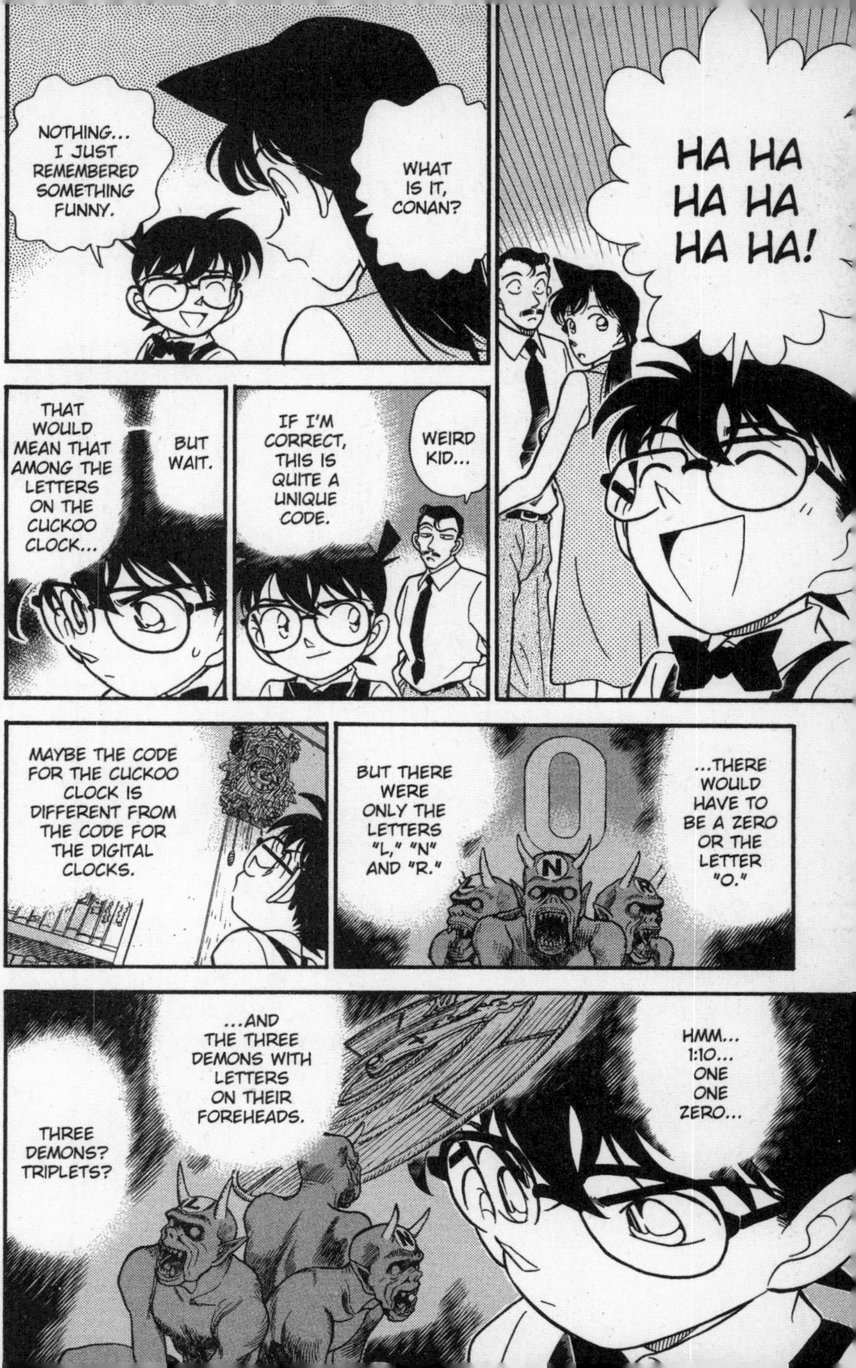
HA HA HA HA HA HA!
WHAT IS IT, CONAN?
NOTHING... I JUST REMEMBERED SOMETHING FUNNY.
WEIRD KID...
IF I'M CORRECT, THIS IS QUITE A UNIQUE CODE.
BUT WAIT.
THAT WOULD MEAN THAT AMONG THE LETTERS ON THE CUCKOO CLOCK...
...THERE WOULD HAVE TO BE A ZERO OR THE LETTER "O."
BUT THERE WERE ONLY THE LETTERS "L," "N" AND "R."
MAYBE THE CODE FOR THE CUCKOO CLOCK IS DIFFERENT FROM THE CODE FOR THE DIGITAL CLOCKS.
HMM... 1:10... ONE ONE ZERO...
...AND THE THREE DEMONS WITH LETTERS ON THEIR FOREHEADS.
THREE DEMONS? TRIPLETS?

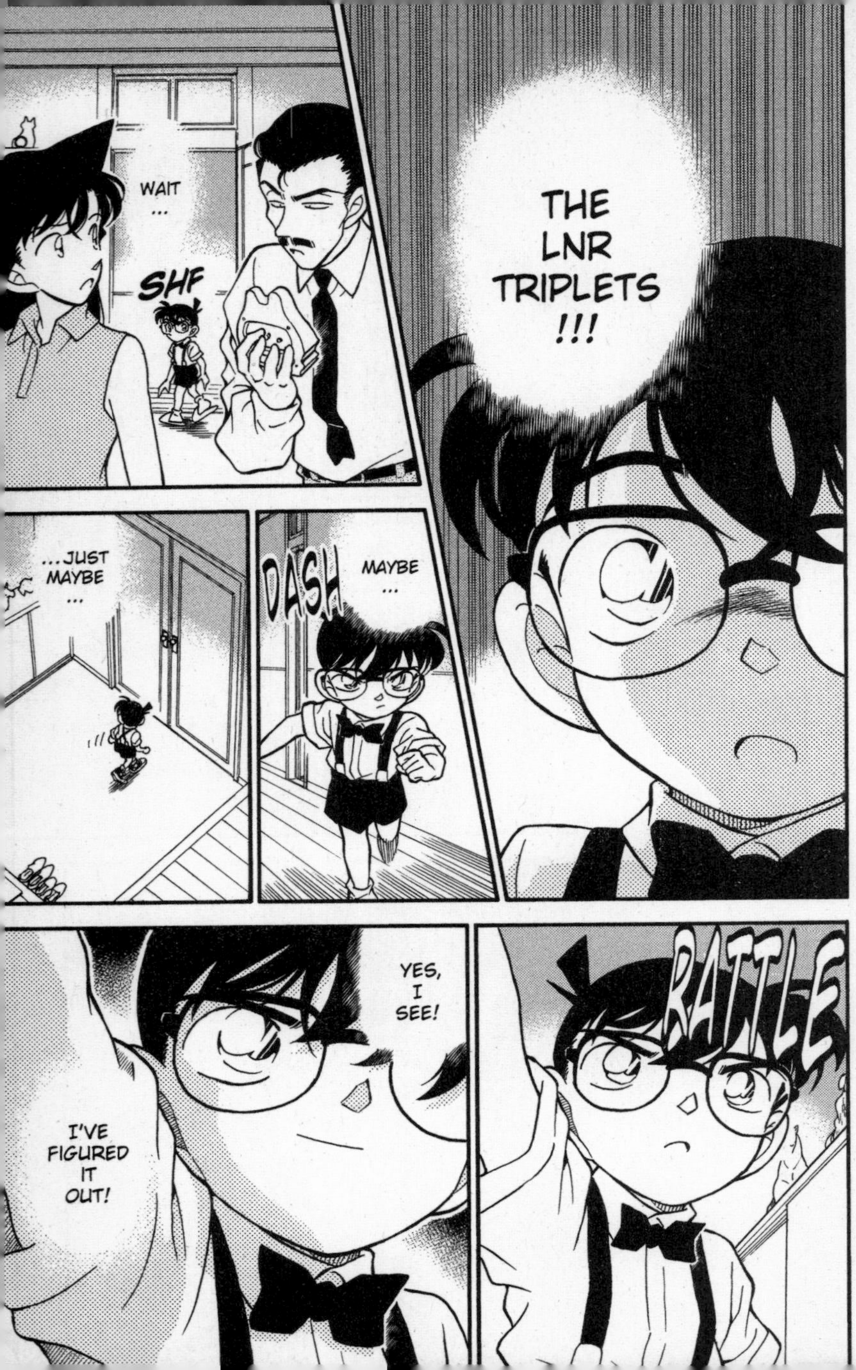

WAIT ...
SHF
MAYBE ...
DASH
...JUST MAYBE ...
THE LNR TRIPLETS !!!
RATTLE
YES, I SEE!
I'VE FIGURED IT OUT!

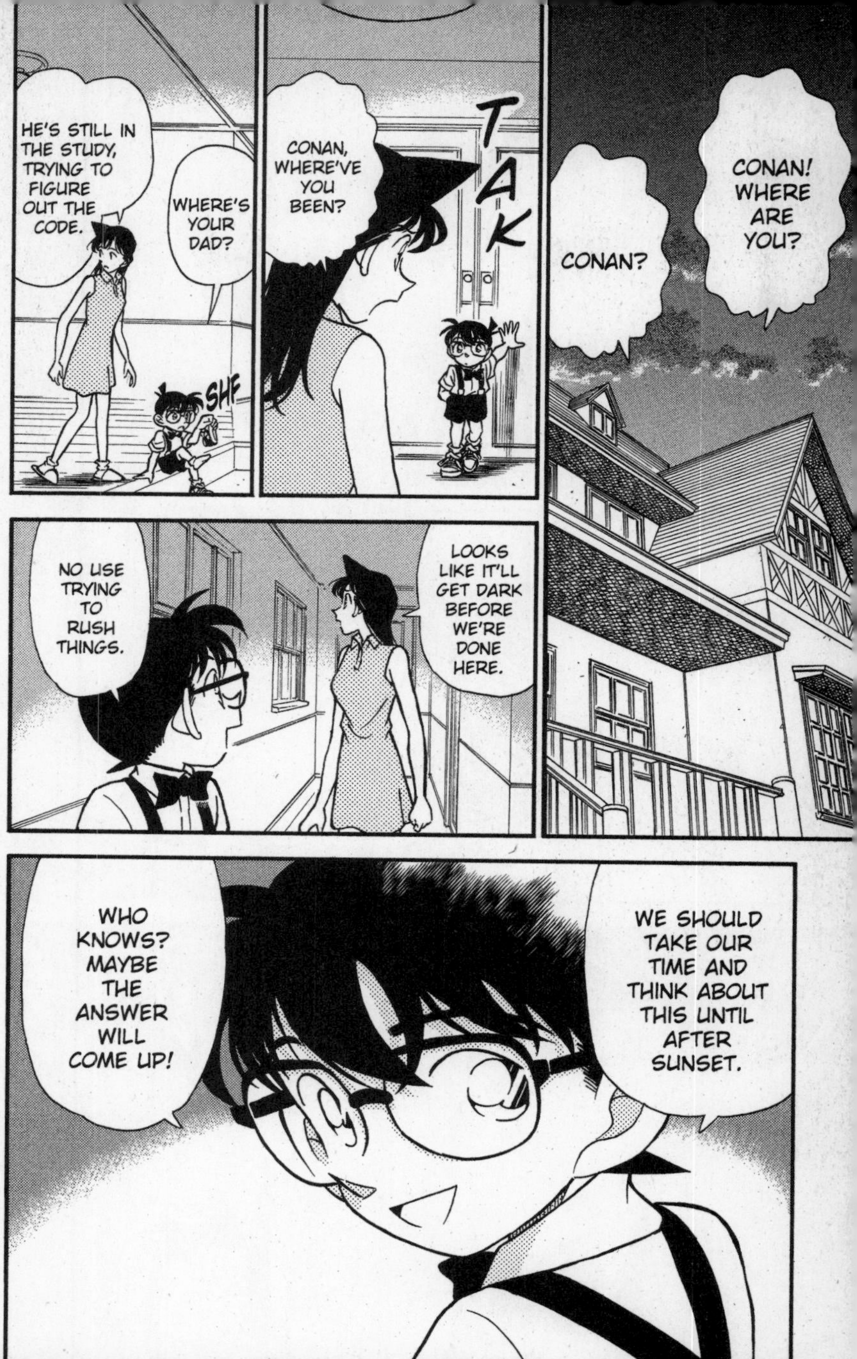
CONAN! WHERE ARE YOU?
CONAN?
TAK
CONAN, WHERE'VE YOU BEEN?
WHERE'S YOUR DAD?
HE'S STILL IN THE STUDY, TRYING TO FIGURE OUT THE CODE.
SHF
LOOKS LIKE IT'LL GET DARK BEFORE WE'RE DONE HERE.
NO USE TRYING TO RUSH THINGS.
WE SHOULD TAKE OUR TIME AND THINK ABOUT THIS UNTIL AFTER SUNSET.
WHO KNOWS? MAYBE THE ANSWER WILL COME UP!

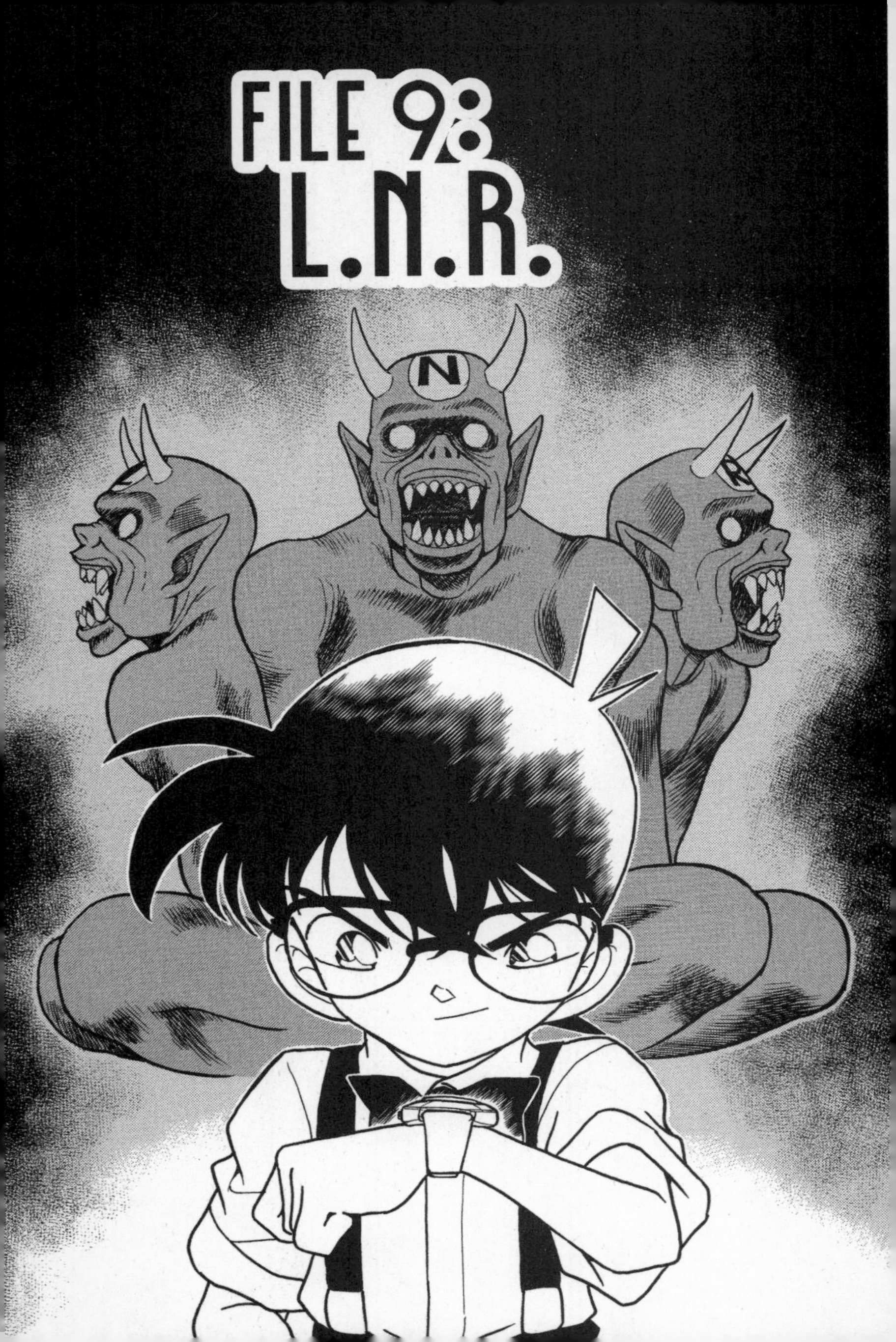
FILE 9:
L.N.R.

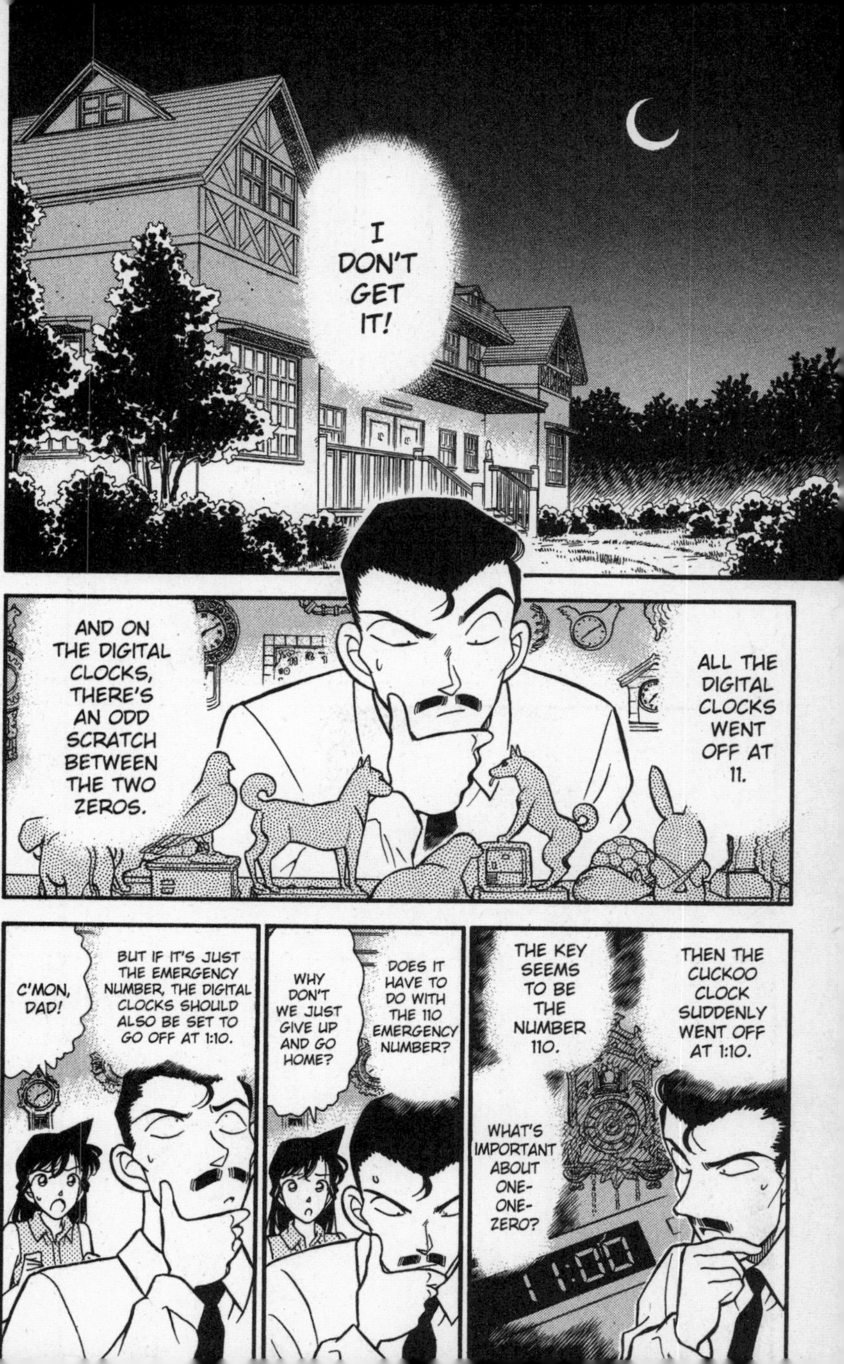
I DON'T GET IT!
ALL THE DIGITAL CLOCKS WENT OFF AT 11.
AND ON THE DIGITAL CLOCKS, THERE'S AN ODD SCRATCH BETWEEN THE TWO ZEROS.
THEN THE CUCKOO CLOCK SUDDENLY WENT OFF AT 1:10.
THE KEY SEEMS TO BE THE NUMBER 110.
WHAT'S IMPORTANT ABOUT ONE-ONE-ZERO?
11:00
DOES IT HAVE TO DO WITH THE 110 EMERGENCY NUMBER?
WHY DON'T WE JUST GIVE UP AND GO HOME?
BUT IF IT'S JUST THE EMERGENCY NUMBER, THE DIGITAL CLOCKS SHOULD ALSO BE SET TO GO OFF AT 1:10.
C'MON, DAD!

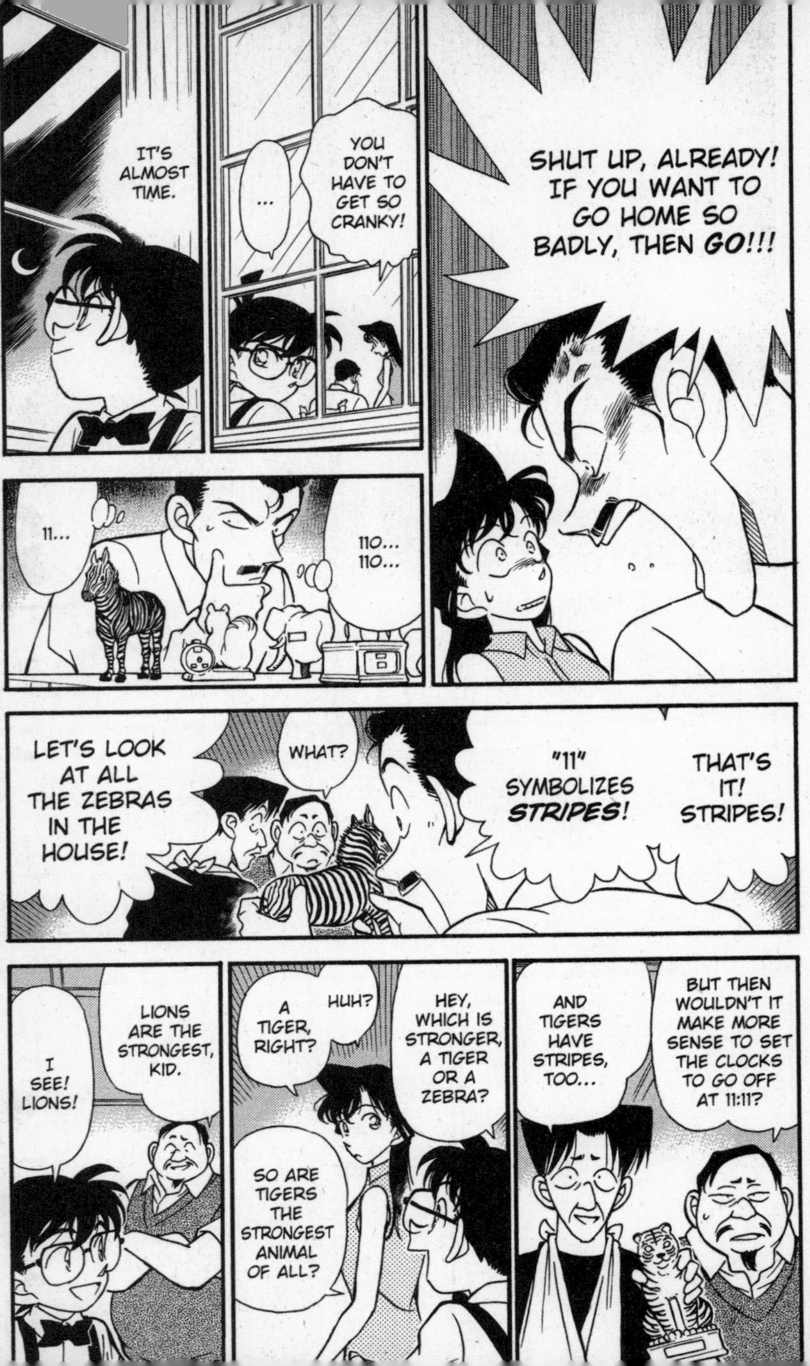
SHUT UP, ALREADY! IF YOU WANT TO GO HOME SO BADLY, THEN GO!!!
YOU DON'T HAVE TO GET SO CRANKY!
...
IT'S ALMOST TIME.
110... 110...
11...
THAT'S IT! STRIPES!
"11" SYMBOLIZES STRIPES!
WHAT?
LET'S LOOK AT ALL THE ZEBRAS IN THE HOUSE!
BUT THEN WOULDN'T IT MAKE MORE SENSE TO SET THE CLOCKS TO GO OFF AT 11:11?
AND TIGERS HAVE STRIPES, TOO...
HEY, WHICH IS STRONGER, A TIGER OR A ZEBRA?
HUH?
A TIGER, RIGHT?
SO ARE TIGERS THE STRONGEST ANIMAL OF ALL?
LIONS ARE THE STRONGEST, KID.
I SEE! LIONS!

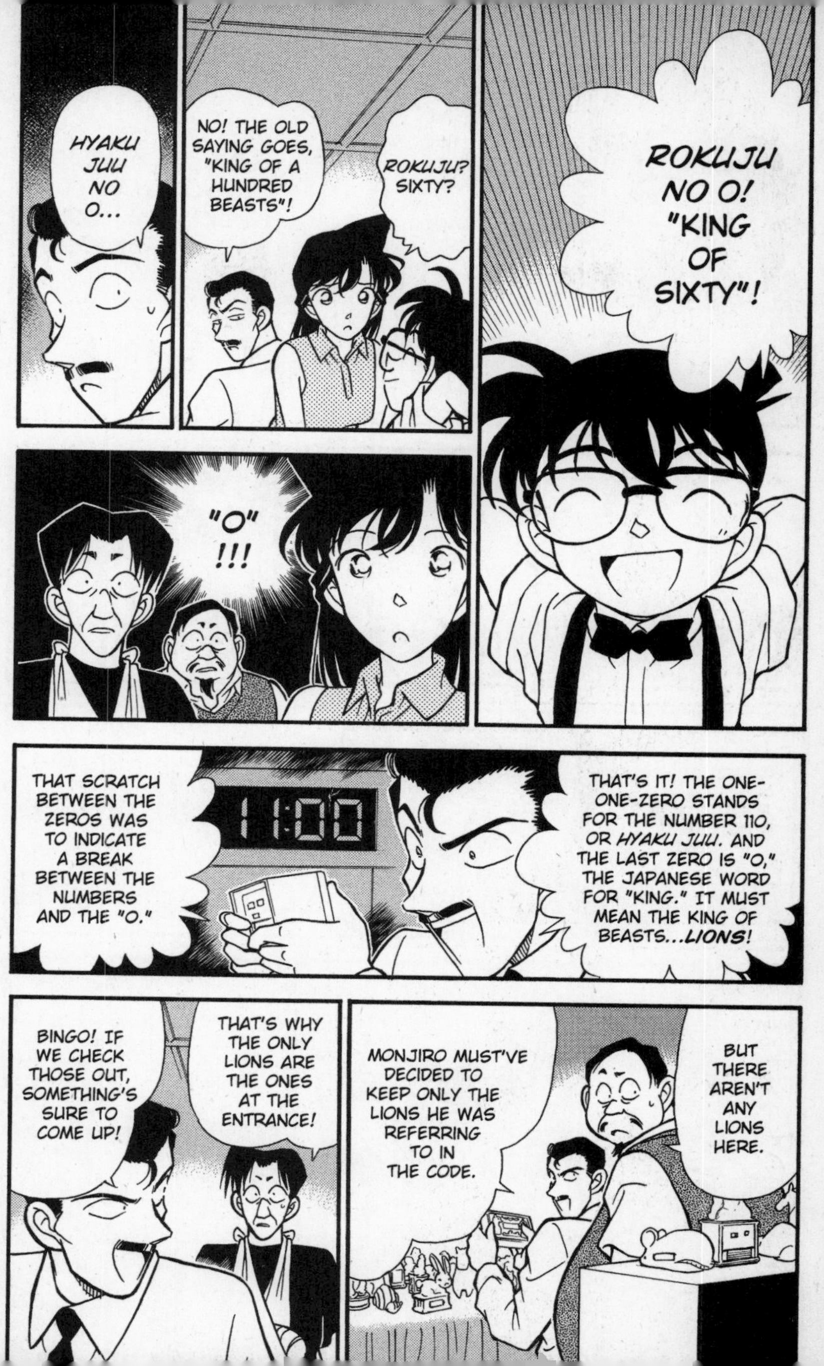

ROKUJU NO O! "KING OF SIXTY"!
ROKUJU? SIXTY?
NO! THE OLD SAYING GOES, "KING OF A HUNDRED BEASTS"!
HYAKU JUU NO O...
"O" !!!
11:00
THAT'S IT! THE ONE-ONE-ZERO STANDS FOR THE NUMBER 110, OR HYAKU JUU. AND THE LAST ZERO IS "O," THE JAPANESE WORD FOR "KING." IT MUST MEAN THE KING OF BEASTS...LIONS!
THAT SCRATCH BETWEEN THE ZEROS WAS TO INDICATE A BREAK BETWEEN THE NUMBERS AND THE "O."
BUT THERE AREN'T ANY LIONS HERE.
MONJIRO MUST'VE DECIDED TO KEEP ONLY THE LIONS HE WAS REFERRING TO IN THE CODE.
THAT'S WHY THE ONLY LIONS ARE THE ONES AT THE ENTRANCE!
BINGO! IF WE CHECK THOSE OUT, SOMETHING'S SURE TO COME UP!

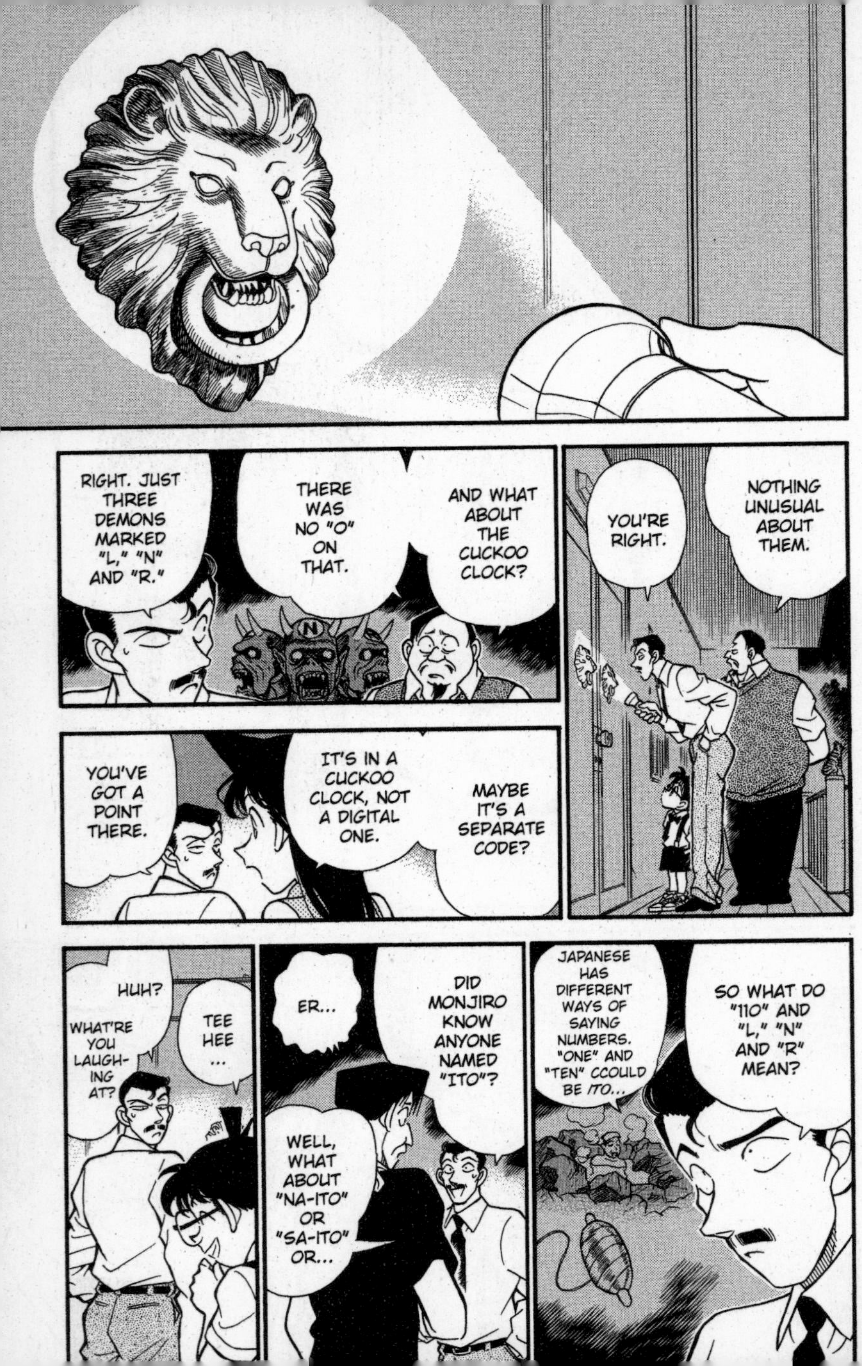
NOTHING UNUSUAL ABOUT THEM.
YOU'RE RIGHT.
AND WHAT ABOUT THE CUCKOO CLOCK?
THERE WAS NO "O" ON THAT.
RIGHT. JUST THREE DEMONS MARKED "L," "N" AND "R."
MAYBE IT'S A SEPARATE CODE?
IT'S IN A CUCKOO CLOCK, NOT A DIGITAL ONE.
YOU'VE GOT A POINT THERE.
SO WHAT DO "110" AND "L," "N" AND "R" MEAN?
JAPANESE HAS DIFFERENT WAYS OF SAYING NUMBERS. "ONE" AND "TEN" CCOULD BE *ITO*...
DID MONJIRO KNOW ANYONE NAMED "ITO"?
ER...
WELL, WHAT ABOUT "NA-ITO" OR "SA-ITO" OR...
TEE HEE ...
HUH?
WHAT'RE YOU LAUGHING AT?

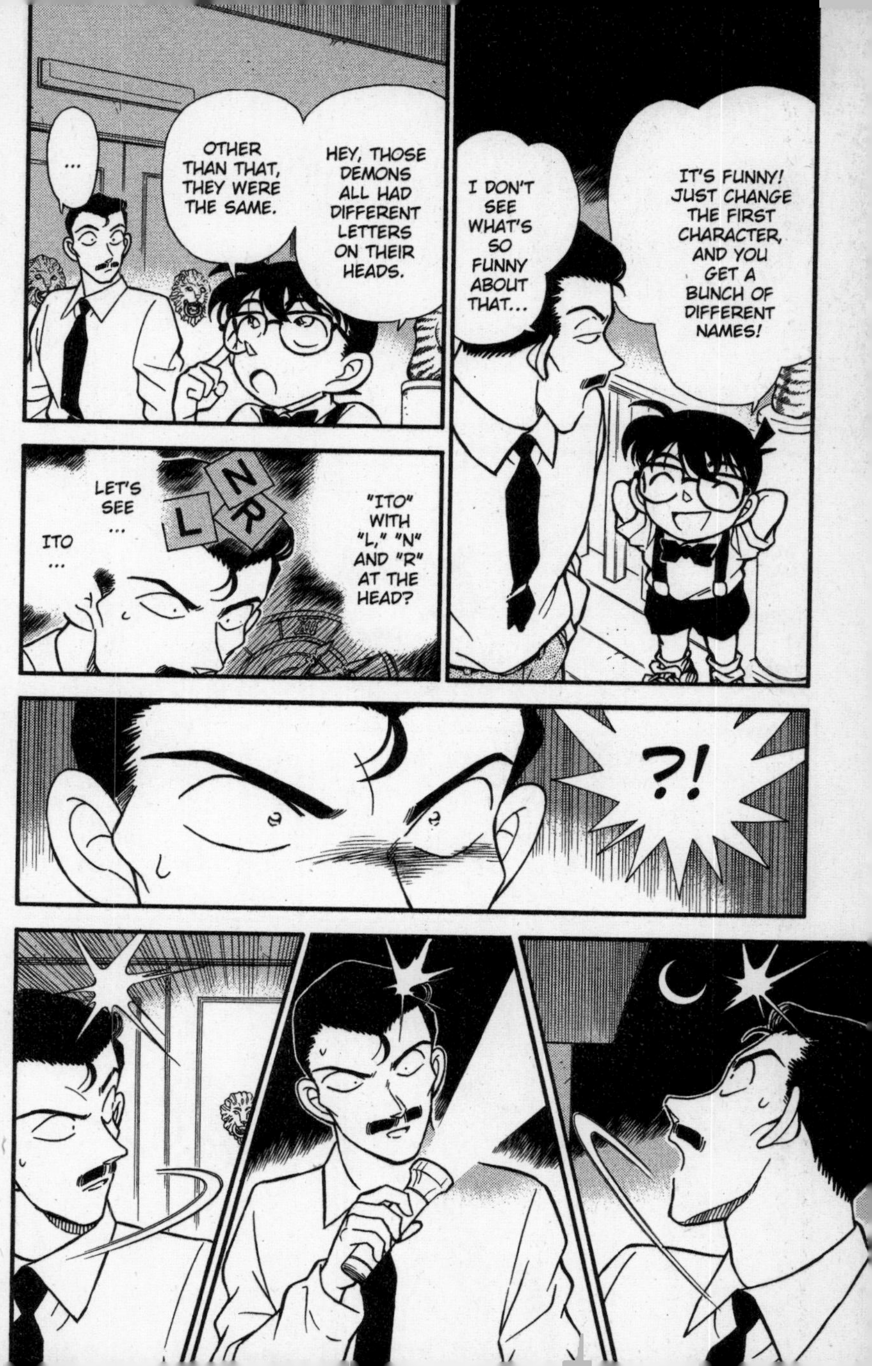
IT'S FUNNY! JUST CHANGE THE FIRST CHARACTER, AND YOU GET A BUNCH OF DIFFERENT NAMES!
I DON'T SEE WHAT'S SO FUNNY ABOUT THAT...
HEY, THOSE DEMONS ALL HAD DIFFERENT LETTERS ON THEIR HEADS.
OTHER THAN THAT, THEY WERE THE SAME.
...
N
R
L
"ITO" WITH "L," "N" AND "R" AT THE HEAD?
LET'S SEE ...
ITO ...
?!

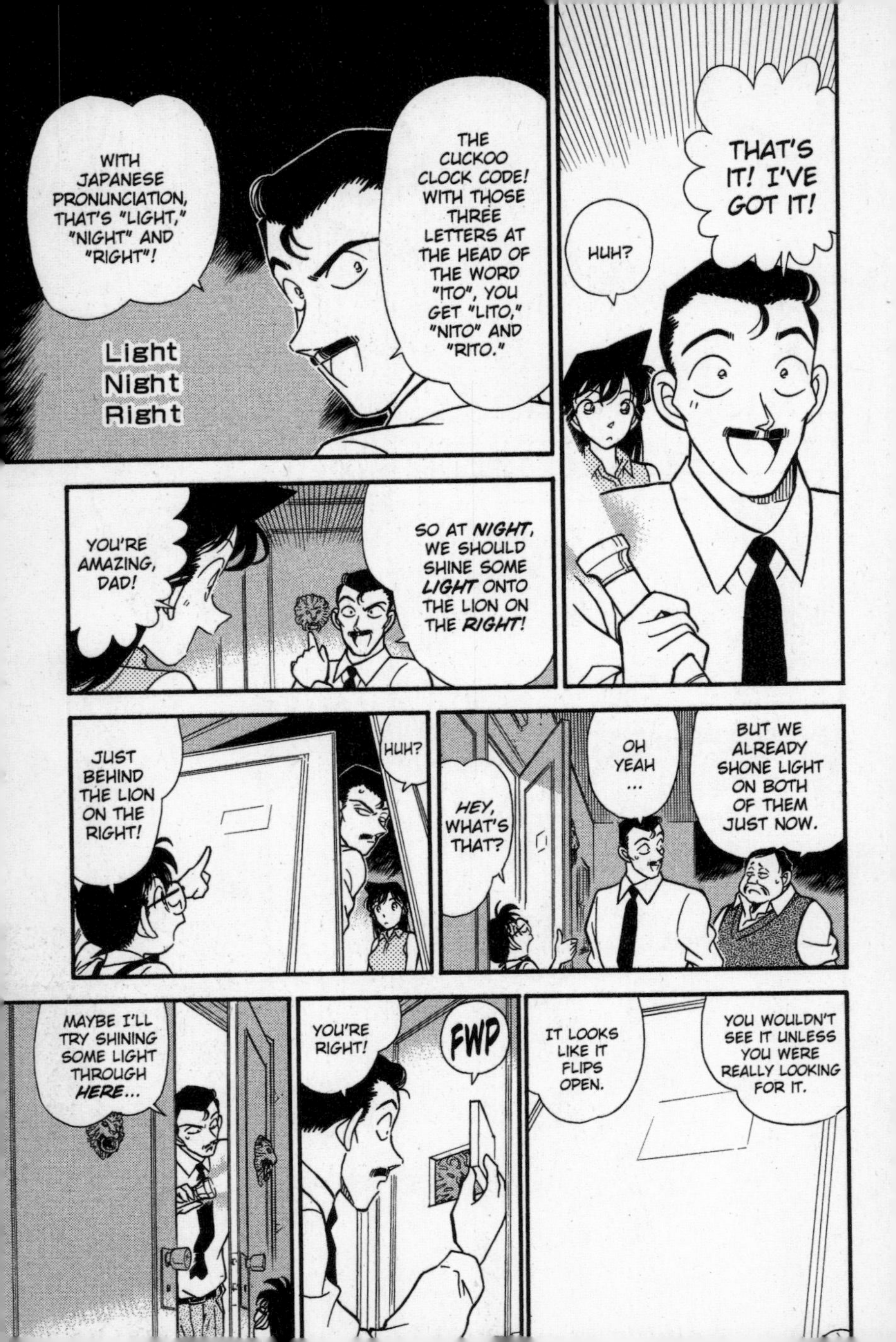
THAT'S IT! I'VE GOT IT!
HUH?
THE CUCKOO CLOCK CODE! WITH THOSE THREE LETTERS AT THE HEAD OF THE WORD "ITO", YOU GET "LITO," "NITO" AND "RITO."
WITH JAPANESE PRONUNCIATION, THAT'S "LIGHT," "NIGHT" AND "RIGHT"!
Light
Night
Right
SO AT NIGHT, WE SHOULD SHINE SOME LIGHT ONTO THE LION ON THE RIGHT!
YOU'RE AMAZING, DAD!
BUT WE ALREADY SHONE LIGHT ON BOTH OF THEM JUST NOW.
OH YEAH ...
HEY, WHAT'S THAT?
HUH?
JUST BEHIND THE LION ON THE RIGHT!
YOU WOULDN'T SEE IT UNLESS YOU WERE REALLY LOOKING FOR IT.
IT LOOKS LIKE IT FLIPS OPEN.
FWP
YOU'RE RIGHT!
MAYBE I'LL TRY SHINING SOME LIGHT THROUGH HERE...

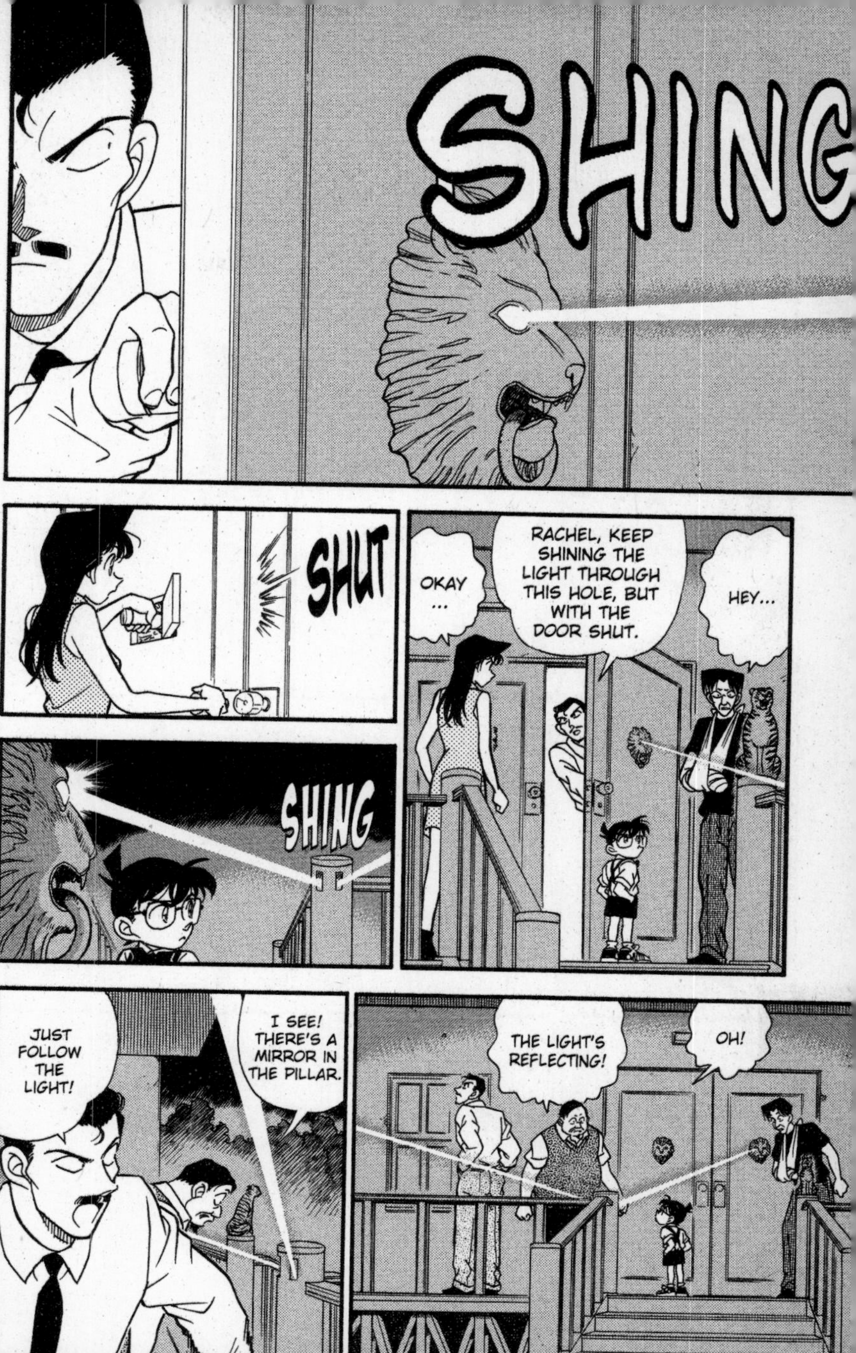
SHING
HEY...
RACHEL, KEEP SHINING THE LIGHT THROUGH THIS HOLE, BUT WITH THE DOOR SHUT.
OKAY ...
SHUT
SHING
OH!
THE LIGHT'S REFLECTING!
I SEE! THERE'S A MIRROR IN THE PILLAR.
JUST FOLLOW THE LIGHT!

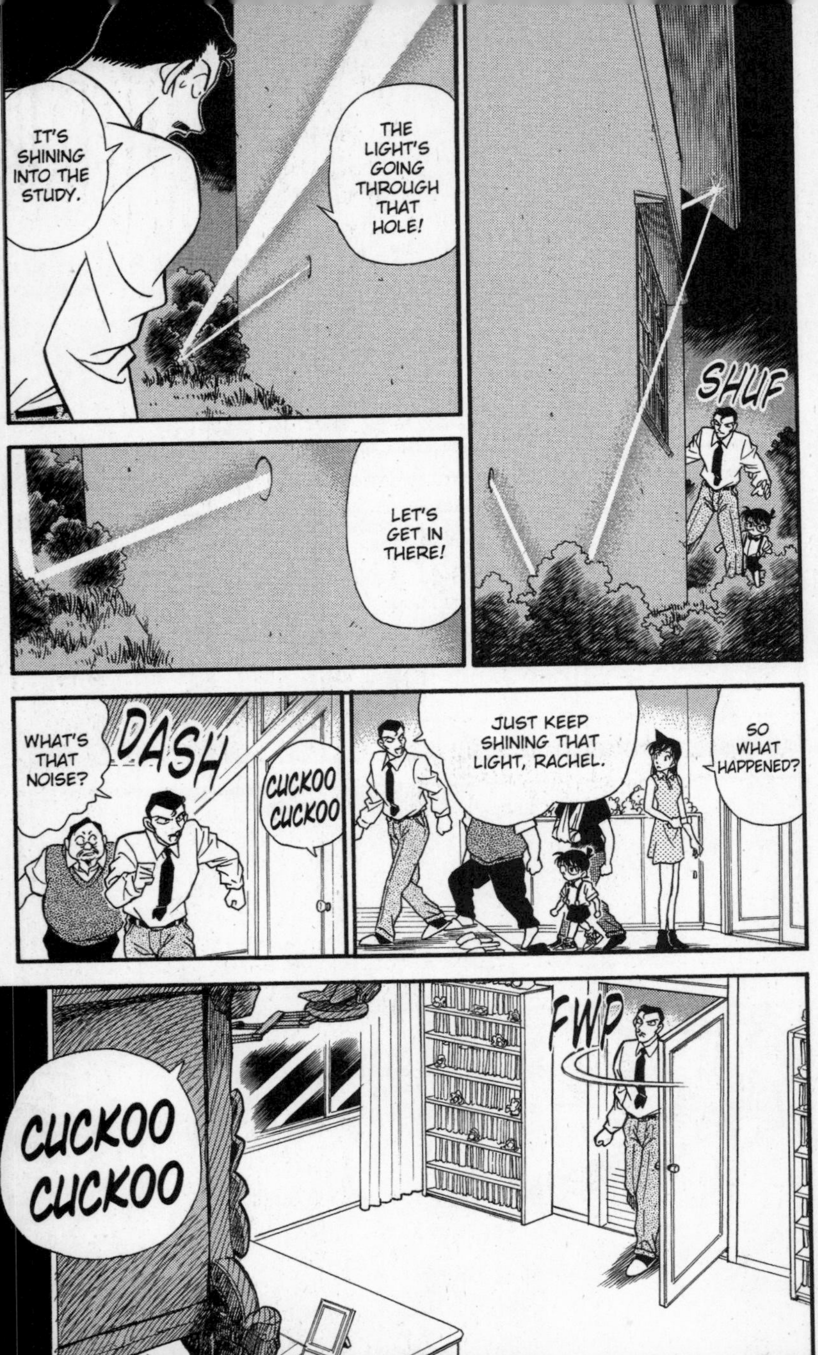
SHUF
THE LIGHT'S GOING THROUGH THAT HOLE!
IT'S SHINING INTO THE STUDY.
LET'S GET IN THERE!
SO WHAT HAPPENED?
JUST KEEP SHINING THAT LIGHT, RACHEL.
CUCKOO CUCKOO
DASH
WHAT'S THAT NOISE?
FWP
CUCKOO CUCKOO

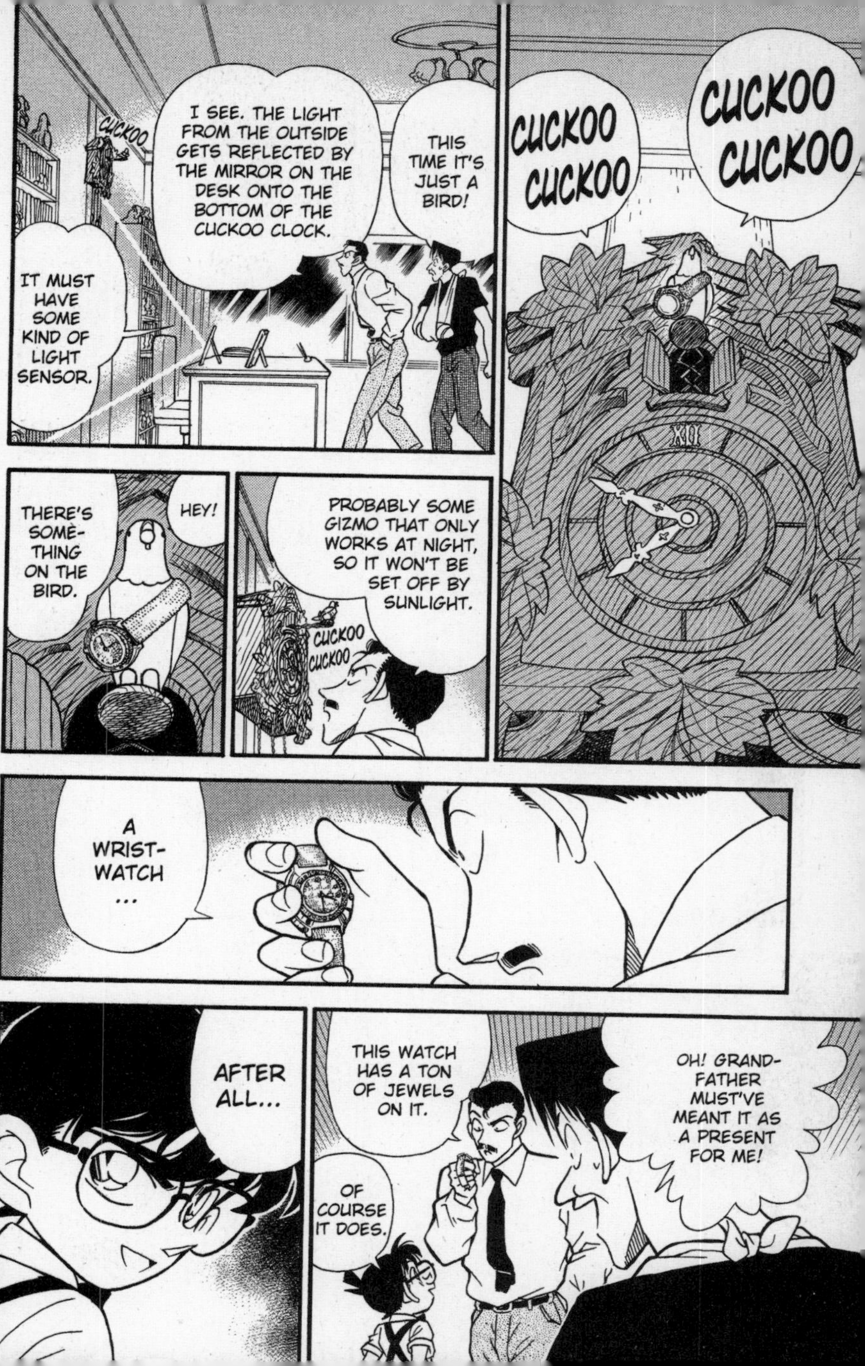

CUCKOO CUCKOO
CUCKOO CUCKOO
THIS TIME IT'S JUST A BIRD!
I SEE. THE LIGHT FROM THE OUTSIDE GETS REFLECTED BY THE MIRROR ON THE DESK ONTO THE BOTTOM OF THE CUCKOO CLOCK.
CUCKOO
IT MUST HAVE SOME KIND OF LIGHT SENSOR.
PROBABLY SOME GIZMO THAT ONLY WORKS AT NIGHT, SO IT WON'T BE SET OFF BY SUNLIGHT.
CUCKOO CUCKOO
HEY!
THERE'S SOME-THING ON THE BIRD.
A WRIST-WATCH ...
OH! GRAND-FATHER MUST'VE MEANT IT AS A PRESENT FOR ME!
THIS WATCH HAS A TON OF JEWELS ON IT.
OF COURSE IT DOES.
AFTER ALL...

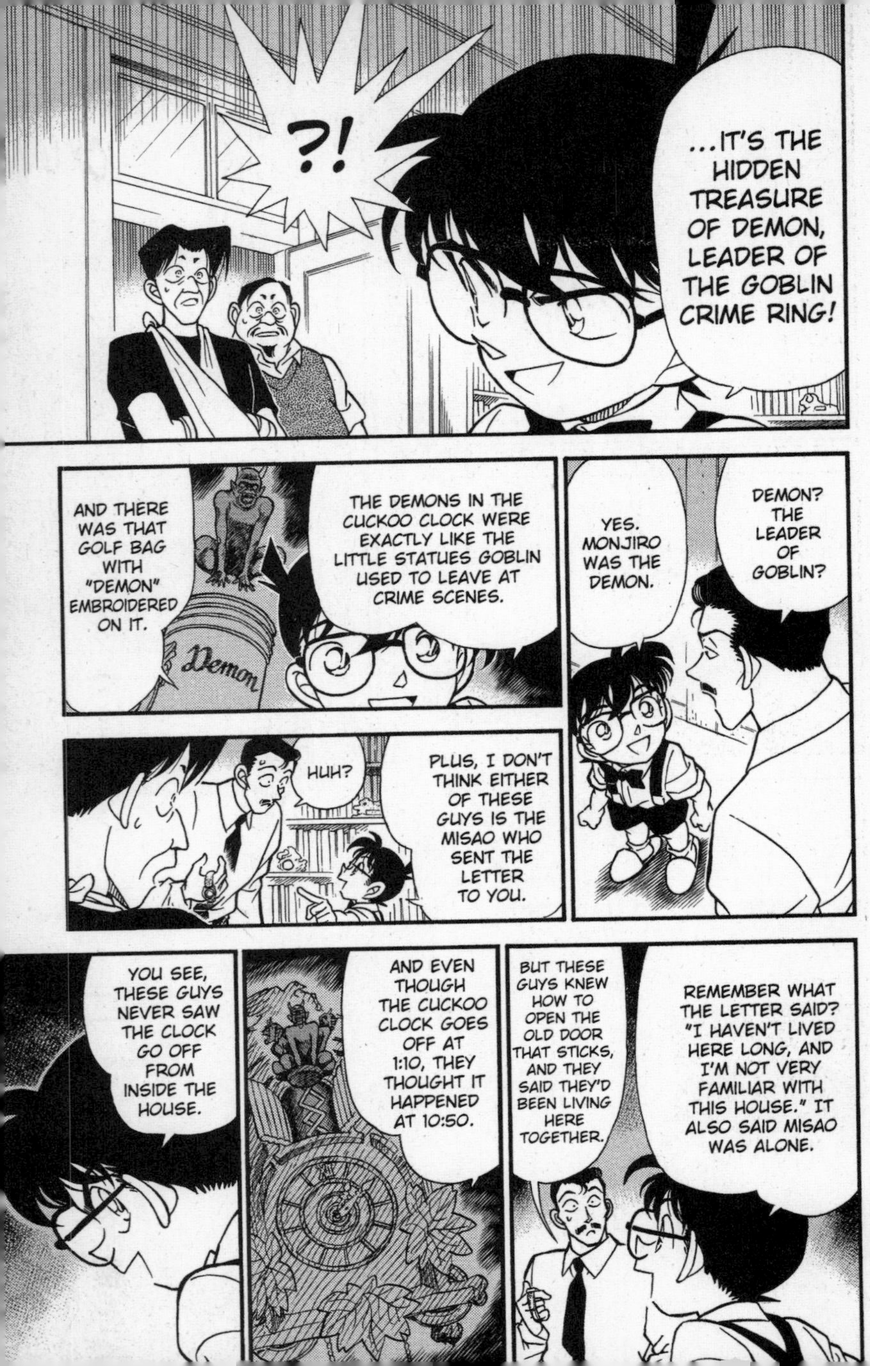
...IT'S THE HIDDEN TREASURE OF DEMON, LEADER OF THE GOBLIN CRIME RING!
?!
DEMON? THE LEADER OF GOBLIN?
YES. MONJIRO WAS THE DEMON.
THE DEMONS IN THE CUCKOO CLOCK WERE EXACTLY LIKE THE LITTLE STATUES GOBLIN USED TO LEAVE AT CRIME SCENES.
AND THERE WAS THAT GOLF BAG WITH "DEMON" EMBROIDERED ON IT.
Demon
PLUS, I DON'T THINK EITHER OF THESE GUYS IS THE MISAO WHO SENT THE LETTER TO YOU.
HUH?
REMEMBER WHAT THE LETTER SAID? "I HAVEN'T LIVED HERE LONG, AND I'M NOT VERY FAMILIAR WITH THIS HOUSE." IT ALSO SAID MISAO WAS ALONE.
BUT THESE GUYS KNEW HOW TO OPEN THE OLD DOOR THAT STICKS, AND THEY SAID THEY'D BEEN LIVING HERE TOGETHER.
AND EVEN THOUGH THE CUCKOO CLOCK GOES OFF AT 1:10, THEY THOUGHT IT HAPPENED AT 10:50.
YOU SEE, THESE GUYS NEVER SAW THE CLOCK GO OFF FROM INSIDE THE HOUSE.

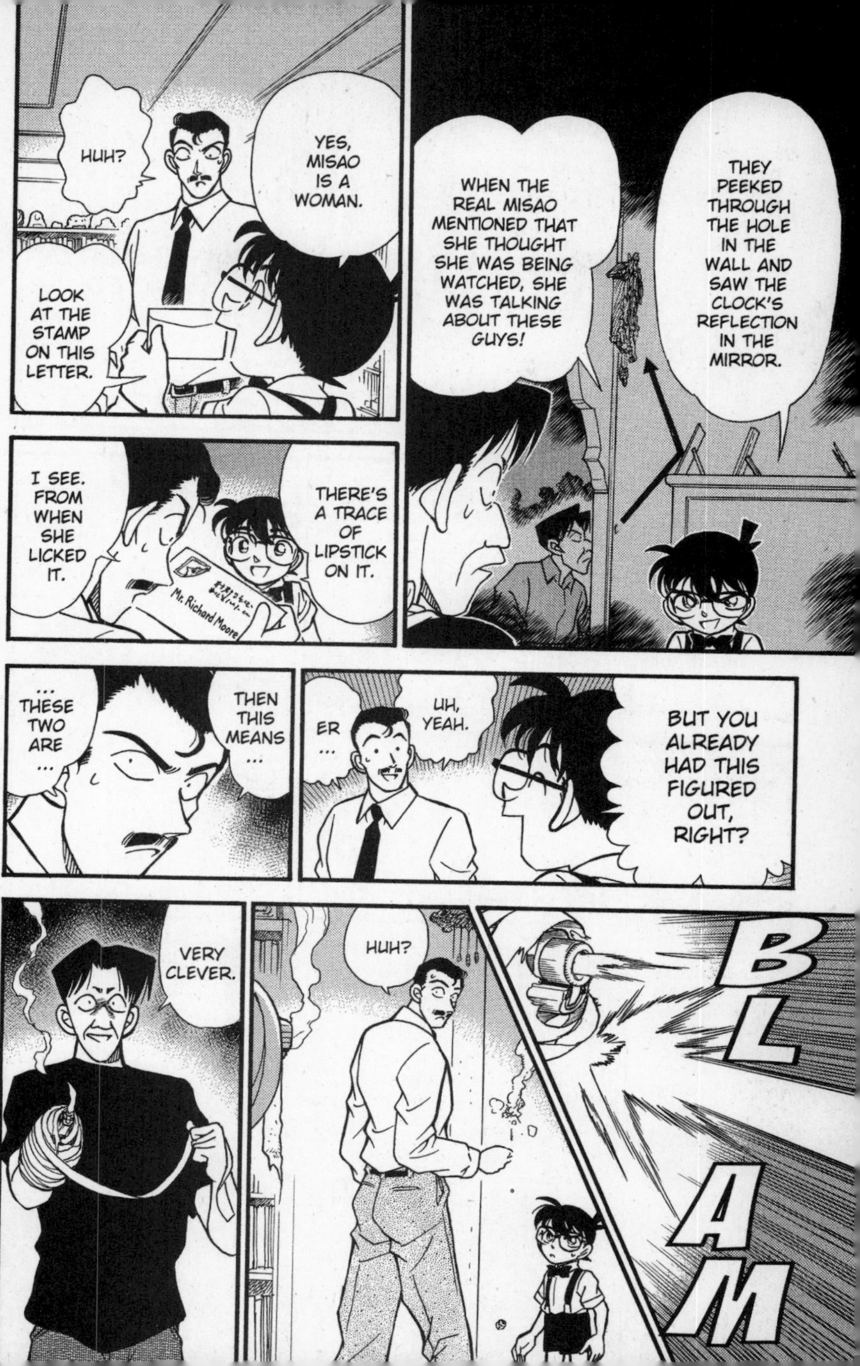
THEY PEEKED THROUGH THE HOLE IN THE WALL AND SAW THE CLOCK'S REFLECTION IN THE MIRROR.
WHEN THE REAL MISAO MENTIONED THAT SHE THOUGHT SHE WAS BEING WATCHED, SHE WAS TALKING ABOUT THESE GUYS!
YES, MISAO IS A WOMAN.
HUH?
LOOK AT THE STAMP ON THIS LETTER.
THERE'S A TRACE OF LIPSTICK ON IT.
I SEE. FROM WHEN SHE LICKED IT.
Mr. Richard Moore
BUT YOU ALREADY HAD THIS FIGURED OUT, RIGHT?
UH, YEAH.
ER ...
THEN THIS MEANS ...
... THESE TWO ARE ...
BLAM
HUH?
VERY CLEVER.

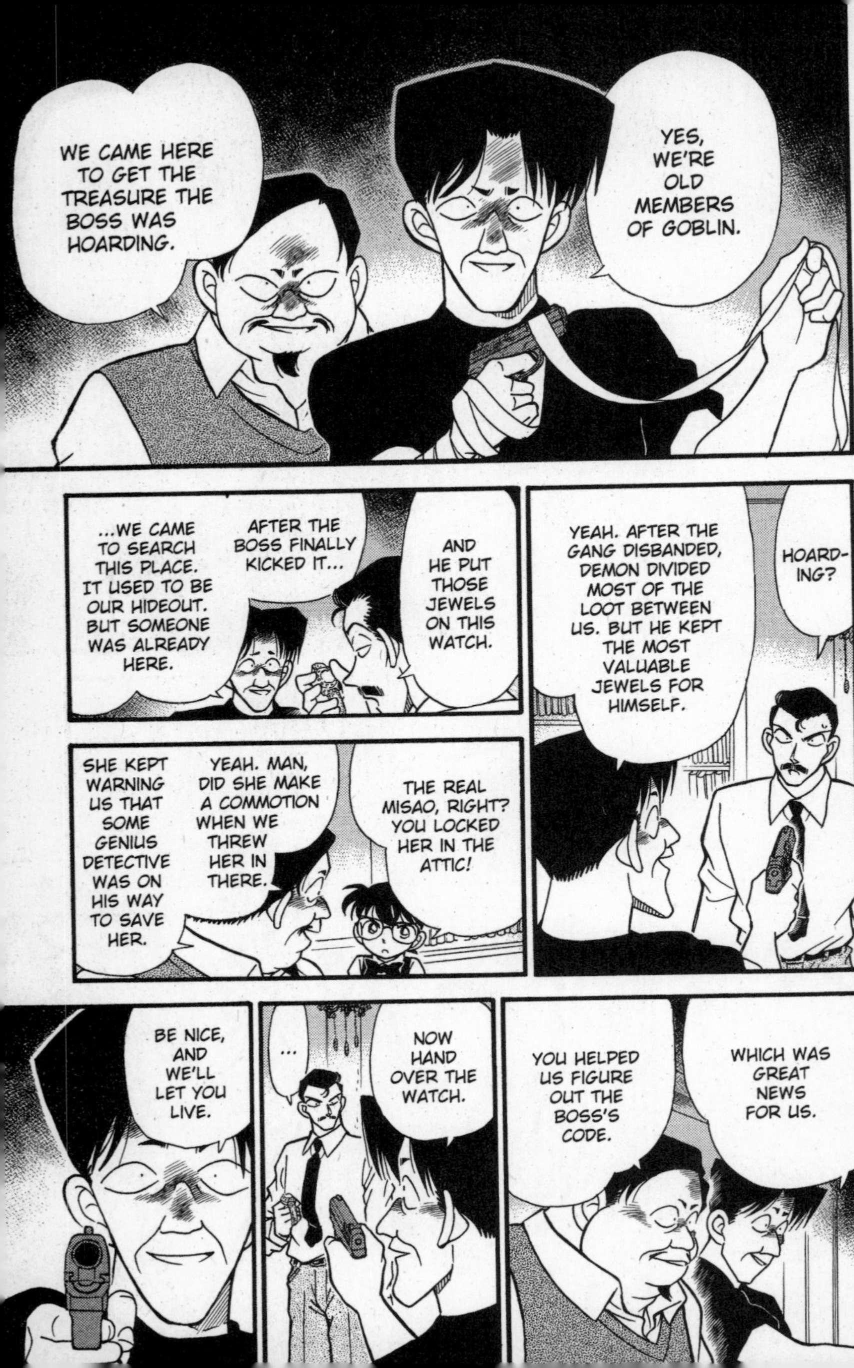
YES, WE'RE OLD MEMBERS OF GOBLIN.
WE CAME HERE TO GET THE TREASURE THE BOSS WAS HOARDING.
HOARD-ING?
YEAH. AFTER THE GANG DISBANDED, DEMON DIVIDED MOST OF THE LOOT BETWEEN US. BUT HE KEPT THE MOST VALUABLE JEWELS FOR HIMSELF.
AND HE PUT THOSE JEWELS ON THIS WATCH.
AFTER THE BOSS FINALLY KICKED IT...
...WE CAME TO SEARCH THIS PLACE. IT USED TO BE OUR HIDEOUT. BUT SOMEONE WAS ALREADY HERE.
THE REAL MISAO, RIGHT? YOU LOCKED HER IN THE ATTIC!
YEAH. MAN, DID SHE MAKE A COMMOTION WHEN WE THREW HER IN THERE.
SHE KEPT WARNING US THAT SOME GENIUS DETECTIVE WAS ON HIS WAY TO SAVE HER.
WHICH WAS GREAT NEWS FOR US.
YOU HELPED US FIGURE OUT THE BOSS'S CODE.
NOW HAND OVER THE WATCH.
...
BE NICE, AND WE'LL LET YOU LIVE.

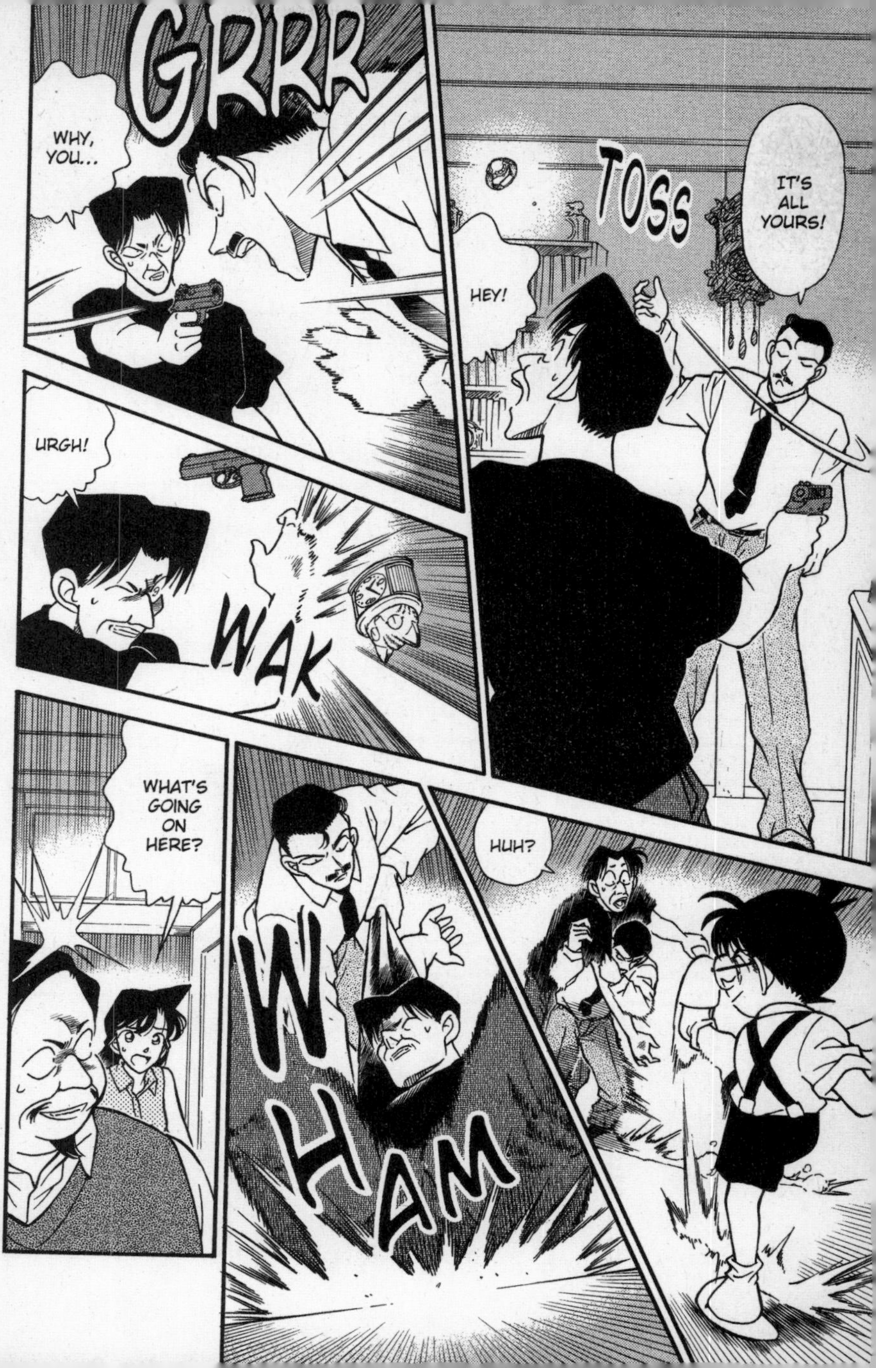
IT'S ALL YOURS!
TOSS
HEY!
GRRR
WHY, YOU...
URGH!
WAK
HUH?
WHAM
WHAT'S GOING ON HERE?

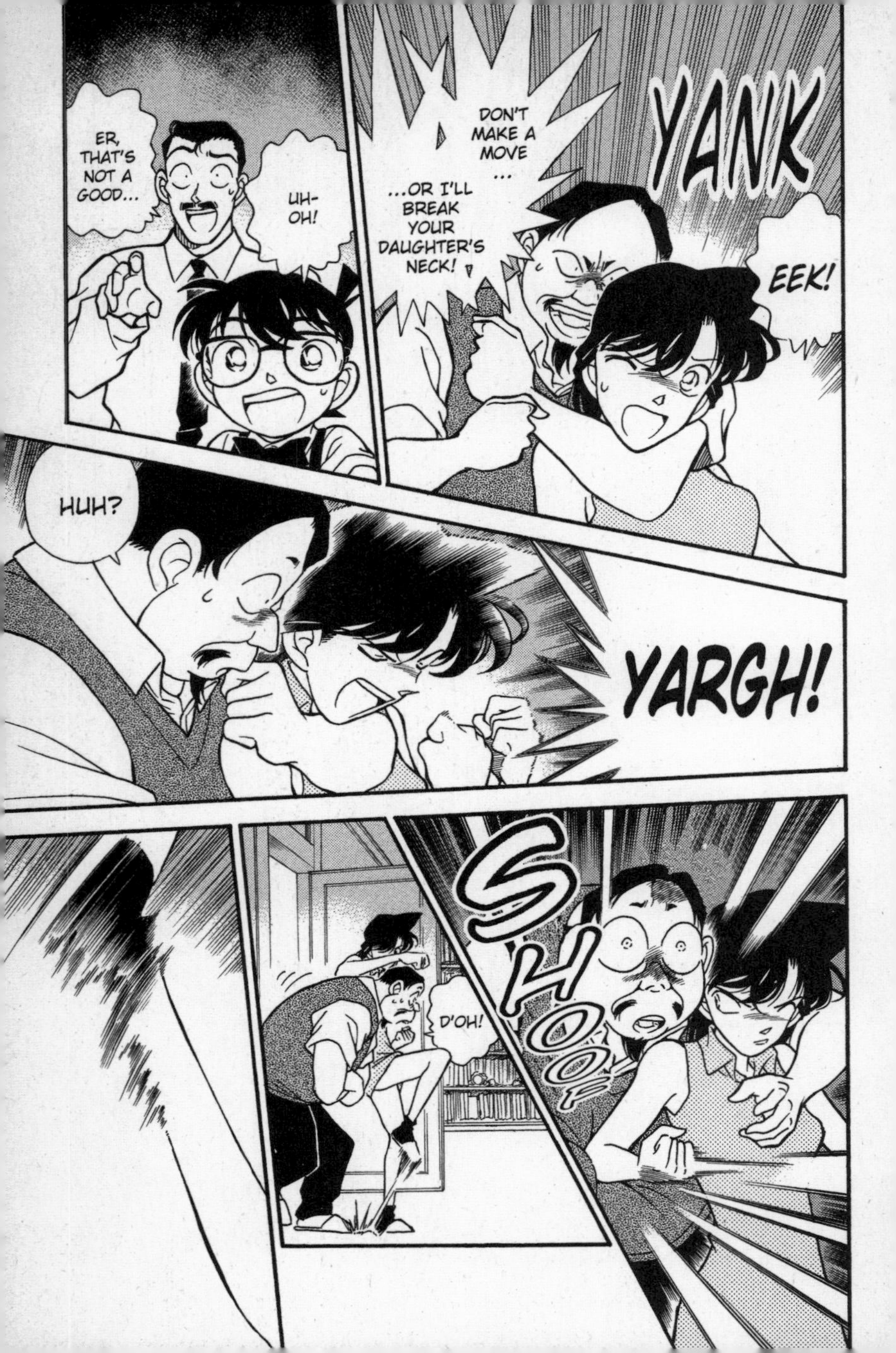
YANK
DON'T MAKE A MOVE ...
...OR I'LL BREAK YOUR DAUGHTER'S NECK!
EEK!
UH-OH!
ER, THAT'S NOT A GOOD...
YARGH!
HUH?
SHOOOF
D'OH!

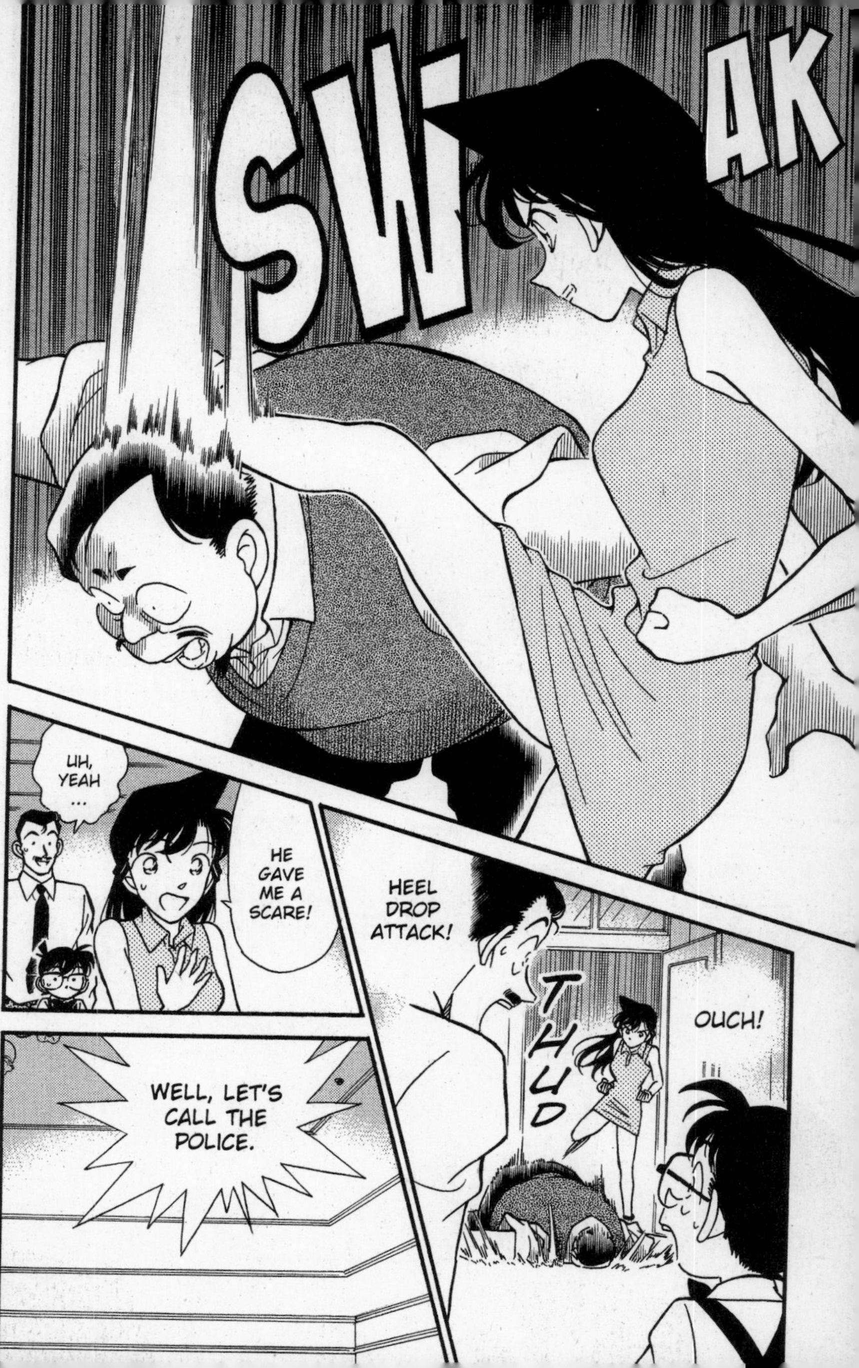
SWAK
HEEL DROP ATTACK!
THUD
OUCH!
HE GAVE ME A SCARE!
UH, YEAH ...
WELL, LET'S CALL THE POLICE.

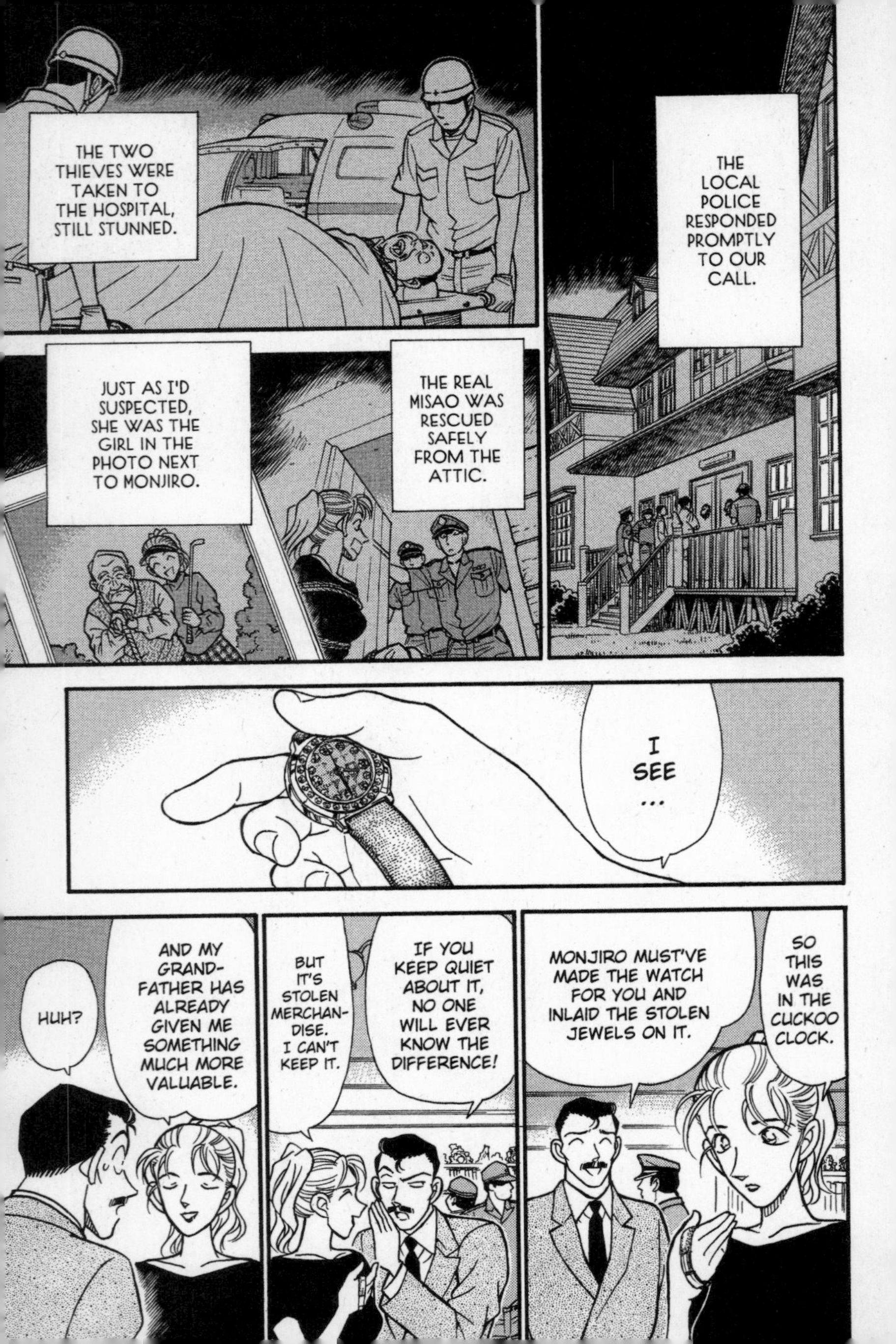
THE LOCAL POLICE RESPONDED PROMPTLY TO OUR CALL.
THE TWO THIEVES WERE TAKEN TO THE HOSPITAL, STILL STUNNED.
THE REAL MISAO WAS RESCUED SAFELY FROM THE ATTIC.
JUST AS I'D SUSPECTED, SHE WAS THE GIRL IN THE PHOTO NEXT TO MONJIRO.
I SEE ...
SO THIS WAS IN THE CUCKOO CLOCK.
MONJIRO MUST'VE MADE THE WATCH FOR YOU AND INLAID THE STOLEN JEWELS ON IT.
IF YOU KEEP QUIET ABOUT IT, NO ONE WILL EVER KNOW THE DIFFERENCE!
BUT IT'S STOLEN MERCHANDISE. I CAN'T KEEP IT.
AND MY GRANDFATHER HAS ALREADY GIVEN ME SOMETHING MUCH MORE VALUABLE.
HUH?

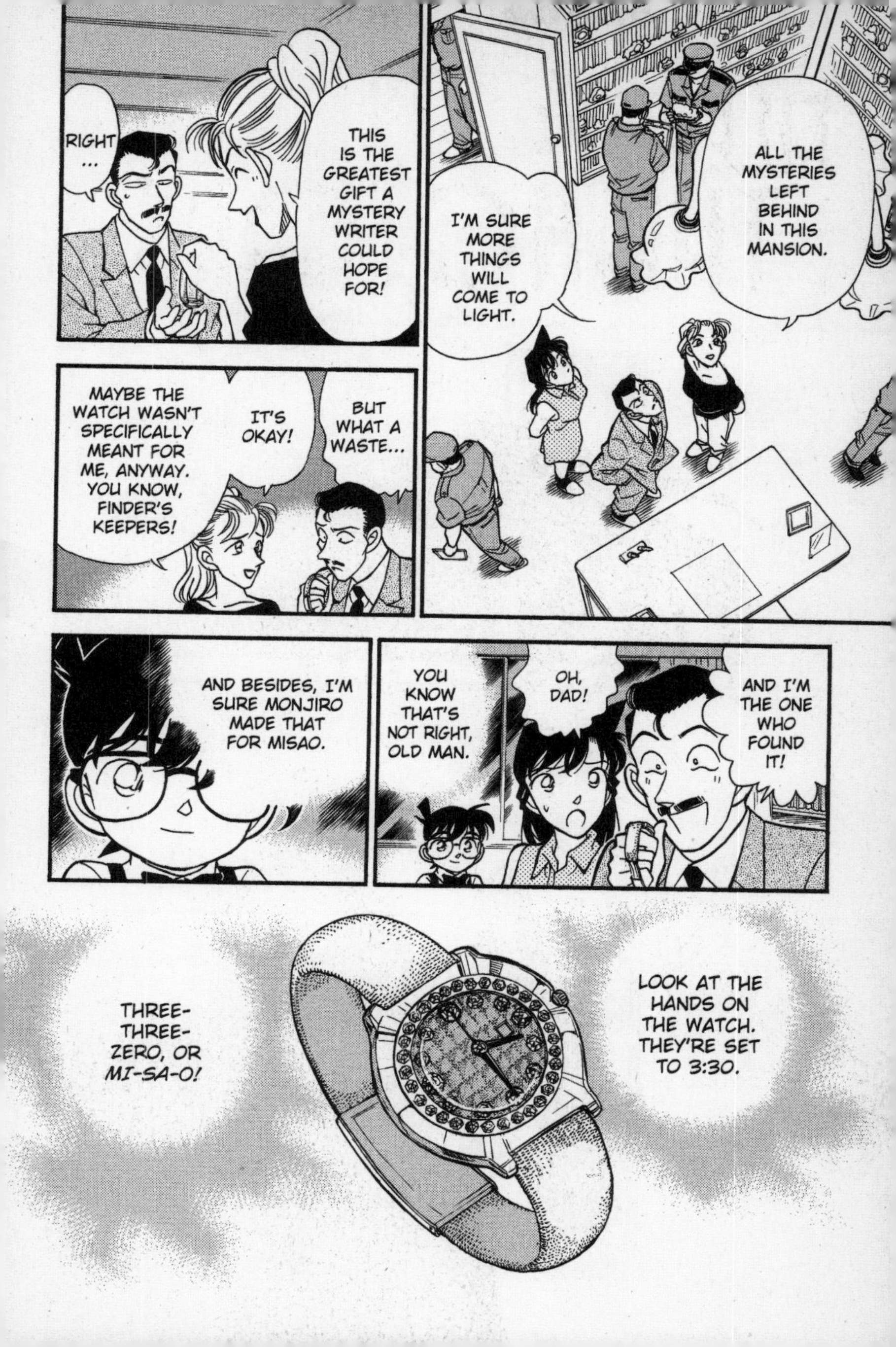
ALL THE MYSTERIES LEFT BEHIND IN THIS MANSION.
I'M SURE MORE THINGS WILL COME TO LIGHT.
THIS IS THE GREATEST GIFT A MYSTERY WRITER COULD HOPE FOR!
RIGHT...
BUT WHAT A WASTE...
IT'S OKAY!
MAYBE THE WATCH WASN'T SPECIFICALLY MEANT FOR ME, ANYWAY. YOU KNOW, FINDER'S KEEPERS!
AND I'M THE ONE WHO FOUND IT!
OH, DAD!
YOU KNOW THAT'S NOT RIGHT, OLD MAN.
AND BESIDES, I'M SURE MONJIRO MADE THAT FOR MISAO.
LOOK AT THE HANDS ON THE WATCH. THEY'RE SET TO 3:30.
THREE-THREE-ZERO, OR *MI-SA-O!*

FILE 10: THE ACTORS

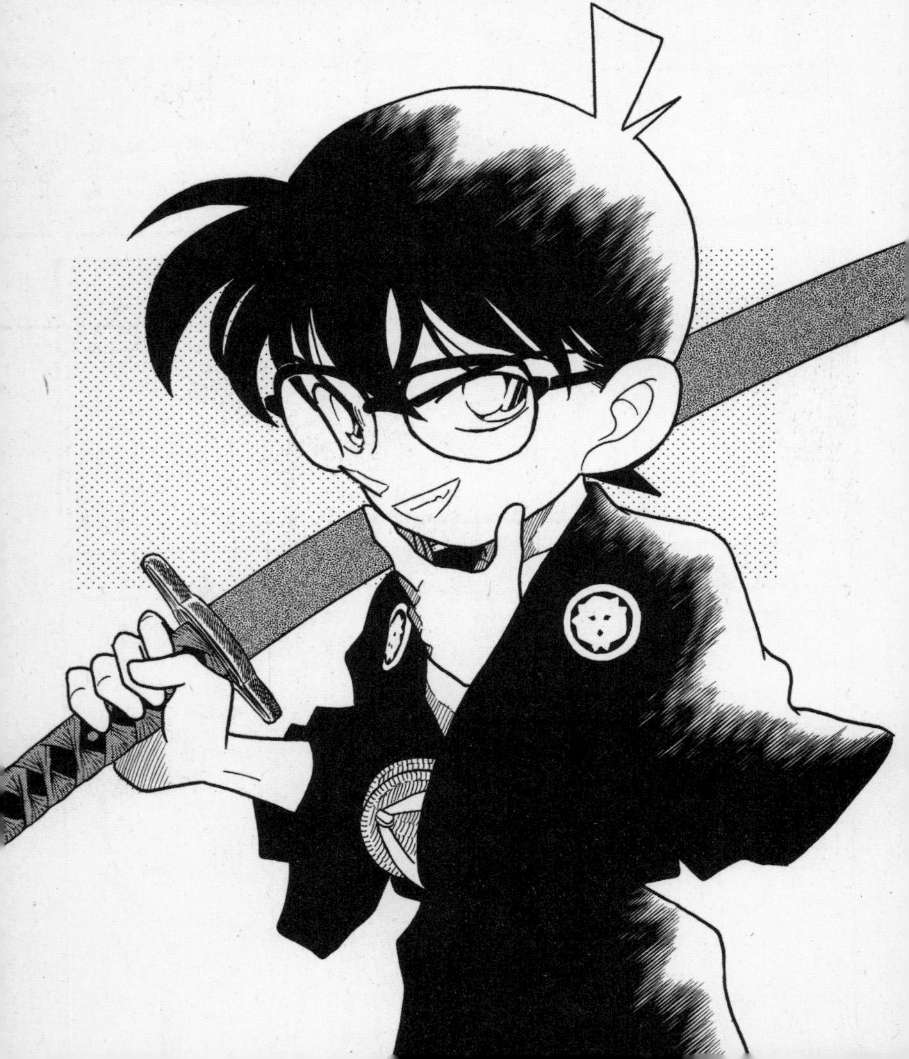

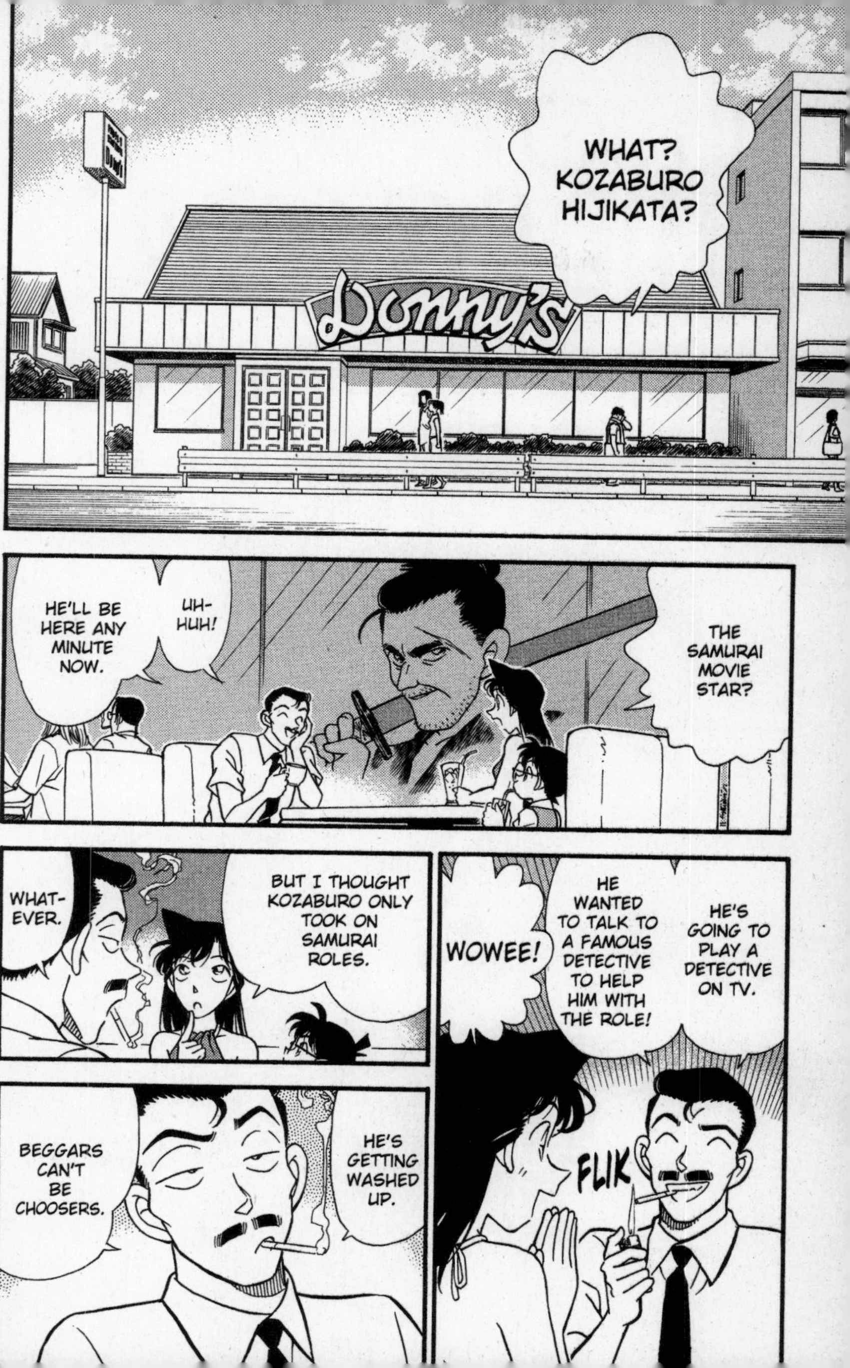
WHAT? KOZABURO HIJIKATA?
THE SAMURAI MOVIE STAR?
UH-HUH!
HE'LL BE HERE ANY MINUTE NOW.
HE'S GOING TO PLAY A DETECTIVE ON TV.
HE WANTED TO TALK TO A FAMOUS DETECTIVE TO HELP HIM WITH THE ROLE!
WOWEE!
FLIK
BUT I THOUGHT KOZABURO ONLY TOOK ON SAMURAI ROLES.
WHAT-EVER.
HE'S GETTING WASHED UP.
BEGGARS CAN'T BE CHOOSERS.

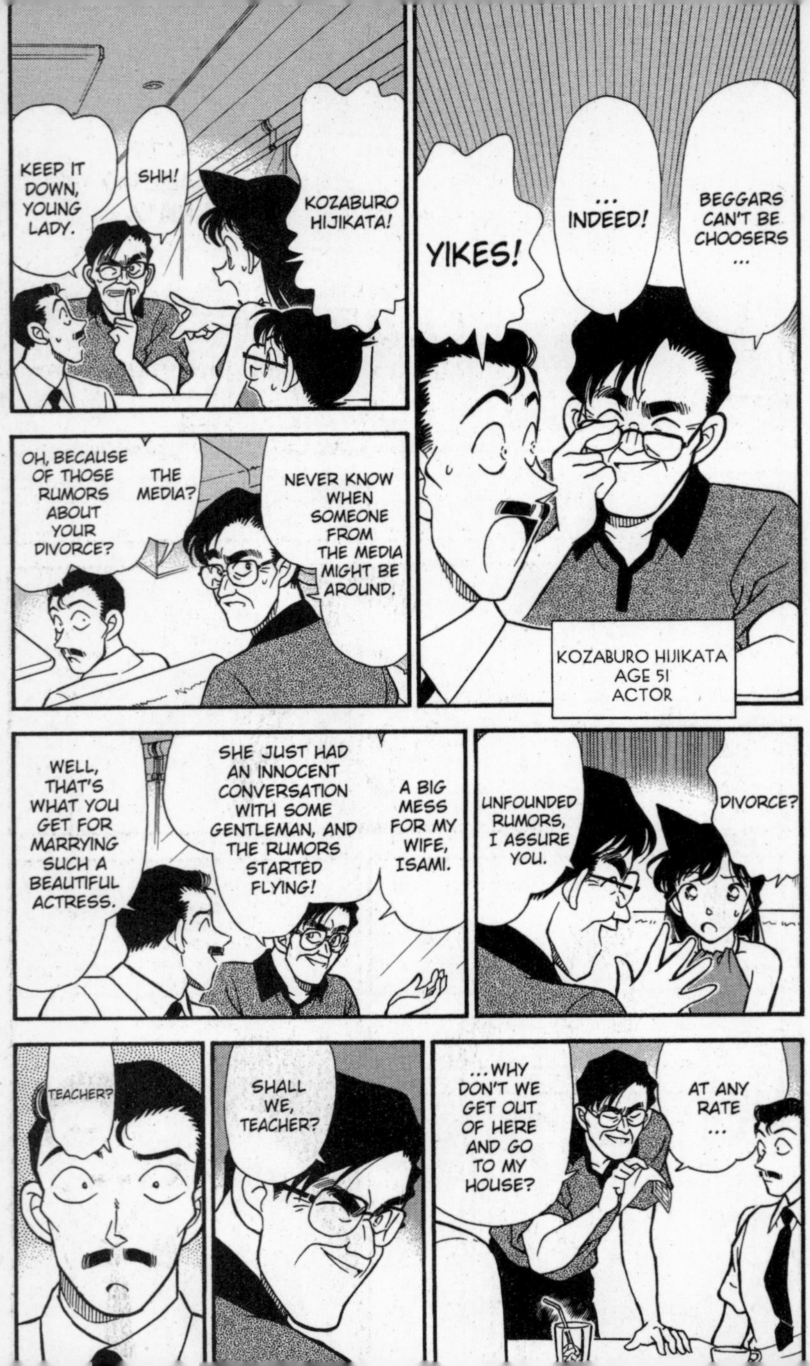
BEGGARS CAN'T BE CHOOSERS ...
... INDEED!
YIKES!
KOZABURO HIJIKATA AGE 51 ACTOR
KOZABURO HIJIKATA!
SHH!
KEEP IT DOWN, YOUNG LADY.
NEVER KNOW WHEN SOMEONE FROM THE MEDIA MIGHT BE AROUND.
THE MEDIA?
OH, BECAUSE OF THOSE RUMORS ABOUT YOUR DIVORCE?
DIVORCE?
UNFOUNDED RUMORS, I ASSURE YOU.
A BIG MESS FOR MY WIFE, ISAMI.
SHE JUST HAD AN INNOCENT CONVERSATION WITH SOME GENTLEMAN, AND THE RUMORS STARTED FLYING!
WELL, THAT'S WHAT YOU GET FOR MARRYING SUCH A BEAUTIFUL ACTRESS.
AT ANY RATE ...
...WHY DON'T WE GET OUT OF HERE AND GO TO MY HOUSE?
SHALL WE, TEACHER?
TEACHER?

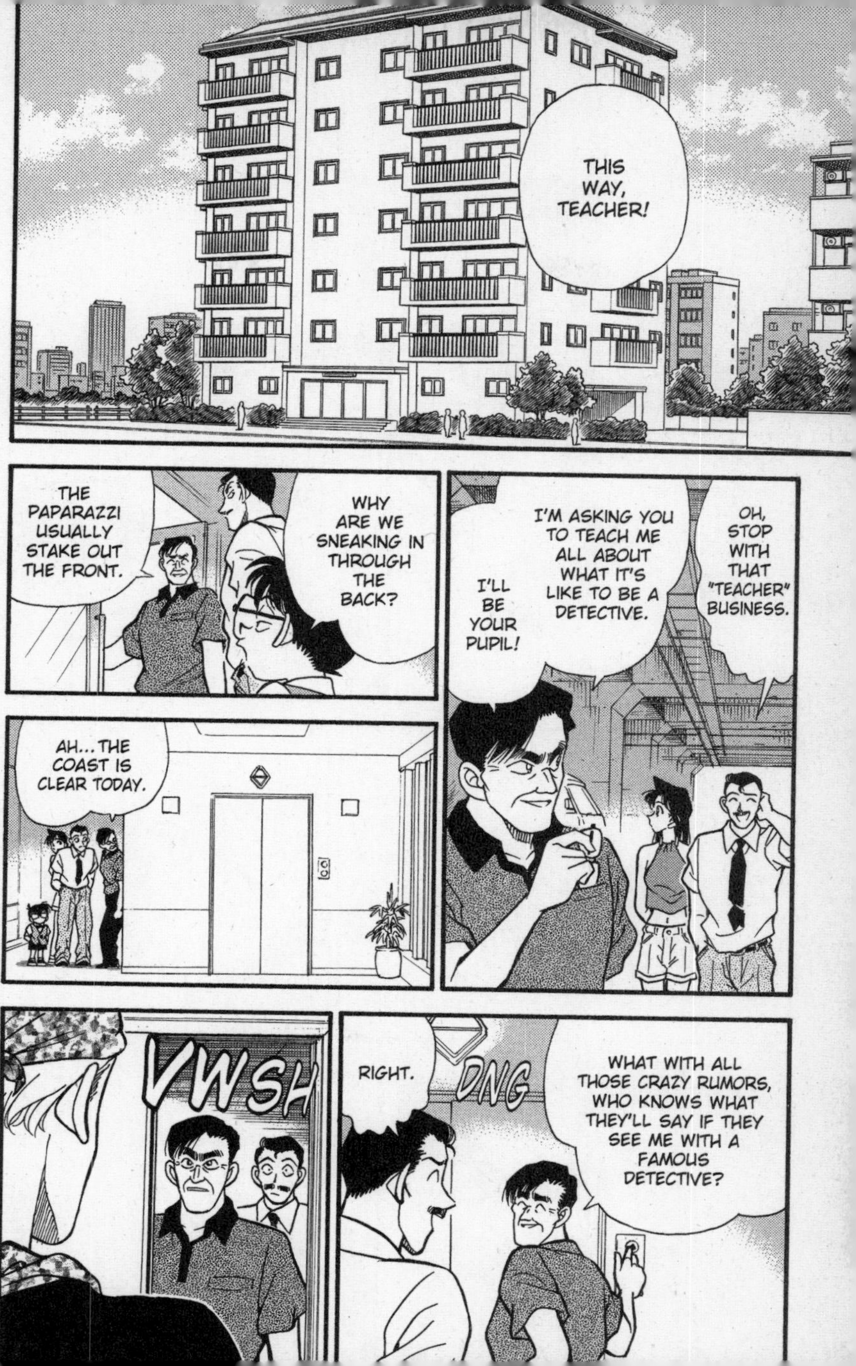
THIS WAY, TEACHER!
OH, STOP WITH THAT "TEACHER" BUSINESS.
I'M ASKING YOU TO TEACH ME ALL ABOUT WHAT IT'S LIKE TO BE A DETECTIVE.
I'LL BE YOUR PUPIL!
WHY ARE WE SNEAKING IN THROUGH THE BACK?
THE PAPARAZZI USUALLY STAKE OUT THE FRONT.
AH...THE COAST IS CLEAR TODAY.
WHAT WITH ALL THOSE CRAZY RUMORS, WHO KNOWS WHAT THEY'LL SAY IF THEY SEE ME WITH A FAMOUS DETECTIVE?
DNG
RIGHT.
VWSH

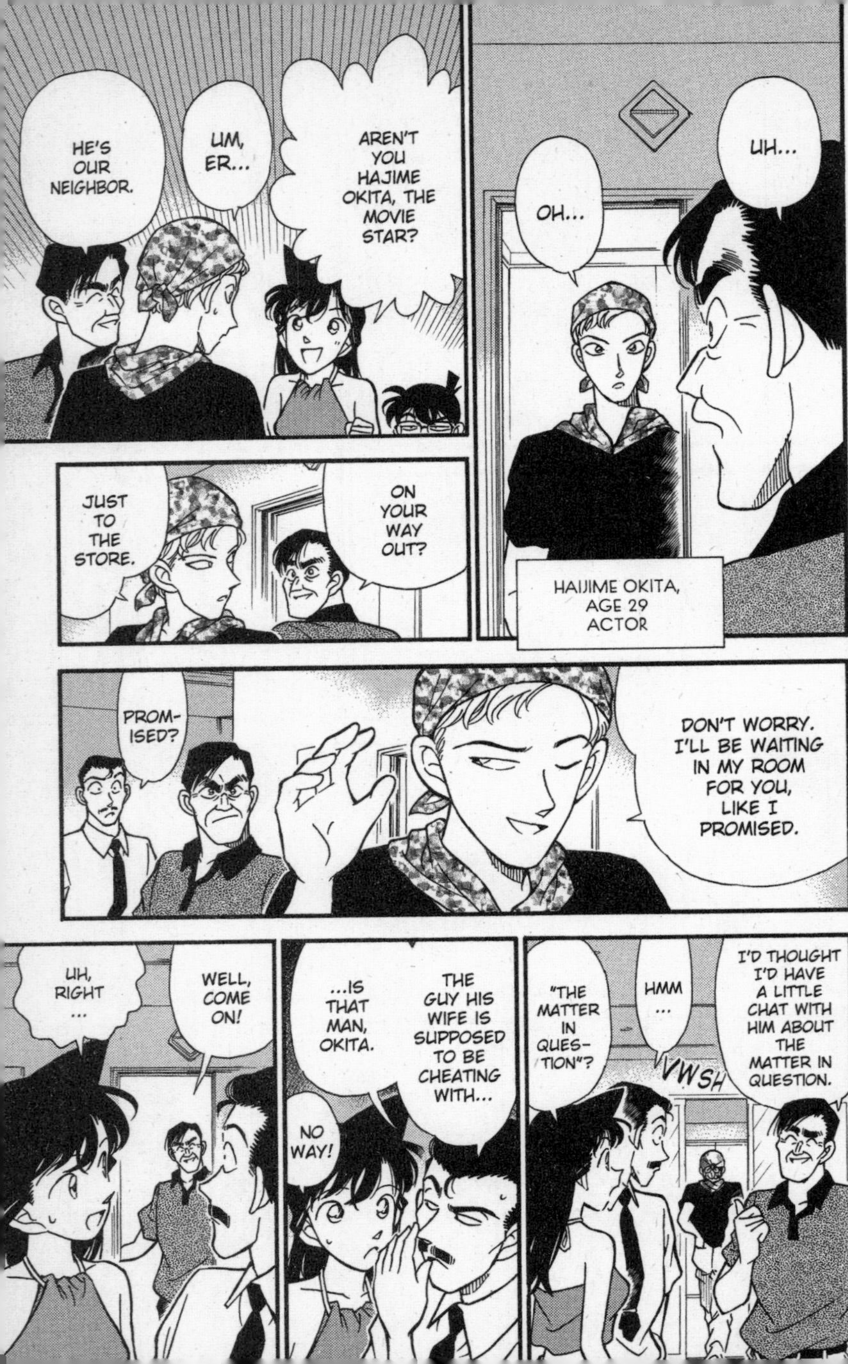
UH...
OH...
HAJIME OKITA, AGE 29 ACTOR
AREN'T YOU HAJIME OKITA, THE MOVIE STAR?
UM, ER...
HE'S OUR NEIGHBOR.
ON YOUR WAY OUT?
JUST TO THE STORE.
DON'T WORRY. I'LL BE WAITING IN MY ROOM FOR YOU, LIKE I PROMISED.
PROM-ISED?
I'D THOUGHT I'D HAVE A LITTLE CHAT WITH HIM ABOUT THE MATTER IN QUESTION.
VWSH
HMM ...
"THE MATTER IN QUES-TION"?
THE GUY HIS WIFE IS SUPPOSED TO BE CHEATING WITH...
...IS THAT MAN, OKITA.
NO WAY!
WELL, COME ON!
UH, RIGHT ...

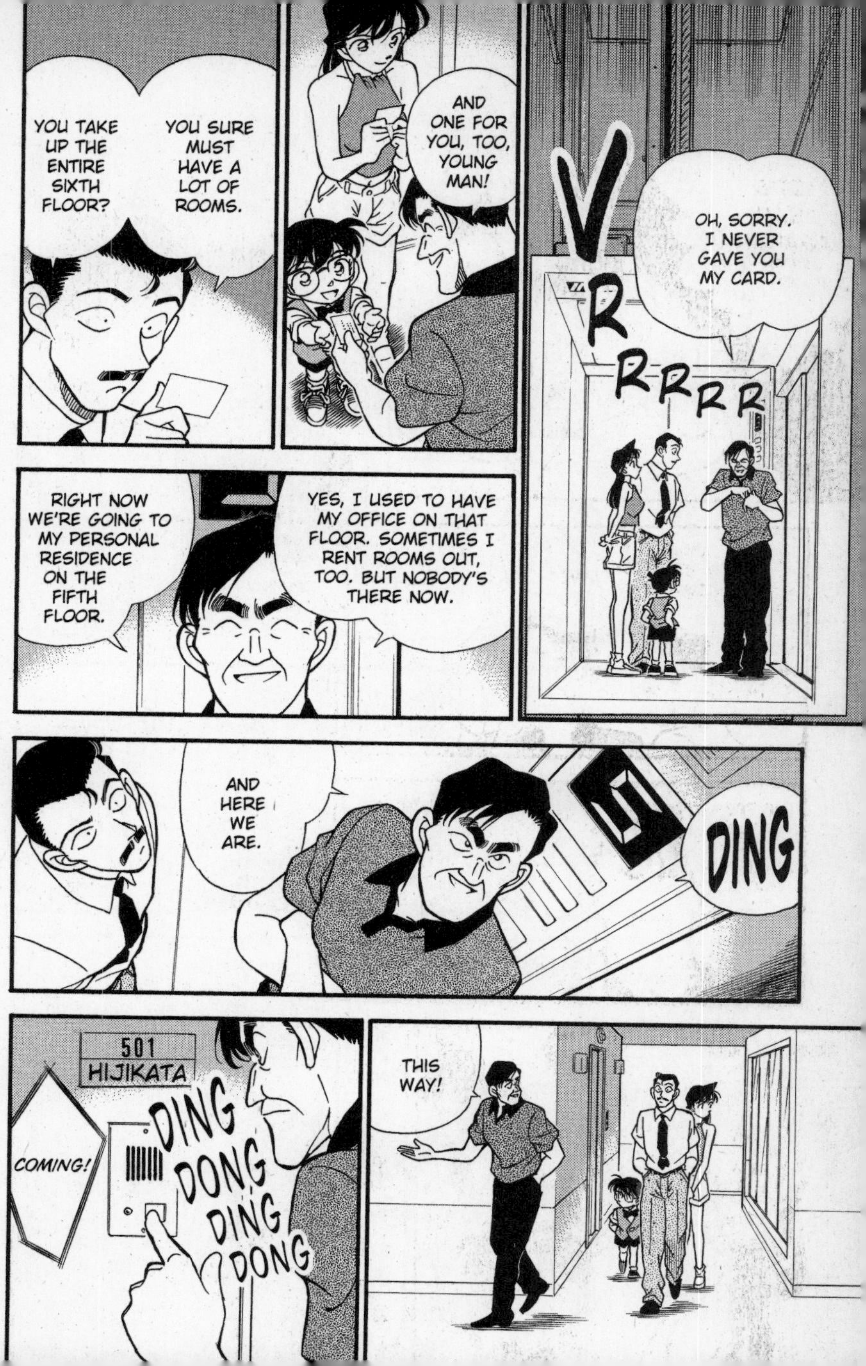
VRRRRRR
OH, SORRY. I NEVER GAVE YOU MY CARD.
AND ONE FOR YOU, TOO, YOUNG MAN!
YOU SURE MUST HAVE A LOT OF ROOMS.
YOU TAKE UP THE ENTIRE SIXTH FLOOR?
YES, I USED TO HAVE MY OFFICE ON THAT FLOOR. SOMETIMES I RENT ROOMS OUT, TOO. BUT NOBODY'S THERE NOW.
RIGHT NOW WE'RE GOING TO MY PERSONAL RESIDENCE ON THE FIFTH FLOOR.
DING
AND HERE WE ARE.
THIS WAY!
501
HIJIKATA
DING DONG DING DONG
COMING!

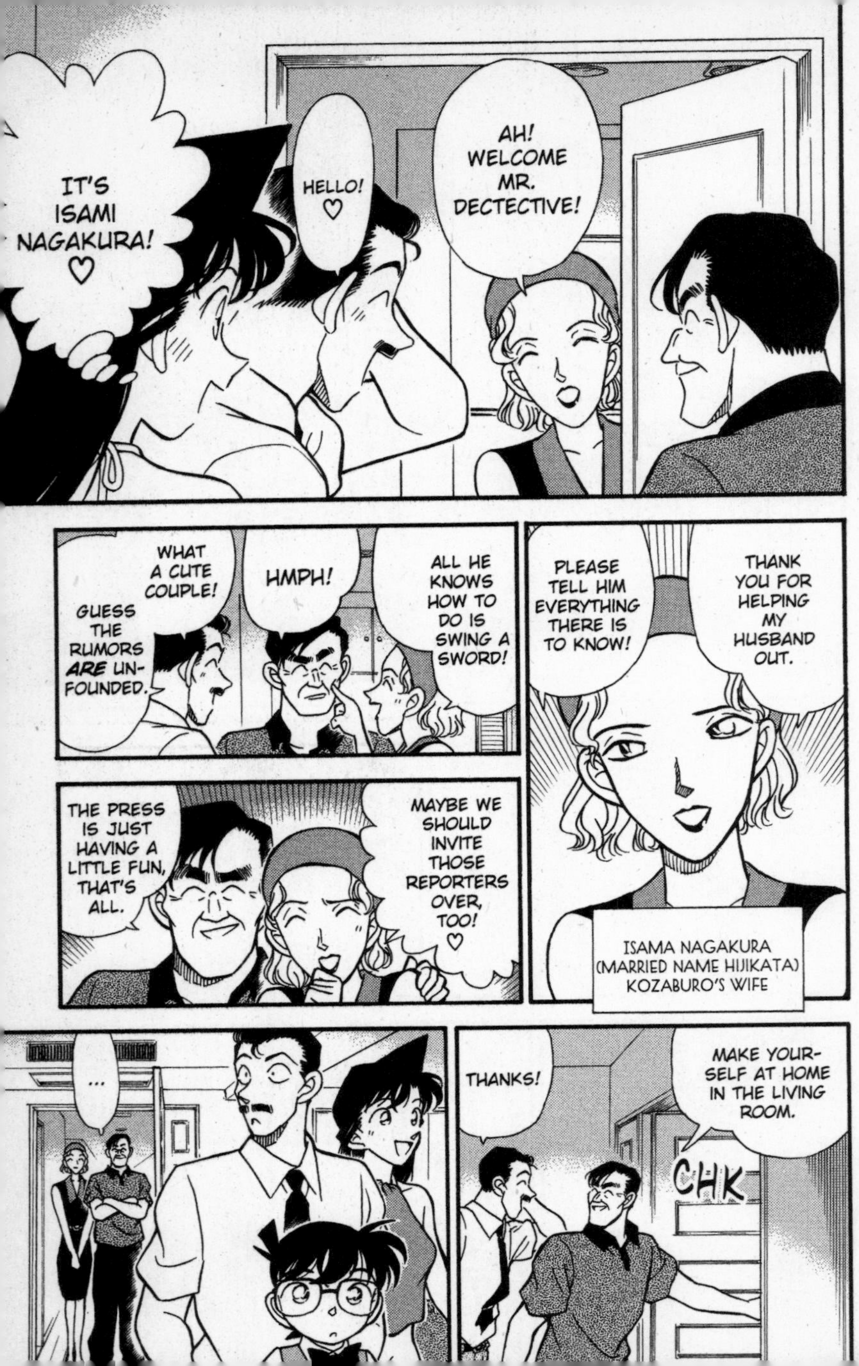
AH! WELCOME MR. DECTECTIVE!
HELLO! ♡
IT'S ISAMI NAGAKURA! ♡
THANK YOU FOR HELPING MY HUSBAND OUT.
PLEASE TELL HIM EVERYTHING THERE IS TO KNOW!
ISAMA NAGAKURA (MARRIED NAME HIJIKATA) KOZABURO'S WIFE
ALL HE KNOWS HOW TO DO IS SWING A SWORD!
HMPH!
WHAT A CUTE COUPLE!
GUESS THE RUMORS ARE UN-FOUNDED.
MAYBE WE SHOULD INVITE THOSE REPORTERS OVER, TOO! ♡
THE PRESS IS JUST HAVING A LITTLE FUN, THAT'S ALL.
MAKE YOUR-SELF AT HOME IN THE LIVING ROOM.
CHK
THANKS!
...

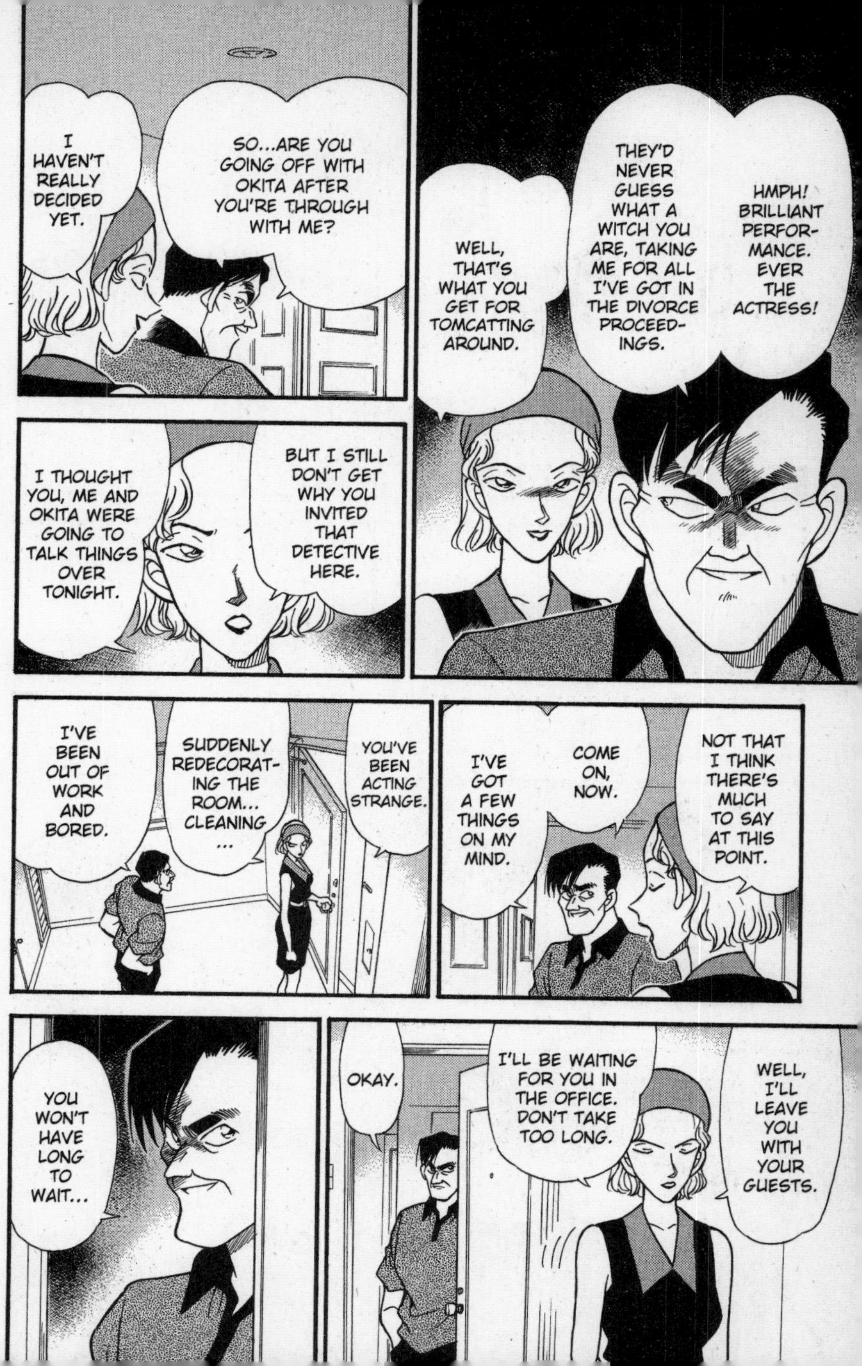
HMPH! BRILLIANT PERFOR-MANCE. EVER THE ACTRESS!
THEY'D NEVER GUESS WHAT A WITCH YOU ARE, TAKING ME FOR ALL I'VE GOT IN THE DIVORCE PROCEED-INGS.
WELL, THAT'S WHAT YOU GET FOR TOMCATTING AROUND.
SO...ARE YOU GOING OFF WITH OKITA AFTER YOU'RE THROUGH WITH ME?
I HAVEN'T REALLY DECIDED YET.
BUT I STILL DON'T GET WHY YOU INVITED THAT DETECTIVE HERE.
I THOUGHT YOU, ME AND OKITA WERE GOING TO TALK THINGS OVER TONIGHT.
NOT THAT I THINK THERE'S MUCH TO SAY AT THIS POINT.
COME ON, NOW.
I'VE GOT A FEW THINGS ON MY MIND.
YOU'VE BEEN ACTING STRANGE.
SUDDENLY REDECORAT-ING THE ROOM... CLEANING ...
I'VE BEEN OUT OF WORK AND BORED.
WELL, I'LL LEAVE YOU WITH YOUR GUESTS.
I'LL BE WAITING FOR YOU IN THE OFFICE. DON'T TAKE TOO LONG.
OKAY.
YOU WON'T HAVE LONG TO WAIT...

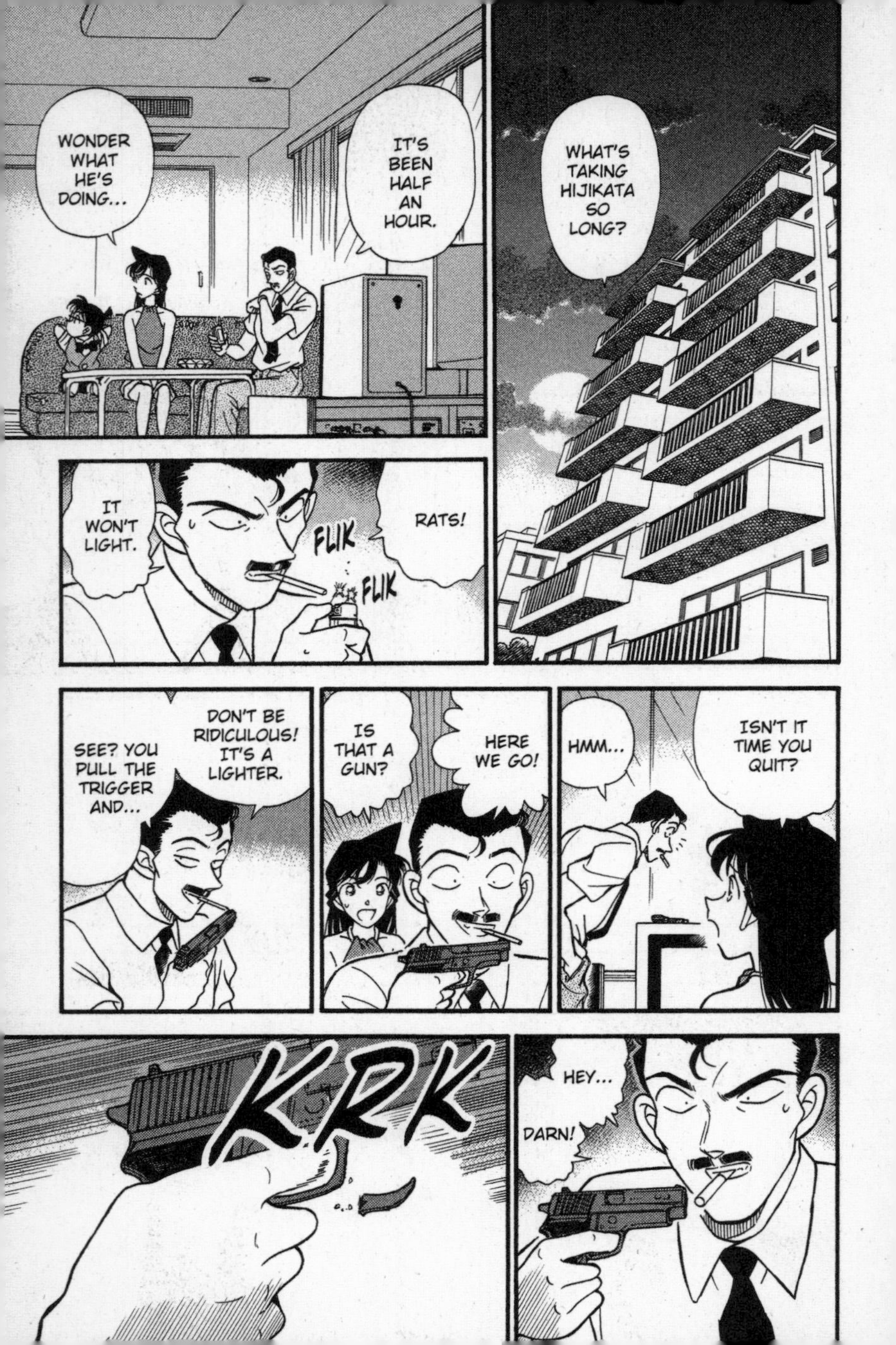
WHAT'S TAKING HIJIKATA SO LONG?
IT'S BEEN HALF AN HOUR.
WONDER WHAT HE'S DOING...
RATS!
FLIK
FLIK
IT WON'T LIGHT.
ISN'T IT TIME YOU QUIT?
HMM...
HERE WE GO!
IS THAT A GUN?
DON'T BE RIDICULOUS! IT'S A LIGHTER.
SEE? YOU PULL THE TRIGGER AND...
HEY...
DARN!
KRK

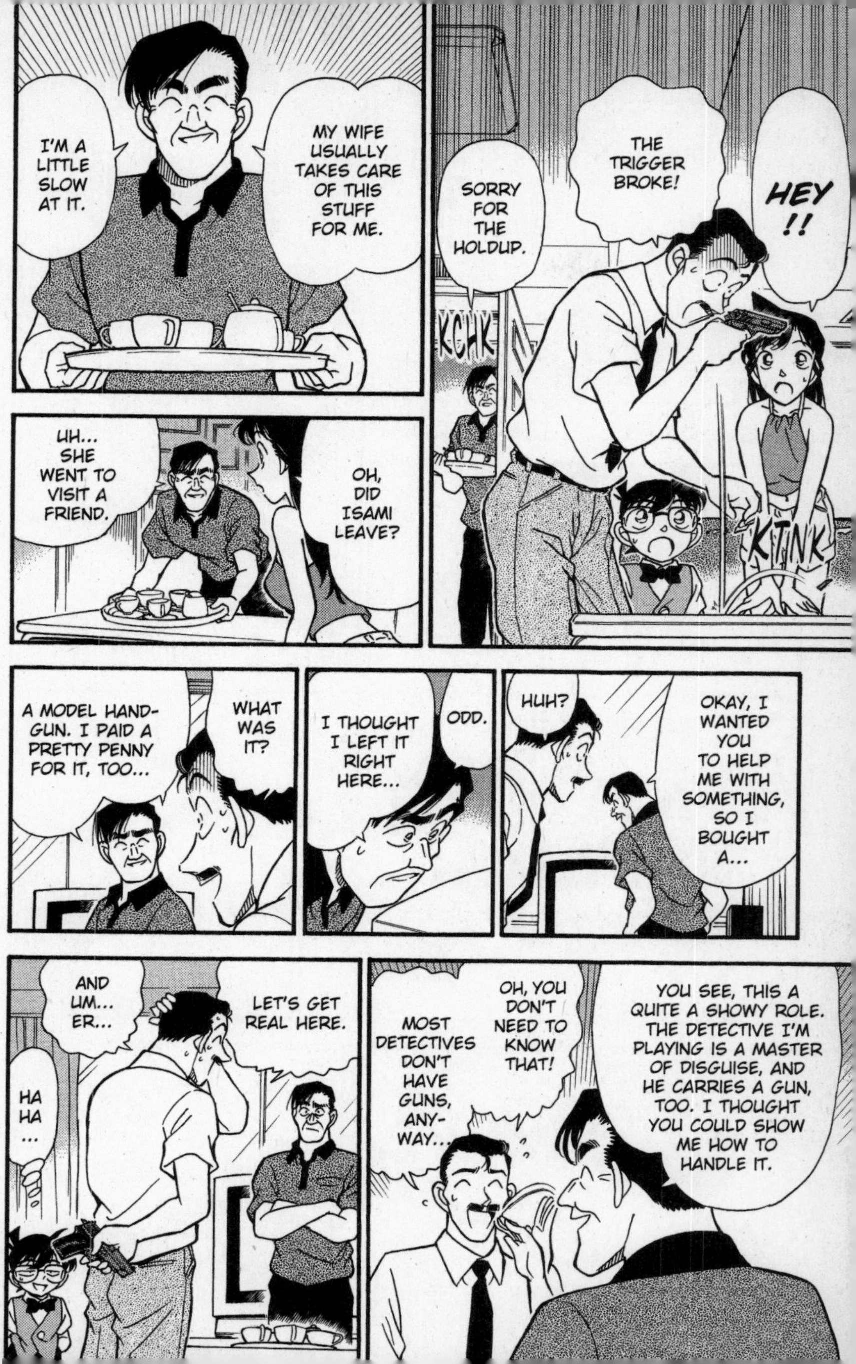
HEY!!
THE TRIGGER BROKE!
SORRY FOR THE HOLDUP.
KCHK
KTNK
MY WIFE USUALLY TAKES CARE OF THIS STUFF FOR ME.
I'M A LITTLE SLOW AT IT.
OH, DID ISAMI LEAVE?
UH... SHE WENT TO VISIT A FRIEND.
OKAY, I WANTED YOU TO HELP ME WITH SOMETHING, SO I BOUGHT A...
HUH?
ODD.
I THOUGHT I LEFT IT RIGHT HERE...
WHAT WAS IT?
A MODEL HAND-GUN. I PAID A PRETTY PENNY FOR IT, TOO...
YOU SEE, THIS A QUITE A SHOWY ROLE. THE DETECTIVE I'M PLAYING IS A MASTER OF DISGUISE, AND HE CARRIES A GUN, TOO. I THOUGHT YOU COULD SHOW ME HOW TO HANDLE IT.
OH, YOU DON'T NEED TO KNOW THAT!
MOST DETECTIVES DON'T HAVE GUNS, ANY-WAY...
LET'S GET REAL HERE.
AND UM... ER...
HA HA ...

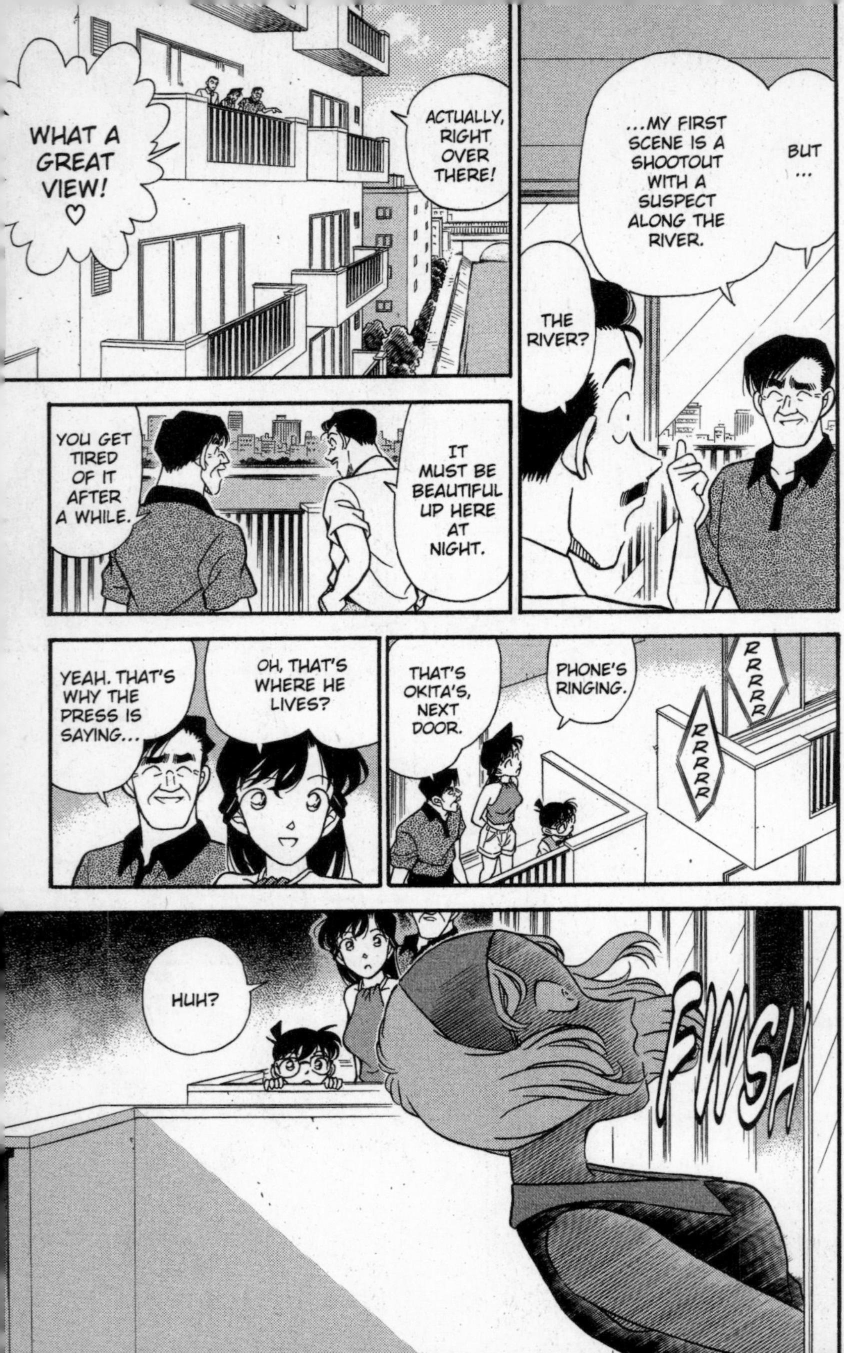
BUT ...
...MY FIRST SCENE IS A SHOOTOUT WITH A SUSPECT ALONG THE RIVER.
THE RIVER?
ACTUALLY, RIGHT OVER THERE!
WHAT A GREAT VIEW! ♡
IT MUST BE BEAUTIFUL UP HERE AT NIGHT.
YOU GET TIRED OF IT AFTER A WHILE.
RRRRR
RRRRR
PHONE'S RINGING.
THAT'S OKITA'S, NEXT DOOR.
OH, THAT'S WHERE HE LIVES?
YEAH. THAT'S WHY THE PRESS IS SAYING...
FWISH
HUH?

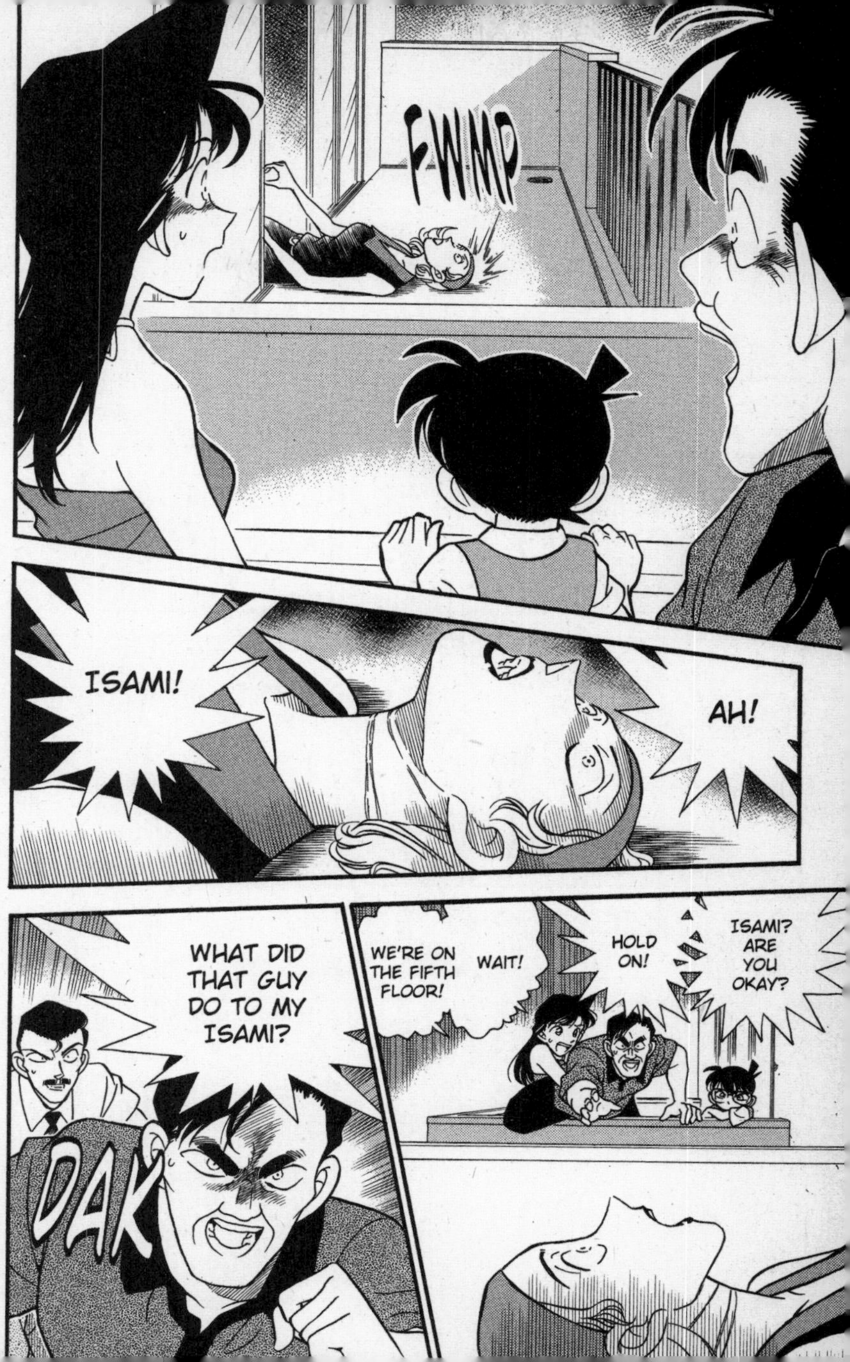
FWMP
AH!
ISAMI!
ISAMI? ARE YOU OKAY?
HOLD ON!
WAIT!
WE'RE ON THE FIFTH FLOOR!
WHAT DID THAT GUY DO TO MY ISAMI?
DAK

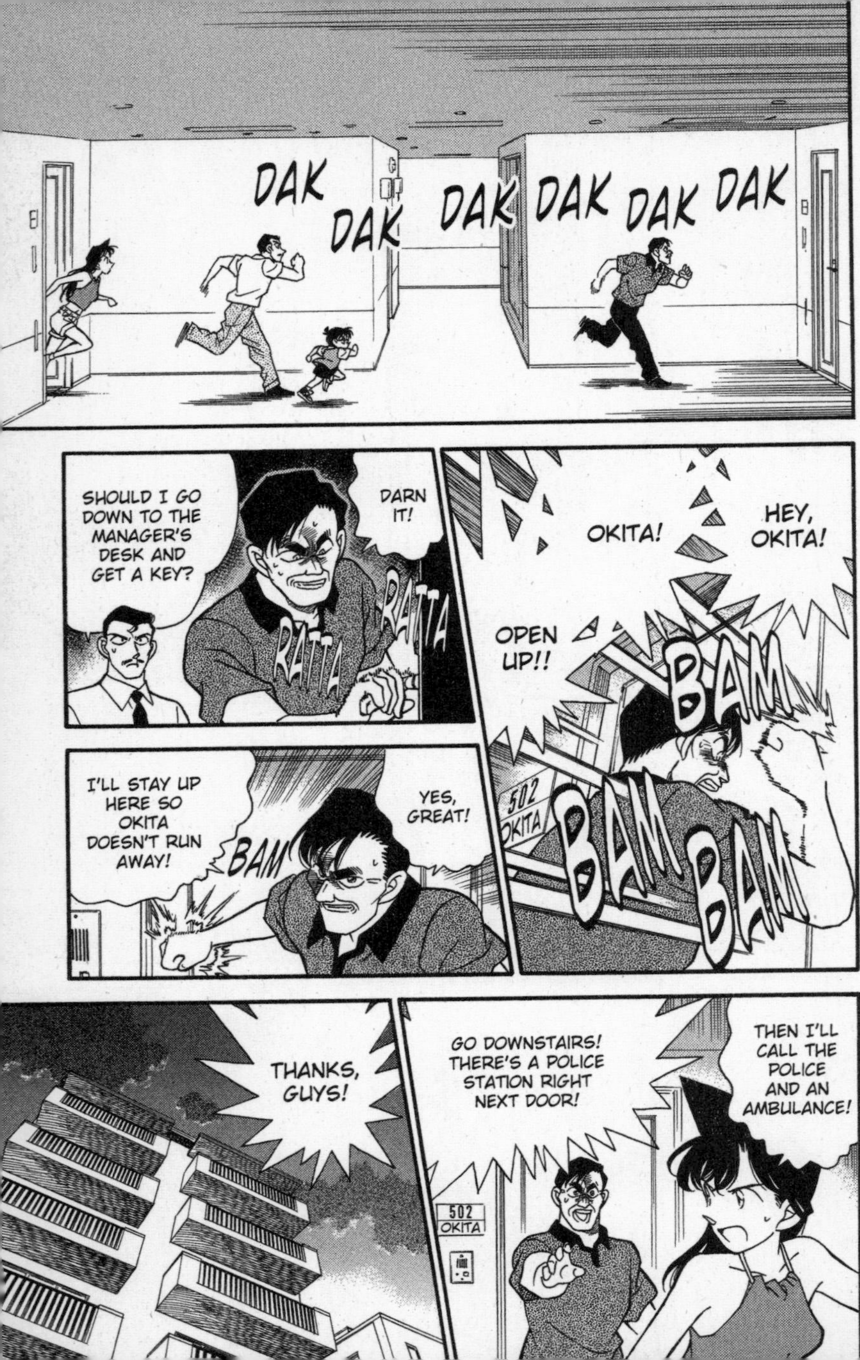
DAK
DAK
DAK
DAK
DAK
DAK
HEY, OKITA!
OKITA!
OPEN UP!!
BAM
502 OKITA
BAM
BAM
DARN IT!
SHOULD I GO DOWN TO THE MANAGER'S DESK AND GET A KEY?
RATTA
RATTA
YES, GREAT!
I'LL STAY UP HERE SO OKITA DOESN'T RUN AWAY!
BAM
THEN I'LL CALL THE POLICE AND AN AMBULANCE!
GO DOWNSTAIRS! THERE'S A POLICE STATION RIGHT NEXT DOOR!
502 OKITA
THANKS, GUYS!

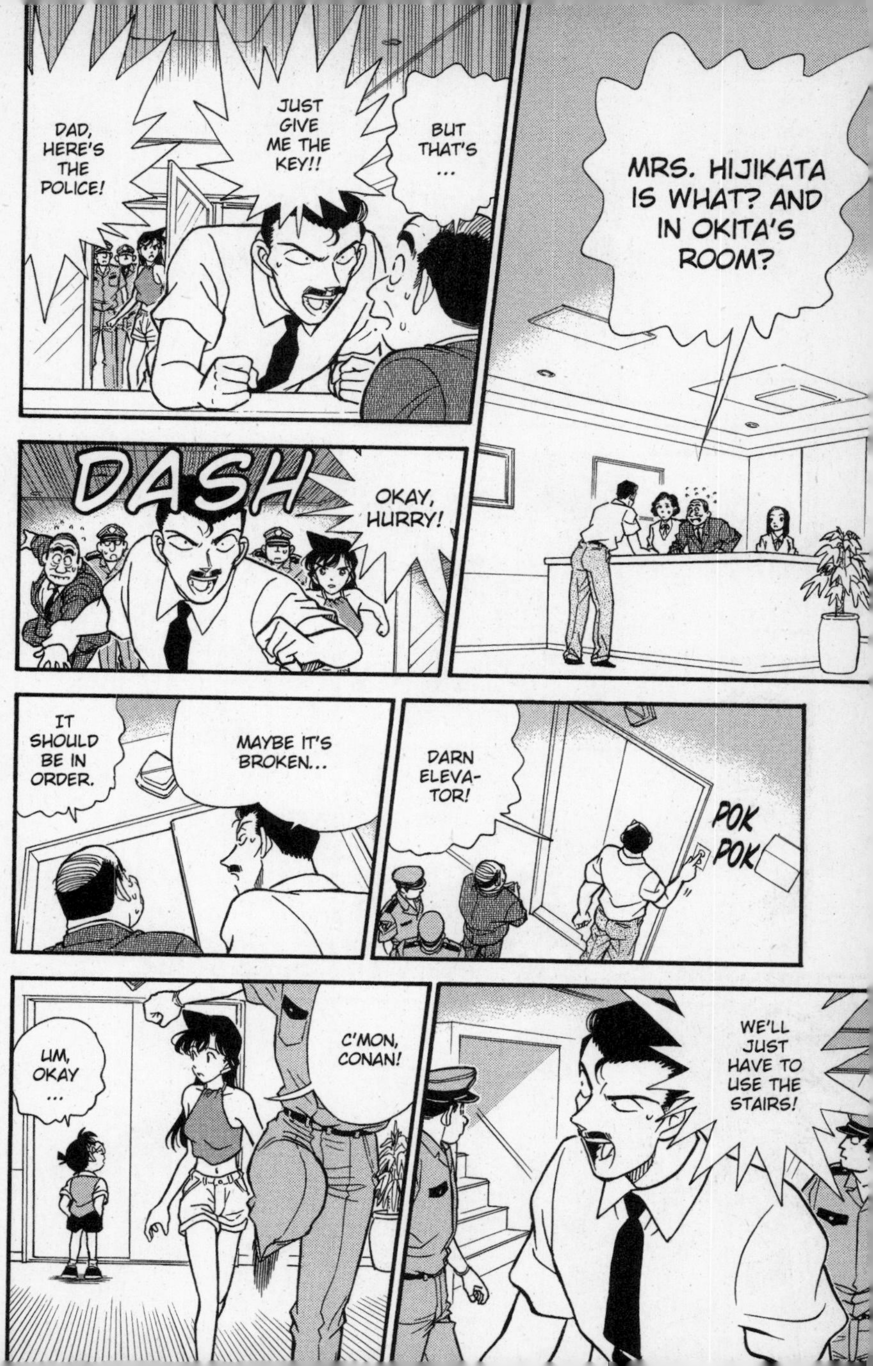

MRS. HIJIKATA IS WHAT? AND IN OKITA'S ROOM?
BUT THAT'S ...
JUST GIVE ME THE KEY!!
DAD, HERE'S THE POLICE!
OKAY, HURRY!
DASH
POK POK
DARN ELEVATOR!
MAYBE IT'S BROKEN...
IT SHOULD BE IN ORDER.
WE'LL JUST HAVE TO USE THE STAIRS!
C'MON, CONAN!
UM, OKAY ...

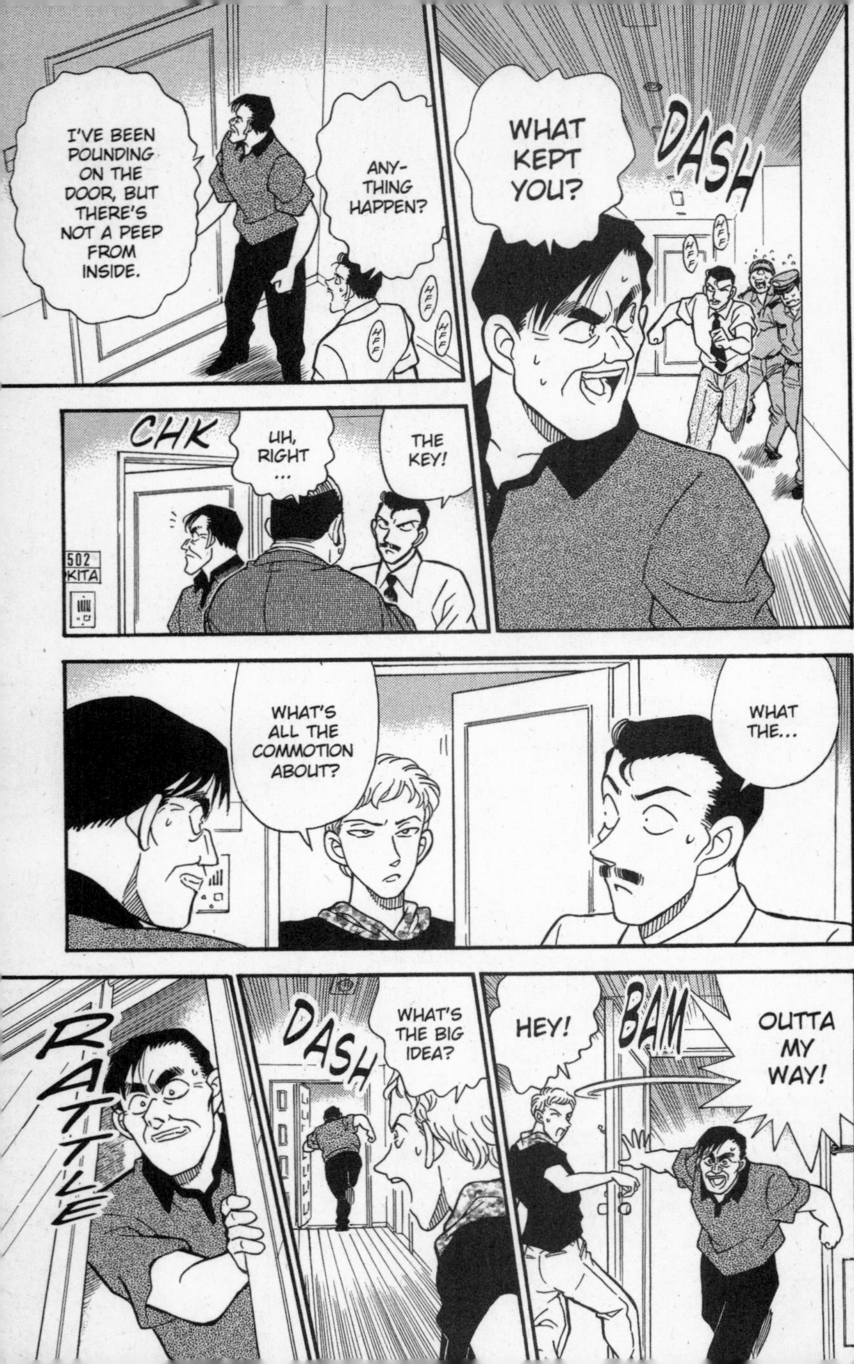
WHAT KEPT YOU?
DASH
HFF
HFF
HFF
ANY-THING HAPPEN?
HFF
HFF
HFF
I'VE BEEN POUNDING ON THE DOOR, BUT THERE'S NOT A PEEP FROM INSIDE.
THE KEY!
UH, RIGHT ...
CHK
502
KITA
WHAT THE...
WHAT'S ALL THE COMMOTION ABOUT?
OUTTA MY WAY!
BAM
HEY!
WHAT'S THE BIG IDEA?
DASH
RATTLE

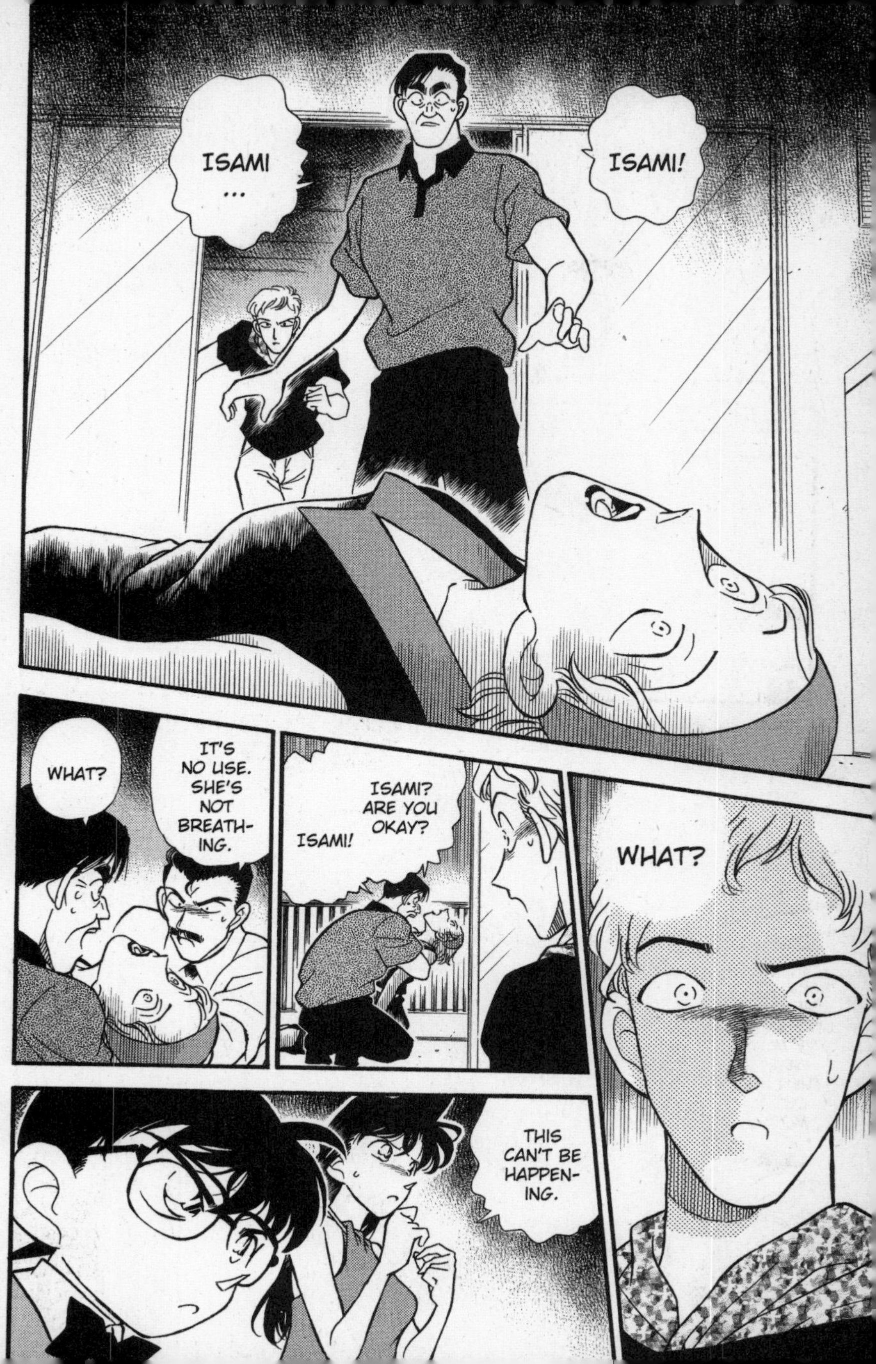
ISAMI!
ISAMI ...
WHAT?
ISAMI? ARE YOU OKAY?
ISAMI!
IT'S NO USE. SHE'S NOT BREATH-ING.
WHAT?
THIS CAN'T BE HAPPEN-ING.

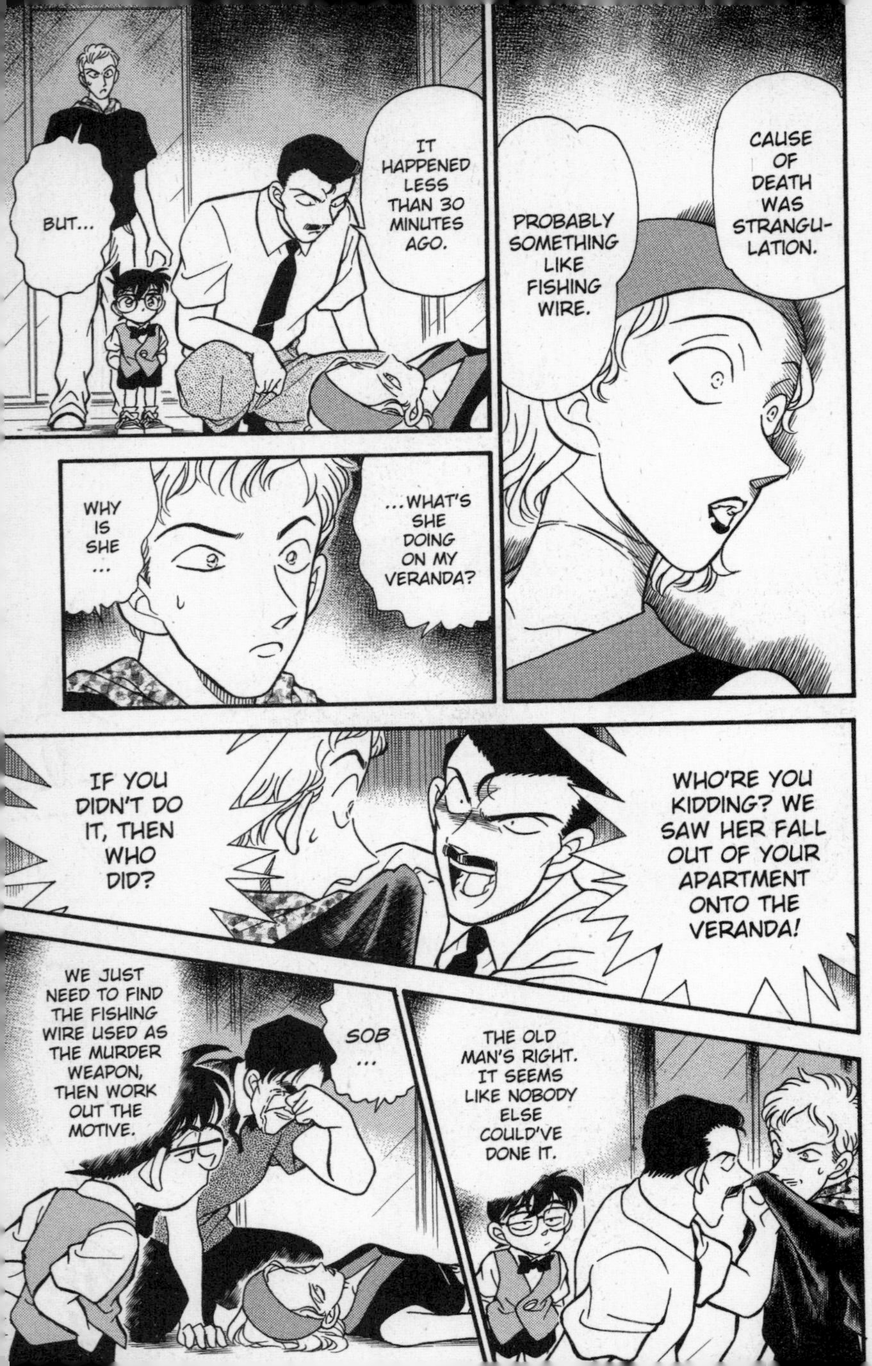
CAUSE OF DEATH WAS STRANGULATION.
PROBABLY SOMETHING LIKE FISHING WIRE.
IT HAPPENED LESS THAN 30 MINUTES AGO.
BUT...
WHY IS SHE ...
...WHAT'S SHE DOING ON MY VERANDA?
WHO'RE YOU KIDDING? WE SAW HER FALL OUT OF YOUR APARTMENT ONTO THE VERANDA!
IF YOU DIDN'T DO IT, THEN WHO DID?
THE OLD MAN'S RIGHT. IT SEEMS LIKE NOBODY ELSE COULD'VE DONE IT.
SOB ...
WE JUST NEED TO FIND THE FISHING WIRE USED AS THE MURDER WEAPON, THEN WORK OUT THE MOTIVE.

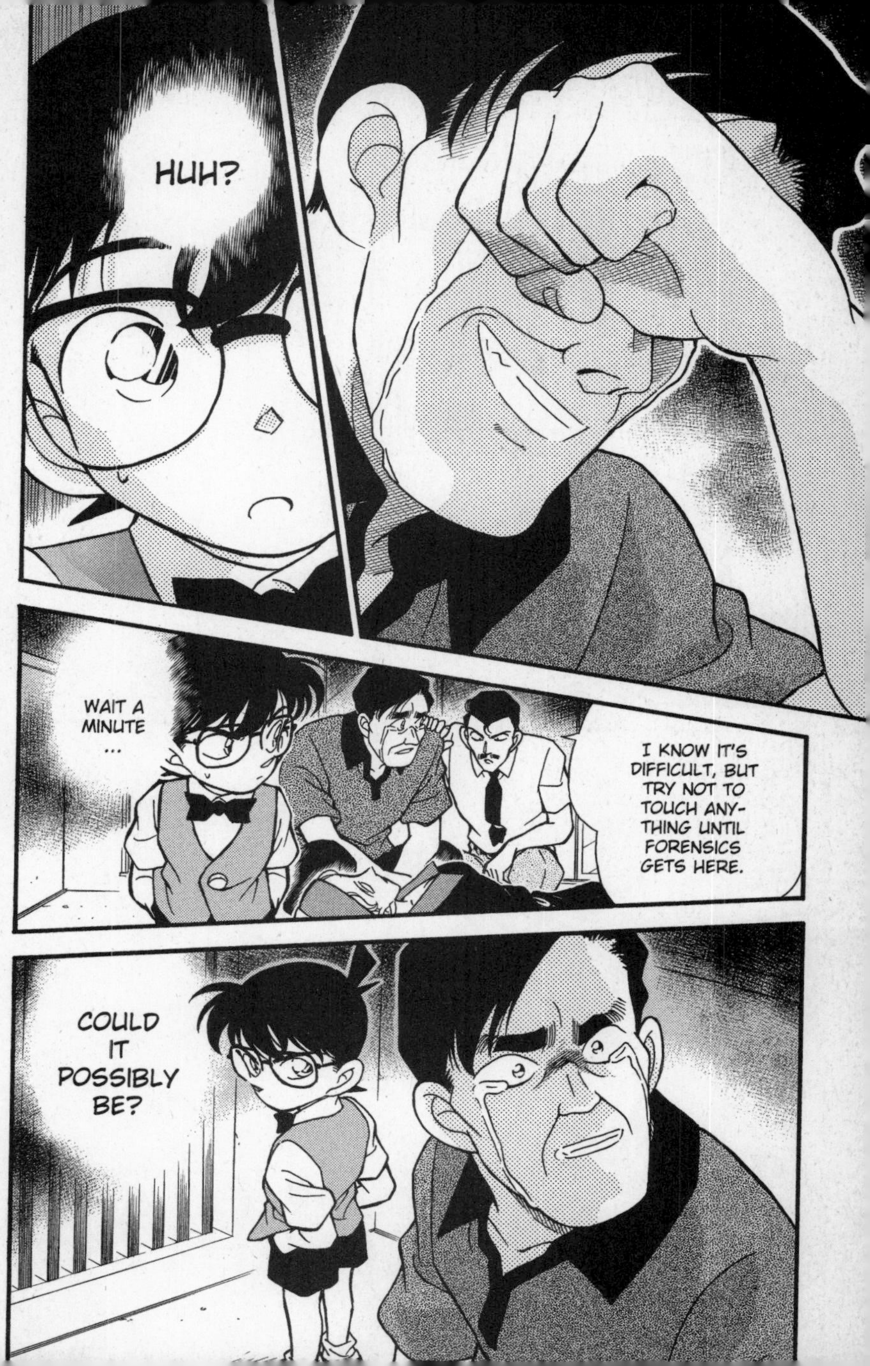
HUH?
I KNOW IT'S DIFFICULT, BUT TRY NOT TO TOUCH ANY-THING UNTIL FORENSICS GETS HERE.
WAIT A MINUTE ...
COULD IT POSSIBLY BE?

Hello, Aoyama here.

Guess what? I heard there was a Conan float in the Midosuji Parade in Osaka the other day! Apparently, they had a lively group of about 60 kids dressed up as Conan around the float!! Ms. Takayama, Mr. Kamiya and Ms. Yamazaki were all there. It sounds like it was a fun festival. Boy, I wish I could have been there (laughs)!

(Editor's note: Minami Takayama is the actress who plays Conan in the Japanese version of the *Case Closed* anime (known in Japan as *Detective Conan*). Akira Kamiya plays Detective Moore, and Wakana Yamazaki plays Rachel.)

Gosho Aoyama's
Mystery Library
17

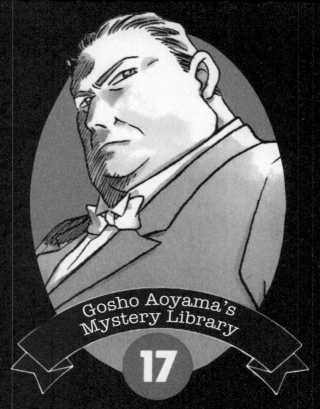

NERO WOLFE

Detectives can be an eccentric lot, but this character stands out even among his fellow detectives. I'm talking about Nero Wolfe! He's hugely overweight, weighing one-seventh of a ton. He's a gourmet whose typical day includes a dozen beers and fancy epicurean dishes. He dislikes leaving home and doesn't care for women. This extreme eccentric's favorite hobby is growing orchids. During the times set aside for his orchids and his meals, he refuses to be disturbed by anyone for any reason. His fees are extravagant and his attitude haughty. So why do the cases keep pouring in? Because his deductive skills are extraordinary, of course! But with his massive bulk, he hates moving around. His assistant Archie goes out and does the investigative legwork for him. Always exchanging sarcastic comments, they're a great detective duo! By the way, author Rex Stout was a gourmet just like his character. A guy like me who rarely sees fancy food could never come up with a detective like Wolfe. I recommend *Too Many Cooks*.

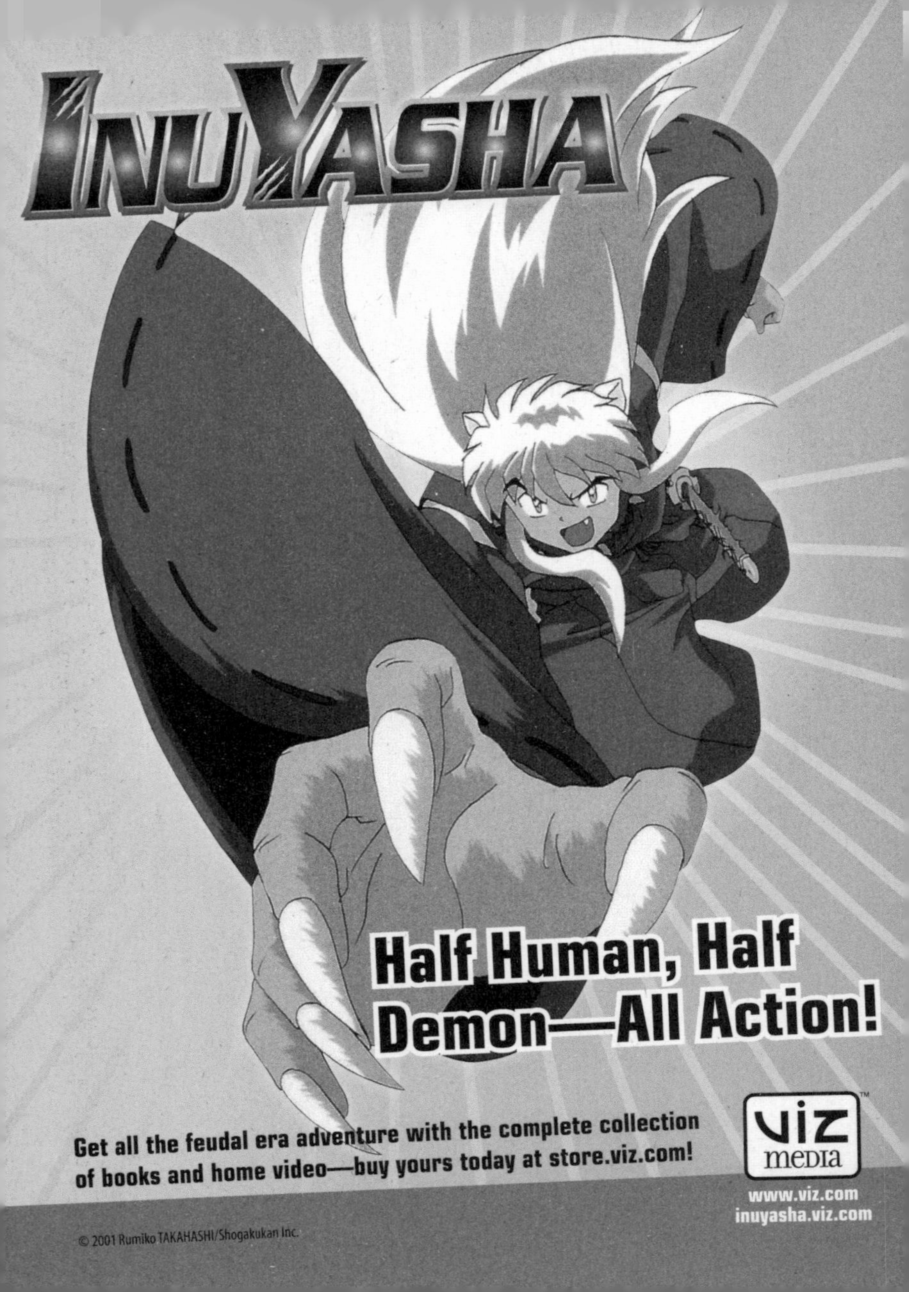
INUYASHA
Half Human, Half Demon—All Action!
Get all the feudal era adventure with the complete collection of books and home video—buy yours today at store.viz.com!
VIZ media
www.viz.com
inuyasha.viz.com
© 2001 Rumiko TAKAHASHI/Shogakukan Inc.

INUYASHA

Read the action from the start with the original manga series

Full color adaptation of the popular TV series

Art book with cel art, paintings, character profiles and more

TV SERIES & MOVIES ON DVD!

See more of the action in Inuyasha full-length movies

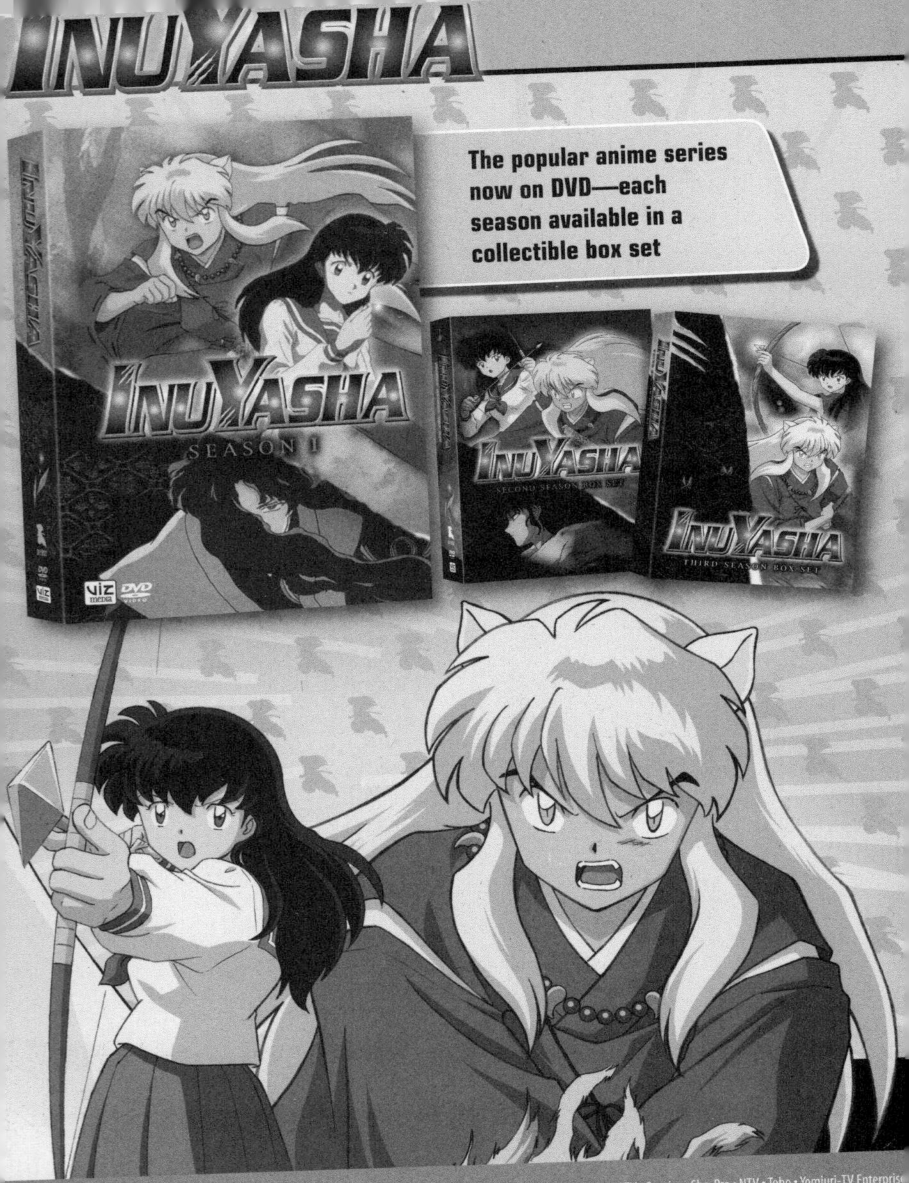
INUYASHA
The popular anime series now on DVD—each season available in a collectible box set
INUYASHA SEASON 1
INUYASHA
INUYASHA THIRD SEASON BOX SET

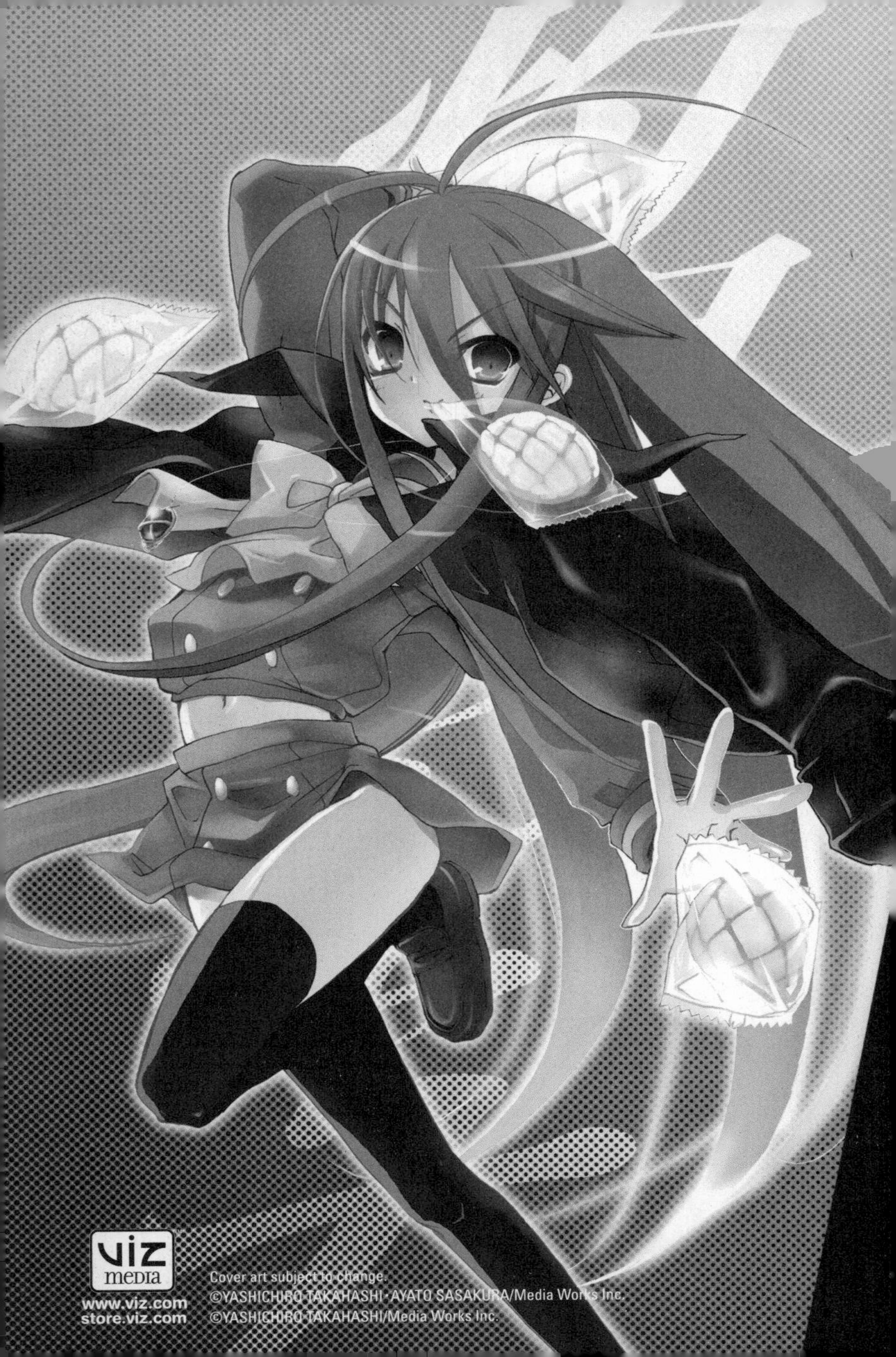

www.viz.com
store.viz.com

Cover art subject to change.

LOVE MANGA?
LET US KNOW WHAT YOU THINK!

OUR MANGA SURVEY IS NOW
AVAILABLE ONLINE. PLEASE VISIT:
VIZ.COM/MANGASURVEY

HELP US MAKE THE MANGA
YOU LOVE BETTER!